7th Workshop on Asian Language Resources 2009

(ALR-7)

Held at ACL-IJCNLP 2009

Singapore
6-7 August 2009

ISBN: 978-1-61738-456-1

Printed from e-media with permission by:

Curran Associates, Inc.
57 Morehouse Lane
Red Hook, NY 12571

Printed by Curran Associates, Inc. (2010)

Association for Computational Linguistics
209 N. Eighth Street
Stroudsburg, Pennsylvania 18360

Phone: 1-570-476-8006
Fax: 1-570-476-0860

acl@aclweb.org

Additional copies of this publication are available from:

Curran Associates, Inc.
57 Morehouse Lane
Red Hook, NY 12571 USA
Phone: 845-758-0400
Fax: 845-758-2634
Email: curran@proceedings.com
Web: www.proceedings.com

Introduction

This volume contains the papers presented at the Seventh Workshop on Asian Language Resources, held on August 6-7, 2009 in conjunction with the joint conference of the 47th Annual Meeting of the Association for Computational Linguistics and the 4th International Joint Conference on Natural Language Processing of the Asian Federation of Natural Language Processing (ACL-IJCNLP 2009).

Language resources have played an essential role in empirical approaches to natural language processing (NLP) for the last two decades. Previous concerted efforts on construction of language resources, particularly in the US and European countries, have laid a solid foundation for the pioneering NLP research in these two communities. In comparison, the availability and accessibility of many Asian language resources are still very limited except for a few languages. Moreover, there is a greater diversity in Asian languages with respect to character sets, grammatical properties and the cultural background.

Motivated by such a context, we have organized a series of workshops on Asian language resources since 2001. This workshop series has contributed to the activation of the NLP research in Asia particularly of building and utilizing corpora of various types and languages. In this seventh workshop, we had 37 submissions encompassing the research from NLP community as well as the speech processing community thanks to the contributions from Oriental COCOSDA. The paper selection was highly competitive compared with the last six workshops. The program committee selected 21 papers for regular presentation, 5 papers for short presentation, and one panel discussion to enlightening the information exchange between ALR and FLaReNet initiatives.

This Seventh Workshop on Asian Language Resources would not have been succeeded without the hard work of the program committee. We would like to thank all the authors and the people who attend this workshop to share their research experiences. Last but not least, we would like to express our deep appreciation to the arrangement of the ACL-IJCNLP 2009 organizing committee and secretariat. We deeply hope this workshop further accelerates the already thriving NLP research in Asia.

Hammam Riza
Virach Sornlertlamvanich
Workshop Co-chairs

Organizers

Program Chairs:

Hammam Riza	IPTEKnet-BPPT
Virach Sornlertlamvanich	NECTEC

Program Committee:

Pushpak Bhattacharyya	*IIT-Bombay*
Thatsanee Charoenporn	*NECTEC*
Key-Sun Choi	*KAIST*
Chu-Ren Huang	*Hong Kong Polytechnic University*
Sarmad Hussain	*National University of Computer & Emerging Sciences*
Hitoshi Isahara	*NICT*
Shuichi Itahashi	*NII*
Lin-Shan Lee	*National Taiwan University*
Haizhou Li	*I2R*
Chi Mai Luong	*Institute of Information Technology, Vietnamese Academy of Science and Technology*
Yoshiki Mikami	*Nagaoka University of Technology*
Sakrange Turance Nandasara	*University of Colombo School of Computing*
Thein Oo	*Myanmar Computer Federation*
Phonpasit Phissamay	*NAST*
Oskar Riandi	*ICT Center-BPPT*
Rachel Edita O Roxas	*De La Salle University*
Kiyoaki Shirai	*JAIST*
Myint Myint Than	*Myanmar Computer Federation*
Takenobu Tokunaga	*Tokyo Institute of Technology*
Chiuyu Tseng	*Academia Sinica*
Chai Wutiwiwatchai	*NECTEC*

Book Chair:

Takenobu Tokunaga	*Tokyo Institute of Technology*

Table of Contents

Workshop Program

Thursday, August 6, 2009

8:30–9:00	Registration
9:00–9:10	Opening
9:10–9:35	*Enhancing the Japanese WordNet* Francis Bond, Hitoshi Isahara, Sanae Fujita, Kiyotaka Uchimoto, Takayuki Kuribayashi and Kyoko Kanzaki
9:35–10:00	*An Empirical Study of Vietnamese Noun Phrase Chunking with Discriminative Sequence Models* Le Minh Nguyen, Huong Thao Nguyen, Phuong Thai Nguyen, Tu Bao Ho and Akira Shimazu
10:00–10:30	Break
10:30–10:55	*Corpus-based Sinhala Lexicon* Ruvan Weerasinghe, Dulip Herath and Viraj Welgama
10:55–11:20	*Analysis and Development of Urdu POS Tagged Corpus* Ahmed Muaz, Aasim Ali and Sarmad Hussain
11:20–11:45	*Annotating Dialogue Acts to Construct Dialogue Systems for Consulting* Kiyonori Ohtake, Teruhisa Misu, Chiori Hori, Hideki Kashioka and Satoshi Nakamura
11:45–12:10	*Assas-band, an Affix-Exception-List Based Urdu Stemmer* Qurat-ul-Ain Akram, Asma Naseer and Sarmad Hussain
12:10–13:50	Lunch break
13:50–14:15	*Automated Mining Of Names Using Parallel Hindi-English Corpus* R. Mahesh K. Sinha
14:15–14:40	*Basic Language Resources for Diverse Asian Languages: A Streamlined Approach for Resource Creation* Heather Simpson, Kazuaki Maeda and Christopher Cieri
14:40–15:05	*Finite-State Description of Vietnamese Reduplication* Le Hong Phuong, Nguyen Thi Minh Huyen and Roussanaly Azim
15:05–15:30	*Construction of Chinese Segmented and POS-tagged Conversational Corpora and Their Evaluations on Spontaneous Speech Recognitions* Xinhui Hu, Ryosuke Isotani and Satoshi Nakamura
15:30–16:00	Break
16:00–16:15	*Bengali Verb Subcategorization Frame Acquisition - A Baseline Model* Somnath Banerjee, Dipankar Das and Sivaji Bandyopadhyay
16:15–16:30	*Phonological and Logographic Influences on Errors in Written Chinese Words* Chao-Lin Liu, Kan-Wen Tien, Min-Hua Lai, Yi-Hsuan Chuang and Shih-Hung Wu
16:30–16:45	*Resource Report: Building Parallel Text Corpora for Multi-Domain Translation System* Budiono, Hammam Riza and Chairil Hakim
16:45–17:00	*A Syntactic Resource for Thai: CG Treebank* Taneth Ruangrajitpakorn, Kanokorn Trakultaweekoon and Thepchai Supnithi
17:00–17:15	*Part of Speech Tagging for Mongolian Corpus* Purev Jaimai and Odbayar Chimeddorj

Friday, August 7, 2009

8:45–9:10	*Interaction Grammar for the Persian Language: Noun and Adjectival Phrases* Masood Ghayoomi and Bruno Guillaume
9:10–9:35	*KTimeML: Specification of Temporal and Event Expressions in Korean Text* Seohyun Im, Hyunjo You, Hayun Jang, Seungho Nam and Hyopil Shin
9:35–10:00	*CWN-LMF: Chinese WordNet in the Lexical Markup Framework* Lung-Hao Lee, Shu-Kai Hsieh and Chu-Ren Huang
10:00–10:30	Break
10:30–10:55	*Philippine Language Resources: Trends and Directions* Rachel Edita Roxas, Charibeth Cheng and Nathalie Rose Lim
10:55–11:20	*Thai WordNet Construction* Sareewan Thoongsup, Thatsanee Charoenporn, Kergrit Robkop, Tan Sinthurahat, Chumpol Mokarat, Virach Sornlertlamvanich and Hitoshi Isahara
11:20–11:45	*Query Expansion using LMF-Compliant Lexical Resources* Takenobu Tokunaga, Dain Kaplan, Nicoletta Calzolari, Monica Monachini, Claudia Soria, Virach Sornlertlamvanich, Thatsanee Charoenporn, Yingju Xia, Chu-Ren Huang, Shu-Kai Hsieh and Kiyoaki Shirai
11:45–12:10	*Thai National Corpus: A Progress Report* Wirote Aroonmanakun, Kachen Tansiri and Pairit Nittayanuparp
12:10–13:50	Lunch break
13:50–14:15	*The FLaReNet Thematic Network: A Global Forum for Cooperation* Nicoletta Calzolari and Claudia Soria
14:15–14:40	*Towards Building Advanced Natural Language Applications - An Overview of the Existing Primary Resources and Applications in Nepali* Bal Krishna Bal
14:40–15:05	*Using Search Engine to Construct a Scalable Corpus for Vietnamese Lexical Development for Word Segmentation* Doan Nguyen
15:05–15:30	*Word Segmentation Standard in Chinese, Japanese and Korean* Key-Sun Choi, Hitoshi Isahara, Kyoko Kanzaki, Hansaem Kim, Seok Mun Pak and Maosong Sun
15:30–16:00	Break
16:00–17:50	Panel discussion “ALR and FLaReNet”
17:50–18:00	Closing

Enhancing the Japanese WordNet

Francis Bond,† **Hitoshi Isahara,**‡ **Sanae Fujita,**♡
Kiyotaka Uchimoto,† **Takayuki Kuribayashi**† and **Kyoko Kanzaki**‡
† NICT Language Infrastructure Group, ‡ NICT Language Translation Group
`<bond@ieee.org,{isahara,uchimoto,kuribayashi,kanzaki}@nict.go.jp>`
♡ Sanae Fujita, NTT Communications Science Laboratory
`<sanae@kecl.cslab.ntt.co.jp>`

Abstract

The Japanese WordNet currently has 51,000 synsets with Japanese entries. In this paper, we discuss three methods of extending it: increasing the cover, linking it to examples in corpora and linking it to other resources (SUMO and GoiTaikei). In addition, we outline our plans to make it more useful by adding Japanese definition sentences to each synset. Finally, we discuss how releasing the corpus under an open license has led to the construction of interfaces in a variety of programming languages.

1 Introduction

Our goal is to make a semantic lexicon of Japanese that is both **accesible** and **usable**. To this end we are constructing and releasing the Japanese WordNet (`WN-Ja`) (Bond et al., 2008a).

We have almost completed the first stage, where we automatically translated the English and Euro WordNets, and are hand correcting it. We introduce this in Section 2. Currently, we are extending it in three main areas: the first is to add more concepts to the Japanese WordNet, either by adding Japanese to existing English synsets or by creating new synsets (§ 3). The second is to link the synsets to text examples (§ 4). Finally, we are linking it to other resources: the Suggested Upper Merged Ontology (SUMO) (Niles and Pease, 2001), the Japanese semantic lexicon GoiTaikei (Ikehara et al., 1997), and a collection of illustrations taken from the Open ClipArt Library (Phillips, 2005) (§ 5).

2 Current State

Currently, the `WN-Ja` consists of 157,000 senses (word-synset pairs) 51,000 concepts (synsets) and 81,000 unique Japanese words (version 0.91). The relational structure (hypernym, meronym, domain, ...) is based entirely on the English WordNet 3.0 (Fellbaum, 1998). We have Japanese words for 43.0% of the synsets in the English WordNet. Of these synsets, 45% have been checked by hand, 8% were automatically created by linking through multiple languages and 46% were automatically created by adding non-ambiguous translations, as described in Bond et al. (2008a). There are some 51,000 synsets with Japanese candidate words that have not yet been checked. For up-to-date information on `WN-Ja` see: `nlpwww.nict.go.jp/wn-ja`.

An example of the entry for the synset 02076196-n is shown in Figure 1. Most fields come from the English WordNet. We have added the underlined fields (Ja Synonyms, Illustration, links to GoiTaikei, SUMO) and are currently adding the translated definition (Def (Ja)). In the initial automatic construction there were 27 Japanese words associated with the synset,[1] including many inappropriate translations for other senses of *seal* (e.g., 判こ *hanko* "stamp"). These were reduced to three after checking: アザラシ, 海豹 *azarashi* "seal" and シール *shi-ru* "seal". Synsets with ? in their names are those for which there is currently no Japanese entry in the WordNet.

The main focus of this year's work has been this manual trimming of badly translated words. The result is a WordNet with a reasonable coverage of common Japanese words. The precision per sense is just over 90%. We have aimed at high coverage at the cost of precision for two reasons: (i) we think that the WordNet must have a rea-

[1] アザラシ, シール, スタンプ, 上封, 判, 判こ, 判子, 刻印, 加判, 印, 印判, 印形, 印章, 印鎰, 印鑑, 印鑰, 印顆, 墨引, 墨引き, 封, 封じ目, 封印, 封目, 封着, 封緘, 押し手, 押印, 押手, 押捺, 捺印, 極印, 海豹, 版行, 符節, 緘, 証印, 調印

Proceedings of the 7th Workshop on Asian Language Resources, ACL-IJCNLP 2009, pages 1–8,
Suntec, Singapore, 6-7 August 2009. ©2009 ACL and AFNLP

sonable coverage to be useful for NLP tasks and (ii) we expect to continue refining the accuracy over the following years. Our strategy is thus different from Euro WordNet (Vossen, 1998), where initial emphasis was on building a consistent and complete upper ontology.

3 Increasing Coverage

We are increasing the coverage in two ways. The first is to continue to manually correct the automatically translated synsets. This is being done both by hand, as time permits, and also by comparing against other resources such as GoiTaikei and Wikipedia. When we check for poor candidates, we also add in missing words as they occur to us.

More interestingly, we wish to add synsets for Japanese concepts that may not be expressed in the English WordNet. To decide which new concepts to add, we will be guided by the other tasks we are doing: annotation and linking. We intend to create new synsets for words found in the corpora we annotate that are not currently covered, as well as for concepts that we want to link to. An example for the first is the concept 御飯 *gohan* "cooked rice", as opposed to the grain 米 *kome* "rice". An example of the second is シングル *shinguru* "single: a song usually extracted from a current or upcoming album to promote the album". This is a very common hypernym in Wikipedia but missing from the English WordNet.

As far as possible, we want to coordinate the creation of new synsets with other projects: for example KorLex: the Korean WordNet already makes the cooked rice/grain distinction, and the English WordNet should also have a synset for this sense of *single.*

4 Text Annotation

We are in the process of annotating four texts (Table 1). The first two are translations of WordNet annotated English Texts (SemCor and the WordNet definitions), the third is the Japanese newspaper text that forms the Kyoto Corpus and the fourth is an open corpus of bilingual Japanese-English sentences (Tanaka). In 2009, we expect to finish translating and annotate all of SemCor, translate the WordNet definitions and start annotation on the Kyoto and Tanaka Corpora.

Name	Sentences	Words	Content Words
SemCor	12,842	224,260	120,000
Definitions	165,977	1,468,347	459,000
Kyoto	38,383	969,558	527,000
Tanaka	147,190	1,151,892	360,000

Table 1: Corpora to be Sense Tagged

This annotation is essential for finding missing senses in the Japanese WordNet, as well as getting the sense distributions that are needed for supervised word sense disambiguation.

4.1 SemCor

SemCor is a textual corpus in which words have been both syntactically and semantically tagged. The texts included in SemCor were extracted from the Brown corpus (Francis and Kucera, 1979) and then linked to senses in the English WordNet. The frequencies in this corpus were used to give the sense frequencies in WordNet (Fellbaum, 1998). A subset of this corpus (MultiSemCor) was translated into Italian and used as a corpus for the Italian WordNet (Bentivogli et al., 2004). We are translating this subset into Japanese.

In the same way as Bentivogli et al. (2004), we are exploiting Cross-Language Annotation Transfer to seed the Japanese annotation. For example, consider (1)[2]. The content words *answer, was, simple, honest* are tagged in SemCor. They can be aligned with their translations 答え *kotae* "answer", 簡単 *kantan* "simple", 率直 *socchoku* "honest" and だった *datta* "was". This allows us to tag the Japanese translation with the same synsets as the English, and thus disambiguate them.

(1) His answer$_i$ was$_j$ simple$_k$ but honest$_l$.
答え$_i$ は 簡単$_k$ ながらも 率直$_l$ な もの だった$_j$ 。

However, just because all the English words have sysnets in WordNet, it is not always the case for the translations. For example, the English phrase *last night* can be translated into 前夜 *zen'ya* "last-night". Here the two English words (and synsets) link to a single Japanese

[2]Sentence 96 in b13.

Synset	02076196-n
Synonyms	ja 海豹, アザラシ, シール en $seal_9$ fr phoque
Illustration	 animal/seal.png
Def (en)	"any of numerous marine mammals that come on shore to breed; chiefly of cold regions"
Def (ja)	「繁殖のために岸に上がる海洋性哺乳動物の各種；主に寒帯地域に」
Hypernyms	アシカ亜目/pinniped
Hyponyms	？/crabeater_seal ？/eared_seal 海驢/earless_seal
GoiTaikei	⟨⟨537:beast⟩⟩
SUMO	⊂ Carnivore

Figure 1: Example Entry for Seal/海豹

word which has no suitable synset in the English WordNet. In this case, we need to create a new synset unique to the Japanese WordNet.[3]

We chose a translated SemCor as the basis of annotation for two main reasons: (i) the corpus can be freely redistributed — we expect the glosses to be useful as an aligned corpus of Japanese-English-Italian and (ii) it has other annotations associated with it: Brown corpus POS annotation, Penn Treebank syntactic annotation.

4.2 WordNet Definitions

Our second translated corpus is formed from the WordNet definitions (and example sentences) themselves (e.g., the **def** field shown in Figure 1). The English definitions have been annotated with word senses in the *Princeton WordNet Gloss Corpus*. In the same way that we do for SemCor, we are translating the definitions and examples, and using the existing annotation to seed our annotation.

Using the definitions as the base for a sense annotated corpus is attractive for the following reasons: (i) the translated corpus can be freely redistributed — we expect the definitions to be useful as an aligned corpus and also to be useful for many other open lexicons; (ii) the definitions are useful for Japanese native speakers using the WordNet, (iii) the definitions are useful for unsupervised sense disambiguation techniques such as LESK (Baldwin et al., 2008); (iv) other projects have also translated synset definitions (e.g. Spanish and Korean), so we can hope to create a multilingual corpus here as well and (v) the definitions can be used as a machine readable dictionary, and various information extracted from there (Barnbrook, 2002; Nichols et al., 2006)

4.3 Kyoto Text Corpus

The Kyoto Text Corpus consists of newspaper text from the Mainichi Newspaper (1995), segmented and annotated with Japanese POS tags and dependency trees (Kurohashi and Nagao, 2003). The corpus is made up of two parts. The first consists of 17 full days of articles and the second of one year's editorials. We hope to annotate at least parts of it during 2009.

Even though the Kyoto Text Corpus is not freely redistributable, we have chosen to annotate it due to the wealth of annotation associated with it: dependency trees, predicate-argument relations and co-reference (Iida et al., 2007), translations into English and Chinese (Uchimoto et al., 2004) and sense annotations from the Hinoki project (Bond et al., 2006). We also felt it was important to tag some native Japanese text, not only translated text.

4.4 Tanaka Corpus

Finally, we will also tag the Tanaka Corpus, an open corpus of Japanese-English sentence pairs compiled by Professor Yasuhito Tanaka at Hyogo University and his students (Tanaka, 2001) and released into the public domain. The corrected version we use has around 140,000 sentence pairs.

This corpus is attractive for several reasons. (i) it is freely redistributable; (ii) it has been indexed to entries in the Japanese-English dictio-

[3]Arguably, the fact that one says *last night* (not *yesterday night*) for the night proceeding today and *tomorrow night* (not *next night*) for the night following today suggests that these multi-word expressions are lexicalized and synsets should be created for them in the English WordNet. However, in general we expect to create some synsets that will be unique to the Japanese WordNet.

nary JMDict (Breen, 2003); (iii) part of it has also been used in an open HPSG-based treebank (Bond et al., 2008b); (iv) further, translations in other languages, most notably French, have been added by the TATOEBA project.[4] Our plan is to tag this automatically using the tools developed for the Kyoto corpus annotation, and then to open the data to the community for refinement. We give a typical example sentence in (2).

(2) あの木の枝に数羽の鳥がとまっている。

"Some birds are sitting on the branch of that tree." (en)

"Des oiseaux se reposent sur la branche de cet arbre." (fr)

5 Linking to other resources

We currently link the Japanese WordNet to three other resources: the Suggested Upper Merged Ontology; GoiTaikei, a Japanese Lexicon; and a collection of pictures from the Open Clip Art Library (OCAL: Phillips (2005)).

For SUMO we used existing mappings. For the other resources, we find confident matches automatically and then generalize from them. We find matches in three ways:

MM Monosemous monolingual matches
e.g. *cricket bat* or 海豹 *azarashi* "seal"

MB Monosemous bilingual matches
e.g. ⟨海豹↔*seal*⟩

HH Hypernym/Hyponym pairs
e.g. ⟨seal ⊂ mammal⟩

We intend to use the same techniques to link other resources, such as the concepts from the EDR lexicon (EDR, 1990) and the automatically extracted hypernym-hyponym links from Torishiki-kai (Kuroda et al., 2009).

5.1 SUMO

The Suggested Upper Merged Ontology (SUMO) is a large formal public ontology freely released by the IEEE (Niles and Pease, 2001).

Because the structure of the Japanese WordNet is closely linked to that of the English WordNet, we were able to take advantage of the existing mappings from the English WordNet to SUMO. There are 102,669 mappings from SUMO to WordNet: 3,593 equivalent, 10,712 where the WordNet synset subsumes the SUMO concept, 88,065 where the SUMO concept subsumes the WordNet concept, 293 where the negation of the SUMO concept subsumes the WordNet synset and 6 where the negation of the SUMO concept is equivalent to the WordNet synset. According to the mapping, synset 02076196-n 海豹 *azarashi* "seal", shown in Figure 1 is subsumed by the SUMO concept ⟨⟨Carnivore⟩⟩. There is no link between *seal* and *carnivore* in WordNet, which shows how different ontologies can complement each other.

Carnivore Business Competition

Figure 2: SUMO illustrations

Linking to SUMO also allowed us to use the SUMO illustrations.[5] These consist of 12,237 links linking 4,607 concepts to the urls of 10,993 illustrations. These are mainly taken from from Wikimedia (`upload.wikimedia.org`), with around 1,000 from other sources. The pictures can be linked quite loosely to the concepts. For example, ⟨⟨Carnivore⟩⟩ is illustrated by a lion eating meat, and ⟨⟨BusinessCompetition⟩⟩ by a picture of Wall Street.

As we wanted our illustrations to be more concrete, we only use SUMO illustrations where the SUMO-WordNet mapping is equivalence. This gave 4,384 illustrations for 999 synsets.

5.2 GoiTaikei

Linking Goi-Taikei, we used not only the Japanese dictionary published in Ikehara et al. (1997), but also the Japanese-English dictionary used in the machine translation system ALT-J/E (Ikehara et al., 1991). We attempted to match synsets to semantic categories by matching the

[4] `wwwcyg.utc.fr/tatoeba/`

[5] Available at `http://sigmakee.cvs.sourceforge.net/viewvc/sigmakee/KBs/pictureList.kif`, thanks to Adam Pease for letting us know about them.

Japanese, English and English-Japanese pairs to unambiguous entries in Goi-Taikei. For example, the synset shown in Figure 1 was automatically assigned the semantic category ⟨⟨537:beast⟩⟩, as 海豹 appears only once in `WN-Ja`, with the synset shown, and once in the Japanese dictionary for ALT-J/E with a single semantic category.

We are currently evaluating our results against an earlier attempt to link WordNet and GoiTaikei that also matched synset entries to words in Goi-Taikei (Asanoma, 2001), but did not add an extra constraint (that they must be either monosemous or match as a hypernym-hyponym pair).

Once we have completed the mapping, we will use it to check for inconsistencies in the two resources.

5.3 Open ClipArt Library

In order to make the sense distinctions more visible we have semi-automatically linked synsets to illustrations from the Open Clip Art Library (OCAL: Phillips (2005)) using the mappings produced by Bond et al. (2008a).

We manually checked the mappings and added a goodness score. Illustrations are marked as:

3 the best out of multiple illustrations

2 a good illustration for the synset

1 a suitable illustration, but not perfect
This tag was used for black and white images, outlines, and so forth.

After the scoring, there were 874 links for 541 synsets (170 scored 1, 642 scored 2 and 62 scored 3). This is only a small subset of illustrations in OCAL and an even smaller proportion of wordnet. However, because any illustrated synset also (in theory) illustrates its hypernyms, we have indirectly illustrated far more than 541 synsets: these figures are better than they seem.

There are far fewer OCAL illustrations than the SUMO linked illustrations. However, they are in general more representative illustrations (especially those scored 2 and above), and the source of the clipart is available as SVG source so it is easy to manipulate them. We think that this makes them particularly useful for a variety of tasks. One is pedagogical — it is useful to have pictures in learners' dictionaries. Another is in cross-cultural communication - for example in Pangea, where children use pictons (small concept representing pictures) to write messages (Takasaki and Mori, 2007).

The OCAL illustrations mapped through WordNet to 541 SUMO concepts. We have given these links to the SUMO researchers.

6 Interfaces

We released the Japanese WordNet in three formats: tab-delimited text, XML and as an SQLite database. The license was the same as English WordNet. This is a permissive license, the data can be reused within proprietary software on the condition that the license is distributed with that software (similar to the MIT X license). The license is also GPL-compatible, meaning that the GPL permits combination and redistribution with software that uses it.

The tab delimited format consists of just a list of synsets, Japanese words and the type of link (hand, multi-lingual or monosemous):

02076196-n	海豹	hand
02076196-n	アザラシ	hand
02076196-n	シール	hand

We also output in WordNet-LMF (Francopoulo et al., 2006; Soria et al., 2009), to make the program easily available for other WordNet researchers. In this case the synset structure was taken from the English WordNet and the lemmas from the Japanese WordNet. Because of the incomplete coverage, not all synsets contain lemmas. This format is used by the Kyoto Project, and we expect it to become the standard exchange format for WordNets (Vossen et al., 2008).

Finally, we also created an SQL database. This contains information from the English WordNet, the Japanese WordNet, and links to illustrations. We chose SQLite,[6] a self-contained, zero-configuration, SQL database engine whose source code is in the public domain. The core structure is very simple with six tables, as shown in Figure 3.

As we prepared the release we wrote a perl module for a basic interface. This was used to develop a web interface: Figure 4 shows a screenshot.

[6] `http://www.sqlite.org`

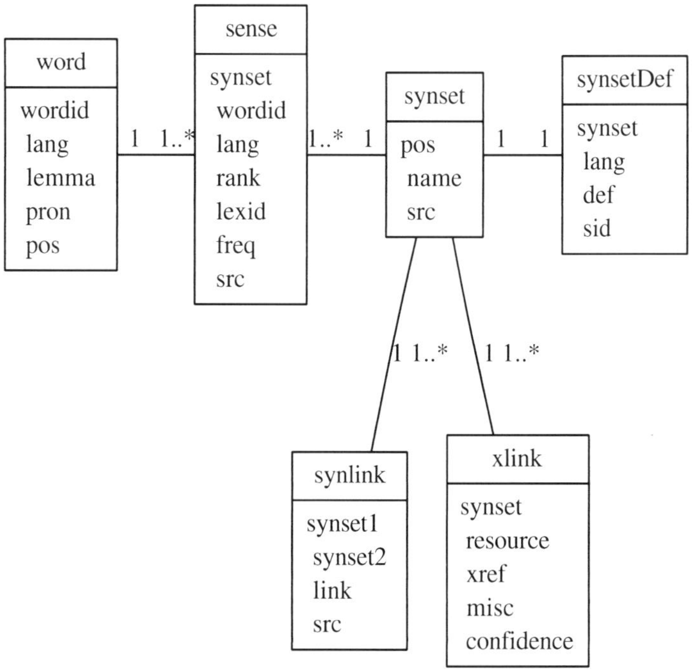

Figure 3: Database Schema

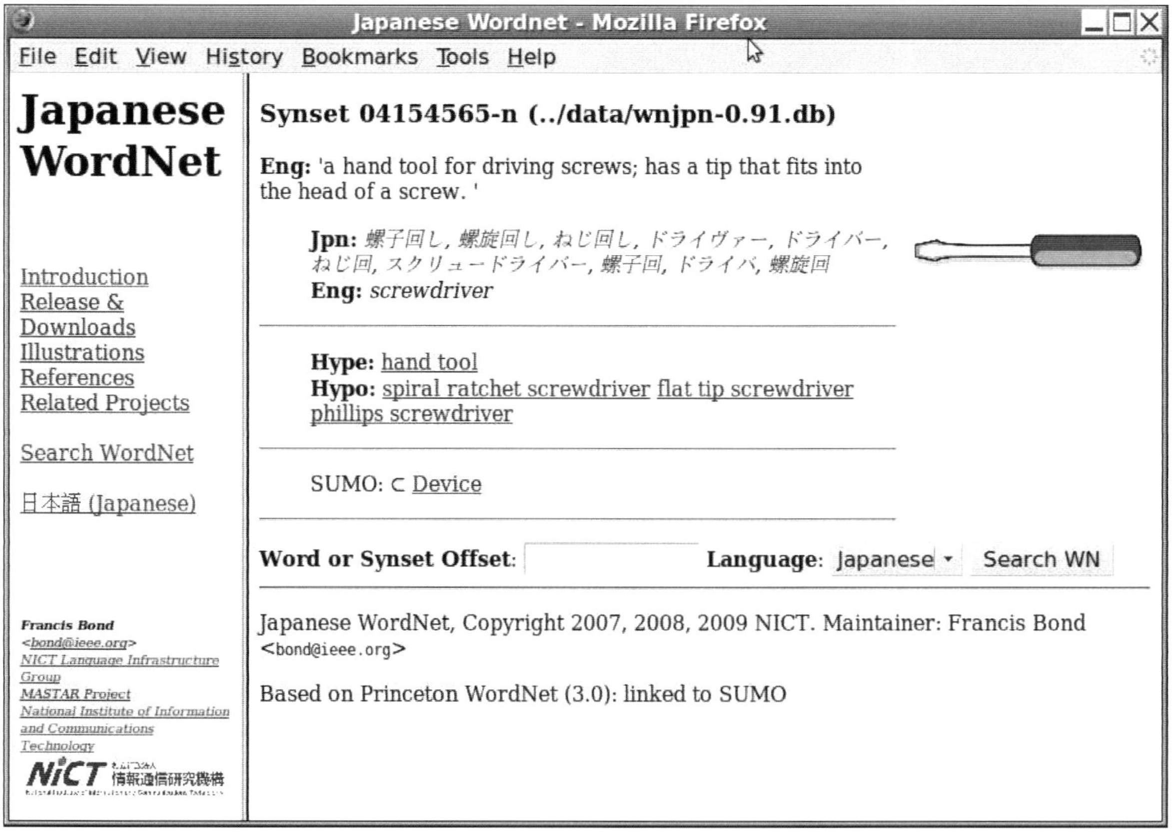

Figure 4: Web Search Screenshot

7 Discussion

In contrast to earlier WordNets, the Japanese WordNet was released with two known major imperfections: (i) the concept hierarchy was entirely based on English with no adaptation to Japanese and (ii) the data was released with some unchecked automatically created entries. The result was a WordNet that did not fully model the lexical structure of Japanese and was known to contain an estimated 5% errors. The motivation behind this was twofold. Firstly, we wanted to try and take advantage of the open source model. If the first release was good enough to be useful, we hoped to (a) let people use it and (b) get feedback from them which could then be incorporated into the next release. This is the strategy known as *release early, release often* (Raymond, 1999).

Secondly, we anticipated the most common use of the WordNet to be in checking whether one word is a hypernym of another. In this case, even if one word is wrong, it is unlikely that the other will be, so a small percentage of errors should be acceptable.

From the practical point of view, the early release appears to have been a success. The SQL database proved very popular, and within two weeks of the first release someone produced a python API. This was soon followed by interfaces in java, ruby, objective C and gauche. We also received feedback on effective indexing of the database and some corrections of entries — these have been included in the most recent release (0.91).

The data from the Japanese WordNet has already been incorporated into other projects. The first was the Multi-Lingual Semantic Network (MLSN) (Cook, 2008) a WordNet based network of Arabic, Chinese, English, German and Japanese. Because both the Japanese WordNet and MLSN use very open licenses, it is possible to share entries directly. We have already received useful feedback and over a thousand new entries from MLSN. The second project using our data is the Asian WordNet (Charoenporn et al., 2008). They have a well developed interface for collaborative development of linguistic resources, and we hope to get corrections and additions from them in the future. Another project using the Japanese WordNet data is the Language Grid (Ishida, 2006) which offers the English and Japanese WordNets as concept dictionaries.

We have also been linked to from other resources. The Japanese-English lexicon project JMDict (Breen, 2004) now links to the Japanese WordNet, and members of that project are using WordNet to suggest new entries. We used JMDict in the first automatic construction stage, so it is particularly gratifying to be able to help JMDict in turn.

Finally, we believe that data about language should be shared — language is part of the common heritage of its speakers. In our case, the Japanese WordNet was constructed based on the work that others made available to us and thus we had a moral obligation to make our results freely available to others. Further, projects that create WordNets but do not release them freely hinder research on lexical semantics in that language — people cannot use the unreleased resource, but it is hard to get funding to duplicate something that already exists.

In future work, in addition to the planned extensions listed here, we would like to work on the following: Explicitly marking lexical variants; linking to instances in Wikipedia; adding derivational and antonym links; using the WordNet for word sense disambiguation.

8 Conclusion

This paper presents the current state of the Japanese WordNet (157,000 senses, 51,000 concepts and 81,000 unique Japanese words, with links to SUMO, Goi-Taikei and OCAL) and outlined our plans for further work (more words, links to corpora and other resources). We hope that `WN-Ja` will become a useful resource not only for natural language processing, but also for language education/learning and linguistic research.

References

Naoki Asanoma. 2001. Alignment of ontologies:wordnet and goi-taikei. In *NAACL Wokshop on WordNet & Other Lexical Resources*, pages 89–94. Pittsburgh, USA.

Timothy Baldwin, Su Nam Kim, Francis Bond, Sanae Fujita, David Martinez, and Takaaki Tanaka. 2008. MRD-based word sense disambiguation: Further extending Lesk. In *Proc. of the 3rd International Joint Conference on Natural Language Processing (IJCNLP-08)*, pages 775–780. Hyderabad, India.

Geoff Barnbrook. 2002. *Defining Language — A local*

grammar of definition sentences. Studies in Corpus Linguistics. John Benjamins.

Luisa Bentivogli, Pamela Forner, and Emanuele Pianta. 2004. Evaluating cross-language annotation transfer in the MultiSemCor corpus. In *20th International Conference on Computational Linguistics: COLING-2004*, pages 364–370. Geneva.

Francis Bond, Sanae Fujita, and Takaaki Tanaka. 2006. The Hinoki syntactic and semantic treebank of Japanese. *Language Resources and Evaluation*, 40(3–4):253–261. (Special issue on Asian language technology).

Francis Bond, Hitoshi Isahara, Kyoko Kanzaki, and Kiyotaka Uchimoto. 2008a. Boot-strapping a WordNet using multiple existing WordNets. In *Sixth International conference on Language Resources and Evaluation (LREC 2008)*. Marrakech.

Francis Bond, Takayuki Kuribayashi, and Chikara Hashimoto. 2008b. Construction of a free Japanese treebank based on HPSG. In *14th Annual Meeting of the Association for Natural Language Processing*, pages 241–244. Tokyo. (in Japanese).

James W. Breen. 2003. Word usage examples in an electronic dictionary. In *Papillon (Multi-lingual Dictionary) Project Workshop*. Sapporo.

James W. Breen. 2004. JMDict: a Japanese-multilingual dictionary. In *Coling 2004 Workshop on Multilingual Linguistic Resources*, pages 71–78. Geneva.

Thatsanee Charoenporn, Virach Sornlerlamvanich, Chumpol Mokarat, and Hitoshi Isahara. 2008. Semi-automatic compilation of Asian WordNet. In *14th Annual Meeting of the Association for Natural Language Processing*, pages 1041–1044. Tokyo.

Darren Cook. 2008. MLSN: A multi-lingual semantic network. In *14th Annual Meeting of the Association for Natural Language Processing*, pages 1136–1139. Tokyo.

EDR. 1990. Concept dictionary. Technical report, Japan Electronic Dictionary Research Institute, Ltd.

Christine Fellbaum, editor. 1998. *WordNet: An Electronic Lexical Database*. MIT Press.

W. Nelson Francis and Henry Kucera. 1979. *BROWN CORPUS MANUAL*. Brown University, Rhode Island, third edition.

Gil Francopoulo, Monte George, Nicoletta Calzolari, Monica Monachini, Nuria Bel, Mandy Pet, and Claudia Soria. 2006. Lexical markup framework (LMF). In *Proceedings of the 5th International Conference on Language Resources and Evaluation (LREC 2006)*. Genoa, Italy.

Ryu Iida, Mamoru Komachi, Kentaro Inui, and Yuji Matsumoto. 2007. Annotating a Japanese text corpus with predicate-argument and coreference relations. In *ACL Workshop: Linguistic Annotation Workshop*, pages 132–139. Prague.

Satoru Ikehara, Masahiro Miyazaki, Satoshi Shirai, Akio Yokoo, Hiromi Nakaiwa, Kentaro Ogura, Yoshifumi Ooyama, and Yoshihiko Hayashi. 1997. *Goi-Taikei — A Japanese Lexicon*. Iwanami Shoten, Tokyo. 5 volumes/CDROM.

Satoru Ikehara, Satoshi Shirai, Akio Yokoo, and Hiromi Nakaiwa. 1991. Toward an MT system without pre-editing — effects of new methods in **ALT-J/E** —. In *Third Machine Translation Summit: MT Summit III*, pages 101–106. Washington DC.

Toru Ishida. 2006. Language grid: An infrastructure for intercultural collaboration. In *IEEE/IPSJ Symposium on Applications and the Internet (SAINT-06)*, pages 96–100. (keynote address).

Kow Kuroda, Jae-Ho Lee, Hajime Nozawa, Masaki Murata, and Kentaro Torisawa. 2009. Manual cleaning of hypernyms in Torishiki-Kai. In *15th Annual Meeting of The Association for Natural Language Processing*, pages C1–3. Tottori. (in Japanese).

Sadao Kurohashi and Makoto Nagao. 2003. Building a Japanese parsed corpus — while improving the parsing system. In Anne Abeillé, editor, *Treebanks: Building and Using Parsed Corpora*, chapter 14, pages 249–260. Kluwer Academic Publishers.

Eric Nichols, Francis Bond, Takaaki Tanaka, Sanae Fujita, and Daniel Flickinger. 2006. Robust ontology acquisition from multiple sources. In *Proceedings of the 2nd Workshop on Ontology Learning and Population: Bridging the Gap between Text and Knowledge*, pages 10–17. Sydney.

Ian Niles and Adam Pease. 2001. Towards a standard upper ontology. In Chris Welty and Barry Smith, editors, *Proceedings of the 2nd International Conference on Formal Ontology in Information Systems (FOIS-2001)*. Maine.

Jonathan Phillips. 2005. Introduction to the open clip art library. `http://rejon.org/media/writings/ocalintro/ocal_intro_phillips.html`. (accessed 2007-11-01).

Eric S. Raymond. 1999. *The Cathedral & the Bazaar*. O'Reilly.

Claudia Soria, Monica Monachini, and Piek Vossen. 2009. Wordnet-LMF: fleshing out a standardized format for wordnet interoperability. In *Second International Workshop on Intercultural Collaboration (IWIC-2009)*. Stanford.

Toshiyuki Takasaki and Yumiko Mori. 2007. Design and development of a pictogram communication system for children around the world. In *First International Workshop on Intercultural Collaboration (IWIC-2007)*, pages 144–157. Kyoto.

Yasuhito Tanaka. 2001. Compilation of a multilingual parallel corpus. In *Proceedings of PACLING 2001*, pages 265–268. Kyushu.

Kiyotaka Uchimoto, Yujie Zhang, Kiyoshi Sudo, Masaki Murata, Satoshi Sekine, and Hitoshi Isahara. 2004. Multilingual aligned parallel treebank corpus reflecting contextual information and its applications. In Gilles Sérasset, editor, *COLING 2004 Multilingual Linguistic Resources*, pages 57–64. COLING, Geneva, Switzerland.

P Vossen, E. Agirre, N. Calzolari, C. Fellbaum, S. Hsieh, C. Huang, H. Isahara, K. Kanzaki, A. Marchetti, M. Monachini, F. Neri, R. Raffaelli, G. Rigau, and M. Tescon. 2008. KYOTO: A system for mining, structuring and distributing knowledge across languages and cultures. In *Proceedings of the Sixth International Language Resources and Evaluation (LREC'08)*. Marrakech, Morocco.

Piek Vossen, editor. 1998. *Euro WordNet*. Kluwer.

An Empirical Study of Vietnamese Noun Phrase Chunking with Discriminative Sequence Models

Le Minh Nguyen
School of Information Science, JAIST
nguyenml@jaist.ac.jp

Huong Thao Nguyen and **Phuong Thai Nguyen**
College of Technology, VNU
{thaonth, thainp}@vnu.edu.vn

Tu Bao Ho and **Akira Shimazu**
Japan Advanced Institute of Science and Technology
{bao,shimazu}@jaist.ac.jp

Abstract

This paper presents an empirical work for Vietnamese NP chunking task. We show how to build an annotation corpus of NP chunking and how discriminative sequence models are trained using the corpus. Experiment results using 5 fold cross validation test show that discriminative sequence learning are well suitable for Vietnamese chunking. In addition, by empirical experiments we show that the part of speech information contribute significantly to the performance of there learning models.

1 Introduction

Many Natural Language Processing applications (i.e machine translation) require syntactic information and tools for syntactic analysis. However, these linguistic resources are only available for some languages(i.e English, Japanese, Chines). In the case of Vietnamese, currently most researchers have focused on word segmentation and part of speech tagging. For example, Nghiem et al (Nghiem, Dinh, Nguyen, 2008) has developed a Vietnamese POS tagging. Tu (Tu, Phan, Nguyen, Ha, 2006) (Nguyen, Romary, Rossignol, Vu, 2006)(Dien, Thuy, 2006) have developed Vietnamese word segmentation.

The processing of building tools and annotated data for other fundamental tasks such as chunking and syntactic parsing are currently developed. This can be viewed as a bottleneck for developing NLP applications that require a deeper understanding of the language. The requirement of developing such tools motives us to develop a Vietnamese chunking tool. For this goal, we have been looking for an annotation corpus for conducting a Vietnamese chunking using machine learning methods. Unfortunately, at the moment, there is still no common standard annotated corpus for evaluation and comparison regarding Vietnamese chunking.

In this paper, we aim at discussing on how we can build annotated data for Vietnamese text chunking and how to apply discriminative sequence learning for Vietnamese text chunking. We choose discriminative sequence models for Vietnamese text chunking because they have shown very suitable methods for several languages(i.e English, Japanese, Chinese) (Sha and Pereira, 2005)(Chen, Zhang, and Ishihara, 2006) (Kudo and Matsumoto, 2001). These presentative discriminative models which we choose for conducting empirical experiments including: Conditional Random Fields (Lafferty, McCallum, and Pereira, 2001), Support Vector Machine (Vapnik, 1995) and Online Prediction (Crammer et al, 2006). In other words, because Noun Phrase chunks appear most frequently in sentences. So, in this paper we focus mainly on empirical experiments for the tasks of Vietnamese NP chunking.

We plan to answer several major questions by using empirical experiments as follows.

- Whether or not the discriminative learning models are suitable for Vietnamese chunking problem?
- We want to know the difference of SVM, Online Learning, and Conditional Random Fields for Vietnamese chunking task.
- Which features are suitable for discriminative learning models and how they contribute to the performance of Vietnamese text chunking?

The rest of this paper is organized as follows: Section 2 describes Vietnamese text chunking with discriminative sequence learning models. Section 3 shows experimental results and Section 4 dis-

Proceedings of the 7th Workshop on Asian Language Resources, ACL-IJCNLP 2009, pages 9–16,
Suntec, Singapore, 6-7 August 2009.

cusses the advantage of our method and describes future work.

2 Vietnamese NP Chunking with Discriminative Sequence Learning

Noun Phrase chunking is considered as the task of grouping a consecutive sequence of words into a NP chunk lablel. For example: "[NP Anh Ay (He)] [VP thich(likes)] [NP mot chiec oto(a car)] "

Before describing NP chunking tasks, we summarize the characteristic of Vietnamese language and the background of Conditional Random Fields, Support Vector Machine, and Online Learning. Then, we present how to build the annotated corpus for the NP chunking task.

2.1 The characteristic of Vietnamese Words

Vietnamese syllables are elementary units that have one way of pronunciation. In documents, they are usually delimited by white-space. Being the elementary units, Vietnamese syllables are not undivided elements but a structure. Generally, each Vietnamese syllable has all five parts: first consonant, secondary vowel, main vowel, last consonant and a tone mark. For instance, the syllable tu.n (week) has a tone mark (grave accent), a first consonant (t), a secondary vowel (u), a main vowel () and a last consonant (n). However, except for main vowel that is required for all syllables, the other parts may be not present in some cases. For example, the syllable anh (brother) has no tone mark, no secondary vowel and no first consonant. In other case, the syllable hoa (flower) has a secondary vowel (o) but no last consonant.

Words in Vietnamese are made of one or more syllables which are combined in different ways. Based on the way of constructing words from syllables, we can classify them into three categories: single words, complex words and reduplicative words (Mai,Vu, Hoang, 1997).

The past of speechs (Pos) of each word in Vietnamese are mainly sketched as follows.

A Noun Phrase (NP) in Vietnamese consists of three main parts as follows: the noun center, the prefix part, and the post fix part. The prefix and postfix are used to support the meaning of the NP. For example in the NP "ba sinh vien nay", the noun center is "sinh vien", and the prefix is "ba (three)", the postfix is "nay".

Vietnamese Tag	Equivalent to English Tag
CC	Coordinating conjunction)
CD	Cardinal number)
DT	Determiner)
V	Verb
P	Preposition
A	Adjective
LS	List item marker
MD	Modal
N	Noun

Table 1: Part of Speeches in Vietnamese

2.2 The Corpus

We have collected more than 9,000 sentences from several web-sites through the internet. After that, we then applied the segmentation tool (Tu, Phan, Nguyen, Ha, 2006) to segment each sentences into a sequence of tokens. Each sequence of tokens are then represented using the format of CONLL 2000. The details are sketched as follows.

Each line in the annotated data consists of three columns: the token (a word or a punctuation mark), the part-of-speech tag of the token, and the phrase type label (label for short) of the token. The label of each token indicates whether the token is outside a phrase (O), starts a phrase (B-⟨PhraseType⟩), or continues a phrase (I-⟨PhraseType⟩).

In order to save time for building annotated data, we made a set of simple rules for automatically generating the chunking data as follows. If a word is not a "noun", "adjective", or "article" it should be assigned the label "O". The consecutive words are NP if they is one of type as follows: "noun noun"; "article noun", "article noun adjective". After generating such as data, we ask an expert about Vietnamese linguistic to correct the data. Finally, we got more than 9,000 sentences which are annotated with NP chunking labels.

Figure 1 shows an example of the Vietnamese chunking corpus.

2.3 Discriminative Sequence Learning

In this section, we briefly introduce three discriminative sequence learning models for chunking problems.

2.3.1 Conditional Random Fields

Conditional Random Fields (CRFs) (Lafferty, McCallum, and Pereira, 2001) are undirected graphical models used to calculate the conditional

Ngày	B
thứ	I
ba	I
phúc_thẩm	O
vụ_án	B
Lã_Thị_Kim_Oanh	I
:	O
.	O
Ngày	B
thứ	I
ba	I
...	

Figure 1: An Example of the Vietnamese chunking corpus

probability of values on designated output nodes, given values assigned to other designated input nodes for data sequences. CRFs make a first-order Markov independence assumption among output nodes, and thus correspond to finite state machine (FSMs).

Let **o** = $(o_1, o_2, \ldots, o_T)$ be some observed input data sequence, such as a sequence of words in a text (values on T input nodes of the graphical model). Let **S** be a finite set of FSM states, each is associated with a label l such as a clause start position. Let **s** = $(s_1, s_2, \ldots, s_T)$ be some sequences of states (values on T output nodes). CRFs define the conditional probability of a state sequence given an input sequence to be

$$P_\Lambda(s|o) = \frac{1}{Z_o} exp\left(\sum_{t=1}^{T} F(s, o, t)\right) \tag{1}$$

where $Z_o = \sum_s exp\left(\sum_{t=1}^{T} F(s, o, t)\right)$ is a normalization factor over all state sequences. We denote δ to be the Kronecker-δ. Let $F(s, o, t)$ be the sum of CRFs features at time position t:

$$\sum_i \lambda_i f_i(s_{t-1}, s_t, t) + \sum_j \lambda_j g_j(o, s_t, t) \tag{2}$$

where $f_i(s_{t-1}, s_t, t) = \delta(s_{t-1}, l')\delta(s_t, l)$ is a *transition* feature function which represents sequential dependencies by combining the label l' of the previous state s_{t-1} and the label l of the current state s_t, such as the previous label l' = AV (adverb) and the current label l = JJ (adjective). $g_j(o, s_t, t) = \delta(s_t, l)x_k(o, t)$ is a *per-state* feature function which combines the label l of current state s_t and a context predicate, i.e., the binary function $x_k(o, t)$ that captures a particular property of the observation sequence o at time position t. For instance, the current label is JJ and the current word is *"conditional"*.

Training CRFs is commonly performed by maximizing the likelihood function with respect to the training data using advanced convex optimization techniques like L-BFGS. Recently, there are several works apply Stochastic Gradient Descent (SGD) for training CRFs models. SGD has been historically associated with back-propagation algorithms in multilayer neural networks.

And inference in CRFs, i.e., searching the most likely output label sequence of an input observation sequence, can be done using Viterbi algorithm.

2.3.2 Support Vector Machines

Support vector machine (SVM)(Vapnik, 1995) is a technique of machine learning based on statistical learning theory. The main idea behind this method can be summarized as follows. Suppose that we are given l training examples (x_i, y_i), $(1 \le i \le l)$, where x_i is a feature vector in n dimensional feature space, and y_i is the class label {-1, +1 } of x_i.

SVM finds a hyperplane $w.x+b = 0$ which correctly separates training examples and has maximum margin which is the distance between two hyperplanes $w \cdot x + b \ge 1$ and $w \cdot x + b \le -1$. Finally, the optimal hyperplane is formulated as follows:

$$f(x) = \text{sign}\left(\sum_{1}^{l} \alpha_i y_i K(x_i, x) + b\right) \tag{3}$$

where α_i is the Lagrange multiple, and $K(x', x'')$ is called a kernel function, which calculates similarity between two arguments x' and x''. For instance, the Polynomial kernel function is formulated as follows:

$$K(x', x'') = (x' \cdot x'')^p \tag{4}$$

SVMs estimate the label of an unknown example x whether the sign of $f(x)$ is positive or not.

Basically, SVMs are binary classifier, thus we must extend SVMs to multi-class classifier in order to classify three or more classes. The pairwise classifier is one of the most popular methods to extend the binary classification task to that of K classes. Though, we leave the details to (Kudo and Matsumoto, 2001), the idea of pairwise classification is to build K.(K-1)/2 classifiers considering all pairs of classes, and final decision is given by their weighted voting. The implementation of Vietnamese text chunking is based on Yamcha (V0.33)[1].

2.3.3 Online Passive-Aggressive Learning

Online Passive-Aggressive Learning (PA) was proposed by Crammer (Crammer et al, 2006) as an alternative learning algorithm to the maximize margin algorithm. The Perceptron style for natural language processing problems as initially proposed by (Collins, 2002) can provide to state of the art results on various domains including text segmentation, syntactic parsing, and dependency parsing. The main drawback of the Perceptron style algorithm is that it does not have a mechanism for attaining the maximize margin of the training data. It may be difficult to obtain high accuracy in dealing with hard learning data. The online algorithm for chunking parsing in which we can attain the maximize margin of the training data without using an optimization technique. It is thus much faster and easier to implement. The details of PA algorithm for chunking parsing are presented as follows.

Assume that we are given a set of sentences x_i and their chunks y_i where $i = 1, ..., n$. Let the feature mapping between a sentence x and a sequence of chunk labels y be: $\Phi(x, y) = \Phi_1(x, y), \Phi_2(x, y), ..., \Phi_d(x, y)$ where each feature mapping Φ_j maps (x, y) to a real value. We assume that each feature $\Phi(x, y)$ is associated with a weight value. The goal of PA learning for chunking parsing is to obtain a parameter w that minimizes the hinge-loss function and the margin of learning data.

Algorithm 1 shows briefly the Online Learning for chunking problem. The detail about this algorithm can be referred to the work of (Crammer et al, 2006). In Line 7, the argmax value is computed by using the Viterbi algorithm which is similar to the one described in (Collins, 2002). Algorithm 1 is terminated after T round.

[1]Yamcha is available at http://chasen.org/ taku/software/yamcha/

1 Input: $S = (x_i; y_i), i = 1, 2, ..., n$ in which x_i is the sentence and y_i is a sequence of chunks
2 Aggressive parameter C
3 Output: the model
4 Initialize: $w_1 = (0, 0, ..., 0)$
5 **for** t=*1, 2...* **do**
6 Receive an sentence x_t
7 Predict $y_t^* = \arg\max_{y \in Y}(w_t.\Phi(x_t, y_t))$ Suffer loss: $l_t = w_t.\Phi(x_t, y_t^*) - w_t.\Phi(x_t, y_t) + \sqrt{\rho(y_t, y_t^*)}$
8 Set:$\tau_t = \frac{l_t}{||\Phi(x_t, y_t^*) - \Phi(x_t, y_t)||^2}$
9 Update: $w_{t+1} = w_t + \tau_t(\Phi(x_t, y_t) - \Phi(x_t, y_t^*))$
10 **end**

Algorithm 1: The Passive-Aggressive algorithm for NP chunking.

2.3.4 Feature Set

Feature set is designed through features template which is shown in Table 2. All edge features obey the first-order Markov dependency that the label (l) of the current state depends on the label (l') of the previous state (e.g., "l = I-NP" and "l' = B-NP"). Each observation feature expresses how much influence a statistic ($x(\mathbf{o}, i)$) observed surrounding the current position i has on the label (l) of the current state. A statistic captures a particular property of the observation sequence. For instance, the observation feature "l = I-NP" and "word$_{-1}$ is *the*" indicates that the label of the current state should be I-NP (i.e., continue a noun phrase) if the previous word is *the*. Table 2 describes both edge and observation feature templates. Statistics for observation features are identities of words, POS tags surrounding the current position, such as words and POS tags at -2, -1, 1, 2.

We also employ 2-order conjunctions of the current word with the previous ($w_{-1}w_0$) or the next word (w_0w_1), and 2-order and 3-order conjunctions of two or three consecutive POS tags within the current window to make use of the mutual dependencies among singleton properties. With the feature templates shown in Table 2 and the feature rare threshold of 1 (i.e., only features with occurrence frequency larger than 1 are included into the discriminative models)

Edge feature templates	
Current state: s_i	Previous state: s_{i-1}
l	l'

Observation feature templates	
Current state: s_i	Statistic (or context predicate) templates: $x(\mathbf{o}, i)$
l	$w_{-2}; w_{-1}; w_0; w_1; w_2; w_{-1}w_0; w_0w_1;$ $t_{-2}; t_{-1}; t_0; t_1; t_2;$ $t_{-2}t_{-1}; t_{-1}t_0; t_0t_1; t_1t_2; t_{-2}t_{-1}t_0;$ $t_{-1}t_0t_1; t_0t_1t_2$

Table 2: Feature templates for phrase chunking

3 Experimental Results

We evaluate the performance of using several sequence learning models for the Vietnamese NP chunking problem. The data of more than 9,000 sentences is evaluated using an empirical experiment with 5 fold cross validation test. It means we used 1,800 and 7,200 sentences for testing and training the discriminative sequence learning models, respectively. Note that the evaluation method is used the same as CONLL2000 did. We used Precision, Recall, and F-Measure in which Precision measures how many chunks found by the algorithm are correct and the recall is percentage of chunks defined in the corpus that were found by the chunking program.

$$Precision = \frac{\#\text{correct}-\text{chunk}}{\#\text{numberofchunks}}$$
$$Recall = \frac{\#\text{correct}-\text{chunks}}{\#\text{numerofchunksinthecorpus}}$$

$$\mathrm{F-measure} = \frac{2 \times \text{Precision} \times \text{Recall}}{\text{Precision} + \text{Recall}}$$

To compute the scores in our experiments, we utilized the evaluation tool (conlleval.pl) which is available in CONLL 2000 (Sang and Buchholz, 2000,).

Figure 2 shows the precision scores of three methods using 5 Folds cross validation test. It reports that the CRF-LBFGS attain the highest score. The SVMs and CRF-SGD are comparable to CRF-LBFGS. The Online Learning achieved the lowest score.

Figure 3 shows the recall scores of three CRFs-LBFGS, CRFs-SGD, SVM, and Online Learning. The results show that CRFs-SGD achieved the highest score while the Online Learning obtained the lowest score in comparison with others.

Figure 4 and Figure 5 show the F-measure and accuracy scores using 5 Folds Cross-validation Test. Similar to these results of Precision and Recall, CRFs-LBFGS was superior to the other ones while the Online Learning method obtained the lowest result.

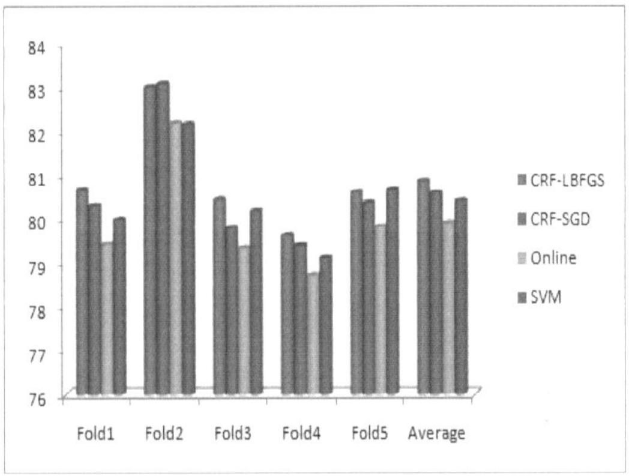

Figure 2: Precision results in 5 Fold cross validation test

Table 3 shows the comparison of three discriminative learning methods for Vietnamese Noun Phrase chunking. We compared the three sequence learning methods including: CRFs using the LBFGS method, CRFs with SGD, and Online Learning. Experiment results show that the CRFs-LBFGS is the best in comparison with others. However, the computational times when training the data is slower than either SGD or Online Learning. The SGD is faster than CRF-LBFS approximately 6 times. The SVM model obtained a comparable results with CRFs models and it was superior to Online Learning. It yields results that were 0.712% than Online Learning. However, the SVM's training process take slower than CRFs and Online Learning. According to our empirical investigation, it takes approximately slower than CRF-SGF, CRF-LBFGS as well as Online Learning.

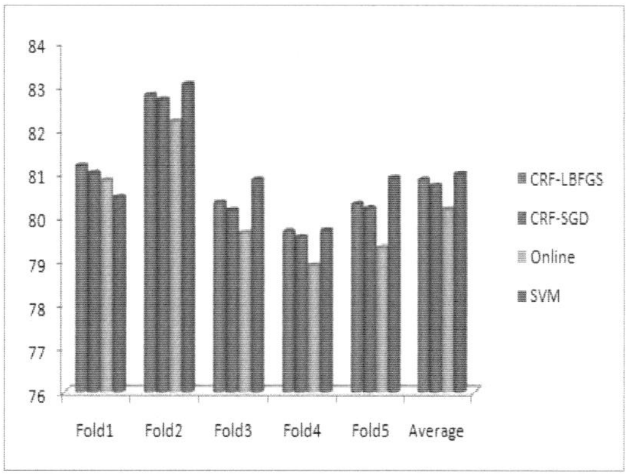

Figure 3: Recall result in 5 Fold cross validation test

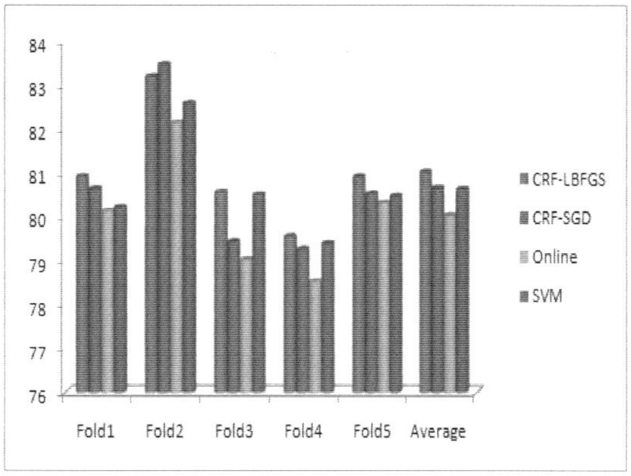

Figure 4: The F-measure results of 5 Folds Cross-validation Test

Note that we used FlexCRFs (Phan, Nguyen, Tu , 2005) for Conditional Random Fields using LBFGS, and for Stochastic Gradient Descent (SGD) we used SGD1.3 which is developed by Leon Bottou [2].

Methods	Precision	Recall	F_1
CRF-LBGS	80.85	81.034	80.86
CRF-SGD	80.74	80.66	80.58
Online-PA	80.034	80.13	79.89
SVM	80.412	80.982	80.638

Table 3: Vietnamese Noun Phrase chunking performance using Discriminative Sequence Learning (CRFs, SVM, Online-PA)

In order to investigate which features are major effect on the discriminative learning models for Vietnamese Chunking problems, we conduct three experiments as follows.

[2] http://leon.bottou.org/projects/sgd

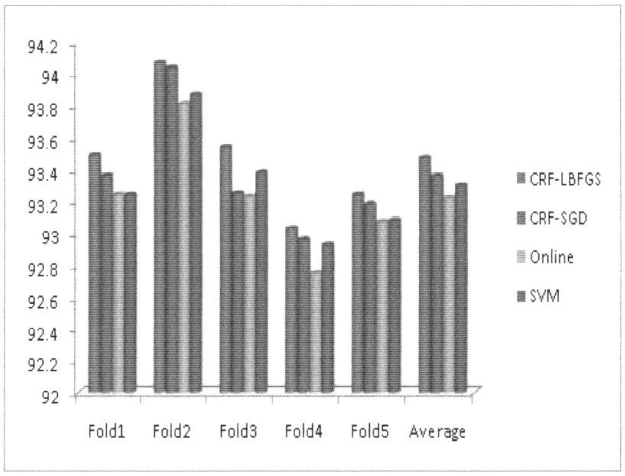

Figure 5: The accuracy scores of four methods with 5 Folds Cross-validation Test

- Cross validation test for three modes without considering the edge features
- Cross validation test for three models without using POS features
- Cross validation test for three models without using lexical features
- Cross validation test for three models without using "edge features template" features

Note that the computational time of training SVMs model is slow, so we skip considering feature selection for SVMs. We only consider feature selection for CRFs and Online Learning.

Feature Set	LBFGS	SGD	Online
Full-Features	80.86	80.58	79.89
Without-Edge	80.91	78.66	80.13
Without-Pos	62.264	62.626	59.572
Without-Lex	77.204	77.712	75.576

Table 4: Vietnamese Noun Phrase chunking performance using Discriminative Sequence Learning (CRFs, Online-PA)

Table 4 shows that the Edge features have an impact to the CRF-SGD model while it do not affect to the performance of CRFs-LBFGS and Online-PA learning. Table 4 also indicates that the POS features are severed as important features regarding to the performance of all discriminative sequence learning models. As we can see, if one do not use POS features the F1-score of each model is decreased more than 20%. We also remark that the lexical features contribute an important role to the performance of Vietnamese text

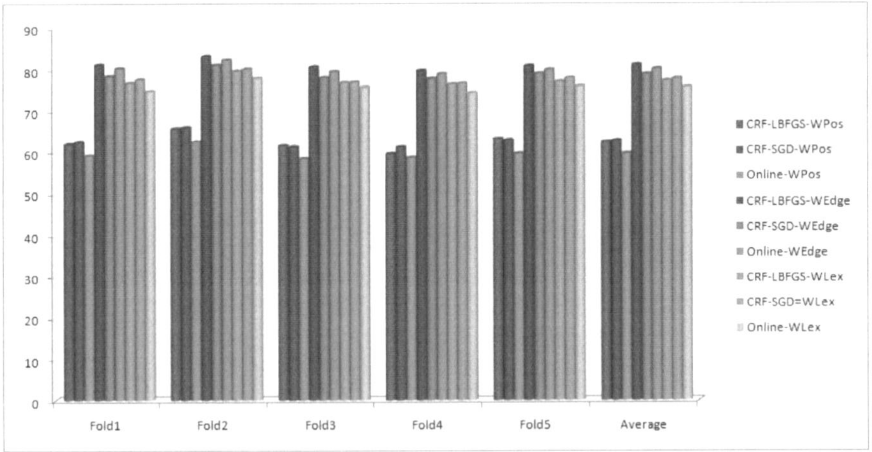

Figure 6: F-measures of three methods with different feature set

chunking. If we do not use lexical features the F1-score of each model is decreased till approximately 3%. In conclusion, the POS features significantly effect on the performance of the discriminative sequence models. This is similar to the note of (Chen, Zhang, and Ishihara, 2006).

Figure 6 reports the F-Measures of using different feature set for each discriminative models. Note that WPos, WLex, and WEdge mean without using Pos features, without using lexical features, and without using edge features, respectively. As we can see, the CRF-LBFGs always achieved the best scores in comparison with the other ones and the Online Learning achieved the lowest scores.

4 Conclusions

In this paper, we report an investigation of developing a Vietnamese Chunking tool. We have constructed an annotation corpus of more than 9,000 sentences and exploiting discriminative learning models for the NP chunking task. Experimental results using 5 Folds cross-validation test have showed that the discriminative models are well suitable for Vietnamese phrase chunking. Conditional random fields show a better performance in comparison with other methods. The part of speech features are known as the most influence features regarding to the performances of discriminative models on Vietnamese phrases chunking.

What our contribution is expected to be useful for the development of Vietnamese Natural Language Processing. Our results and corpus can be severed as a very good baseline for Natural Language Processing community to develop the Vietnamese chunking task.

There are still room for improving the performance of Vietnamese chunking models. For example, more attention on features selection is necessary. We would like to solve this in future work.

Acknowledgments

The constructive comments and helpful suggestions from three anonymous reviewers are greatly appreciated. This paper is supported by JAIST Grant for Research Associates and a part from a national project named Building Basic Resources and Tools for Vietnamese Language and Speech Processing, KC01.01/06-10.

References

M. Collins. 2002. Discriminative training methods for hidden markov models: Theory and experiments with perceptron algorithms. In Proceedings of EMNLP 2002.

K. Crammer et al. 2006. Online Passive-Aggressive Algorithm. Journal of Machine Learning Research, 2006

W. Chen, Y. Zhang, and H. Ishihara 2006. An empirical study of Chinese chunking. In Proceedings COLING/ACL 2006

Dinh Dien, Vu Thuy 2006. A maximum entropy approach for vietnamese word segmentation. In Proceedings of the IEEE - International Conference on Computing and Telecommunication Technologies RIVF 2006: 248-253

J. Lafferty, A. McCallum, and F. Pereira. 2001. Conditional random fields: Probabilistic models for segmenting and labeling sequence data. In the proceedings of International Conference on Machine Learning (ICML), pp.282-289, 2001

N.C. Mai, D.N. Vu, T.P. Hoang. 1997. Foundations of linguistics and Vietnamese. Education Publisher (1997) 142. 152

Thi Minh Huyen Nguyen, Laurent Romary, Mathias Rossignol, Xuan Luong Vu. 2006. A lexicon for Vietnamese language processing. Language Reseourse Evaluation (2006) 40:291-309.

Minh Nghiem, Dien Dinh, Mai Nguyen. 2008. Improving Vietnamese POS tagging by integrating a rich feature set and Support Vector Machines. In Proceedings of the IEEE - International Conference on Computing and Telecommunication Technologies RIVF 2008: 128–133.

X.H. Phan, M.L. Nguyen, C.T. Nguyen. FlexCRFs: Flexible Conditional Random Field Toolkit. http://flexcrfs.sourceforge.net, 2005

T. Kudo and Y. Matsumoto. 2001. Chunking with Support Vector Machines. The Second Meeting of the North American Chapter of the Association for Computational Linguistics (2001)

F. Sha and F. Pereira. 2005. Shallow Parsing with Conditional Random Fields. Proceedings of HLT-NAACL 2003 213-220 (2003)

C.T. Nguyen, T.K. Nguyen, X.H. Phan, L.M. Vietnamese Word Segmentation with CRFs and SVMs: An Investigation. 2006. The 20th Pacific Asia Conference on Language, Information, and Computation (PACLIC), 1-3 November, 2006, Wuhan, China

Tjong Kim Sang and Sabine Buchholz. 2000. Introduction to the CoNLL-2000 Shared Task: Chunking. Proceedings of CoNLL-2000 , Lisbon, Portugal, 2000.

V. Vapnik. 1995. The Natural of Statistical Learning Theory. New York: Springer-Verlag, 1995.

Corpus-based Sinhala Lexicon

Ruvan Weerasinghe[1], Dulip Herath[2], Viraj Welgama[3]
Language Technology Research Laboratory,
University of Colombo School of Computing
35, Reid Avenue, Colombo 07,
Sri Lanka
{arw[1], dlh[2], wvw[3]}@ucsc.cmb.ac.lk

Abstract

Lexicon is in important resource in any kind of language processing application. Corpus-based lexica have several advantages over other traditional approaches. The lexicon developed for Sinhala was based on the text obtained from a corpus of 10 million words drawn from diverse genres. The words extracted from the corpus have been labeled with parts of speech categories defined according to a novel classification proposed for Sinhala. The lexicon reports 80% coverage over unrestricted text obtained from online sources. The lexicon has been implemented in Lexical Mark up Framework.

1 Introduction

The availability of lexical resources is central to many natural language processing tasks as words play a crucial role in defining higher level constructions such as phrases, clauses and sentences of any language. The most generic and basic lexical resource for such work is a lexicon, preferably with part of speech annotation and information about possible word forms. The latter is important especially for morphologically rich languages such as Sinhala. This kind of resource is extremely useful for part of speech tagging, grammar development and parsing, machine translations, speech processing applications, among others. As new knowledge is created, new concepts are introduced to the language in terms of words. Non-corpus-based lexicon development approaches are not capable of acquiring these new words into lexica due to their inherent limitations such as reliance on introspection and linguistic exposure of the human compiler(s). Therefore it is essential to adopt less expensive (less time consuming, labor intensive and robust) alternative strategies to develop wide-coverage lexica for less studied languages.

This paper presents a lexicon for Sinhala which has nearly 35,000 entries based on the text drawn from the UCSC Text Corpus of Contemporary Sinhala consisting of 10 million words from diverse genres. The corpus-based approach taken in this work can overcome the limitations that traditional approaches suffering from such as less reliance on less expert knowledge, the ability to capture modern usage based on recently introduced words and wide coverage.

The lexical entries defined in this approach are classified according to a novel classification in order to fulfill the requirements of language processing tasks. The broad classes defined are significantly different from those described in traditional Sinhala grammar. For declensional classes such as Nouns and Verbs, further subdivisions have been proposed based on their morpho-phonemic features. Each of the subdivision classes is associated with a set of rules that can be used to generate all possible morphological forms of that group. This has made a significant contribution to improve the coverage of the lexicon as for a given lexical entry it is hard to guarantee that all possible forms exist in the original corpus. However, the rules defined in each class guarantee recognize such unseen forms in the test data set.

In addition, a comprehensive set of function words has been defined based on some of the indeclinable classes such as Post-positions, Particles, Determiners, Conjunctions and Interjections. The lexicon also consists of the most commonly used named entities such as person and city names. Syllabified phonetic transcriptions of the lexical entries are also incorporated in order to make this resource useful in speech processing applications.

Proceedings of the 7th Workshop on Asian Language Resources, ACL-IJCNLP 2009, pages 17–23,
Suntec, Singapore, 6-7 August 2009. ©2009 ACL and AFNLP

These characteristics are essential in building effective practical natural language processing applications. To the best of our knowledge, this is the first attempt to build a wide coverage lexicon for Sinhala from a computational linguistic perspective reported in the literature.

The rest of the paper describes the work carried out in detail. Section 2 gives a detailed description of the data acquisition stage, the part of speech categories and the subdivisions based on morphology and the phonetic transcription with syllabification. The implementation details of the lexicon and schemas defined for lexical entries using Lexical Mark up Framework (LMF) is given in Section 3. Section 4 comments on the results of the experiments conducted to measure the coverage of the lexicon. Finally, Section 5 discusses the issues and limitations of the current work with insights for future work.

2 Sinhala Lexicon

2.1 Data Acquisition

The data for the lexicon was obtained from the UCSC Sinhala Corpus which has text drawn from diverse genres namely, Creative Writing, Technical Writing and News Reportage. The corpus represents the modern usage of Sinhala in the above mentioned genres. This guarantees the robustness of the lexicon in practical language processing applications. The text distribution across genres in the corpus is given in Table 1.

Genre	Number of Words	% Number of Words
Creative Writing	2,340,999	23%
Technical Writing	4,357,680	43%
News Reportage	3,433,772	34%

Table 1. Distribution of Corpus Text across Genres

It is clear from the Table 1 that the corpus is fairly balanced across genres while Creative Writing and Technical Writing genres respectively make the lowest and the highest contributions to the total word count of the corpus.

In order to extract the candidate words for the lexicon, a distinct word list with frequencies was obtained by running a simple tokenizer on the corpus text. Misspelt and irrelevant tokens (numbers, foreign words, etc) were removed from the list after manual inspection. Further, the resultant words were manually classified into their respective parts of speech for subsequent processing based on a predefined classification. This was carried out by a team of five members including one senior linguist. At the initial stage of this phase, a substantial effort was made to train the manual classifiers to classify words according to the predefined set of classification criteria. In order to automate this process, the high frequency words were first classified into their respective parts of speech and then certain word ending patterns peculiar to each class were identified. These patterns were used to classify the rest of the list automatically by running regular expression matching followed by manual cleaning. This strategy significantly accelerated the data acquisition process.

In addition to the words taken from the corpus, a comprehensive list of named entities such as person, village/city, country, capital, product names was added to the lexicon after processing data sources obtained from the Departments of Census & Statistics and Inland Revenue. These entries were absorbed into the lexicon on the basis of complete enumeration.

2.2 Parts of Speech and Morphology

In traditional Sinhala grammar, several classifications have been proposed for parts of speech. This is mainly due to the existence of different grammatical schools in Sinhala language studies. They can be broadly classified into three main categories namely, notions based on Sanskrit grammar (Dharmarama, 1913), ideas inspired by language purism significantly different from those based on Sanskrit grammar (Kumaratunaga, 1963), and classifications proposed in the light of modern linguistics (Karunatilake, 2004). From a computational linguistic point of view, each of these classifications while having their own strengths is unable to capture phenomena which are useful for computational linguistics. They are mainly descriptive treatments of language which are used for pedagogical purposes whereas a computational model requires a formal analytical treatment in order to be of any use. Due to the limitations of the existing classifications of Sinhala words, a novel classification of part-of-speech categories was developed after studying the existing classifications closely; consulting linguists and reviewing part of speech tag set design initiatives for other Indic languages. Widely accepted and used tag sets for English were also taken into account when proposed classification was developed. As described in section 1, the current classification has improved the predictive power of each class and this has in turn improved the coverage that is essential for robustness of the lexicon in computational linguistic and natural language processing tasks.

Part of Speech	Frequency	
Noun	12264	35.89%
Verb	1018	3.00%
Adjective	2869	8.40%
Adverb	315	0.92%
Postposition	146	0.43%
Particle	145	0.42%
Conjunction	29	0.08%
Numeral	382	1.12%
Determiner	76	0.22%
Pronoun	150	0.44%
Proper Noun	16585	48.52%
Verb Particle	158	0.46%
Interjection	44	0.13%

Table 2. Part of Speech Categories and their Frequencies

Table 2 shows the thirteen broad classes of parts of speech used in the proposed lexicon. Names of these categories are self-explanatory except for *Verb Particle* which stands for a category of words that are used in Sinhala compound verbs, exemplified best by the terms ඉකුත් (Sinhala: *ikuth*, Sanskrit: *athikränthə*), පත් (Sinhala: *path*, Sanskrit: *präpthə*), and පළ (Sinhala: *palə*, Sanskrit: *prəkətə*). Most of these Verb Particles are localized forms of past participle forms of some Sanskrit verbs. For some historical reason, only past participle forms of these verbs are present in modern usage of Sinhala but not the other forms.

According to the frequency distribution of parts of speech categories given in Table 2, it is clear that nearly 50% of the lexical entries are Proper Nouns. Overall 85% of the total number of entries is nouns with only 3% being Verbs. This is mainly due to the fact that Sinhala has many compound verbs. Compound verbs are usually formed by using Nouns, Adjectives, Verb Particles and Participles of some verbs together with the helper verbs such as කරනවා (English: *do*), වෙනවා (English: *be*), දෙනවා (English: *give*), ගන්නවා (English: *take*), and දානවා (English: *put*). As this contextual information is absent it is hard to determine whether a particular noun or adjective or any other word has occurred as a constituent of a compound verb or not. Therefore they were classified as if they occurred in their primary category.

Even though the number of entries under Verb category is relatively small i.e. nearly 3%, it was found that the number of instances of those verbs is significantly high. In the distinct word list obtained from the original corpus, 4.64% of the entries were verbs (including inflected forms). The total number of instances of verbs (including inflected forms) in the corpus is 19.4% of the total number of words in the corpus. This implies that 3% of the lexicon has coverage of nearly 20% of the corpus. In addition, it was found that 27.7% of the verbs in the corpus are compound verbs since verbs that are essentially part of compound verbs (කරනවා, වෙනවා, දෙනවා, ගන්නවා, දානවා) have occurred 27.7% of the corpus.

It was also possible to identify a set of words which plays only functional roles in Sinhala sentences and have no lexical meaning. In the traditional treatments of grammar they are classified as *nipa:thə* which literally means "*things that fall in either initial or medial or final position of a sentence to express the relationships among elements of the sentence*". This definition does not take into account the different functional roles played by those words and therefore classifies them into one single class called *nipa:thə*. In the work described here, these words were classified into five classes namely, Postpositions, Particles, Conjunctions, Determiners and Interjections. A list of 440 words that belong to these five classes form the first function (stop) word list reported for Sinhala. Identifying the function words is important for applications such as information retrieval, prosody modeling in speech synthesis, semantic role labeling, and dependency parsing.

Nouns and Verbs are further classified into subclasses according to their inflectional/declension paradigms given in Table 3 and 4. These subclasses are mainly specified by the morphophonemic characteristics of stems/roots.

Gender	Subclass	Frequency
Masculine	Consonant-1	63
	Consonant-2	13
	Consonant Reduplication	973
	Front-Mid Vowel	1231
	Back Vowel	191
	Retroflex-1	81
	Retroflex-2	61
	Kinship	180
	Irregular	41
Feminine	Consonant	12

	Front-Mid Vowel	168
	Back Vowel	78
	Irregular	17
Neuter	Consonant	2303
	Consonant Reduplication	206
	Front-Mid Vowel	4379
	Mid Vowel	115
	Back Vowel	1097
	Retroflex-1	127
	Retroflex-2	523
	Uncountable	404
	Irregular	12

Table 3. Noun Subclasses

Nouns are primarily classified with respect to the phone type of the final position of the stem: *Consonant-1* and *Consonant-2* classes have stems that have a consonant ending. The difference between these two classes is defined by the phonological changes that take place when nominal and accusative suffixes are added to the stem. The noun stems belong Consonant-1 has the plural suffix (*-u*) and their final position consonant is reduplicated when the suffix is appended whereas noun stems belong to Consonant-2 has null suffix to mark plurality.

The noun stems that belong to *Consonant Reduplication* have either vowel /i/ or /u/ at the final position. When a nominative or accusative suffix (-a: / -O: / -an) is appended to the noun stem the final position vowel is deleted and the penultimate non-retroflex consonant is reduplicated. If the consonant is retroflex they are classified under *Retroflex-1*. If the noun stems that have vowel /ə/ at the final position and the penultimate consonant is retroflex then the vowel is deleted and the nominative or accusative suffix is appended to the remaining part of the stem. This class is named as *Retroflex-2*.

When a nominative or accusative suffix is appended to a noun stem that belongs to *Front-Mid Vowel* subclass, the semi-consonant /y/ is inserted between the noun stem and the suffix. Similarly, /w/ is inserted if the noun stem belongs to *Back Vowel* category.*Kinship* and *Uncountable* nouns[1] are inflected in a unique manner irrespective of the phonetic characteristics of stem endings. Each subcategory (*Masculine, Feminine*, and *Neuter*) has a set of stems that behaves irregularly.

Each category has a unique set of phonological rules and inflectional suffixes to generate 130 possible word forms.

Verbs have been classified into four main subclasses according to the phonetic characteristics of their roots.

Subclass	Frequency
ə-ending	488
e-ending	325
i-ending	90
irregular	115

Table 4. Verb Subclasses

As shown in Table 4 the most frequently occurring verbs belong to the ə-ending category. Each of these verb categories except for the irregular category has a unique set of phonological rules and suffixes to generate 240 possible word forms.

2.3 Phonetic Transcriptions

Sinhala orthography is relatively unambiguous as each character corresponds to a unique speech sound. However there are a few ambiguous cases that have to be resolved by taking the context into account. Though Sinhala orthography has different symbols to denote aspirated and unaspirated consonants, in present usage aspiration is not present. Similarly, the alveolar consonants such as ළ (/l/) and ණ (/n/) are now pronounced as their dental counterparts ල and න. Schwa epenthesis also plays a crucial role in Sinhala pronunciation as it leads to significant meaning changes of Sinhala words.

Having considered all these issues, it was decided to incorporate phonetic transcriptions of lexical entries in order to make the current lexicon general purpose. This piece of information is very useful for speech synthesis and recognition application development. Syllabified phonetic transcriptions were automatically derived by applying the grapheme to phoneme (G2P) rules and the syllabification algorithm described in (Wasala et al, 2006) and (Weerasinghe et al, 2005) respectively that report 98% on G2P and 99% accuracy on syllabification. All phonetic transcriptions are given in International Phonetic Alphabet (IPA) symbols.

[1] These two classes have been defined on a semantic basis whereas the other classes are based on phonetic and morphological characteristics of stems.

3 Implementation

The lexicon has been implemented in XML according to the specification given in Lexical Mark-up Framework (Francopoulo et al, 2006) which is now the ISO standard for lexicon development. The XML schema defined for Nouns and Verbs with some examples are shown in Figure 1 and 2 respectively.

```
- <LexicalEntry>
    <feat att="partOfSpeech" val="NOUN" />
    <feat att="subClass" val="Masc.GerminatedConsonant" />
  - <Lemma>
      <feat att="citationForm" val="බල්ලා" />
      <feat att="pronunciation" val="bal-lä" />
    </Lemma>
  - <WordForm>
      <feat att="writtenForm" val="බල්ලා" />
      <feat att="pronunciation" val="e-lu-vä" />
      <feat att="gender" val="masculine" />
      <feat att="number" val="singular" />
      <feat att="definiteness" val="definite" />
      <feat att="case" val="nominative" />
    </WordForm>
  </LexicalEntry>
- <LexicalEntry>
    <feat att="partOfSpeech" val="NOUN" />
    <feat att="subClass" val="Masc.BackVowel" />
  - <Lemma>
      <feat att="citationForm" val="එළුවා" />
      <feat att="pronunciation" val="e-lu-vä" />
    </Lemma>
  - <WordForm>
      <feat att="writtenForm" val="එළුවා" />
      <feat att="pronunciation" val="e-lu-vä" />
      <feat att="gender" val="masculine" />
      <feat att="number" val="singular" />
      <feat att="definiteness" val="definite" />
      <feat att="case" val="nominative" />
    </WordForm>
  </LexicalEntry>
```

Figure 1. Lexical Entries for **Nouns බල්ලා and එළුවා.**

```
- <LexicalEntry>
    <feat att="partOfSpeech" val="VERB" />
    <feat att="subClass" val="Regular.a" />
  - <Lemma>
      <feat att="citationForm" val="බලනවා" />
      <feat att="pronunciation" val="ba-la-na-vä" />
    </Lemma>
  - <WordForm>
      <feat att="writtenForm" val="බලමි" />
      <feat att="pronunciation" val="ba-la-mi" />
      <feat att="tense" val="present" />
      <feat att="aspect" val="finite" />
      <feat att="modality" val="indicative" />
      <feat att="number" val="singular" />
      <feat att="person" val="first" />
    </WordForm>
  </LexicalEntry>
- <LexicalEntry>
    <feat att="partOfSpeech" val="VERB" />
    <feat att="subClass" val="Regular.e" />
  - <Lemma>
      <feat att="citationForm" val="සිනාසෙනවා" />
      <feat att="pronunciation" val="si-nä-se-na-vä" />
    </Lemma>
  - <WordForm>
      <feat att="writtenForm" val="සිනාසෙයි" />
      <feat att="pronunciation" val="si-na:-se-yi" />
      <feat att="tense" val="present" />
      <feat att="aspect" val="finite" />
      <feat att="modality" val="indicative" />
      <feat att="number" val="singular" />
      <feat att="person" val="third" />
    </WordForm>
  </LexicalEntry>
```

Figure 2. Lexical Entries for Verbs **බලනවා** (see) and **සිනාසෙනවා** (smile)

As shown in Figure 1, a typical noun entry has main part of speech category (**partOfSpeech**), sub category (**subClass**). Each Lemma has two feature attributes namely citation form and pronunciation. **WordForm** has several feature attributes called *writtenForm* which is the *orthographic representation, pronunciation, number, gender, person, definiteness* and *case* of the particular word form.

In addition to the attributes available in Nouns, schema defined for Verbs have some attributes peculiar to verbs such as tense, aspect and modality. For Verb, only the present tense.

4 Evaluation

4.1 Test Data Sets

The coverage of the current lexicon was measured by conducting a set of experiments on test data prepared for each of the three genres: News Reportage, Technical Writing, and Creative Writing. This data was obtained from text available online: online newspapers, Sinhala Wikipedia, blogs and other websites. From this data two types of test data sets were prepared namely uncleaned and cleaned test data sets. The uncleaned test data contains all the text as they were whereas the cleaned test data contains words that have occurred more than once. Tables 5 and 6 respectively give the details of uncleaned and cleaned data sets.

Genre	Type	Size
Creative Writing	Full Text	108,018
	Distinct List	22,663
Technical Writing	Full Text	107,004
	Distinct List	25,786
News Reportage	Full Text	103,194
	Distinct List	20,225

Table 5. Un-Cleaned Test Data for Three Main Genres

Genre	Type	Size
Creative Writing	Full Text	94,971
	Distinct List	9,616
Technical Writing	Full Text	91,323
	Distinct List	10,105
News Reportage	Full Text	91,838
	Distinct List	8,869

Table 6. Cleaned Test Data for Three Main Genres

4.2 Lexicon Coverage

Initially, coverage of the lexicon was measured for each genre for both Full Text (FT) and Distinct Wordlist (DW) obtained from full text on each data sets: un-cleaned and cleaned. According to the results of this experiment shown in Table 7, the lexicon reports its highest coverage in Creative Writing genre and the lowest is reported in News Reportage.

Genre	Data Set			
	Un-cleaned		Cleaned	
	DW	FT	DW	FT
Creative Writing	60.11%	82.42%	72.21%	86.71%
Technical Writing	58.74%	80.32%	70.73%	84.15%
News Reportage	55.20%	79.82%	71.1%	85.81%

Table 7. Coverage Reported for each Genre on Un-cleaned and Cleaned Data Sets

There is a significant difference between the coverage reported on the Distinct Wordlists obtained from Un-cleaned and Cleaned datasets that is 60% to 72% in Creative Writing, 58% to 70% in Technical Writing and 55% to 71% in News Reportage. This consistent difference proves that a significant number of the words that could not be found in the lexicon were occurred only once in the test data set.

Relatively higher coverage can be achieved when the full text is used rather than a distinct list of words. As high frequency words occur in text more than once in practical situations the lexicon covers a large area of the text though it cannot recognize some low frequency words in the text. This is evident from the differences of coverage reported on Distinct Wordlists and Full Text for both un-cleaned and cleaned data sets (see Table 7). Around 20% coverage difference between Distinct Wordlist and Full Text was reported for each genre.

The average coverage of the lexicon was computed by averaging the coverage reported for three different genres on un-cleaned full-text (FT) data set, which is 80.9%.

In addition, a similar experiment was conducted to measure the significance of the classification proposed in the current work. In that experiment, the coverage of the lexicon was measured by taking only the word forms occurred in the original corpus but not all the forms of the words occurred in the original corpus. Then the rules defined in each subdivision of nouns and verbs were used to generate all possible forms of the words occurred in the original corpus. This experiment was carried out on the distinct word list obtained from the un-cleaned data set. The results show that there were 3.8%, 3.4% and 3.2% improvements in the coverage of creative writing, technical writing and news reportage genres respectively after introducing the generation rules for each subdivision of nouns and verbs.

4.3 Error Analysis

A comprehensive error analysis was done on the words that could not be found in the lexicon to identify the issues behind the errors reported. It was found that there were several types of errors that have contributed to the overall error. The identified error types are given in Table 8.

Error Type	Description
Word Division Errors (D)	Word does not follow standard word division policy
Spelling Error (E)	Word is incorrectly spelt
Foreign Word (F)	Foreign word written in Sinhala script
Non Standard Spelling (N)	Word does not follow standard spelling
Proper Nouns (P)	Word is a Proper Noun
Spoken Forms (S)	Word is a spoken form
Typographic Errors (T)	Word had typographic errors
Wrong Word Forms (W)	Word is an incorrect morphological form
Correct Forms (C)	Correct word not found in the lexicon

Table 8. Typical Errors Found in the Error Analysis

The distribution of these errors across three different genres is given in Table 9. These results were taken only for the cleaned data set. According to the reported results, it is clear that some errors are prominent in some genres are some are consistently present in all the genres. For example, word division errors (D), correct form errors (C), wrong word form errors (W), and non standard spelling errors (N) are consistently occurring in all three genres whereas spoken form errors (S) are prominent in Creative Writing genre (8.52%), Spelling Errors (E) are more prominent in Technical Writing genre, more foreign word errors (F) are found in Technical Writing genre, typographic errors (T) are prominent in found in News Reportage.

Error Type	Creative Writing		Technical Writing		News Reportage	
	DW	FT	DW	FT	DW	FT

C	38.88	39.59	25.81	25.20	17.16	10.57
D	31.84	32.28	23.16	25.36	33.82	33.15
E	5.01	4.49	6.31	5.72	2.31	2.60
F	3.01	2.27	5.27	3.37	2.12	2.19
N	2.30	2.77	6.34	5.94	5.40	6.44
P	2.86	1.89	11.37	11.59	11.03	7.88
S	8.52	8.64	3.20	2.14	5.40	4.34
T	6.22	6.84	14.96	17.88	18.97	29.10
W	1.36	1.22	3.58	2.79	3.78	3.73

Table 9. Different Error Types Distributed across Three Genres Reported on Distinct Wordlist (DW) and Full Text (FT)

It can be concluded from these observations that the errors that are genre independent occur more frequently than genre dependent error and they are the most general mistakes that writers make in their writings. The typographic errors that more frequent in Technical Writing and News Reportage genres are mainly due to the complications in Sinhala typing and Unicode representation. As Sinhala Unicode uses Zero Width Joiner character very often to represent combined characters typists make errors when typing by inserting this character incorrectly. It is hard for them to correct it by deleting that character as it is invisible to the typist on the computer screen. It is clear that from the results shown in Table 9 that there is no significant difference between the error distributions in distinct wordlist and full text test data.

5 Issues and Future Work

The current lexicon has 80% coverage over unrestricted text selected from online sources. In order to make this lexicon robust in practical language processing applications it is important to further improve its coverage in different domains.

It was observed that the number of verbs in the lexicon is relatively small due to the fact that fairly large numbers of Sinhala verbs are compound verbs. In the future it is expected to incorporate those compound verbs so that the coverage of verbs of the lexicon is relatively higher.

In the current implementation the word forms of nouns and verbs are generated by using third party commercial software. It is expected to incorporate a morphological analyzer and generator so that all the possible word forms can be generated by the lexicon itself.

6 Acknowledgements

Authors are very grateful to Prof Tissa Jayawardana at the University of Colombo for his generous support extended to linguistic aspect of this project. The contribution made by the members of the Development Team at the Language Technology Research Laboratory of the University of Colombo of School of Computing-Sri Lanka for manual data classification process is highly appreciated. Authors would also like to acknowledge the feedback given by three unknown reviewers as they have been extremely useful in improving the quality of the work reported.

References

Asanka Wasala, Ruvan Weerasinghe, Kumudu Gamage. 2006. *Sinhala Grapheme-toPhoneme Conversion and Rules for Schwa Epenthesis*. Proceedings of the COLING/ACL 2006 Main Conference Poster Sessions, Sydney, Australia. pp. 890—897

Gil Francopoulo, Monte George, Nicoletta Calzolari, Monica Monachini, Nuria Bel, Mandy Pet, Claudia Soria. 2006. *Lexical Markup Framework*. LREC 2006

Kumaratunga Munidasa. 1963. *Vyakarana Vivaranaya*. M. D. Gunasena Publishers, Colombo

Rathmalane Dharmarama. 1913. *Sidath Sangarawa*. Author Publication.

Ruvan Weerasinghe Asanka Wasala, and Kumudu Gamage. 2005 *A Rule Based Syllabification Algtoithm for Sinhala*. Proceedings of the 2nd International Joint Conference on Natural Language Processing (IJCNLP-05), Jeju Island, Korea. pp. 438-449

W S Karunatilaka. 2004. *Sinhala Bhasa Vyakaranaya*. 5th Edition, M. D Gunasena Publishers, Colombo

Analysis and Development of Urdu POS Tagged Corpus

Ahmed Muaz
Center for Research in Urdu Language Processing
NUCES, Pakistan
ahmed.muaz@nu.edu.pk

Aasim Ali
Center for Research in Urdu Language Processing,
NUCES, Pakistan
aasim.ali@nu.edu.pk

Sarmad Hussain
Center for Research in Urdu Language Processing
NUCES, Pakistan
sarmad.hussain@nu.edu.pk

Abstract

In this paper, two corpora of Urdu (with 110K and 120K words) tagged with different POS tagsets are used to train TnT and Tree taggers. Error analysis of both taggers is done to identify frequent confusions in tagging. Based on the analysis of tagging, and syntactic structure of Urdu, a more refined tagset is derived. The existing tagged corpora are tagged with the new tagset to develop a single corpus of 230K words and the TnT tagger is retrained. The results show improvement in tagging accuracy for individual corpora to 94.2% and also for the merged corpus to 91%. Implications of these results are discussed.

1 Introduction

There is increasing amount of work on computational modeling of Urdu language. As various groups work on the language, diversity in analysis is also developed. In this context, there has been some work on Urdu part of speech (POS) tagging, which has caused multiple tagsets to appear. Thus, there is also need to converge these efforts.

Current work compares the existing tagsets of Urdu being used for tagging corpora in an attempt to look at the differences, and understand the reasons for the variation. The work then undertakes experiments to develop a common tagset, which is syntactically and computationally coherent. The aim is to make a robust tagset and then to port the differently tagged Urdu corpora onto the same tagset. As Urdu already has very few annotated corpora, this will help consolidating them for better modeling.

The next sections present the existing tagsets and accuracies of the POS taggers reported using them. Sections 4 and 5 present baseline experiment and the methodology used for the analysis for updating the tagset. Section 6 describes the proposed tagset. Section 7 reports experiments comparing the new tagset with existing ones. Section 8 discusses the results achieved and future directions.

2 Relevant Resources of Urdu

2.1 Urdu Corpora

Several annotated corpora have been built during last few years to facilitate computational processing for Urdu language. The initial work was undertaken through EMILLE project to build multi-lingual corpora for South Asian languages (McEnery et al., 2000). They released 200,000 words parallel corpus of English, Urdu, Bengali, Gujarati, Hindi and Punjabi. In addition, there are 1,640,000 words of Urdu text in this corpus. These text collections are also annotated with part of speech tags (Hardie 2003).

Center for Research in Urdu Language Processing (CRULP[1]) gathered 18 million words corpus in order to build a lexicon. It has cleaned text from news websites from multiple domains (Ijaz et.al. 2007). Following this work, a syntactic tagset was developed based on work by existing grammarians and a corpus of 110,000 words was manually tagged. This annotated corpus is available through the center (Sajjad 2007, Hussain 2008).

Recently an English-Urdu parallel corpus has also been developed by CRULP, by translating the first 140,000 words of PENN Treebank corpus. In addition, a tagset has also been designed following the PENN Treebank guidelines. These words have been tagged manually with this new tagset. This collection is also available from CRULP, and the tagset is still unpublished.

2.2 Urdu Part of Speech tagsets

Hardie (2003) developed the first POS tagset for Urdu using EAGLES guidelines for computational processing. The tagset contains 282 morpho-syntactic tags, differentiating on the basis of number, gender and other morphological details

[1] www.crulp.org

Proceedings of the 7th Workshop on Asian Language Resources, ACL-IJCNLP 2009, pages 24–31,
Suntec, Singapore, 6-7 August 2009.

in addition to the syntactic categories. Punctuation marks are tagged as they are, and not included in 282 tags. The tags include the gender and number agreement, in addition to syntactic information.

The complications of Urdu tagset design are also discussed. One of these complexities is word segmentation issue of the language. Suffixes in Urdu are written with an orthographic space. Words are separated on the basis of space and so suffixes are treated same as lexical words. Hence it is hard to assign accurate tag for an automatic tagger. Although the tagset is designed considering details, but due to larger number of tags it is hard to get a high accuracy with a small sized corpus. Due to its morphological dependence and its large size, this tagset is not considered in our analysis.

Two much smaller tagsets are considered for this work. They are compared in detail in Section 6. The first tagset, containing 42 tags, is designed by Sajjad (2007), based on the work of Urdu grammarians (e.g. Schmidt 1999, Haq 1987, Javed 1981, Platts 1909) and computational work by Hardie (2003). The main features of the tagset include multiple pronouns (PP, KP, AKP, AP, RP, REP, G, and GR) and demonstratives (PD, KD, AD, and RD). It has only one tag for all forms of verbs (VB), except for auxiliaries to show aspect (AA) and tense (TA) information about the verb. All noun types are assigned single tag (NN) except for Proper Nouns (PN). It also has a special tag NEG to mark any occurrence negation words (نہیں "not" and نہ "no" or "neither") regardless of context. It also has a tag SE to mark every occurrence of سے ("from") without considering the context. Another example of such a context-free lexical tag is WALA to mark every occurrence (including all the inflections) of the word والا. This tagset is referred to as T1 subsequently in this paper.

Recently Sajjad and Schmid (2009) used the tagged data of 107,514 words and carried out an experiment for tagger comparison. A total of 100,000 words are used as training set and rest as test data. Four taggers (TnT, Tree, RF and SVM) are trained using training corpus and then tested accordingly. Reported results of this work show that SVM tagger is the most accurate, showing 94.15% correct prediction of tags. Remaining three taggers have accuracies of 93.02% (Tree tagger), 93.28% (RF tagger) and 93.40% (TnT tagger).

Another tagset has recently been developed as a part of a project to develop English-Urdu parallel corpus at CRULP, following the Penn Treebank guidelines (Santorini 1990). It contains 46 tags, with fewer grades of pronouns (PR, PRP$, PRRF, PRRFP$, and PRRL) and demonstratives (DM and DMRL), as compared to T1. It has several tags for verbs on the basis of their forms and semantics (VB, VBI, VBL, VBLI, and VBT) in addition to the tags for auxiliaries showing aspect (AUXA) and tense (AUXT). The NN tag is assigned for both singular and plural nouns and includes adverbial *kaf* pronoun, *kaf* pronoun, and adverbial pronoun categories of T1. Yet, it has several other grades of common nouns (NNC, NNCR, NNCM). It also has two shades of Proper Nouns (NNP, NNPC), which are helpful in identifying phrase boundary of compound proper nouns. It also has a tag WALA that is assigned to every occurrence (and inflection) of word والا (wala). However, marking of token سے ("from") is context dependent: either it is CM when marking case or it is RBRP when occurring as an adverbial particle. This tagset is referred to as T2 subsequently in this paper.

3 Tools and Resource Selection

The decision of selecting the tagger, the tagset, and the data is the starting point for the task of POS tagging. This section gives details of the taggers chosen and the corpora used for the experiments conducted.

3.1 Selection of taggers

There are a number of existing taggers available for tagging. Two POS taggers are used in the initial step of this work to compare the initial tagging accuracies.

One of the selected taggers is Trigram-and-Tag (TnT). It is a trigram based HMM tagger in which two preceding tags are used to find the transition probability of a tag. Brants (2000) tested PENN Treebank (English) and NEGRA (German) corpora and reported 96-97% accuracy of the tagger.

Schmid (1994) proposed probabilistic POS tagger that uses decision trees to store the transition probabilities. The trained decision tree is used for identification of highest probable tags. Schmid reported an accuracy of 95-96% on PENN Treebank for this tagger.

Both taggers give good accuracy for Urdu tagging, as reported by Sajjad and Schmid (2009).

3.2 Data Used for Experimentation

Corpora annotated with the different tagsets are acquired from CRULP. The corpus originally tagged with T1 tagset is referred to as C1 (news from non-business domain) and the corpus initially annotated with T2 tagset is referred to as C2 (news from business domain), subsequently in the current work. Both C1 and C2 are taken and cleaned. The data is re-counted and approximately 100,000 words are separated for training and rest are kept for testing. The details of data are given in Tables 1 and 2 below.

Table 1. Number of tokens in Urdu corpora

Tokens	C1	C2
Training	101,428	102,454
Testing	8,670	21,181
Total	110,098	123,635

Table 2. Number of sentences in Urdu corpora

Sentences	C1	C2
Training	4,584	3,509
Testing	404	755
Total	4,988	4,264

4 Baseline Estimation

The comparison is initiated with training of existing tagsets on their respective annotated data (T1 on C1 and T2 on C2). Both corpora are tested on TnT and Tree Tagger to obtain the confusion matrices for errors. These confusion matrices are used to analyze misclassification of tags. TnT tagger shows that overall accuracy of using T1 with C1 is 93.01% and is significantly better than using T2 with C2, which gives 88.13% accuracy. Tree tagger is also trained on the corpora. The overall accuracy of T1 on C1 (93.37%) is better than that of T2 on C2 (90.49%). The results are shown in Table 3.

Table 3. Results of both tagsets on their respective corpora with TnT and Tree taggers

	T1 on C1	T2 on C2
TnT Tagger	93.01%	88.13%
Tree Tagger	93.37%	90.49%

The accuracies reported (for T1 on C1) by Sajjad and Schmid (2009) are comparable to these accuracies. They have reported 93.40% for TnT Tagger and 93.02% for Tree Tagger.

Further experimentation is performed only using TnT tagger.

5 Methodology

The current work aims to build a larger corpus of around 230,000 manually tagged words for Urdu by combining C1 and C2. These collections are initially annotated with two different tagsets (T1 and T2 respectively, and as described above). For this unification, it was necessary to indentify the differences in the tagsets on which these corpora are annotated, analyzed the differences and then port them to unified tagset.

The work starts with the baseline estimation (described in Section 4 above). The results of baseline estimation are used to derive a new tagset (detailed in Section 6 below), referred to as T3 in this paper. Then a series of experiments are executed to compare the performance of three tagsets (T1, T2, and T3) on data from two different domains (C1 and C2), as reported in Section 7 below and summarized in Table 4.

Table 4. Summary of experiments conducted

	Experiment	Tagset	Corpus
0	Baseline Estimation: Original tagsets with respective corpora	T1	C1
		T2	C2
1	Experiment1: For comparison of results of T1 and T3 on C1	T3	C1
2	Experiment2: For comparison of T1, T2 and T3 on C2	T3	C2
		T1	C2
3	Experiment3: Comparison of T1 and T3 with no unknowns	T3	C2
		T1	C2
4	Experiment4: Comparison of T1 and T3 over complete corpus	T3	C1+C2
		T1	C1+C2

The performance of T1 on C1 is already better than T2 on C2, so the first comparison for the merged tagset T3 is with T1 on C1, which is the basis of the first experiment. Then the performance of better performing tagsets (T1 and T3) are compared on the corpus C2 in the second experiment to compare them with T2. One possible reason of relatively better performance could be the difference in application of open classes for unknown words in the test data. Therefore, the third experiment is performed using the same data as in second experiment (i.e. corpus C2) with combined lexicon of training and test data (i.e. no unknown words). Finally, an experiment is conducted with the merged corpus. Following table summarizes these experiments.

6 Tagset design

After establishing the baseline, the existing tagsets are reviewed with the following guidelines:

- Focus on the syntactic variation (instead of morphological or semantic motivation) to either collapse existing tags or introduce new ones
- Focus on word level tagging and not try to accommodate phrase level tagging (e.g. to support chunking, compounding or other similar tasks)
- Tag according to the syntactic role instead of having a fixed tag for a string, where possible
- Use PENN Treebank nomenclature to keep the tagset easy to follow and share

Comparison of T1 and T2 showed that there are 33 tags in both tagsets which represent same syntactic categories, as shown in Appendix A. The tag I (Intensifier) in T2 labels the words which are marked as ADV in T1. The words annotated as NNC, NNCR and NNCM (under T2) are all labeled as NN under T1. The words tagged as VBL, VBLI, VBI, and VBLI (under T2) are all labeled as VB under T1. Range of distinct tags for demonstratives of T1 are all mapped to DM in T2 except RD (of T1) which maps to DMRL (of T2).

In order to identify the issues in tagging, a detailed error analysis of existing tagsets is performed. Following tables represent the major tag confusions for tagging C2 with T2 using Tree and TnT taggers.

Table 5. Major misclassifications in C2 with T2 tagset using Tree tagger

Tag	Total tokens	Errors	Maximum misclassification	
VB	888	214	183	VBL
VBL	328	168	151	VB
VBI	202	47	38	VBLI
VBLI	173	52	46	VBI
AUXT	806	145	121	VBT

Table 6. Major misclassifications in C2 with T2 tagset using TnT-tagger

Tag	Total tokens	Error	Maximum misclassification	
VB	888	240	181	VBL
VBL	328	154	135	VB
VBI	202	46	34	VBLI
VBLI	173	61	55	VBI
AUXT	806	136	111	VBT

The proposed tagset for Urdu part-of-speech tagging contains 32 tags. The construction of new tagset (T3) is initiated by adopting T2 as the baseline, because T2 uses the tagging conventions of PENN Treebank. There are 17 tags in T3 that are same as in T1 and T2. These tags (CC, CD, DM, DMRL, JJ, NN, OD, PM, PRP, PRP$, PRRF, PRRF$, PRRL, Q, RB, SM, SYM) are not discussed in detail. The complete tagset along with short description and examples of each tag is given in Appendix B.

RBRP (Adverbial Particle) and CM (Case Marker) are merged to make up a new tag PP (Postposition), so every postposition particle comes under this new tag ignoring semantic context. I (Intensifier) is used to mark the intensification of an adjective, which is a semantic gradation, and syntactically merged with Q (Quantifier). NNCM (Noun after Case Marker), NNC (Noun Continuation), NNCR (Continuing Noun Termination) are merged into NN (Noun) because syntactically they always behave similarly and the difference is motivated by phrase level marking. U (Unit) is also merged with NN because the difference is semantically motivated.

DATE is not syntactic, and may be either treated as NN (Noun) or CD (Cardinal), depending upon the context. Similarly, R (Reduplication), MOPE (Meaningless Pre-word), and MOPO (Meaningless Post-word) always occur in pair with NN, JJ, or another tag. Thus they are phrasal level tags, and can be replaced by relevant word level tag in context. NNPC (Proper Noun Continuation) tag identifies compounding but syntactically behaves as NNP (Proper Noun), and is not used.

VBL (Light Verb) is used in complex predicates (Butt 1995), but its syntactic similarity with VB (Verb) is a major source of confusion in automatic tagging. It is collapsed with VB (Verb). Similarly, VBLI (Light Verb Infinitive) is merged with VBI (Verb Infinitive). AUXT (Tense Auxiliary) is highly misclassified as VBT (To be Verb) because both occur as last token in a clause or sentence, and both include tense information. The word is labeled as VBT only when there is no other verb in the sentence or clause, otherwise these words are tagged as AUXT. The syntactic similarity of both tags is also evident from statistically misclassifying AUXT as VBT. Therefore both are collapsed into single tag VBT (Tense Verb).

In T1, NEG (Negation) is used to mark all the negation words without context, but they mostly occur as adverbs. Therefore, NEG tag is removed. Similarly, SE (Postposition سے, "from") is not separated from postpositions and marked accordingly. PRT (Pre-Title) and POT (Post-Title) always occur before or after Proper Noun, respectively. Therefore, they behave as Proper Nouns, hence proposed to be labeled as NNP (Proper Noun).

7 Experiments

After designing a new tagset, a series of experiments are conducted to investigate the proposed changes. The rationale of the sequence of experiments has been discussed in Section 5 above, however the reasoning for each experiment is also given below. As T2 tags have much more semantic and phrasal information, and C2 tagged with T2 shows lower accuracy than T1 on C1, therefore further experiments are conducted to compare the performance of T1 and T3 only. Comparisons on C2 with T3 may also be drawn.

7.1 Experiment 1

As baseline estimation shows that T1 on C1 outperforms T2 on C2, the first experiment is to compare the performance of T3 on C1. In this experiment C1 is semi-automatically tagged with T3. TnT tagger is then trained and tested. T3 gives 93.44% accuracy, which is slightly better than the results already obtained for T1 (93.01%). The results are summarized in Table 7.

Table 7. Accuracies of T3 and T1 on C1

Corpus	Tagset	Accuracy
C1	T3	93.44%
C1	T1	93.01%

7.2 Experiment 2

Now to test the effect of change in domain of the corpus, the performance T1 and T3 on C2 is compared in this experiment. C2 is manually tagged with T3, then trained and tested using TnT tagger. The results obtained with T3 are 91.98%, which are significantly better than the results already obtained for T2 on C2 (88.13%).

C2 is also semi-automatically re-tagged with T1. T1 shows better performance (91.31%) than T2 (88.13%). However, the accuracy of using T3 (on C2) is still slightly higher. The results are summarized in Table 8.

Table 8. Accuracies of T3 on C1, and accuracies of T3 and T1 on C2

Corpus	Tagset	Accuracy
C2	T3	91.98%
C2	T1	91.31%

7.3 Experiment 3

Due to the change in open class set there may be a difference of performance on unknown words, therefore in this experiment, all the unknown words of test set are also included in the vocabulary. This experiment again involves T3 and T1 with C2. Combined lexica are built using testing and training parts of the corpus, to eliminate the factor of unknown words. This experiment also shows that T3 performs better than T1, as shown in Table 9.

Table 9. Accuracies of T3 and T1 with ALL known words in test data

Corpus	Tagset	Accuracy
C2	T3	94.21%
C2	T1	93.47%

7.4 Experiment 4

Finally both corpora (C1 and C2) were combined, forming a training set of 203,882 words and a test set of 29,851 words. The lexica are generated only from the training set. Then TnT tagger is trained separately for both T1 and T3 tagsets and the accuracies are compared. The results show that T3 gives better tagging accuracy, as shown in Table 10.

Table 10. Accuracies of T3 and T1 using combined C1 and C2 corpora

Corpus	Tagset	Accuracy
C1+C2	T3	90.99%
C1+C2	T1	90.00%

Partial confusion matrices for both the tagsets are given in Tables 11 and 12.

The error analysis shows that the accuracy drops for both tagsets when trained on multi-domain corpus, which is expected. The highest error count is for the confusion between noun and adjective. There is also confusion between proper and common nouns. T3 also gives significant confusion between personal pronouns and demonstratives, as they represent the same lexical entries.

Table 11. Major misclassifications in merged corpus with T1 using TnT tagger

Tag	Total tokens	Error	Maximum misclassification	
A	18	5	3	ADJ
AD	18	7	4	ADJ
ADJ	2510	551	371	NN
ADV	431	165	59	ADJ
INT	8	6	6	ADV
KD	16	9	6	Q
KER	77	28	19	P
NN	7642	548	218	PN
OR	75	24	9	Q
PD	205	55	12	PP
PN	2246	385	264	NN
PP	239	51	11	PD
Q	324	119	53	ADJ
QW	24	12	11	VB
RD	71	62	61	RP
RP	11	5	2	NN
U	24	8	8	NN

Table 12. Major misclassifications in merged corpus with T3 using TnT tagger

Tag	Total tokens	Error	Maximum misclassification	
CVRP	77	24	15	PP
DM	242	77	58	PRP
DMRL	71	64	63	PRRL
INJ	8	6	6	RB
JJ	2510	547	376	NN
JJRP	18	4	4	JJ
NN	7830	589	234	NNP
NNP	2339	390	267	NN
OD	75	23	8	JJ
PRP	642	119	33	DM

8 Discussion and Conclusion

The current work looks at the existing tagsets of Urdu being used for tagging corpora and analyzes them from two perspectives. First, the tagsets are analyzed to see their linguistic level differences. Second, they are compared based on their inter-tag confusion after training with two different POS taggers. These analyses are used to derive a more robust tagset.

The results show that collapsing categories which are not syntactically motivated improves the tagging accuracy in general. Specifically, light and regular verbs are merged, because they may come in similar syntactic frames. Reduplicated categories are given the same category tag (instead of a special repetition tag). Units and dates are also not considered separately as the differences have been semantically motivated and they can be categorized with existing tags at syntactic level.

Though, the measuring unit is currently treated as a noun, it could be collapsed as an adjective as well. The difference is sometimes lexical, where *kilogram* is more adjectival, vs. *minute* is more nominal in nature in Urdu, though both are units.

NNP (Proper Noun) tag could also have been collapsed with NN (Common Noun), as Urdu does not make clear between them at syntactic level. However, these two tags are kept separate due to their cross-linguistic importance.

One may expect that extending the genre or domain of corpus reduces accuracy of tagging because of increase in the variety in the syntactic patterns and diverse use of lexical items. One may also expect more accuracy with increase in size. The current results show that effect on additional domain (when C1 and C2 are mixed) is more pronounced than the increase in size (from approximately 100k to 200k), reducing accuracy from 94.21% (T3 with C2) to 90.99% (T3 with C1 + C2). The increase in accuracy for T3 vs. T1 may be caused by reduced size of T3. However, the proposed reduction does not compromise the syntactic word level information, as the collapsed categories are where they were either semantically motivated or motivated due to phrasal level tags.

The work has been motivated to consolidate the existing Urdu corpora annotated with different tagsets. This consolidation will help build more robust computational models for Urdu.

References

Brants, T. 2000. TnT – A statistical part-of-speech tagger. *Proceedings of the Sixth Applied Natural Language Processing Conference ANLP-2000* Seattle, WA, USA.

Butt, M. 1995. *The structure of complex predicates in Urdu.* CSLI, USA. ISBN: 1881526585.

Haq, A,. 1987. اردو صرف و نحو Amjuman-e-Taraqqi Urdu.

Hardie, A. 2003. Developing a tag-set for automated part-of-speech tagging in Urdu. Archer, D, Rayson, P, Wilson, A, and McEnery, T (eds.) *Proceedings of the Corpus Linguistics 2003 conference. UCREL Technical Papers Volume 16. Department of Linguistics, Lancaster University, UK.*

Hussain, S. 2008. Resources for Urdu Language Processing. *The Proceedings of the 6th Workshop on Asian Language Resources, IJCNLP'08,* IIIT Hyderabad, India.

Ijaz, M. and Hussain, S. 2007. Corpus Based Urdu Lexicon Development. *The Proceedings of Conference on Language Technology (CLT07), University of Peshawar, Pakistan.*

Javed, I. 1981. نئی اردو قواعد Taraqqi Urdu Bureau, New Delhi, India.

Platts, J. 1909. *A grammar of the Hindustani or Urdu language.* Reprinted by Sang-e-Meel Publishers, Lahore, Pakistan.

Sajjad, H. 2007. Statistical Part of Speech Tagger for Urdu. Unpublished MS Thesis, National University of Computer and Emerging Sciences, Lahore, Pakistan.

Sajjad, H. and Schmid, H. 2009. Tagging Urdu Text with Parts Of Speech: A Tagger Comparison. *12th conference of the European chapter of the association for computational Linguistics*

Santorini, B. 1990. Part_of_Speech Tagging Guidelines for the Penn Treebank Project (3rd printing, 2nd revision). Accessed from ftp://ftp.cis.upenn.edu/pub/treebank/doc/tagguide.ps.gz on 3rd May, 2009.

Schmid, H. 1994. Probabilistic part-of-speech tagging using decision trees. Institut für Maschinelle Sprachverarbeitung, Universität Stuttgart, Germany.

Schmidt, R. 1999. *Urdu: an essential grammar.* Routledge, London, UK.

McEnery, A., Baker, J. Gaizauskas, R. and Cunningham, H. 2000. EMILLE: towards a corpus of South Asian languages, British Computing Society Machine Translation Specialist Group, London, UK.

Appendix A: Mappings of tags between Tagsets T1 and T2.

	Tagset T1	Tagset T2
1.	A	JJRP
2.	AA	AUXA
3.	ADJ	JJ
4.	ADV	RB
5.	CA	CD
6.	CC	CC
7.	DATE	DATE
8.	EXP	SYM
9.	FR	FR
10.	G	PRP$
11.	GR	PRRFP$
12.	I	ITRP
13.	INT	INJ
14.	KER	KER
15.	MUL	MUL
16.	NN	NN
17.	OR	OD
18.	P	CM
19.	PD	DM
20.	PM	PM
21.	PN	NNP
22.	PP	PR
23.	Q	Q
24.	QW	QW
25.	RD	DMRL
26.	REP	PRRL
27.	RP	PRRF
28.	SC	SC
29.	SE	RBRP
30.	SM	SM
31.	TA	AUXT
32.	U	U
33.	WALA	WALA

Appendix B: New Tagset T3.

	Tag	Meaning	Example	
1.	AUX	Auxiliary	منتقل کر **سکتے** ہو	May
2.	CC	Coordinate Conjunction	ملازمین **یا** حکومتی عہدہ داروں کے ذریع	Or
3.	CD	Cardinal	**ایک** موجودہ اداکار کو	One
4.	CVRP	Conjunctive Verb Particle	فرانسیسی قلعے بیچ **کر** بھی فنڈز بڑھانے پر راضی نہ	After
5.	DM	Demonstrative	پہلے **ایسے** واقعات نہ ہونے کے برابر تھے	Like this
6.	DMRL	Demonstrative Relative	وہ اشاعتی ادارہ سے **جو** وہ 23 سال تک چلا چکے ہیں	That
7.	FR	Fraction	**آدھے** گھنٹے میں	Half
8.	INJ	Interjection	**واہ!** کیا بات ہے	Hurrah
9.	ITRP	Intensive Particle	نہ گہرا تھا نہ **ہی** باقی رہنے والا	Too
10.	JJ	Adjective	**بلند** تر لاگتوں کے ساتھ	Taller
11.	JJRP	Adjective Particle	باہر رہنے کی بہت **سی** وجوہات کو سوچ سکتے ہیں	As
12.	MRP	Multiplicative Particle	**دگنی** رقم	Double
13.	NN	Noun	**سال** کے آغاز میں **افواہوں** پر	Year
14.	NNP	Proper Noun	**رابرٹ** نے کہا	Robert
15.	OD	Ordinal	**پہلا** ریٹائرمنٹ منصوبہ	First
16.	PM	Phrase Marker	،	,
17.	PP	Postposition	بورڈ رکنیت نو تک بڑھاتے ہوئے	To
18.	PRP	Pronoun Personal	**وہ** طریق کار کو استعمال کے اہل ہونا پسند کریں گے	They
19.	PRP$	Pronoun Personal Possessive	**میری** تیز گیند اچھی ہے	My
20.	PRRF	Pronoun Reflexive	کمپنی نے اپنے **آپ** کو بخوبی	Oneself
21.	PRRF$	Pronoun Reflexive Possessive	**اپنے** اجتماعی دفاتر	Own
22.	PRRL	Pronoun Relative	وہ اشاعتی ادارہ سے **جو** وہ 23 سال تک چلا چکے ہیں	That
23.	Q	Quantitative	**چند** لوگ	Some
24.	QW	Question Word	ایک مصنف **کیوں** یقین کرے گا	Why
25.	RB	Adverb	**ہمیشہ** بیچی گئی	Always
26.	SC	Subordinate Conjunction	کتنا رکھے گی **کیونکہ** کچھ نوکریاں	Because
27.	SM	Sentence Marker	؟	?
28.	SYM	any Symbol	**$**	$
29.	VB	Verb	مہنگے کپڑے **چاہتے** تھے	Wanted
30.	VBI	Verb Infinitive form	اسے لے **جانے** کے لیے	To go
31.	VBT	Verb Tense	تصور قابل عمل **ہے**	Is
32.	WALA	Association Marking Morpheme	رکھنے **والے** جاری کرنے **والا**	Associated Bearing

Annotating Dialogue Acts to Construct Dialogue Systems for Consulting

Kiyonori Ohtake Teruhisa Misu Chiori Hori Hideki Kashioka Satoshi Nakamura
MASTAR Project, National Institute of Information and Communications Technology
Hikaridai, Keihanna Science City, JAPAN
kiyonori.ohtake (at) nict.go.jp

Abstract

This paper introduces a new corpus of consulting dialogues, which is designed for training a dialogue manager that can handle consulting dialogues through spontaneous interactions from the tagged dialogue corpus. We have collected 130 h of consulting dialogues in the tourist guidance domain. This paper outlines our taxonomy of dialogue act annotation that can describe two aspects of an utterances: the communicative function (speech act), and the semantic content of the utterance. We provide an overview of the Kyoto tour guide dialogue corpus and a preliminary analysis using the dialogue act tags.

1 Introduction

This paper introduces a new dialogue corpus for consulting in the tourist guidance domain. The corpus consists of speech, transcripts, speech act tags, morphological analysis results, dependency analysis results, and semantic content tags. In this paper, we describe the current status of a dialogue corpus that is being developed by our research group, focusing on two types of tags: speech act tags and semantic content tags. These speech act and semantic content tags were designed to express the dialogue act of each utterance.

Many studies have focused on developing spoken dialogue systems. Their typical task domains included the retrieval of information from databases or making reservations, such as airline information e.g., DARPA Communicator (Walker et al., 2001) and train information e.g., ARISE (Bouwman et al., 1999) and MASK (Lamel et al., 2002). Most studies assumed a definite and consistent user objective, and the dialogue strategy was usually designed to minimize the cost of information access. Other target tasks include tutoring and trouble-shooting dialogues (Boye, 2007). In such tasks, dialogue scenarios or agendas are usually described using a (dynamic) tree structure, and the objective is to satisfy all requirements.

In this paper, we introduce our corpus, which is being developed as part of a project to construct consulting dialogue systems, that helps the user in making a decision. So far, several projects have been organized to construct speech corpora such as CSJ (Maekawa et al., 2000) for Japanese. The size of CSJ is very large, and a great part of the corpus consists of monologues. Although, CSJ includes some dialogues, the size of dialogues is not enough to construct a dialogue system via recent statistical techniques. In addition, relatively to consulting dialogues, the existing large dialogue corpora covered very clear tasks in limited domains.

However, consulting is a frequently used and very natural form of human interaction. We often consult with a sales clerk while shopping or with staff at a concierge desk in a hotel. Such dialogues usually form part of a series of information retrieval dialogues that have been investigated in many previous studies. They also contains various exchanges, such as clarifications and explanations. The user may explain his/her preferences vaguely by listing examples. The server would then sense the user's preferences from his/her utterances, provide some information, and then request a decision.

It is almost impossible to handcraft a scenario that can handle such spontaneous consulting dialogues; thus, the dialogue strategy should be bootstrapped from a dialogue corpus. If an extensive dialogue corpus is available, we can model the dialogue using machine learning techniques such as partially observable Markov decision processes (POMDPs) (Thomson et al., 2008). Hori et al. (2008) have also proposed an efficient approach to organize a dialogue system using weighted finite-state transducers (WFSTs); the system obtains the

Proceedings of the 7th Workshop on Asian Language Resources, ACL-IJCNLP 2009, pages 32–39,
Suntec, Singapore, 6-7 August 2009.

Table 2: Overview of Kyoto tour guide dialogue corpus

dialogue type	F2F	WOZ	TEL
# of dialogues	114	80	62
# of guides	3	2	2
avg. # of utterance / dialogue (guide)	365.4	165.2	324.5
avg. # of utterance / dialogue (tourist)	301.7	112.9	373.5

structure of the transducers and the weight for each state transitions from an annotated corpus. Thus, the corpus must be sufficiently rich in information to describe the consulting dialogue to construct the statistical dialogue manager via such techniques.

In addition, a detailed description would be preferable when developing modules that focus on spoken language understanding and generation modules. In this study, we adopt dialogue acts (DAs) (Bunt, 2000; Shriberg et al., 2004; Bangalore et al., 2006; Rodriguez et al., 2007; Levin et al., 2002) for this information and annotate DAs in the corpus.

In this paper, we describe the design of the Kyoto tour guide dialogue corpus in Section 2. Our design of the DA annotation is described in Section 3. Sections 4 and 5 respectively describe two types of the tag sets, namely, the speech act tag and the semantic content tag.

2 Kyoto Tour Guide Dialogue Corpus

We are currently developing a dialogue corpus based on tourist guidance for Kyoto City as the target domain. Thus far, we have collected itinerary planning dialogues in Japanese, in which users plan a one-day visit to Kyoto City. There are three types of dialogues in the corpus: face-to-face (F2F), Wizard of OZ (WOZ), and telephonic (TEL) dialogues. The corpus consists of 114 face-to-face dialogues, 80 dialogues using the WOZ system, and 62 dialogues obtained from telephone conversations with the interface of the WOZ system.

The overview of these three types of dialogues is shown in Table 2. Each dialogue lasts for almost 30 min. Most of all the dialogues have been manually transcribed. Table 2 also shows the average number of utterances per a dialogue.

Each face-to-face dialogue involved a professional tour guide and a tourist. Three guides, one male and two females, were employed to collect the dialogues. All three guides were involved in almost the same number of dialogues. The guides used maps, guidebooks, and a PC connected to the internet.

In the WOZ dialogues, two female guides were employed. Each of them was participated in 40 dialogues. The WOZ system consists of two internet browsers, speech synthesis program, and an integration program for the collaborative work. Collaboration was required because in addition to the guide, operators were employed to operate the WOZ system and support the guide. Each of the guide and operators used own computer connected each other, and they collaboratively operate the WOZ system to serve a user (tourist).

In the telephone dialogues, two female guides who are the same for the WOZ dialogues were employed. In these dialogues, we used the WOZ system, but we did not need the speech synthesis program. The guide and a tourist shared the same interface in different rooms, and they could talk to each other through the hands-free headset.

Dialogues to plan a one-day visit consist of several conversations for choosing places to visit. The conversations usually included sequences of requests from the users and provision of information by the guides as well as consultation in the form of explanation and evaluation. It should be noted that in this study, enabling the user to access information is not an objective in itself, unlike information kiosk systems such as those developed in (Lamel et al., 2002) or (Thomson et al., 2008). The objective is similar to the problem-solving dialogue of the study by Ferguson and Allen (1998), in other words, accessing information is just an aspect of consulting dialogues.

An example of dialogue via face-to-face communication is shown in Table 1. This dialogue is a part of a consultation to decide on a sightseeing spot to visit. The user asks about the location of a spot, and the guide answers it. Then, the user provides a follow-up by evaluating the answer. The task is challenging because there are many utterances that affect the flow of the dialogue during a consultation. The utterances are listed in the order of their start times with the utterance ids (UID). From the column "Time" in the table, it is easy to see that there are many overlaps.

Table 1: Example dialogue from the Kyoto tour guide dialogue corpus

UID	Time (ms)	Speaker	Transcript	Speech act tag**	Semantic content tag
56	76669–78819	User	*Ato* (And,) *Ohara ga* (Ohara is) *dono henni* (where) *narimasuka* (I'd like to know)	WH–Question_Where	null (activity),location (activity),(demonstrative),interr (activity),predicate
57	80788–81358	Guide	*kono* (here) *hendesune* (is around)	State_Answer→56	(demonstrative),kosoa (demonstrative),noun
58	81358–81841	Guide	*Ohara ha* (Ohara)	State_Inversion	location
59	81386–82736	User	*Chotto* (a bit) *hanaresugitemasune* (is too far)	State_Evaluation→57	(transp),(cost),(distance),adverb-phrase (transp),(cost),(distance),predicate
60	83116–83316	Guide	*A* (Yeah,)	Pause_Grabber	null
61	83136–85023	User	*Kore demo* (it) *ichinichi dewa* (in a day) *doudeshou* (Do you think I can do)	Y/N–Question	null (activity),(planning),duration (activity),(planning),(demonstrative),interr
62	83386–84396	Guide	*Soudesune* (right.)	State_Acknowledgment→59	null
63	85206–87076	Guide	*Ichinichi* (One day) *areba* (is) *jubuN* (enough) *ikemasu* (to enjoy it.)	State_AffirmativeAnswer→61	(activity),(planning),(entity),day-window (activity),(planning),predicate (consulting),(activity),adverb-phrase (consulting),(activity),action
64	88392–90072	Guide	*Oharamo* (Ohara is) *sugoku* (very) *kireidesuyo* (a beautiful spot)	State_Opinion	(activity),location (recommendation),(activity),adverb-phrase (recommendation),(activity),predicate
65	89889–90759	User	*Iidesune* (that would be nice.)	State_Acknowledgment→64 _Evaluation→64	(consulting),(activity),predicate

* Tags are concatenated using a delimiter '_' and omitting null values.
The number following the '→' symbol denotes the target utterance of the function.

3 Annotation of Communicative Function and Semantic Content in DA

We annotate DAs in the corpus in order to describe a user's intention and a system's (or the tour guide's) action. Recently, several studies have addressed multilevel annotation of dialogues (Levin et al., 2002; Bangalore et al., 2006; Rodriguez et al., 2007); in our study, we focus on the two aspects of a DA indicated by Bunt (2000). One is the communicative function that corresponds to how the content should be used in order to update the context, and the other is a semantic content that corresponds to what the act is about. We consider both of them important information to handle the consulting dialogue. We designed two different tag sets to annotate DAs in the corpus. The speech act tag is used to capture the communicative functions of an utterance using domain-independent multiple function layers. The semantic content tag is used to describe the semantic contents of an utterance using domain-specific hierarchical semantic classes.

4 Speech Act Tags

In this section, we introduce the speech act (SA) tag set that describes communicative functions of utterances. As the base units for tag annotation, we adopt clauses that are detected by applying the clause boundary annotation program (Kashioka and Maruyama, 2004) to the transcript of the dialogue. Thus, in the following discussions, "utterance" denotes a clause.

4.1 Tag Specifications

There are two major policies in SA annotation. One is to select exactly one label from the tag set (e.g., the AMI corpus[1]). The other is to annotate with as many labels as required. MRDA (Shriberg et al., 2004) and DIT++ (Bunt, 2000) are defined on the basis of the second policy. We believe that utterances are generally multifunctional and this multifunctionality is an important aspect for managing consulting dialogues through spontaneous interactions. Therefore, we have adopted the latter policy.

By extending the MRDA tag set and DIT++, we defined our speech act tag set that consists of six layers to describe six groups of function: *General*, *Response*, *Check*, *Constrain*, *ActionDiscussion*, and *Others*. A list of the tag sets (excluding the *Others layer* is shown in Table 3. The *General* layer has two sublayers under the labels, *Pause* and *WH-Question*, respectively. The two sublayers are used to elaborate on the two labels, respectively. A tag of the *General* layer must be labeled to an utterance, but the other layer's tags are optional, in other words, layers other than the *General* layer can take null values when there is no tag which is appropriate to the utterance. In the practical annotation, the most appropriate tag is selected from each layer, without taking into account any of the other layers.

The descriptions of the layers are as follows:

General: It is used to represent the basic form

[1] `http://corpus.amiproject.org`

Table 3: List of speech act tags and their occurrence in the experiment

Tag	Percentage(%)		Tag	Percentage(%)		Tag	Percentage(%)		Tag	Percentage(%)	
	User	Guide		User	Guide		User	Guide		User	Guide
(General)			**(Response)**			**(ActionDiscussion)**			**(Constrain)**		
Statement	45.25	44.53	Acknowledgment	19.13	5.45	Opinion	0.52	2.12	Reason	0.64	2.52
Pause	12.99	15.05	Accept	4.68	6.25	Wish	1.23	0.05	Condition	0.61	3.09
Backchannel	26.05	9.09	PartialAccept	0.02	0.10	Request	0.22	0.19	Elaboration	0.28	4.00
Y/N-Question	3.61	2.19	AffirmativeAnswer	0.08	0.20	Suggestion	0.16	1.12	Evaluation	1.35	2.01
WH-Question	1.13	0.40	Reject	0.25	0.11	Commitment	1.15	0.29	**(Check)**		
Open-Question	0.32	0.32	PartialReject	0.04	0.03				RepetitionRequest	0.07	0.03
OR–after-Y/N	0.05	0.02	NegativeAnswer	0.10	0.10				UnderstandingCheck	0.19	0.20
OR-Question	0.05	0.03	Answer	1.16	2.57				DoubleCheck	0.36	0.15
Statement==	9.91	27.79							ApprovalRequest	2.01	1.07

of the unit. Most of the tags in this layer are used to describe forward-looking functions. The tags are classified into three large groups: "Question," "Fragment," and "Statement." "Statement==" denotes the continuation of the utterance.

Response: It is used to label responses directed to a specific previous utterance made by the addressee.

Check: It is used to label confirmations that are along a certain expected response.

Constrain: It is used to label utterances that restrict or complement the target of the utterance.

ActionDiscussion: It is used to label utterances that pertain to a future action.

Others: It is used to describe various functions of the utterance, e.g., Greeting, SelfTalk, Welcome, Apology, etc.

In the *General* layer, there are two sublayers:— (1) the *Pause* sublayer that consists of Hold, Grabber, Holder, and Releaser and (2) the *WH* sublayer that labels the WH-Question type.

It should be noted that this taxonomy is intended to be used for training spoken dialogue systems. Consequently, it contains detailed descriptions to elaborate on the decision-making process. For example, checks are classified into four categories because they should be treated in various ways in a dialogue system. *UnderstandingCheck* is often used to describe clarifications; thus, it should be taken into account when creating a dialogue scenario. In contrast, *RepetitionRequest*, which is used to request that the missed portions of the previous utterance be repeated, is not concerned with the overall dialogue flow.

An example of an annotation is shown in Table 1. Since the *Response* and *Constrain* layers are not necessarily directed to the immediately preceding utterance, the target utterance ID is specified.

4.2 Evaluation

We performed a preliminary annotation of the speech act tags in the corpus. Thirty dialogues (900 min, 23,169 utterances) were annotated by three labellers. When annotating the dialogues, we took into account textual information, audio information, and contextual information The result was cross-checked by another labeller.

4.2.1 Distributional Statistics

The frequencies of the tags, expressed as a percentages, are shown in Table 3. In the General layer, nearly half of the utterances were *Statement*. This bias is acceptable because 66% of the utterances had tag(s) of other layers.

The percentages of tags in the *Constrain layer* are relatively higher than those of tags in the other layers. They are also higher than the percentages of the corresponding tags of MRDA (Shriberg et al., 2004) and SWBD-DAMSL(Jurafsky et al., 1997).

These statistics characterize the consulting dialogue of sightseeing planning, where explanations and evaluations play an important role during the decision process.

4.2.2 Reliability

We investigated the reliability of the annotation. Another two dialogues (2,087 utterances) were annotated by three labelers and the agreement among them was examined. These results are listed in Table 4. The agreement ratio is the average of all the combinations of the three individual agreements. In the same way, we also computed the average Kappa statistic, which is often used to measure the agreement by considering the chance rate.

A high concordance rate was obtained for the *General layer*. When the specific layers and sublayers are taken into account, Kappa statistic was

Table 4: Agreement among labellers

	General layer	All layers
Agreement ratio	86.7%	74.2%
Kappa statistic	0.74	0.68

0.68, which is considered a good result for this type of task. (cf. (Shriberg et al., 2004) etc.)

4.2.3 Analysis of Occurrence Tendency during Progress of Episode

We then investigated the tendencies of tag occurrence through a dialogue to clarify how consulting is conducted in the corpus. We annotated the boundaries of episodes that determined the spots to visit in order to carefully investigate the structure of the decision-making processes. In our corpus, users were asked to write down their itinerary for a practical one day tour. Thus, the beginning and ending of an episode can be determined on the basis of this itinerary.

As a result, we found 192 episodes. We selected 122 episodes that had more than 50 utterances, and analyzed the tendency of tag occurrence. The episodes were divided into five segments so that each segment had an equal number of utterances. The tendency of tag occurrence is shown in Figure 1. The relative occurrence rate denotes the number of times the tags appeared in each segment divided by the total number of occurrences throughout the dialogues. We found three patterns in the tendency of occurrence. The tags corresponding to the first pattern frequently appear in the early part of an episode; this typically applies to Open-Question, WH-Question, and Wish. The tags of the second pattern frequently appear in the later part, this typically applies to Evaluation, Commitment, and Opinion. The tags of the third pattern appear uniformly over an episode, e.g., Y/N-Question, Accept, and Elaboration. These statistics characterize the dialogue flow of sightseeing planning, where the guide and the user first clarify the latter's interests (Open, WH-Questions), list and evaluate candidates (Evaluation), and then the user makes a decision (Commitment).

This progression indicates that a session (or dialogue phase) management is required within an episode to manage the consulting dialogue, although the test-set perplexity[2], which was calculated by a 3-gram language model trained with the SA tags, was not high (4.25 using the general layer and 14.75 using all layers).

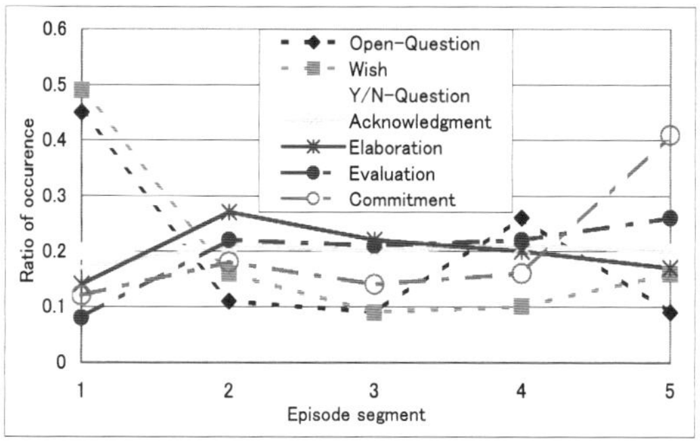

Figure 1: Progress of episodes vs. occurrence of speech act tags

5 Semantic Content Tags

The semantic content tag set was designed to capture the contents of an utterance. Some might consider semantic representations by HPSG (Pollard and Sag, 1994) or LFG (Dalrymple et al., 1994) for an utterance. Such frameworks require knowledge of grammar and experiences to describe the meaning of an utterance. In addition, the utterances in a dialogue are often fragmentary, which makes the description more difficult.

We focused on the predicate-argument structure that is based on dependency relations. Annotating dependency relations is more intuitive and is easier than annotating the syntax structure; moreover, a dependency parser is more robust for fragmentary expressions than syntax parsers.

We introduced semantic classes to represent the semantic contents of an utterance. Semantic class labels are applied to each unit of the predicate-argument structure. The task that identifies the semantic classes is very similar to named entity recognition, because the classes of the named entities can be equated to the semantic classes that are used to express semantic content. However, both nouns and predicates are very important for capturing the semantic contents of an utterance. For example, "10 a.m." might denote the current time in the context of planning, or it might signify the opening time of a sightseeing spot. Thus, we represent the semantic contents on the basis of the predicate-argument structure. Each predicate and argument is assigned a semantic category.

For example, the sentence "I would like to see

[2]The perplexity was calculated by 10-fold cross validation of the 30 dialogues.

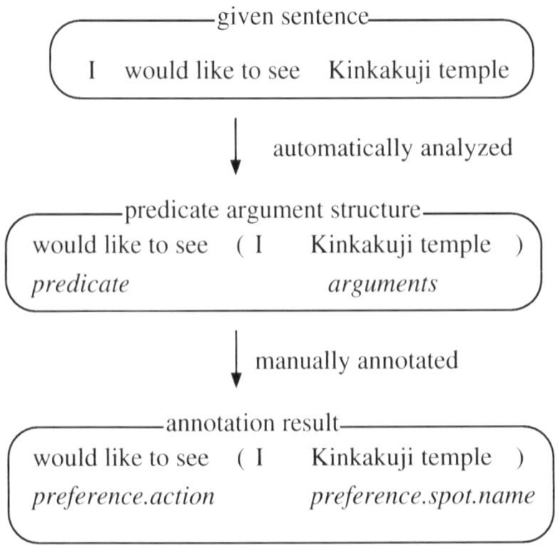

Figure 2: Example of annotation with semantic content tags

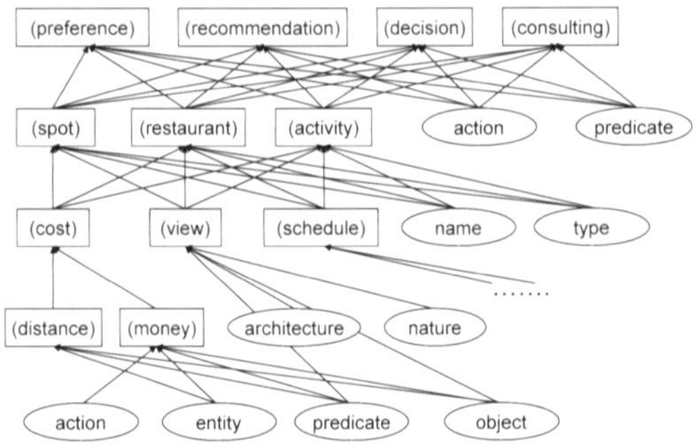

Figure 3: A part of the semantic category hierarchy

Kinkakuji temple." is annotated as shown in Figure 2. In this figure, the semantic content tag *preference.action* indicates that the predicate portion expresses the speaker's *preference* for the speaker's action, while the semantic content tag *preference.spot.name* indicates the *name* of the *spot* as the object of the speaker's *preference*.

Although we do not define semantic the role (e.g., object (*Kinakuji temple*) and subject (*I*)) of each argument item in this case, we can use conventional semantic role labeling techniques (Gildea and Jurafsky, 2002) to estimate them. Therefore, we do not annotate such semantic role labels in the corpus.

5.1 Tag Specifications

We defined hierarchical semantic classes to annotate the semantic content tags. There are 33 labels (classes) at the top hierarchical level. The labels are, for example, **activity**, **event**, **meal**, **spot**, **transportation**, **cost**, **consulting**, and **location**, as shown in Figure 3. There two kinds of labels, nodes and leaves. A node must have at least one child, a node or a leaf. A leaf has no children. The number of kinds for nodes is 47, and the number of kinds for leaves is 47. The labels of leaves are very similar to the labels for named entity recognition. For example, there are "year, date, time, organizer, name, and so on." in the labels of the leaves.

One of the characteristics of the semantic structure is that the lower level structures are shared by many upper nodes. Thus, the lower level structure can be used in any other domains or target tasks.

5.2 Annotation of semantic contents tags

The annotation of semantic contents tags is performed by the following four steps. First, an utterance is analyzed by a morphological analyzer, ChaSen[3]. Second, the morphemes are chunked into dependency unit (*bunsetsu*). Third, dependency analysis is performed using a Japanese dependency parser, CaboCha[4]. Finally, we annotate the semantic content tags for each *bunsetsu* unit by using our annotation tool. An example of an annotation is shown in Table 1. Each row in column "Transcript" denotes the divided *bunsetsu* units.

The annotation tool interface is shown in Figure 4. In the left side of this figure, the dialogue files and each utterance of the dialogue information are displayed. The dependency structure of an utterance is displayed in the upper part of the figure. The morphological analysis results and chunk information are displayed in the lower part of the figure.

At present, the annotations of semantic content tags are being carried out for 10 dialogues. Approximately 22,000 paths, including paths that will not be used, exist if the layered structure is fully expanded. In the 10 dialogues, 1,380 tags (or paths) are used.

In addition, not only to annotate semantic content tags, but to correct the morphological analyze results and dependency analyzed results are being carried out. If we complete the annotation, we will also obtain these correctly tagged data of Kyoto tour guide corpus. These corpora can be used to develop analyzers such as morphological analyz-

[3] http://sourceforge.jp/projects/chasen-legacy/

[4] http://chasen.org/~taku/software/cabocha/

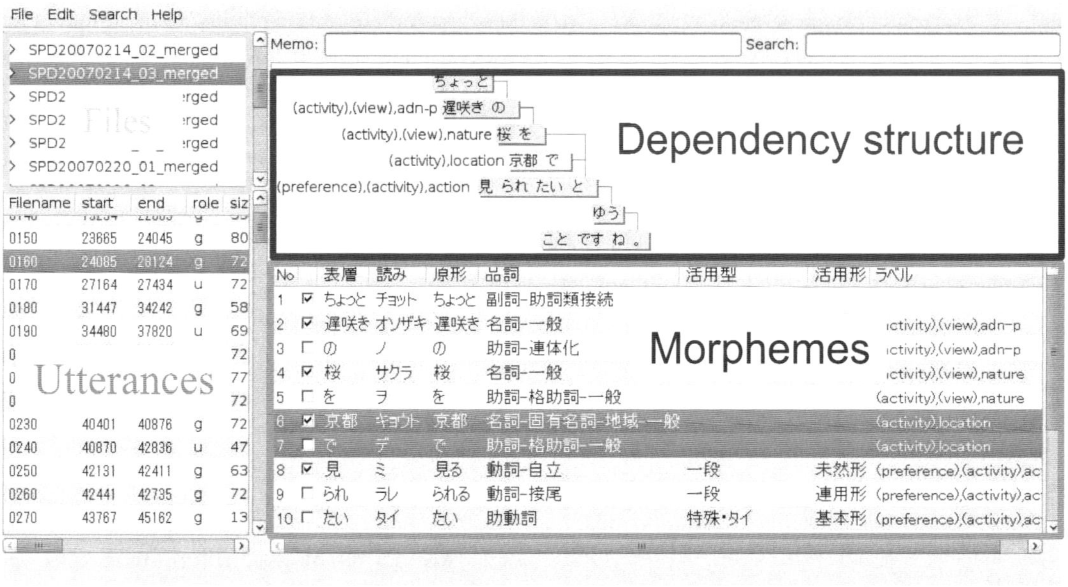

Figure 4: Annotation tool interface for annotating semantic content tags

ers and dependency analyzers via machine learning techniques or to adapt analyzers for this domain.

6 Conclusion

In this paper, we have introduced our spoken dialogue corpus for developing consulting dialogue systems. We designed a dialogue act annotation scheme that describes two aspects of a DA: speech act and semantic content. The speech act tag set was designed by extending the MRDA tag set. The design of the semantic content tag set is almost complete. If we complete the annotation, we will obtain speech act tags and semantic content tags, as well as manual transcripts, morphological analysis results, dependency analysis results, and dialogue episodes. As a preliminary analysis, we have evaluated the SA tag set in terms of the agreement between labellers and investigated the patterns of tag occurrences.

In the next step, we will construct automatic taggers for speech act and semantic content tags by using the annotated corpora and machine learning techniques. Our future work also includes a condensation or selection of dialogue acts that directly affect the dialogue flow in order to construct a consulting dialogue system using the DA tags as an input.

References

Srinivas Bangalore, Giuseppe Di Fabbrizio, and Amanda Stent. 2006. Learning the structure of task-driven human-human dialogs. In *Proceedings of COLING/ACL*, pages 201–208.

Gies Bouwman, Janienke Sturm, and Louis Boves. 1999. Incorporating Confidence Measures in the Dutch Train Timetable Information System Developed in the ARISE Project. In *Proc. ICASSP*.

Johan Boye. 2007. Dialogue Management for Automatic Troubleshooting and Other Problem-solving Applications. In *Proc. of 8th SIGdial Workshop on Discourse and Dialogue*, pages 247–255.

Harry Bunt. 2000. Dialogue pragmatics and context specification. In Harry Bunt and William Black, editors, *Abduction, Belief and Context in Dialogue*, pages 81–150. John Benjamins.

Mary Dalrymple, Ronald M. Kaplan, John T. Maxwell III, and Anni e Zaenen, editors. 1994. *Formal Issues in Lexical-Functional Grammar*. CSLI Publications.

George Ferguson and James F. Allen. 1998. TRIPS: An intelligent integrated problem-solving assistant. In *Proc. Fifteenth National Conference on Artificial Intelligence*, pages 567–573.

Daniel Gildea and Daniel Jurafsky. 2002. Automatic labeling of semantic roles. *Computational Linguistics*, 28(3):245–288.

Chiori Hori, Kiyonori Ohtake, Teruhisa Misu, Hideki Kashioka, and Satoshi Nakamura. 2008. Dialog Management using Weighted Finite-state Transducers. In *Proc. Interspeech*, pages 211–214.

Daniel Jurafsky, Elizabeth Shriberg, and Debra Biasca. 1997. Switchboard SWBD-DAMSL shallow-discourse-function annotation coders manual, draft 13. Technical report, University of Colorado at Boulder & SRI International.

Hideki Kashioka and Takehiko Maruyama. 2004. Segmentation of Semantic Unit in Japanese Monologue. In *Proc. ICSLT-O-COCOSDA*.

Lori F. Lamel, Samir Bennacef, Jean-Luc Gauvain, H. Dartigues, and J. N. Temem. 2002. User evaluation of the MASK kiosk. *Speech Communication*, 38(1):131–139.

Lori Levin, Donna Gates, Dorcas Wallace, Kay Peterson, Along Lavie, Fabio Pianesi, Emanuele Pianta, Roldano Cattoni, and Nadia Mana. 2002. Balancing expressiveness and simplicity in an interlingua for task based dialogue. In *Proceedings of ACL 2002 workshop on Speech-to-speech Translation: Algorithms and Systems*.

Kikuo Maekawa, Hanae Koiso, Sadaoki Furui, and Hitoshi Isahara. 2000. Spontaneous speech corpus of Japanese. In *Proceedings of the Second International Conference of Language Resources and Evaluation (LREC2000)*, pages 947–952.

Carl Pollard and Ivan A. Sag. 1994. *Head-Driven Phrase Structure Grammar*. The University of Chicago Press.

Kepa Joseba Rodriguez, Stefanie Dipper, Michael Götze, Massimo Poesio, Giuseppe Riccardi, Christian Raymond, and Joanna Rabiega-Wisniewska. 2007. Standoff Coordination for Multi-Tool Annotation in a Dialogue Corpus. In *Proc. Linguistic Annotation Workshop*, pages 148–155.

Elizabeth Shriberg, Raj Dhillon, Sonali Bhagat, Jeremy Ang, and Hannah Carvey. 2004. The ICSI Meeting Recorder Dialog Act (MRDA) Corpus. In *Proc. 5th SIGdial Workshop on Discourse and Dialogue*, pages 97–100.

Blaise Thomson, Jost Schatzmann, and Steve Young. 2008. Bayesian update of dialogue state for robust dialogue systems. In *Proceedings of ICASSP '08*.

Marilyn A. Walker, Rebecca Passonneau, and Julie E. Boland. 2001. Quantitative and Qualitative Evaluation of DARPA Communicator Spoken Dialogue Systems. In *Proc. of 39th Annual Meeting of the ACL*, pages 515–522.

Assas-Band, an Affix-Exception-List Based Urdu Stemmer

Qurat-ul-Ain Akram
Center for Research in Urdu Language Processing
NUCES, Pakistan
ainie.akram@nu.edu.pk

Asma Naseer
Center for Research in Urdu Language Processing
NUCES, Pakistan
asma.naseer@nu.edu.pk

Sarmad Hussain
Center for Research in Urdu Language Processing
NUCES, Pakistan
sarmad.hussain@nu.edu.pk

Abstract

Both Inflectional and derivational morphology lead to multiple surface forms of a word. Stemming reduces these forms back to its stem or root, and is a very useful tool for many applications. There has not been any work reported on Urdu stemming. The current work develops an Urdu stemmer or *Assas-Band* and improves the performance using more precise affix based exception lists, instead of the conventional lexical lookup employed for developing stemmers in other languages. Testing shows an accuracy of 91.2%. Further enhancements are also suggested.

1. Introduction

A stemmer extracts stem from various forms of words, for example words *actor, acted,* and *acting* all will reduce to stem *act.* Stemmers are very useful for a variety of applications which need to acquire root form instead of inflected or derived forms of words. This is especially true for Information Retrieval tasks, which search for the base forms, instead of inflected forms. The need of stemmers becomes even more pronounced for languages which are morphologically rich, and have a variety of inflected and derived forms.

Urdu is spoken by more than a 100 million people (accessed from http://www.ethnologue.com/show_ language.asp ?code =urd). It is the national language of Pakistan and a state language of India. It is an Indo-Aryan language, and is morphologically rich. Currently there is no stemmer for Urdu, however recent work has shown that it may have much utility for a variety of applications, much wider than some other languages. Due to the morphological richness of Urdu, its application to information retrieval tasks is quite apparent. However, there are also a few other areas of application, including automatic diacritization for text to speech systems, chunking, word sense disambiguation and statistical machine translation. In most of these cases, stemming addresses the sparseness of data caused by multiple surface forms which are caused mostly by inflections, though also applicable to some derivations.

Due to urgent need for some applications, an Urdu stemmer called *Assas-Band*[1], has been developed. The current work explains the details of *Assas-Band* and its enhancements using exceptions lists instead of lexical lookup methods, to improve its accuracy. Finally results are reported and discussed.

2. Literature Review

Urdu is rich in both inflectional and derivational morphology. Urdu verbs inflect to show agreement for number, gender, respect and case. In addition to these factors, verbs in Urdu also have different inflections for infinitive, past, non-past, habitual and imperative forms. All these forms (twenty in total) for a regular verb are duplicated for transitive and causative (di-transitive) forms, thus giving a total of more than sixty inflected variations. Urdu nouns also show agreement for number, gender and case. In addition, they show diminutive and vocative affixation. Moreover, the nouns show derivational changes into adjectives and nouns. Adjectives show similar agreement changes for number, gender and case. A comprehensive computational analysis of Urdu morphology is given by Hussain (2004).

Stemmers may be developed by using either rule-based or statistical approaches. Rule-based stemmers require prior morphological knowledge of the language, while statistical stemmers use corpus to calculate the occurrences of stems and affixes. Both rule-based and statistical stemmers have been developed for a variety of languages.

A rule-based stemmer is developed for English by Krovetz (1993) using machine-readable dictionaries. Along with a dictionary, rules for inflectional and derivational morphology are defined. Due to high dependency on dictionary the systems lacks consistency (Croft and Xu 1995). In Porter Stemmer (Porter 1980) the algorithm enforces some terminating conditions of a stem. Until any of the conditions is achieved, it keeps on removing endings of the word iteratively. Thabet has proposed a stemmer that performs stemming of classical Arabic

[1] In Urdu *Assas* means stem and *Assas-Band* means stemmer

Proceedings of the 7th Workshop on Asian Language Resources, ACL-IJCNLP 2009, pages 40–47,
Suntec, Singapore, 6-7 August 2009.

in Quran (Thabet 2004) using stop-word list. The main algorithm for prefix stemming creates lists of words from each *surah*. If words in the list do not exist in stop-word list then prefixes are removed. The accuracy of this algorithm is 99.6% for prefix stemming and 97% for postfix stemming. An interesting stemming approach is proposed by Paik and Parui (2008), which presents a general analysis of Indian languages. With respect to the occurrences of consonants and vowels, characters are divided into three categories. Different equivalence classes are made of all the words in the lexicon using the match of prefix of an already defined length. This technique is used for Bengali[2], Hindi and Marathi languages. A rule-based stemming algorithm is proposed for Persian language by Sharifloo and Shamsfard (2008), which uses bottom up approach for stemming. The algorithm identifies substring (core) of words which are derived from some stem and then reassembles these cores with the help of some rules. Morpheme clusters are used in rule matching procedure. An anti-rule procedure is also employed to enhance the accuracy. The algorithm gives 90.1 % accuracy.

Besides rule-based stemmers there are a number of statistical stemmers for different languages. Croft and Xu provide two methods for stemming i.e. Corpus-Specific Stemming and Query-Specific Stemming (Croft and Xu 1995). Corpus-Specific Stemming gathers unique words from the corpus, makes equivalence classes, and after some statistical calculations and reclassification makes a dictionary. Query-Based Stemming utilizes dictionary that is created by Corpus-Based Stemming. Thus the usual process of stemming is replaced with dictionary lookup. Kumar and Siddiqui (2008) propose an algorithm for Hindi stemmer which calculates n-grams of the word of length *l*. These n-grams are treated as postfixes. The algorithm calculates probabilities of stem and postfix. The combination of stem and postfix with highest probability is selected. The algorithm achieves 89.9% accuracy. Santosh et.al. (2007) presents three statistical techniques for stemming Telugu language. In the first technique the word is divided into prefix and postfix. Then scores are calculated on the basis of frequency of prefix, length of prefix, frequency of postfix, and length of postfix. The accuracy of this approach is 70.8%. The second technique is based on n-grams. Words are clustered using n-grams. Within the cluster a smallest word is declared as the stem of the word. The algorithm gives 65.4% accuracy. In the third approach a successive verity is calculated for each word's prefix. This approach increases accuracy to 74.5%.

Looking at various techniques, they can generally be divided into rule based or statistical methods. Rule based methods may require cyclical application of rules. Stem and/or affix look-ups are needed for the rules and may be enhanced by maintaining a lexicon. Statistical stemmers are dependent on corpus size, and their performance is influenced by morphological features of a language. Morphologically richer languages require deeper linguistic analysis for better stemming. Three different statistical approaches for stemming Telugu (Kumar and Murthy 2007) words reveal very low accuracy as the language is rich in morphology. On the other hand rule-based techniques when applied to morphologically rich languages reveal accuracy up to 99.6% (Thabet 2004). Like other South Asian languages, Urdu is also morphologically rich. Therefore, the current work uses a rule based approach with a variation from lexical look-up, to develop a stemmer for Urdu. The next sections discuss the details of development and testing results of this stemmer.

3. Corpus Collection

An important phase of developing *Assas-Band* is corpus collection. For this four different lexica and corpora[3]: C1 (Sajjad 2007), C2[4], C3 (Online Urdu Dictionary, available at www.crulp.org/oud) and C4 (Ijaz and Hussain 2007) are used for analysis and testing. Furthermore, prefix and postfix lists[5] are also used during the analysis. The summary of each of the resources is given in table 1.

Table 1: Corpora Words Statistics

Corpus	Total No. of Words	Unique Words
C1	63,298	10,604
C2	96,890	7,506
C3	149,486	149,477
C4	19,296,846	50,000

4. Methodology

The proposed technique uses some conventions for the Urdu stemmer *Assas-Band*. The stem returned by this system is the meaningful root e.g. the stem of لڑکیاں *larkiyan* (girls) is لڑکی *larki* (girl) and not the لڑک *larak* (boy/girl-hood; not a surface from). It also maintains distinction between the masculine and

[2] Also see Islam et al. (2007) for Bengali stemming

[3] Available from CRULP (www.crulp.org)

[4] Unpublished, internally developed by CRULP

[5] Internally developed at CRULP

feminine forms of the stem. *Assas-Band* gives the stem لڑکا *larka* (boy) for word لڑکوں *larkon* (boys) and stem لڑکی *larki* (girl) for لڑکیاں *larkiyan* (girls). The reason for maintaining the gender difference is its usability for other tasks in Urdu, e.g. machine translation, automatic diacritization etc. The word can easily be converted to underlying stem (e.g. لڑک *larak* (boy/girl-hood)), if needed.

Assas-Band is trained to work with Urdu words, though it can also process foreign words, e.g. Persian, Arabic and English words, to a limited extent. Proper nouns are considered stems, though only those are handled which appear in the corpora.

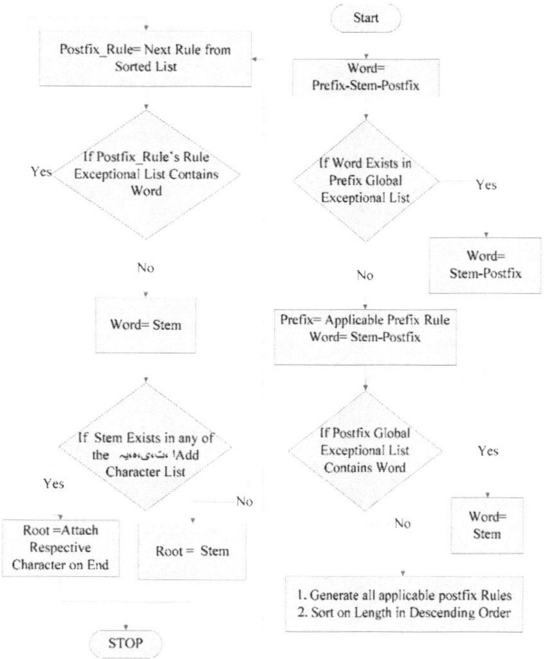

Figure 1: Flow Chart for the Stemming Process

An Urdu word is composed of a sequence of prefixes, stem and postfixes. A word can be divided into *(Prefix)-Stem-(Postfix)*. *Assas-Band* extracts *Stem* from the given word, and then converts it to surface form, as per requirement. The algorithm of the system is as follows. First the prefix (if it exists) is removed from the word. This returns the *Stem-(Postfix)* sequence. Then postfix (if it exists) is removed and *Stem* is extracted. The post-processing step (if required) is performed at the end to generate the surface form.

However, while applying affix rules for any word, the algorithm checks for exceptional cases and applies the affix stripping rules only if the exceptional cases are not found. This is different from other methods which first strip and then repair.

The algorithm for *Assas-Band* is given in Figure 1 and explained in more detail below.

Prefix Extraction: To remove the prefix from the word, first it is checked whether the input word exists in the Prefix-Global-Exceptional-List (PrGEL). If it exists in PrGEL, then it means that the word has an initial string of letters which matches a prefix but is part of the stem and thus should not be stripped. If the word does not exist in PrGEL, then prefix rules list is looked up. If an applicable prefix is found, starting from longest matching prefix to shorter prefix, appropriate rule is applied to separate *prefix* from *stem-postfix*. Both parts of the word are retained for further processing and output.

Postfix Extraction: This process separates the postfix from word and performs the post-processing step, if required, for generating the surface form.

First the remaining *Stem-(Postfix)* is looked up in a general Postfix-Global-Exceptional-List (PoGEL). If the word exists in the list, then it is marked as the stem. If the word does not exist in this list, it indicates that a possible postfix is attached. Postfix matching is then performed. The candidate postfix rules are sorted in descending order according to the postfix length. In addition, a Postfix-Rule-Exception-List (PoREL) is also maintained for each postfix. The first applicable postfix from the list is taken and it is checked if the word to be stemmed exists in PoREL. If the word does not exist in PoREL, then the current postfix rule is applied and the *Stem* and *Postfix* are extracted. If the word exists in the PoREL then the current postfix rule is not applied and the next postfix rule is considered. This process is repeated for all candidate postfix rules, until a rule is applied or the list is exhausted. In both cases the resultant word is marked as *Stem*.

A complete list of prefixes and postfixes are derived by analyzing various lexica and corpora (and using grammar books). In addition, complete rule exception list for each postfix (PoREL), complete general exception list for prefixes PrGEL and general exception list for postfixes PoGEL are developed using C1, C2, C3 and C4. PrGEL and PoGEL are also later extended to include all stems generated through this system.

After applying prefix and postfix rules, post processing is performed to create the surface form of the stem. The stem is looked up in the Add-Character-Lists (ACL). There are only five lists, maintained for each of the following letter(s): ا، ت، ہ، ی، یے (*yay-hay, choti-yah, gol-hay, tay, alif*), because only these can be possibly added. If the stem is listed, the corresponding letter(s) are appended at the end to generate the surface form, else the stem is considered the surface form.

Though the algorithm is straight forward, to the lists have been developed manually after repeated analysis, which has been a very difficult task, as explained in next section. Some sample words in these lists are given in the Appendices A and B.

5. Analysis Phase

The analysis has been divided into two phases. First phase involved the extraction of prefixes and postfixes. The second phase dealt with the development of Prefix and Postfix Global Exceptional Lists (PrGEL, PoGEL), Postfix Rule Exceptional Lists (PoREL) and Add Character Lists (ACL). These are discussed here.

5.1. Extraction of Affixes

C1 and C2 are used for the extraction of affixes. These corpora are POS tagged. The analysis is performed on 11,000 high frequency words. The details of these corpora are given in Table 1. By looking at each word, prefixes and postfixes are extracted. Words may only have a prefix e.g. بدصورت *bud-surat* (ugly), only a postfix, e.g. تصورات *tasawr-aat* (imaginations), or both prefix and postfix, e.g. بداخلاقی *bud-ikhlaq-i* (bad manners). After analysis, 40 prefixes and 300 postfixes are extracted. This list is merged with an earlier list of available postfixes and prefixes[6]. A total of 174 prefixes and 712 postfixes are identified. They are listed in Appendix C. In this phase, the post-processing rules are also extracted separately.

5.2. Extraction of Exception and Word Lists

The following lists are used to improve the accuracy of *Assas-Band*.

1. Prefix and Postfix Global Exceptional Lists (PrGEL, PoGEL)
2. Postfix Rule Exceptional List (PoREL) for each postfix
3. Add Character List (ACL) for each letter/sequence

The second phase of analysis is performed to generate these lists. This analysis is based on C3.

Development of PrGEL: The PrGEL contains all those words from which a prefix cannot be extracted. The list contains words with first few letters which match a prefix but do not contain this prefix, e.g. باندھے *bandh-ay* (tied). This word exists in PrGEL to ensure that the prefix با *ba* (with) is not removed to give invalid stem ندھے *ndhay*. This single list is maintained globally for all prefixes.

Development of PoGEL: There are also many words which do not contain any postfix but their final few letters may match with one. If they are not identified and prevented from postfix removal process, they may result in erroneous invalid stems. For example, ہاتھی *hathi* (elephant) may be truncated to ہاتھhath (hand), which is incorrect removal of the postfix ی (letter *choti-yay)*. All such words are kept in the PoGEL, and considered as a stem. This single list is maintained globally for all the postfixes.

Rule Exceptional Lists: Candidate postfixes are applied in descending order of length. For example, for the word بستیاں *bastiyan* (towns), the following postfixes can be applied: تیاں *tiyan*, یاں *yan*, اں *aan* and ں *noon-gunna*.

First, if the maximal length postfix matches, it is stripped. However, there are cases, when there is a match, but the current postfix should not be detached (a shorter postfix needs to be detached). In this case a postfix specific list is needed to list the exceptions to ensure preventing misapplication of the longer postfix. For this situation PoREL is maintained for each postfix separately. So for بستیاں *bastiyan* (towns), first the maximum length postfix تیاں *tiyan* is matched. However, this creates the stem بس *bas* (bus) which is incorrect. Thus, بستیاں *bastiyan* (towns) is stored in the PrREL of تیاں *tiyan*. Due to this, this postfix is not extracted and the next longest postfix rule is applied. Even in this case nonsense stem بست *bast* is generated. Thus, بستیاں *bastiyan* (towns) is also stored in the PrREL of postfix یاں *yan*. Next the postfix اں *an* is applied. This yields بستی *basti* (town), which is correct. This checking and PrREL development process is manually repeated for all the words in the corpus.

Add Character Lists: During second phase the ACLs (already developed in the first phase) are updated against each of the five possible letter sequences, i.e. ا،ت،ی،ہ،یہ, to generate correct surface forms. For example, when postfix گی *gi* is removed from زندگی *zindagi* (life), it creates the stem زند *zind,* which is not a surface form. The letter ہ *hay* has to be appended at the end to produce the correct surface form زندہ *zinda* (alive). So زند *zind* is stored in the ACL of letter ہ. In the same way the lists are developed and maintained for the five letters separately. After applying a particular postfix rule on

[6] Internally developed at CRULP

the word, the result is checked in each ACL. If the string is found in any of the lists then respective character is attached at the end.

Instead of manually doing all the work, the process is automated using an online Urdu dictionary (OUD) (available at www.crulp.org/oud) using the following algorithm.

1. *Take a word from corpus.*
2. *Generate all applicable rules.*
3. *Sort all rules in descending order according to the maximum length of each.*
4. *Extract upper- most rule from the rules list.*
5. *Apply extracted rule on the word. Check remaining word's existence in the dictionary.*
   a. *If remaining word exists in the dictionary, store that original word in the respective rule's Stem List and stop the loop.*
   b. *Otherwise store original word in the Rule Exceptional List of the respective rule and go to Step 4 for the next rule.*
6. *Repeat steps 4 and 5 until*
   a. *Stop condition (5a) occurs, or*
   b. *All the generated rules have been traversed.*
7. *If termination of the loop is due to step 6b, then the word is stored in the Global Exceptional List which is universal for all the rules.*
8. *Repeat step 1-7 for all the words in the corpus.*

The above algorithm is first run for prefixes. Once a complete manual check is performed on the results, the same algorithm is applied for the postfixes.

6. Manual Corrections

Manual inspection is needed to fix the errors generated by the automated system. The stem list is manually scanned to identify real-word errors, i.e. the stemming is incorrect but results in a valid word. For example when ری *ri* postfix is applied to the word ٹوکری *tokri* (basket), the word ٹوک *tok* (stop) is obtained which exists in the dictionary but is incorrect stemming. The inspection is also needed to ensure that the distinction between the masculine and feminine forms of a word is maintained. As discussed the gender distinction is kept to ensure better use in other applications.

Postfix Rule Exceptional List is scanned manually to check for any missing entries (in case the lexicon contains incomplete information about a word) or spurious entries (in case a word is not in the lexicon). Similarly, the process is also useful in identifying additional missing prefixes and postfixes. For example, the word آنسوؤں *aansuon* (tears) is found in the Exceptional List during manual analysis, because the postfix ؤں *on* was not initially identified. Thus, the algorithm applied the postfix ں *n*, leaving the incorrect stem آنسوؤ *aansuo*. This was (obviously) not found in OUD dictionary, so it was placed in PoGEL. By manually scanning each of the words in this list, new postfix was found, which created the correct stem آنسو *aansu* (tear). ACL is also updated by this manual analysis.

7. Testing

The test results are given in this section.

Testing Phase 1: The corpora C1 and C2 are used which have combined 11,339 unique words. The following table summarizes the testing results.

Table 2: Initial Testing Results

Testing Results	Values
Total Number of tested words	11339
Accurately Stemmed	7241
Incorrect Stemming	4098
Accuracy Rate	64%
Inaccurate Add Character	278
Inaccurate Prefix Stripping	754
Inaccurate Postfix Stripping	1006
Errors due to Foreign Words	2107
Number of Times Prefix Rules Applied	1656
Correct	942
Incorrect	714
Number of Times Postfix Rules Applied	5990
Correct	4984
Incorrect	1006
Number of Times Character Added	819
Correct	541
Incorrect	278

The accuracy of 64% is achieved. Some of the stems created are not in the lists and are erroneous. They are created by invalid prefix/postfix removal. Analysis showed that some prefixes and postfixes contributed to this error rate because they were derived from foreign words transliterated in Urdu. For example ز *z* postfix is correctly applied to the English word ليڈيز *ladiez* (ladies) yielding the stem ليڈی *ladie* (lady). But this ز *z* postfix rule when applied to Urdu words increases the error rate. Similarly Arabic prefix ال *al (the),* which applies to Arabic words correctly e.g. القرآن *al-Quran* (the Quran), wrongly applies to Urdu words.

Another reason for error in stemming is ineffective post-processing due to insufficient words in the lists. There are also some other sources of errors which are not directly associated with stemming but are common for Urdu corpora. Errors are caused by spelling errors, including space character related errors (Naseem and Hussain 2007). There are also encoding normalization issues, which need to be corrected before string matching. This is caused by the variation in keyboards.

Testing Phase II: On the basis of previous result analysis, prefix and postfix rules which are applicable to only foreign words are removed from the rule lists. Such rules create errors in Urdu word stemming, while trying to cater non-essential task of stemming transliterated foreign words. The foreign words found in C1 and C2 are stored in global lists i.e. PrGEL and PoGEL to ensure that they are not processed.

Table 3: Test Results after Removing Foreign Prefixes and Postfixes Rules

Testing Results	Values
Total Number of tested words	10418
Accurately Stemmed	9476
Incorrect Stemming	942
Accuracy Rate	90.96%
Inaccurate Add Character	35
Inaccurate Prefix Stripping	473
Inaccurate Postfix Stripping	469
Errors due to Foreign Words	0
Number of Times Prefix Rules Applied	660
Correct	187
Incorrect	473
Number of Times Postfix Rules Applied	3445
Correct	2976
Incorrect	469
Number of Times Character Added	626
Correct	591
Incorrect	35

As errors from C1 and C2 have been manually fixed, testing is again performed by using 10,418 high frequency Urdu words from C4 (Ijaz and Hussain 2007). The summary of testing results is in Table 3.

Table 3 shows that removing foreign language affixes improves the results significantly. The prefix error rate is higher than the postfix error rate. In addition, the ACL has to be more comprehensive. There are also some errors because some words require both prefix and postfix to be extracted, but during stemming, if the prefix is wrongly applied and a faulty stem is generated, then the postfix is also incorrectly applied.

Testing Phase III: After analyzing test results of the second phase, amendments are made in the algorithm. Following post-processing, the stem generated is verified in PoGEL. If it does not exist, it is assumed that wrong rule is applied and thus it is skipped and the next rule is applied. This is repeated until the resulting stem is found in PoGEL. By implementing this methodology, the accuracy is enhanced from 90.96% to 91.18% for C4 corpus based word list as shown in Table 4.

Table 4: Test Results after Enhancing Algorithm

Testing Results	Values
Total Number of tested words	10418
Accurately Stemmed	9499
Incorrect Stemming	919
Accuracy Rate	91.18%
Inaccurate Add Character	35
Inaccurate Prefix Stripping	473
Inaccurate Postfix Stripping	446
Errors due to Foreign Words	0
Number of Times Prefix Rules Applied	660
Correct	187
Incorrect	473
Number of Times Postfix Rules Applied	3445
Correct	2999
Incorrect	446
Number of Times Character Added	626
Correct	591
Incorrect	35

The methodology does not affect prefix removal and the process of adding characters. The improvement made by this methodology is only in the accuracy of postfixes because this modification is only performed on the second phase i.e. extraction of postfixes.

8. Conclusion

The current paper presents work performed to develop an Urdu stemmer. It first removes the prefix, then the postfix and then adds letter(s) to generate the surface form of the stem. In the first two steps it uses exception lists if a prefix and/or postfix can be applied. A successful lookup bypasses the stripping process. This is different from lexical or stem look up in other work which triggers the stripping process. The current stemming accuracy can be further improved by making the lists more comprehensive. ACL should also be maintained against each postfix for more accuracy. The developed system is currently being used for various other applications for Urdu language processing, including automatic diacritization.

Acknowledgements

The work has been partially supported by PAN Localization Project grant by International Development Research Center (IDRC) of Canada.

References

Croft, W. B. and Xu, J. 1995. Corpus-Specific Stemming using Word Form Co-occurrences. In Fourth Annual Symposium on Document Analysis and Information Retrieval.

Krovetz, R. 1993. View Morphology as an Inference Process. In the Proceedings of 5th International Conference on Research and Development in Information Retrieval.

Porter, M. 1980. An Algorithm for Suffix Stripping. *Program,* 14(3): 130-137.

Thabet, N. 2004. Stemming the Qur'an. In the Proceedings of the Workshop on Computational Approaches to Arabic Script-based Languages.

Hussain, Sara. 2004. *Finite-State Morphological Analyzer for Urdu.* Unpublished MS thesis, Center for Research in Urdu Language Processing, National University of Computer and Emerging Sciences, Pakistan.

Sajjad, H. 2007. *Statistical Part-of-Speech for Urdu.* Unpublished MS Thesis, Center for Research in Urdu Language Processing, National University of Computer and Emerging Sciences, Pakistan.

Ijaz, M and Hussain, S. 2007. Corpus Based Urdu Lexicon Development. In the Proceedings of Conference on Language Technology (CLT07), Pakistan.

Naseem, T., Hussain, S. 2007. Spelling Error Trends in Urdu. In the Proceedings of Conference on Language Technology (CLT07), Pakistan.

Kumar, M. S. and Murthy, K. N. 2007. Corpus Based Statistical Approach for Stemming Telugu. Creation of Lexical Resources for Indian Language Computing and Processing (LRIL), C-DAC, Mumbai, India.

Paik, J. H. and Parui, S. K. 2008. A Simple Stemmer for Inflectional Languages. Forum for Information Retrieval Evaluation,

Islam, M. Z., Uddin, M. N. and Khan, M. 2007. A Light Weight Stemmer for Bengali and Its Use in Spelling Checker. In the Proceedings of 1st Intl. Conf. on Digital Comm. and Computer, Amman, Jordan.

Sharifloo, A. A. and Shamsfard, M. 2008. A Bottom up Approach to Persian Stemming. In the Proceedings of the Third International Joint Conference on Natural Language Processing. Hyderabad, India.

Kumar, A. and Siddiqui, T. 2008. An Unsupervised Hindi Stemmer with Heuristics Improvements. In Proceedings of the Second Workshop on Analytics for Noisy Unstructured Text Data.

Appendix A

A.1 Postfix Rule Exceptional List Samples

Postfix	Some Exceptional Words
بات	ترکیبات
اۓ	سرسراۓ,گڑاۓ,روشاۓ,تلملاۓ
ۓ	آیئنے,قرینے,مہینے,خزاۓ,شامیاۓ,تراۓ,تھاۓ
ہیں	افواہیں,نگاہیں,کراہیں,جاپناہیں,چراگاہیں,سراہیں

A.2 Postfix Global Exception List Samples

بشیر	پیروی	مسلح	مشہور	راوی
سکون	فائرنگ	جذب	ذہن	ایوانِ
راستہ	سیبل	چونکہ	حاوی	آفتاب

A.3 Prefix Global Exception List Samples

یکایک	نکالتے	نالیوں	مہنگی
یکساں	نکھارۓ	ناشپاتی	مناۓ
یکسانیت	نکالیں	نایاب	منائی
ہمدانی	نکالی	نادار	منگوا

Appendix B

Add Character List Samples

ا Add	ت Add
انتہ + ا = انتہا	قیاد + ت = قیادت
ایذ + ا = ایذا	کاش + ت = کاشت
ایس + ا = ایسا	سس + ت = سست
کت + ا = کتا	شدّ + ت = شدّت
ی Add	ہ Add
ترق + ی = ترقی	آزمود + ہ = آزمودہ
	امریک + ہ = امریکہ
	افتاد + ہ = افتادہ
	آزمود + ہ = آزمودہ

Appendix C

C.1 List of Sample Prefixes

مس	صاحب	تو	باد	ما
بالا	فور	اشک	غم	نا
شپس	ان	ناز	گلو	پا
پس	سوڈو	تنگ	شہ	براۓ
پارہ	بال	بن	نیل	بازی
زود	قبل	براۓ	صد	انڈر
ٹرائی	پاک	روبہ	مابعد	نو
طالع	آبی	آن	بد	ادا
آرام	خرد	پر	دم	ایکس
مافوق	من	غیر	ابو	روۓ
آہن	آتش	تہ	ام	گراں
زبر	باطنی	مے	ڈی	دل

C.2 List of Sample Postfixes

آہنگیوں	انوں	گاہی	وائزرز	ائی	سوزی
نگیں	ہندی	دست	ویز	آرائی	نمائی
پروریوں	پروریاں	ارتے	یز	رنگی	نفسی
برداریوں	ٹیگیاں	اۓ	وائز	فروشی	انگیزی
راں	نوازیوں	نامے	گرافیز	سرائی	نامی
سازیاں	لیواؤں	ۓ	ز	گردانی	ونی
آرائیاں	خیزیوں	ے	سوز	رسانی	تھانی
شکنوں	واں	چ	آمےز	پروری	دلی
بوسیوں	گاہئیں	اتے	گرافز	آمیزی	پوشی
ریزیاں	نوازیاں	واۓ	ازمز	ائی	بیانی
گریوں	بیانیاں	ۓ	اندوز	نشینی	برداری
کناں	فشانیاں	خاۓ	ریز	ستانی	اتی
ورزیاں	اندوزوں	ینے	آموز	آزاری	خوری
سراؤں	بریوں	کدے	کیسز	گردی	نگاہی
کاریوں	نویسوں	یلے	نواز	وتی	چاری
خوانیوں	گوئیوں	وے	راز	بندی	سنجی
رانیوں	تراشیاں	اۓ	پرداز	آفرینی	فشانی

Automated Mining Of Names Using Parallel Hindi-English Corpus

R. Mahesh K. Sinha
Indian Institute of Technology, Kanpur, India
rmk@iitk.ac.in

Abstract

Machine transliteration has a number of applications in a variety of natural language processing related tasks such as machine translation, information retrieval and question-answering. For automated learning of machine transliteration, a large parallel corpus of names in two scripts is required. In this paper we present a simple yet powerful method for automatic mining of Hindi-English names from a parallel corpus. An average 93% precision and 85% recall is achieved in mining of proper names. The method works even with a small corpus. We compare our results with Giza++ word alignment tool that yields 30% precision and 63% recall on the same corpora. We also demonstrate that this very method of name mining works for other Indian languages as well.

1 Introduction

Transliteration of names from one script/language to another has a number of applications in a variety of natural language processing tasks. These include machine translation, information retrieval, question-answering, multilingual directories, reservation charts, name lists etc.

Machine transliteration has been studied by a number of researchers (Knight et al., 1998; Al-Onaizan et al., 2002; Goto et al., 2003; Huang et al., 2003; Feng et al., 2004; Asif et al., 2006; Kuo et al. 2006); Knight and Graehl(1998) use a modular approach in which five probability distributions are obtained for various phases of the transliteration - generation and pronunciation of English word sequences, conversion of English sounds to Japanese and then Japanese sounds to Katakana writing. Al-Onaizan and Knight (2002) present work on transliteration from English to Arabic. It relies on an existing named entity recognition system, which identifies possible named entities in English. A predefined phoneme mapping is used to generate all possible transliterations. The validity of transliterations is examined by rating it based on web counts, and co-references by querying for the candidate transliteration on popular search engines such as Google. Huang et al. (2003) have worked on extracting Hindi-English named entity pairs through alignment of a parallel corpus. Chinese-English pairs are first extracted using a dynamic programming string matching. This Chinese-English model is then adapted to Hindi-English iteratively, by using already extracted Hindi-English named entity pairs to bootstrap the model. The precision achieved by this model is 91.8%. Feng et al. (2004) have used a maximum entropy model, in which an alignment probability for target/source named entities is defined over 4 features - translation score, transliteration score, co-occurrence score and distortion score. The extraction of each feature is involved, but the maximum entropy model over these features is straightforward. Kuo et al. (2006) uses a syllable alignment algorithm for cross-language syllable-phoneme conversion. Asif et al. (2006) have considered Bengali to English transliteration. They present a model which upon supervised training provides direct orthographical mapping. They report an accuracy of 69-89%. The success of all of these works depends upon the volume and nature of name corpora used.

In this paper, we present a simple yet powerful method for mining of Hindi-English names from a parallel text corpus. In Hindi, the words are written as they are spoken i.e. it is phonetic in nature. On the other hand, English is non-phonetic in the sense that there is a specified usage of a spelling for every word. Hindi names when written in English have a similar problem that the users have developed their own spellings for names that are commonly accepted. Though these English spellings do retain the phonetic structure of Hindi to a large extent, there are variations that cannot be easily captured through rules. In table 1 a few illustrative examples are given. It is evident that the Hindi vowel modifiers (called 'matra') do not have unique mappings to English vowel combinations. It is difficult to derive simple mapping rules for these. The map-

Proceedings of the 7th Workshop on Asian Language Resources, ACL-IJCNLP 2009, pages 48–54,
Suntec, Singapore, 6-7 August 2009.

ping of semivowels 'y' and 'v' and 'schwa' deletions are highly contextual. However, for the consonants, the mappings are straightforward barring a few exceptions.

Our strategy for automatic mining of Hindi-English proper names from parallel corpus exploits this near-invariance in consonant mapping. We compare our results with Giza++ word alignment. In the following section, we present our design methodology followed by experimental results and conclusions.

Hindi word in Devanagari	Hindi word in IITK-Roman (Appendix-A)	Corresponding commonly used English (Roman) transliteration	Unacceptable English (Roman) transliterations	Observations
हरीश	harISa	Harish	Hareesh / Hariesh / Hareish	i. long vowel mapping ii. 'schwa' deletion iii. consonant cluster mapping
संजीव	saMjIva	Sanjeev or Sanjiv	Sanjiiv / Sanjiev /Sanjeiv	i. variation in long vowel mapping ii. 'schwa' deletion
फाल्गुनी	PAlgunI	Phalguni	Falguni	i. long vowel mapping ii. consonant mapping
मूना	mUnA	Moona	Muna / Muuna / Moonaa	preferred long vowel mapping
सूरज	sUraja	Suraj	Sooraj / Suuraj / Suraz /Surag	i. long vowel mapping ii. 'schwa' deletion iii. consonant mapping
सोमनाथ	somanAWa	Somenath or Somnath	Somanath / Somanaath	i. long vowel mapping ii. 'schwa' deletion iii. peculiar vowel mapping to 'e'
सक्सेना	saksenA	Saxena	Saksena	i. long vowel mapping ii. preferred consonant mapping
दीक्षित	xIkSiwa	Dixit or Dikshit	Deexit / Dikchhit etc.	i. long vowel mapping ii. 'schwa' deletion iii. preferred consonant mapping
मोदी	moxI	Modi	Modee / Modii / Mody etc.	preferred long vowel mapping
सोनिया	soniyA	Sonia	Soniya	preferred semivowel mapping
रामदेव देव	rAmaxeva xeva	Ramdeo Deva	Ramdev /Ramadev / Ramadeo Deo / Dev	preferred semivowel mapping

Table 1: An Illustration of Hindi to English Name Transliteration Variations

2 Hindi-English Name Corpus Creation

We use an aligned parallel Hindi-English text corpus for creation of Hindi-English name corpus. The size of the corpus is immaterial and it could be as small as a few lines. The sentence alignment also need not be perfect as long as the aligned set of sentences contain the translated sentences. Our methodology is even capable of capturing to some extent mapping between old city names with new city names such as Bombay and Mumbai. Figure 1 depicts the process of name mining diagrammatically.

The Hindi text written in Devanagari is first converted to IITK-Roman form (appendix-A). IITK-Roman has become a de-facto standard used by a large number of researchers in India. The conversion to IITK-Roman form is straightforward and is a direct representation of UTF-8 or ISSCII-8 coding schemes without any loss of constituent information in terms of phonemes or constituent symbols. The usage of IITK-Roman form is more for entry and programming convenience.

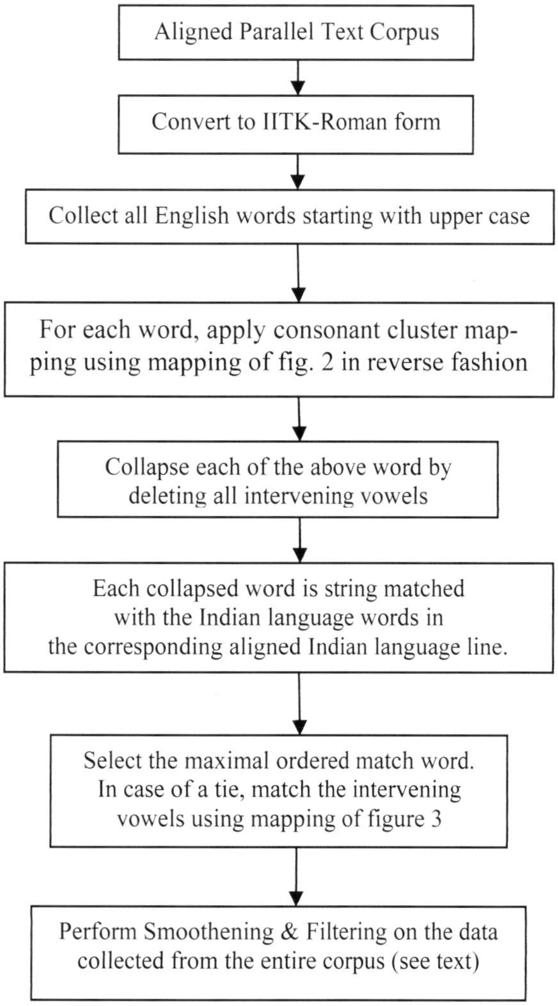

Figure 1: Schematic flow diagram of the name mining process

As outlined earlier, in order to simplify the learning process, the trivial consonant (C) and consonant cluster (C^+) mappings are provided separately in the form of rules. The main consonant mappings from IITK-Roman to English are shown in figure 2.

k(क)→k/c/ck; K(ख)→kh; g(ग)→g; G(घ)→gh; f(ङ)→n;

c(च)→ch; C(छ)→chh; j(ज)→j/z; J(झ)→jh; F(ञ)→n;

t(ट)→t; T(ठ)→th; d(ड)→d; D(ढ)→dh; N(ण)→n;

w(त)→t; W(थ)→th; x(द)→d; X(ध)→dh; n(न)→n;

p(प)→p; P(फ)→ph/f; b(ब)→b; B(भ)→bh; m(म)→m;

y(य)→y; r(र)→r; l(ल)→l; v(व)→v/w;

s(स)→s; S(श)→sh; R(ष)→sh; h(ह)→h;

kR(क्ष)→x; jF(ज्ञ)→ gy; dZ(ड़) →r;

q (◌ृ)→r/k; M(◌ं)→n; H(◌ः)→h;

ks(क्स)→x; kZ (क़)→q; jZ (ज़)→z; PZ (फ़)→f

Figure 2: IITK-Roman to English consonant mapping

A (◌ा)→ a; i (ि◌)→ i; I (◌ी)→ i; u (◌ु)→u;

U(◌ू)→u; e(◌े)→e; E(◌ै)→ai; o (◌ो)→o;

O(◌ौ)→ou;

Figure 3: IITK-Roman to English vowel mapping

The consonant mappings are exploited in hypothesizing plausible name transliterations. Following steps explain the process of mining of Hindi-English name pairs:

i. For each aligned line, collect all the words in the English sentence that have first letter in upper case. These are potential English proper names excepting the first word that may or may not be a proper name.

ii. For each word, apply consonant cluster map-ping from English to Hindi (using the mapping as given in figure 2 in reverse fashion). In absence of a defined mapping, the consonant is ignored. This yields one or more plausible Hindi names as there are one to many reverse mappings. The following three mappings are very rare and so are ignored for efficiency: f→n; F→n; H→h. Further, the semivowel 'y' is not treated as a consonant if it is the last character of the word. It is treated as a consonant if it is preceded or followed by a vowel.

iii. Collapse each of the above word into being part of the plausible Hindi name by deleting all vowels in it.

iv. Each collapsed plausible Hindi name, as de-rived in the preceding step, is string-matched with the Hindi words in the corresponding aligned Hindi line. The process of matching looks for maximal ordered string match omitting the Hindi vowels.

- In case no match is found, it is ignored.
- In case of multiple matches, minimal word length distance is taken as the criterion for selection.

- In order to avoid false matching, length must be greater than 1 and at least 30% of characters must match.
- Further, a constraint that the first character of the mapped words must both be either a consonant or both be a vowel, is imposed.

v. In case two or more matches have same maximal length match, then the maximal match with the plausible un-collapsed (i.e. including the intervening vowels with their mapping using figure 3) Hindi name is matched and the ordered maximal length match is selected. Usually such a situation is encountered when two or more similar names are encountered in the aligned lines. An example of this would be say the two names 'Hindi' and 'Hindu' occur in the same sentence. These will get matched to the same degree by step (iv) above. The way to resolve this is to also take intervening vowels into account. The IITK Roman vowel mapping to English used here is given in figure 3. It may be noted that only one vowel mapping out of the many possibilities, has been taken. This is the most frequent mapping and is taken as the baseline vowel mapping.

vi. The final stage is that of filtering and smoothening.

- For every English name, the corresponding Hindi name mapping(s) with their frequency of occurrence is recorded for the entire corpus.
- In case of multiple mappings, each mapping is examined. The suffix that represent the post-position markers such as ne (ne ने), ka(kA का), ko (ko को), ki(kI की), ke(ke के), se(se से), men(meM में), par(para पर), vala (vA-lA वाला) etc. in Hindi are stemmed. Further, other morphological co-joiners ('sandhi') for other Indian scripts are also stemmed.
- After stemming, the frequency is re-computed.
- The mapping with the highest frequency is selected.

Although these post-position markers in Hindi are separate words and are usually written with a preceding blank, many a time it is not properly observed and appears as a suffix.

Given below is an illustrative example:
English sentence:
It goes daily from Delhi to Mumbai, Bangalore, Varanasi and Lucknow.
Aligned Hindi Sentence:
यह रोजाना दिल्ली से मुम्बई, बैंगलुरु, वाराणसी और लखनऊ जाती है ।
(Converted to IITK-Roman)
yaha rojAnA xillI se mumbaI, bEMgaluru, vArANasI Ora laKanaU jAwI hE.
Probable English Proper Nouns:
It Delhi Mumbai Bangalore Varanasi Lucknow
Plausible Hindi Names after reverse consonant substitutions:
{it iw} {delhi xelhi} {mumbai}
{bangalore baMgalore} {varanasi varaNasi vaMasi}{luknov lukNov lukMov}
Collapsed plausible corresponding Hindi Names:
{t w} {dlh xlh} {mmb} {bnglr bMglr}
{vrns vrNs vrMs} {lknv lkNv lkMv}
Hypothesized Hindi Names after matching:
Delhi→ xillI दिल्ली ;
Mumbai →mumbaI मुम्बई;
Bangalore →bEMgaluru बैंगलुरु;
Varanasi → vArANasI वाराणसी;
Lucknow →laKanaU लखनऊ.

In the above example, the first word 'It' does not get matched to any of the Hindi words because of the constraint that the matching length has to be greater than 1 and a minimum of 30% of length must match.

It is interesting to note the method outlined captures even those names that differ in their forms or spelling such as Delhi & दिल्ली (xillI), Bangalore & बैंगलुरु (bEMgaluru) and Lucknow & लखनऊ (laKanaU) based on maximal match. For transliteration, these have to made table driven.

Given below is an illustration of step (v) of the procedure:
English sentence:
Mr. Handa speaks Hindi and he is a Hindu.
Aligned Hindi Sentence:
श्री हांडा हिन्दी बोलते हैं और वह एक हिन्दू हैं ।
(Converted to IITK-Roman)
SrI hAMdA hinxI bolawe hEM Ora vaha eka hinxU hEM.

Probable English Proper Nouns:

Mr Handa Hindi Hindu.

Plausible Hindi Names after reverse consonant substitutions:

{mr mq} {haNda handa haMda haNxa hanxa haMxa} {hiNdi hindi hiMdi hiNxi hinxi hiMxi} {hiNdu hindu hiMdu hiNxu hinxu hiMxu}

Collapsed plausible corresponding Hindi Names:

{mr mq} {hNd hnd hMd hNx hnx hMx} {hNd hnd hMd hNx hnx hMx} {hNd hnd hMd hNx hnx hMx}

Hypothesized Hindi Names after matching:

Handa→ *hAMdA* हांडा*; hinxI* हिन्दी; *hinxU* हिन्दू;

Hindi → *hAMdA* हांडा*; hinxI* हिन्दी; *hinxU* हिन्दू;

Hindu → *hAMdA* हांडा*; hinxI* हिन्दी; *hinxU* हिन्दू;

Now since these are equiprobable multiple matches, step (v) will get invoked. For each matching target word, the vowel mapping of figure 3 is applied. This yields the following:

hAMdA हांडा→ *haMda;*

hinxI हिन्दी→*hinxi*;

hinxU हिन्दू→*hinxu*;

Now the English source word is matched and minimal distance word is selected. This finally yields the desired result as follows:

Handa→ *hAMdA* हांडा*;*

Hindi → *hinxI* हिन्दी;

Hindu → *hinxU* हिन्दू;

Given below is an illustration of step (vi) of the procedure:

Suppose in the entire corpus the city name 'Agra' yields the following matches:

i. Agra →*AgarA* आगरा; count=20;

ii. Agra →*Agare* आगरे; count=12;

iii. Agra →*AgarAse* आगरासे; count=5;

iv. Agra →*AgarAmeM* आगरामें; count=4;

v. Agra →*AgarAkA* आगराका; count=2;

Now the process of smoothening will convert *AgarAse* आगरासे to *AgarA* आगरा by deleting post-position suffix 'se'से; *AgarAmeM* आगरामें to *AgarA* आगरा by deleting post-position suffix 'meM'में; and *AgarAkA* आगराका to *AgarA* आगरा by deleting post-position suffix 'kA'का. This will yield the final table as follows:

i. Agra →*AgarA* आगरा; count=31;

ii. Agra →*Agare* आगरे; count=12;

The filtering process will select the mapping of Agra →*AgarA* आगरा.

It may be noted that the word *Agare* आगरे is the oblique form of the name *AgarA* आगरा and such usage is very common in Indian languages. A morphological processing is required to make the conversion and this has not been implemented in the current implementation.

3 Experimentation and Results

For experimentation, we took a text that contained a lot of names. Two sentence aligned files were created from a Indian freedom fighters' story. This story contains a lot of names of individuals and places in the text. The results of our name mining methodology are summarized in table 2. We also used Giza++ word alignment tool (Och and Ney, 2003) on the same files and collected figures pertaining to the alignment of proper names in Hindi and English. In case of multiple mappings for a proper name in which one of them is a correct mapping, it is considered as 'false positive'. These results are also shown in table 2 for comparison.

	File1		File2	
	Name-mapping	Giza++	Name-mapping	Giza++
Total no. of words	2439	2439	4909	4909
Total no. of Names(N)	192	192	343	343
Correct mapping (TP)	155	57	262	74
Incorrect mapping (FP)	13	117	35	200
Not-captured (FN)	24	18	46	69
Accuracy (TP/N)	0.8073	0.2969	0.7638	0.2157
Precision (TP/(TP+FP))	0.9226	0.3276	0.9495	0.2701
Recall (TP/(TP+FN))	0.8659	0.7600	0.8506	0.5175
F-measure (2PR/(P+R))	0.8934	0.4578	0.8968	0.3549

Table 2. Result for name mining and word-alignment algorithms.

Our experimentation reveals that our name mining methodology yields a precision of 92 to 95% and a recall of 85 to 86% resulting in F-measure of 0.89. On the other hand, the Giza++ word alignment tool yields a precision of 27 to 33% and a recall of 52 to 76% resulting in F-measure of 0.35 to 0.46. The results are a clear demonstration of effectiveness our approach of mining proper names from the parallel Hindi-English corpora. Most of the errors using our approach have been found to be due to short names, words not properly delineated in the target text, morphological changes in the target text, the first word in English not being a proper noun or different forms of names that are used denoting the same place. It should be noted that our approach works even for a corpus of a few lines as it is primarily a rule-based method.

The method as outlined above is equally applicable to other Indian languages. In order to demonstrate this, we conducted a limited experiment with Punjabi and Bengali languages. A corpus of about 200 sentences was taken. The same program as was used for Hindi with no change in the mapping tables was used for the experimentation. The results obtained were remarkable and a performance of about 90% and 70% of correct mining of proper names for Punjabi and Bengali respectively is yielded. The poorer performance in case of Bengali is primarily due to morphological changes that take place in the proper names based on their role in the sentence. Unlike in Hindi where the post-positions are written separately or simply suffixed, for most of the other Indian languages, these post-position markers are co-joined ('Sandhi') with the preceding word leading to a morphological change. This is less frequent in Punjabi. Further, Bengali has no consonant for 'va' व and this is mapped to 'ba' ब. So some consonant mapping changes are required to yield better results for another Indian language but the methodology remains the same. Here are some example mappings:

Bengali:

i. Cath hasn't phoned since she went to Berlin.
bArline yAoyZA Weke kyAWa Pona kareni।
বার্লিনে যাওয়া থেকে ক্যাথ ফোন করেনি।

ii. Jo was the next oldest after Martin.
mArtinera parei badZa Cila jo।
মার্টিনের পরেই বড় ছিল জো।

Names extracted:

Cath → kyAWa ক্যাথ;

Berlin → bArline বার্লিনে

Here the correct mapping is 'bArlina বার্লিন' but the name has got morphologically transformed to 'bArline বার্লিনে' (to Berlin) based on co-joining of post-position marker.

Martin → mArtinera মার্টিনের

Here the correct mapping is 'mArtina মার্টিন' but the name has got morphologically transformed to 'mArtinera মার্টিনের' (after Martin)) based on co-joining of post-position marker.

Punjabi:

i. Sam Sand Dunes is one of the best nature's gift to the human beings.
sEma sEzda diUnasa manuYKa xe laI prakirawI xe saraba SreSata wohaPZiAz viYcoz iYka hE.
ਸੈਮ ਸੈਂਡ ਡਿਊਨਸ ਮਨੁੱਖ ਦੇ ਲਈ ਪ੍ਰਕਿਰਤੀ ਦੇ ਸਰਬ ਸ਼੍ਰੇਸ਼ਟ ਤੋਹਫ਼ਿਆਂ ਵਿੱਚੋਂ ਇੱਕ ਹੈ।

ii. Bikaner is located to the north of Rajasthan popularly known as a camel country.
bIkAnera rAjasaWAna xe uYwara viYca saWiwa hE awe saXAraNa wOra we UTa-praxeSa xe rUpa viYca jANiA jAzxA hE.
ਬੀਕਾਨੇਰ ਰਾਜਸਥਾਨ ਦੇ ਉੱਤਰ ਵਿੱਚ ਸਥਿਤ ਹੈ ਅਤੇ ਸਧਾਰਣ ਤੌਰ ਤੇ ਊਠ-ਪ੍ਰਦੇਸ਼ ਦੇ ਰੂਪ ਵਿੱਚ ਜਾਣਿਆ ਜਾਂਦਾ ਹੈ।

Names extracted:

Sam → sEma ਸੈਮ ;

Sand → sEzda ਸੈਂਡ ;

Dunes → diUnasa ਡਿਊਨਸ ;

Bikaner → bIkAnera ਬੀਕਾਨੇਰ ;

Rajasthan → rAjasaWAna ਰਾਜਸਥਾਨ

4 Conclusions

In this paper, we have presented a simple yet powerful method for mining of Hindi-English proper name corpus with a success of mining being 93% precision. In contrast, GIZA+ word alignment tool on same sized corpus yielded 29% precision. The proposed method works even for a single line text. Moreover, there is no strict requirement of sentence alignment as it works equally well for one to many and many to many sentence alignment as long as the target group of sentences contain the corresponding translation.

Thus it works under noisy environments where sentence boundaries are not correctly identified. Our approach also yields a table of similar old city names with new city names that is very frequently encountered in Indian context.

The methodology outlined in this paper for automatic mining of proper names are equally applicable to all Indian languages as all Indian scripts are phonetic in nature in the same way as Devanagari (used for Hindi). We have also demonstrated that this very method of name mining without making any changes in the program or the mapping table as used for Hindi, works for other Indian languages. Our limited experimentation for Punjabi and Bengali and have yielded performance of 90% and 70% respectively of correct mining of proper names.

There are several other advantages of our approach. Since the proper name mining is captured with a high accuracy over a rough or noisy aligned corpus, it is possible to use these as anchors (the same way as numerals) for improvement of the alignment results. These anchors will also be useful in word alignment programs for speedy convergence. Accurate word alignment is crucial to the success of any statistical machine translation system. Another byproduct of our approach is that it also yields the table of old city names with new city names. In India, a large number of city names that were used during British time, have undergone a change and most of these changes are phonetic variations of the old names.

Acknowledgements

Author is thankful to Saleem Siddiqui and Abhay Singh for experimentation and testing.

References

Al-Onaizan Y. and Knight K.2002. Translating Named Entities Using Monolingual and Bilingual Resources. *Proceedings of ACL 2002*, 400-408.

Ekbal Asif, Sudip Kumar Naskar and Sivaji Bandyopadhyay. 2006. A Modified Joint Source-Channel Model for Transliteration, *Proceedings of ACL 2006.*

Feng Dong-Hui, Ya-Juan Lv, and Ming Zhou. 2004.A New Approach for English-Chinese Named Entity Alignment. *Proceedings of ACL 2004.*

Goto I., N. Kato, N. Uratani, and T. Ehara. 2003. Transliteration considering Context Information based on the Maximum Entropy Method. *Proceeding of the MT-Summit IX*, New Orleans, USA, 125-132.

Huang Fei, Stephan Vogel, and Alex Waibel. 2003. Extracting Named Entity Translingual Equivalence with Limited Resources. *ACM Transactions on Asian Language Information Processing (TALIP)*, 2(2):124–129.

Knight K. and J. Graehl. 1998. Machine Transliteration, *Computational Linguistics*, 24(4): 599-612.

Kuo Jin-Shea , Haizhou Li and Ying-Kuei Yang. 2006. Learning Transliteration Lexicons from the Web, *The 44th Annual Meeting of Association for Computational Linguistics (COLING-ACL2006)*, Sydney, Australia, 1129 – 1136.

Och Franz Josef and Hermann Ney. 2003. A Systematic Comparison of Various Statistical Alignment Models, *Computational Linguistics*, 29(1):19-51. (http://www.fjoch.com/GIZA++.html)

Mansur Arbabi, Scott M. Fischthal, Vincent C. Cheng, and Elizabeth Bar. 1994. Algorithms for Arabic name transliteration. *IBM Journal of Research and Development*, 38(2): 183-193.

Paola Virga and Sanjeev Khudanpur. 2003. Transliteration of Proper Names in Crosslingual Information Retrieval. *Proceedings of the ACL 2003 Workshop on Multilingual and Mixedlanguage Named Entity Recognition*, Sapporo, Japan, 57-60.

Appendix-A: IITK-Roman code for Hindi (Devanagari)

अ आ इ ई उ ऊ ऋ ए ऐ ओ औ

◌ा ◌ि ◌ी ◌ु ◌ू ◌ृ ◌े ◌ै ◌ो ◌ौ ◌ं ◌ः ◌ॅ ◌ँ ◌़

a A i I u U q e E o O M H V z Z

क ख ग घ ङ च छ ज झ ञ ट ठ ड ढ ण त थ द ध न

k K g G f c C j J F t T d D N w W x X n

प फ ब भ म य र ल व स श ष ह

p P b B m y r l v s S R h

Basic Language Resources for Diverse Asian Languages: A Streamlined Approach for Resource Creation

Heather Simpson, Kazuaki Maeda, Christopher Cieri
Linguistic Data Consortium
University of Pennsylvania
3600 Market St., Suite 810
Philadelphia, PA 19104, USA
{hsimpson, maeda, ccieri}@ldc.upenn.edu

Abstract

The REFLEX-LCTL (Research on English and Foreign Language Exploitation-Less Commonly Taught Languages) program, sponsored by the United States government, was an effort in simultaneous creation of basic language resources and technologies for under-resourced languages, with the aim to enrich sparse areas in language technology resources and encourage new research. We were tasked to produce basic language resources for 8 Asian languages: Bengali, Pashto, Punjabi, Tamil, Tagalog, Thai, Urdu and Uzbek, and 5 languages from Europe and Africa, and distribute them to research and development also funded by the program. This paper will discuss the streamlined approach to language resource development we designed to support simultaneous creation of multiple resources for multiple languages.

1 Introduction

Over the past decade, the scope of interest in language resource creation has increased across multiple disciplines. The differing approaches of these disciplines are reflected in the terms used for newly targeted groups of languages. Less commonly targeted languages (LCTLs) research may focus on development of basic linguistic technologies or language-aware applications. The REFLEX-LCTL (Research on English and Foreign Language Exploitation-Less Commonly Taught Languages) program, sponsored by the United States government, was an effort in simultaneous creation of basic language resources and technologies for LCTLs, namely languages which have large numbers of speakers, but are nonetheless infrequently studied by language learners or researchers in the U.S.

Under the REFLEX-LCTL program, we produced "language packs" of basic language resources for 13 such languages. This paper focuses on the resources created for the 8 Asian languages: Bengali, Pashto, Punjabi, Tamil, Tagalog, Thai, Urdu and Uzbek.[1]

Our approach to language pack creation was to maximize our resources. We accomplished this in a number of ways. We engaged in thorough planning to identify required tasks and their interdependencies, and the human and technical resources needed to accomplish them. We focused intensely on identifying available digital resources at the start of language pack creation, so we could immediately begin assessment of their usability, and work on filling the resource gaps identified. We developed annotation tools usable for multiple tasks and all languages and designed to make manual annotation more efficient. We developed standards for data representations, to support efficient creation, processing, and end use.

2 Planning For Basic Language Resources Creation

2.1 Language Selection

The selection of REFLEX-LCTL target languages was based on a number of criteria, while operating within a fixed budget. The most basic criterion was that the language be spoken by large number of native speakers, but poorly represented in terms of available language resources. The Indic languages (Bengali, Punjabi, Urdu) were chosen to give researchers the opportunity to experiment with bootstrapping techniques with resources in related languages. In order to maximize the usefulness and generality of our methods, the project adopted the additional goals of variation in the expected availability of raw resources and also variation in linguistic characteristics both within the set of selected languages and in comparison to more well-resourced languages. Though we are focusing, in this paper, on the Asian languages, LCTL languages are linguistically and geographically diverse, representing major language families and major geographical regions.

The following short descriptions of the Asian LCTL languages are intended to provide some context for the language pack discussions. The lan-

[1] The other languages were: Amazigh (Berber), Hungarian, Kurdish, Tigrinya and Yoruba.

Proceedings of the 7th Workshop on Asian Language Resources, ACL-IJCNLP 2009, pages 55–62,
Suntec, Singapore, 6-7 August 2009.

guage demographic information is taken from Ethnologue (Gordon, 2005).

2.2 Bengali

Bengali is spoken mostly in Bangladesh and India. The language pack for Bengali was the first complete language pack we created, and it served as a pilot language pack for the rest of the project. There were a relatively large number of raw materials and existing lexicons to support our lexicon development, and our language pack included the largest lexicon among the Asian language packs.

2.3 Urdu

Urdu, spoken primarily in Pakistan and part of India, is closely related to Hindi. Urdu is traditionally written using Perso-Arabic script, and has vocabulary borrowed from Arabic and Persian. This was a language which had a large amount of available digital resources in comparison with other LCTLs, but did not meet our original expectations for raw digital text.

2.4 Thai

Thai is a Tai-Kadai language spoken by more than 20 million people, mainly in Thailand. Thai was another language which was relatively rich in available digital language resources. The Thai language pack includes the largest amount of monolingual text and found parallel text among the language packs. For Thai, tokenization, or word segmentation, was probably the most challenging aspect of the resource creation effort. For the initial version of the language pack, we used a tokenization tool adopted from an opensource software package.

2.5 Tamil

Tamil is a Dravidian language with more than 60 million speakers in India, Sri Lanka, Singapore and other countries. We benefited from having local language experts available for consultation on this language pack

2.6 Punjabi

Punjabi, also written as Panjabi, is an Indo-European language spoken in both India and Pakistan. Ethnologue and ISO 639-3 distinguish three variations of Punjabi: Eastern, Mirpur and Western, and the Eastern variation has the largest population of speakers. We were able to obtain relatively large amounts of monolingual text and existing parallel text.

2.7 Tagalog

Tagalog is an Austronesian language spoken by 15 million people, primarily in the Philippines. The monolingual text we produced is the smallest (774 K words) among the eight Asian language packs, due in part to the prevalence of English in formal communication mediums such as news publications.

2.8 Pashto

Pashto an Indo-European language spoken primarily in Afghanistan and parts of Pakistan. It is one of the two official languages in Afghanistan. Ethnologue and ISO 639-3 distinguish three varieties of Pashto: Northern, Central and Southern. Major sources of data for this language pack included BBC, Radio Free America and Voice of America.

2.9 Uzbek

Uzbek is primarily spoken in Uzbekistan and in other Asian republics of the former Soviet Union. The creation of the language pack for Uzbek, which is a Turkic language, and the official language of Uzbekistan, was outsourced to BUTE (Budapest University of Technology and Economics) in Hungary. Even though the Uzbek government officially decided to use a Latin script in 1992, the Cyrillic alphabet used between the 1940's and 1990's are still commonly found. Our language pack contains all resources in Latin script and includes an encoding converter for converting between the Latin script and the Cyrillic script.

2.10 Designing Language Packs

Within the REFLEX-LCTL program, a language pack is a standardized package containing the following language resources:

- Documentation
  - Grammatical Sketch
- Data
  - Monolingual Text
  - Parallel Text
  - Bilingual Lexicon
  - Named Entity Annotated Text
  - POS Tagged Text
- Tools
  - Tokenizer
  - Sentence Segmenter
  - Character Encoding Conversion Tool
  - Name Transliterators
  - Named Entity Tagger
  - POS Tagger
  - Morphological Analyzer

Grammatical sketches are summaries (approximately 50 pages) of the features of the written language. The primary target audience are language engineers with a basic grounding in linguistic concepts.

Monolingual text is the foundation for all other language pack resources. We provided monolingual text in both tokenized and non-tokenized format. Parallel text is an important resource for development of machine translation technologies, and allows inductive lexicon creation. The bilingual lexicons also support a variety of language technologies. The named entity annotations and part of speech tagged text can be used to create automatic taggers.

The language packs also include basic data processing and conversion tools, such as tokenizers, sentence segmenters, character encoding converters and name transliterators, as well as more advanced tools, such as POS taggers, named entity taggers, and morphological analyzers.

These language packs include 6 of the 9 text resources and tools in 4 of the 15 text-based modules listed in the current BLARK matrix (ELDA, 2008).

When we had a relatively stable definition of the deliverables for language pack, we were able to begin planning for the downstream processes

3 Standards for Data Representation

An important step in planning was to define standards for language pack data representation, to allow all downstream processes to run more efficiently.

3.1 Language Codes

We decided to use the ISO 639-3[2] (also Ethnologue, 15th edition (Gordon, 2005)) three-letter language codes throughout the language packs. For example, the language code is stored in every text data file in the language packs. The ISO 639-3 language codes for our eight languages are as follows: Urdu (URD), Thai (THA), Bengali (BEN), Tamil (TAM), Punjabi (PAN), Tagalog (TGL), Pashto (PBU) and Uzbek (UZN). When there were multiple ISO 639-3 codes for a target language, the code for the sublanguage for which the majority of the written text can be obtained was used.

3.2 File Formats

One of the first tasks in planning for this data creation effort was to define file formats for the monolingual text, parallel text, lexicons and annotation files. This designing process was led by us and a group of experts selected from the research sites participating in the REFLEX-LCTL program. The requirements included the following:

- Monolingual and parallel text files should be able to represent sentence segmentation, and both tokenized and non-tokenized text.
- For parallel text, the text and the target language and the translations in English should be stored in separate aligned files.
- Unique IDs should be assigned to sentences/segments, so that the segment-level mapping in parallel text is clear.
- Annotation files should be in a *stand-off* format: i.e., annotations should be separate from the source text files.
- Lexicon files should be able to represent at the minimum of word, stem, part-of-speech, gloss and morphological analysis.
- File formats should be XML-based.
- Files should be encoded in UTF-8 (UNICODE).

After several cycles of prototyping and exchanging feedback, we settled on the following original file formats named "LCTL text format" (LTF - file name extension: .ltf.xml), "LCTL annotation format" (LAF - file name extension: .laf.xml), and "LCTL lexicon format" (LLF - file name extension .llf.xml. Appendix A shows the DTD for LTF format.

3.3 Evaluation and Training Data Partition

To support evaluation of language technologies based on the data included in the language packs, we designated approximately 10% of our primary data as the evaluation data and the rest as the training data. Any data that was included as "as-is", (e.g. found parallel text), was included in the training partition.

3.4 Directory Structure and File Naming Conventions

Giving all language packs a consistent design and structure allows users to navigate the contents with ease. As such, we defined the directory structure within each language pack to be the following.

The top directory was named as follows.

```
LCTL_{Language}_{Version}/
```

For example, the version 1.0 of the Urdu language pack would have the top directory named LCTL_Urdu_v1.0.

The top directory name is also used as the official title for the package, so the full name rather than the language code was used for maximum clarity for users not familiar with the ISO coding.

Under the main directory, the following subdirectories are defined:

[2]See `http://www.sil.org/iso639-3/` for more details

```
Documentation/
Grammatical_Sketch/
Tools/
Lexicon/
Monolingual_Text/
Parallel_Text/
Named_Entity_Annotations/
POS_Tagged_Text/
```

The Parallel_Text directory was divided into "Found" and "Translation" directories. The Found directory contains parallel text that was available as raw digital text, which we processed into our standardized formats. The Translation directory contains manually translated text, created by our translators or subcontractors as well as part of found parallel text which we were able to align at the sentence-level. The data directories (e.g., Monolingual Text, Parallel Text, Named Entity Annotation, POS Tagged Text) were further divided into evaluation data ("Eval") and training data ("Train") directories as requested by the program.

We used the following format for text corpora file names wherever possible:

```
{SRC}_{LNG}_{YYYYMMDD}.{SeqID}
```

{SRC} is a code assigned for the source; {LNG} is the ISO 639-3 language code; {YYYYMMDD} is the publication/posting date of the document; and {SeqID} is a unique ID within the documents from the same publication/posting date.

4 Building Technical Infrastructure

In creating the language resources included in the LCTL language packs, we developed a variety of software tools designed for humans, including native speaker informants without technical expertise, to provide data needed for the resource creation efforts as efficiently as possible. In particular, the following tools played crucial roles in the creation of language packs.

4.1 Annotation Collection Kit Interface (ACK)

In order to facilitate efficient annotation of a variety of tasks and materials, we created a web-based judgment/annotation tool, named the Annotation Collection Kit interface (ACK). ACK allows a task manager to create annotation "kits," which consist of question text and predefined list and/or free-form answer categories. Any UTF-8 text may be specified for questions or answers. ACK is ideal for remote creation of multiple types of text-based annotation, by allowing individual "kits" to be uploaded onto a specific server URL which any remote user can access. In fact, using this tool we were able to support native speaker annotators working on part-of-speech (POS) annotation in Thailand.

When annotators make judgments in ACK, they are stored in a relational database. The results can be downloaded in CSV (comma-separated value) or XML format, so anyone with secure access to the server can easily access the results.

ACK was designed so that anyone with even a basic knowledge of a scripting language such as Perl or Python would be able to create the ACK annotation kits, which are essentially sets of data corresponding to a sets of annotation decisions in the form of radio buttons, check boxes, pull-down menus, or comment fields. Indeed some of the linguists on the LCTL project created their own ACK kits when needed. Although they are limited in scope, creative use of ACK kits can yield a great deal of helpful types of annotation.

For example, for POS annotation, the annotators were given monolingual text from our corpus, word by word, in order, and asked to select the correct part of speech for that word in context. We also used ACK to add/edit glosses and part of speech tags for lexicon entries, to perform morphological tagging, and various other tasks that required judgment from native speakers.

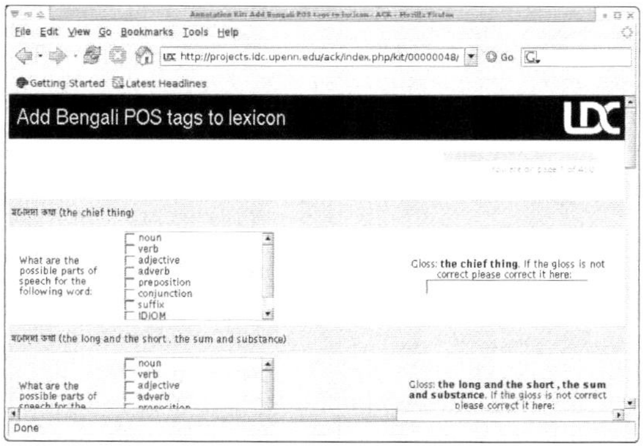

Figure 1: ACK - Annotation Collection Kit

Figure 1 shows a screen shot of ACK.

4.2 Named Entity Annotation Tool

For named entity annotation task, we chose to employ very simple annotation guidelines, to facilitate maximum efficiency and accuracy from native-speaker annotators regardless of linguistic training.

We used an named entity (NE) annotation tool called SimpleNET, which we previously developed for the named entity annotation task for another project. SimpleNET requires almost no training in tool usage, and annotations can be made either with the keyboard or the mouse. The NE annotated text in the LCTL language packs was created with this tool. This tool is written in Python using the QT GUI toolkit, which allows the display of bidirectional text.

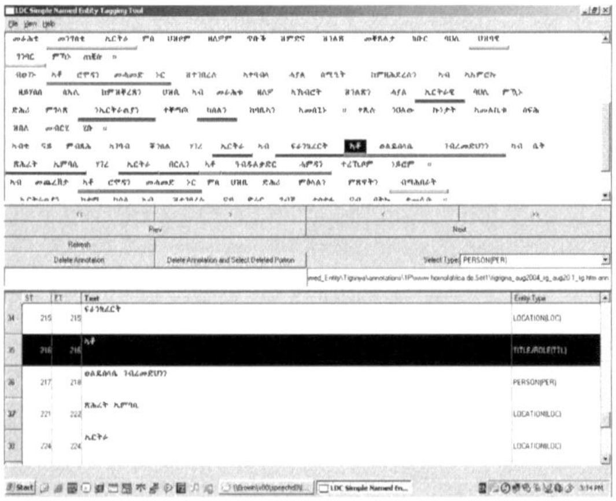

Figure 2: SimpleNET Annotation Tool

Figure 2 shows a screen shot of SimpleNET.

4.3 Named Entity Taggers and POS Taggers

We created common development frameworks for creating named entity taggers and part-of-speech taggers for the LCTL languages. These frameworks allowed us to create taggers for any new language given enough properly-formatted training data and test data. Included are core code written in Java as well as data processing utilities written in Perl and Python. The framework for creating POS taggers was centered around the MALLET toolkit (McCallum, 2002).[3]

4.4 Data Package Creation and Distribution

As per LDC's usual mechanisms for small corpora, language packs were to be packaged as a tar gzip (.tgz) file, and distributed to the REFLEX-LCTL participating research sites. The distribution of the completed languages packs were handled by our secure web downloading system. Access instructions were sent to the participating research sites, and all downloads were logged for future reference.

5 Steps for Creating Each Language Pack

5.1 Identifying Local Language Experts and Native Speakers

An intermediate step between planning and creation was to identify and contact any available local experts in the targeted languages, and recruit additional native speakers to serve as annotators and language informants. Annotators were not necessarily linguists or other language experts, but they were native speakers with reading and writing proficiencies who received training as needed from in-house language experts for creating our annotated corpora, and helped to identify and evaluate harvestable online resources.

Intensive recruiting efforts were conducted for native speakers of each language. Our recruiting strategy utilized such resources as online discussion boards and student associations for those language communities, and we were also able to capitalize on the diversity of the student/staff body at the University of Pennsylvania by recruiting through posted signs on campus.

5.2 Identifying Available Language Resources

The first step in creating each language pack was to identify resources that are already available. To this end we implemented a series of "Harvest Festivals"; intensive sessions where our entire team, along with native speaker informants, convened to search the web for available resources. Available resources were immediately documented on a shared and group editable internal wiki page. By bringing together native speakers, linguists, programmers, information managers and projects managers in the same room, we were able to minimize communications latency, brainstorm as a group, and quickly build upon each other's efforts. This approach was generally quite successful, especially for the text corpora and lexicons, and brought us some of our most useful data.

5.3 Investigating Intellectual Property Rights

As soon as Raw digital resources were identified, our local intellectual property rights specialist began investigation into their usability for the REFLEX-LCTL language packs. It was necessary to contact many individual data providers to obtain an agreement, so the process was quite lengthy and in some cases permission was not granted until shortly before the package was scheduled for release to the REFLEX community. Our general practice was to process all likely candidate data pools and remove data as necessary in later stages, thus ensuring that IPR was not a bottleneck in language pack creation. The exception to this was for large data sources, where removal would have significantly affected the quantity of data in the deliverable.

5.4 Creating Basic Text Processing Tools

The next step was to create the language-specific basic data processing tools, such as encoding converter, sentence segmenter and tokenizer.

The goal for this project was to include whatever encoding converters were needed to convert all of

[3]We thank Partha Pratim Talukdar for providing frameworks for creating taggers.

the raw text and lexical resources collected or created into the standard encoding selected for that target language.

Dividing text into individual sentences is a necessary first step for many processes including the human translation that dominated much of our effort. Simple in principle, LCTL sentence segmentation can prove tantalizingly complex. Our goal was to produce a sentence segmenter that accepts text in our standard encoding as input and outputs segmented sentences in the same encoding.

Word segmentation, or tokenization, is also challenging for languages such as Thai. For Thai, our approach was to utilize an existing opensource word segmentation tool, and enhancing it by using a larger word list than the provided one.

We designed the basic format conversion tools, such as the text-to-LTF converter, to be able to just plug in language-specific tokenizers and segmenters.

5.5 Creating Monolingual Text

The monolingual text corpora in the languages packs were primarily created by identifying and harvesting available resources from the Internet, such as news, newsgroups and weblogs in the target language. Once the IPR expert determined that we can use the resources for the REFLEX-LCTL program, we harvested the document files – recent documents as archived documents. The harvested files were then analyzed and the files that actually have usable contents, such as news articles and weblog postings were kept and converted into the LCTL Text format. The formatting process was typically done in the following steps: 1) convert the harvested document or article in html or other web format to a plain text format, stripping html tags, advertisements, links and other non-contents; 2) convert the plain text files into UTF-8, 2) verify the contents with native speakers, and if necessary, further remove non-contents, or divide a file into multiple files; 3) convert the plain text files into the LCTL Text format, applying sentence segmentation and tokenization. Each document file is assigned a unique document ID. Essential information about the document such as the publication date was kept in the final files.

5.6 Creating Parallel Text

Each language pack contains at least 250,000 words of parallel text. Part of this data was found resources harvested from online resources, such as bilingual news web site. The found parallel documents were converted into the LTF format, and aligned at the sentence level, producing segment-mapping tables between the LTF files in the LCTL language and the LTF files in English.

The rest of this data was created by manually translating documents in the LCTL language into English, or documents in English into the LCTL language. A subset of the monolingual text corpus was selected for translation into English.

In addition, about 65,000 words of English source text were selected as the "Common English Subset" for translation into each LCTL language. Having the same set of parallel documents for all languages will facilitate comparison between any or all of the diverse LCTL languages. The Common Subset included : newswire text, weblogs, a phrasebook and an elicitation corpus. The phrasebook contained common phrases used in daily life, such as "I'm here", and "I have to go". The elicitation corpus, provided by Carnegie Mellon University (Alvarez et al., 2006), included expressions, such as "*male_name_1* will write a book for *female_name_1*, where *male_name_1* and *female_name_1* are common names in the LCTL language. The set of elicitation expressions is designed to elicit lexical distinctions which differ across languages.

The manual translation tasks were outsourced to translation agencies or independent translators. Since the translators were instructed to translate text which had already been sentence-segmented, the creation of sentence-level mappings was trivial. However, we found that it was important to create a sentence-numbered template for the translators to use, otherwise we were likely to receive translations where the source text sentence boundaries were not respected.

5.7 Creating Lexicons

Bilingual lexicons are also an important resource that can support a variety of human language technologies, such as machine translation and information extraction. The goal for this resource was a lexicon of at least 10,000 lemmas with glosses and parts of speech for each language. For most of the languages, we were able to identify existing lexicons, either digital or printed, to consult with and extract information for a subset of the lexical entries; however, in all cases we needed to process them substantially before they could be used efficiently. We performed quality checking, normalizing, added parts of speech and glosses, added entries and removed irrelevant entries.

5.8 Creating Annotated Corpora

A subset of the target language text in each language pack received up to three types of annotations: part-of-speech tags, morphological analysis, and named entity tags. Named entity annotations were created for all language packs.

Annotations were created by native speakers using the annotation tools discussed in section 4.

5.9 Creating Morphological Analyzers

To address the requirement to include some kind of tool for morphological analysis in each language pack, we created either a morphological analyzer implementing hand-written rules or a stemmer using an unsupervised statistical approach, such as the approach described in (Hammarstrom, 2006).

5.10 Creating Named Entity Taggers

We created a named entity tagger for each language pack using our common development framework for named entity taggers4.3. The tagger was created using the named entity annotated text we created for the language packs.

5.11 Creating Part-of-Speech Taggers

Similarly, we created a POS tagger for each language pack using our common development framework for POS taggers (See Section 4.3). We coordinated the POS tag sets for the taggers and lexicons.

5.12 Creating Name Transliterators

A transliterator that converts the language's native script into Latin script is a desired resource. For some languages, this is not a straightforward task. For example, not all vowels are explicitly represented in Bengali script, and there can be multiple pronunciations possible for a given Bengali character. Names, especially names foreign to the target language exhibit a wide variety of spelling, and in HLTs, make up a large percentage of the out-of-vocabulary terms. We focused on creating a transliterator to for romanization of names in the LCTL languages. This resource was generally created by the programming team with consultation from native speakers.

5.13 Writing Grammatical Sketches

The grammatical sketches provide an outline of the features of the written language, to provide the language engineers with description of challenges specific to the languages in creating language technologies. These sketches were written mainly by senior linguists in our group, for readers who do not necessarily have training in linguistics. The format of these documents was either html or pdf.

6 Summary of Completed Language Packs

Table 1 summarizes the contents of the 8 Asian language packs .[4] All of the language packs have already been distributed to REFLEX-LCTL participating research sites. The packs continue to be used to develop and test language technologies. For example, the Urdu pack was used to support a task in the 2006 NIST Open MT Evaluation campaign (of Standards and Technology, 2009). Once a language pack has been used for evaluation it will be placed into queue for general release.

[4]The numbers represent the number of tokens.

7 Conclusion

We have developed an efficient approach for creating basic text language resources for diverse languages. Our process integrated the efforts of software programmers, native speakers, language specialists, and translation agencies to identify and built on already available resources, and create new resources as efficiently as possible.

Using our streamlined processes, we were able to complete language packs for eight diverse Asian languages. We hope that the completed resources will provide valuable support for research and technology development for these languages.

We faced various challenges at the beginning of the project which led us to revisions of our methods, and some of these challenges would surely be encountered during a similar effort. We hope that our approach as described here will be of service to future endeavors in HLT development for under-resourced languages.

References

Alison Alvarez, Lori S. Levin, Robert E. Frederking, Simon Fung, and Donna Gates. 2006. The MILE corpus for less commonly taught languages. In *Proceedings of HLT-NAACL 2006*.

ELDA. 2008. BLARK Resource/Modules Matrix. From Evaluations and Language Resources Distribution Agency (ELDA) web site http://www.elda.org/blark/matrice_res_mod.php , accessed on 2/23/2008.

Raymond G. Gordon, Jr., editor. 2005. *Ethnologue: Languages of the World, Fifteenth edition, Online version*. SIL International. http://www.ethnologue.com/.

Harald Hammarstrom, 2006. *Poor Man's Stemming: Unsupervised Recognition of Same-Stem Words*. Springer Berlin / Heidelberg.

Andrew Kachites McCallum. 2002. MALLET: A machine learning for language toolkit. http://mallet.cs.umass.edu.

National Institute of Standards and Technology. 2009. NIST Open Machine Translation Evaluation. http://www.itl.nist.gov/iad/mig/tests/mt/, accessed on June 7, 2009.

	Urdu	Thai	Bengali	Tamil	Punjabi	Tagalog	Pashto	Uzbek
Mono Text	14,804	39,700	2,640	1,112	13,739	774	5,958	790
Parallel Text (L ⇒ E)	1,300	694	237	308		203	180	206
Parallel Text (Found)	947	1,496	243		230			
Parallel Text (E ⇒ L)	65	65	65	65	65	65	65	65
Lexicon	26	232	482	10	108	18	10	25
Encoding Converter	Yes	Yes	Yes	Yes	Yes	Yes	Yes	Yes
Sentence Segmenter	Yes	Yes	Yes	Yes	Yes	Yes	Yes	Yes
Word Segmenter	Yes	Yes	Yes	Yes	Yes	Yes	Yes	Yes
POS Tagger	Yes	Yes	Yes	Yes	Yes	Yes	Yes	Yes
POS Tagged Text	5	5		59				
Morphological Analyzer	Yes	Yes	Yes	Yes	Yes	Yes	Yes	Yes
Morph-Tagged Text	11			144				
NE Annotated Text	233	218	138	132	157	136	165	93
Named Entity Tagger	Yes	Yes	Yes	Yes	Yes	Yes	Yes	Yes
Name Transliterator	Yes	Yes	Yes	Yes	Yes	Yes	Yes	Yes
Descriptive Grammar	Yes	Yes	Yes	Yes	Yes	Yes	Yes	Yes

Table 1: Language Packs for Asian Languages (Data Volume in 1000 Words)

A DTD for LTF Files

```
<!ELEMENT LCTL_TEXT (DOC+)                          >
<!ATTLIST LCTL_TEXT lang CDATA         #IMPLIED
                    source_file CDATA  #IMPLIED
                    source_type CDATA  #IMPLIED
                    author CDATA       #IMPLIED
                    encoding CDATA     #IMPLIED     >

<!ELEMENT DOC (HEADLINE|DATELINE|AUTHORLINE|TEXT)+ >
<!ATTLIST DOC id     ID      #REQUIRED
              lang   CDATA   #IMPLIED
>

<!ELEMENT HEADLINE (SEG+)                           >
<!ELEMENT DATELINE (#PCDATA)                        >
<!ELEMENT AUTHORLINE (#PCDATA)                      >
<!ELEMENT TEXT (P|SEG)+                             >

<!ELEMENT P (SEG+)                                  >

<!ELEMENT SEG (ORIGINAL_TEXT?, TOKEN*)              >
<!ATTLIST SEG id              ID     #REQUIRED
              start_token     IDREF  #IMPLIED
              end_token       IDREF  #IMPLIED
              start_char      CDATA  #IMPLIED
              end_char        CDATA  #IMPLIED
>
<!ELEMENT ORIGINAL_TEXT (#PCDATA)                   >

<!ELEMENT TOKEN (#PCDATA)                           >
<!ATTLIST TOKEN id            ID     #REQUIRED
                attach        (LEFT|RIGHT|BOTH)
                                     #IMPLIED
                pos           CDATA  #IMPLIED
                morph         CDATA  #IMPLIED
                gloss         CDATA  #IMPLIED
                start_char    CDATA  #IMPLIED
                end_char      CDATA  #IMPLIED
>
```

Finite-State Description of Vietnamese Reduplication

Le Hong Phuong
LORIA, France
lehong@loria.fr

Nguyen Thi Minh Huyen
Hanoi Univ. of Science, Vietnam
huyenntm@vnu.edu.vn

Azim Roussanaly
LORIA, France
azim@loria.fr

Abstract

We present for the first time a computational model for the reduplication of the Vietnamese language. Reduplication is a popular phenomenon of Vietnamese in which reduplicative words are created by the combination of multiple syllables whose phonics are similar. We first give a systematical study of Vietnamese reduplicative words, bringing into focus clear principles for the formation of a large class of bi-syllabic reduplicative words. We then make use of optimal finite-state devices, in particular minimal sequential string-to string transducers to build a computational model for very efficient recognition and production of those words. Finally, several nice applications of this computational model are discussed.

1 Introduction

Finite-state technology has been applied successfully for describing the morphological processes of many natural languages since the pioneering works of (Kaplan and Kay, 1994; Koskenniemi, 1983). It is shown that while finite-state approaches to most natural languages have generally been very successful, they are less suitable for non-concatenative phenomena found in some languages, for example the non-concatenative word formation processes in Semitic languages (Cohen-Sygal and Wintner, 2006). A popular non-concatenative process is reduplication – the process in which a morpheme or part of it is duplicated.

Reduplication is a common linguistic phenomenon in many Asian languages, for example Japanese, Mandarin Chinese, Cantonese, Thai, Malay, Indonesian, Chamorro, Hebrew, Bangla, and especially Vietnamese.

We are concerned with the reduplication of Vietnamese. It is noted that Vietnamese is a monosyllabic language and its word forms never change, contrary to occidental languages that make use of morphological variations. Consequently, reduplication is one popular and important word formation method which is extensively used to enrich the lexicon. This follows that the Vietnamese lexicon consists of a large number of reduplicative words.

This paper presents for the first time a computational model for recognition and production of a large class of Vietnamese reduplicative words. We show that Vietnamese reduplication can be simulated efficiently by finite-state devices. We first introduce the Vietnamese lexicon and the structure of Vietnamese syllables. We next give a complete study about the reduplication phenomenon of Vietnamese language, bringing into focus formation principles of reduplicative words. We then propose optimal finite-state sequential transducers recognizing and producing a substantial class of these words. Finally, we present several nice applications of this computational model before concluding and discussing the future work.

2 Vietnamese Lexicon

In this section, we first present some general characteristics of the Vietnamese language. We then give some statistics of the Vietnamese lexicon and introduce the structure of Vietnamese syllables.

The following basic characteristics of Vietnamese are adopted from (Đoàn, 2003; Đoàn et al. , 2003; Hữu et al. , 1998; Nguyễn et al. , 2006).

2.1 Language Type

Vietnamese is classified in the Viet-Muong group of the Mon-Khmer branch, that belongs to the Austro-Asiatic language family. Vietnamese is also known to have a similarity with languages in the Tai family. The Vietnamese vocabulary features a large amount of Sino-Vietnamese words.

Proceedings of the 7th Workshop on Asian Language Resources, ACL-IJCNLP 2009, pages 63–69,
Suntec, Singapore, 6-7 August 2009. ©2009 ACL and AFNLP

Moreover, by being in contact with the French language, Vietnamese was enriched not only in vocabulary but also in syntax by the calque of French grammar.

Vietnamese is an isolating language, which is characterized by the following properties:

- it is a monosyllabic language;
- its word forms never change, contrary to occidental languages that make use of morphological variations (plural form, conjugation, *etc.*);
- hence, all grammatical relations are manifested by word order and function words.

2.2 Vocabulary

Vietnamese has a special unit called *"tiếng"* that corresponds at the same time to a syllable with respect to phonology, a morpheme with respect to morpho-syntax, and a word with respect to sentence constituent creation. For convenience, we call these *"tiếng"* syllables. The Vietnamese vocabulary contains

- simple words, which are monosyllabic;
- reduplicative words composed by phonetic reduplication;
- compound words composed by semantic coordination and by semantic subodination;
- complex words phonetically transcribed from foreign languages.

The Vietnamese lexicon edited recently by the Vietnam Lexicography Center (Vietlex[1]) contains $40,181$ words and idioms, which are widely used in contemporary spoken language, newspapers and literature. These words are made up of $7,729$ syllables. Table 1 shows some interesting statistics of the word length measured in syllables. $6,303$ syllables (about 81.55% of syllables) are words by themselves. Two-syllable words are the most frequent, consisting of nearly 71% of the vocabulary.

2.3 Syllables

In this paragraph, we introduce phonetic attributes of Vietnamese syllables. In addition of the monosyllabic characteristic, Vietnamese is a tonal language in that each syllable has a certain pitch characteristic. The meaning of a syllable varies with its tone. This phonetic mechanism can also be found in other languages such that Chinese or Thai.

[1] *http://www.vietlex.com/*

Length	#	%
1	$6,303$	15.69
2	$28,416$	70.72
3	$2,259$	5.62
4	$2,784$	6.93
≥ 5	419	1.04
Total	$40,181$	100

Table 1: Length of words measured in syllables

No.	Tones	Notation
1.	low falling	à
2.	creaky rising	ã
3.	creaky falling	ạ
4.	mid level	a
5.	dipping	ả
6.	high rising	á

Table 2: Vietnamese tones

There are six tones in Vietnamese as specified in Table 2. The letter *a* denotes any non-accent syllable. These six tones can be roughly classified into two groups corresponding to low and high pitches in pronunciation. The first half of the table contains three low tones and the second half contains three high tones. In addition, the difference in the tone of two syllables are distinguished by flat property of tones. The 1st and 4th tones in Table 2 are flat (*bằng*), the other tones are non-flat (*trắc*).

The structure of a Vietnamese syllable is given in Table 3. Each syllable can be divided into three parts: onset, rhyme and tone. The onset is usually a consonant, however it may be empty. The rhyme contains a vowel (nucleus) with or without glide /w/, and an optional consonant (coda). It is noticed that the initial consonant of a syllable does not carry information of the tone, the Vietnamese tone has an effect only on the rhyme part of the syllable (Tran et al., 2006). This result reinforces the fact that a tone is always marked by the nucleus composant of the rhyme which is a vowel. Readers who are interested in detail the phonetic composition of Vietnamese syllables may refer to (Tran et al., 2006; Vu et al., 2005).

3 Reduplication in Vietnamese

Reduplication is one of the methods for creating multi-syllable words in Vietnamese. A reduplica-

Tone			
Onset	Rhyme		
	Glide	Nucleus	Coda

Table 3: Phonetic structure of Vietnamese syllables

tive word is characterized by a phenomenon called phonetic interchange, in which one or several phonetic elements of a syllable are repeated following a certain number of specific rules.

From the point of view of sense, the reduplication in Vietnamese usually indicates a diminutive of adjectives, which can also be found in Hebrew, or a pluralization in Malay, in Thai and in Indonesian, or an intensivity as the use of partial reduplication in Japanese, Thai, Cantonese and Chamorro (an Austronesian language spoken on Guam and the Northern Mariana Islands). In this aspect, Vietnamese reduplication serves similar functions as those of reduplication in several Asian languages, as reported in an investigation of Asian language reduplication within the NEDO project (Tokunaga et al. , 2008a; Tokunaga et al. , 2008b).

The Vietnamese reduplication creates an expressional sense connecting closely to the phonetic material of Vietnamese, a language of rich melody. Consequently, there are many Vietnamese reduplicative words which are difficult to interpret to foreigners, though in general, native Vietnamese speakers always use and understand them correctly (Diệp, 1999).

Vietnamese reduplicative words can be classified into three classes basing on the number of syllables they contain: two-syllable (or bi-syllabic) reduplicative words, three-syllable (or tri-syllabic) reduplicative words and four-syllable reduplicative words. The bi-syllabic class is the most important class because of two reasons: (1) bi-syllabic reduplicative words make up more than 98% amount of reduplicative words, that is, almost reduplicative words has two syllables; and (2) bi-syllabic reduplicative words embody principle characteristics of the reduplication phenomenon in both phone aspect and sense formation aspect. For these reasons, in this paper, we address only bi-syllabic reduplicative words and call them reduplicative words for short, if there is no confusion.

As presented in the previous section, a syllable has a strict structure containing three parts: the onset, the rhyme and the tone. Basing on the phonetic interchange of a syllable, we distinguish two types of reduplication:

- full reduplication, where the whole syllable is repeated;
- partial reduplication, where either the onset is repeated or the rhyme and the tone are repeated.

In this work, we constraint ourselves by focusing only on the construction of an efficient computational model applied for reduplicative words which have clear and well-defined formation principles. These words can be classified into three types investigated in detail in the following subsections. In given examples, the base syllables (or root syllable, or root for short) are the ones which are underlined. The reduplication that has undefined or incomplete formation rules will be tackled in future works.

3.1 Full Reduplication

In this type of reduplication, the root is identically repeated; there is only a slight difference on stress in pronunciation. For example, *hao hao* (a little similar), *lăm lăm* (intentional), *đùng đùng* (accidentally dertermined), *lừ lừ* (silently). In the Vietnamese lexicon there are 274 reduplicative words of this type.

In principle, there appears to be many reduplicative words of this type whose their roots may be whatever syllables bearing whatever tone, for instance *đỏ đỏ*, *hớ hớ*, *sững sững*, *chậm chậm*. However, in consequence of the difference of stress between the root and the reduplicant, the tone of the reduplicant is changed in order to be in harmony with the root, for the sake of more readability and audibility ("easier to read, easier to hear"). This consequence leads to the formation of reduplicative words of the second type which we call reduplication with tone according.

3.2 Reduplication with Tone According

As presented above, the difference between tone of the root and the reduplicant is a consequence of the difference between their stress which is expressed by their tones. This creates reduplicative words of the second type; for example, *đo đỏ* (reddish), *hơ hớ* (in the bloom of youth), *sừng sững* (statly, high and majestic), *chầm chậm* (rather slow). The tone properties (low or high pitch, flat or non-flat) are now put into use.

Reduplicant	Root	#
a	*ả*	72
a	*á*	128
à	*ã*	27
à	*ạ*	80
	Sum	307

Table 4: Statistic of the second type reduplication

The prosodic influence is responsible for the creation of the reduplicant from its root. As a result, the combination of tones between two syllables is realized in the following principle: *non-flat tones of the roots are matched against a corresponding flat tones of their reduplicants*. That is, the non-flat root has to select for it the flat reduplicant belonging to the same pitch, *i.e.*, in the same row. In this type of reduplicative words, the root is stressed in pronunciation.

A detailed statistic about these reduplicative words with respect to the combination of tones is given in Table 4. There are 307 reduplicative words of the second type.

3.3 Reduplication with Final Consonant According

In this type of reduplication, there is not only the difference between tones of the root and the reduplicant but also the difference between their final consonants (hence their penultimates). Some examples of this type of reduplication which we call the third reduplication type are:

- *cầm cập* (clatter, shiver), *lôm lốp* (pop pop), *xăm xắp* (a little full), *thiêm thiếp* (fall asleep), *nơm nớp* (be in a state of suspense)
- *giôn giốt* (sourish), *ngùn ngụt* (burn violently), *phơn phớt* (light red), *hun hút* (profound), *san sát* (be very close to, adjoining)
- *vằng vặc* (very clear), *nhưng nhức* (a little ache), *rừng rực* (brightly), *phăng phắc* (very silent), *chênh chếch* (a little oblique), *anh ách* (feeling bloated).

The practical observation shows that the modification of final consonant from the root to the duplicate also has a clear rule: *the noisy phone of the root is transformed to a nasal phone of the reduplicant* as shown in Table 5.

Example	At root	At reduplicant
	Noisy phone	Nasal phone
ăm ắp	*-p*	*-m*
phơn phớt	*-t*	*-n*
vằng vặc	*-c*	*-ng*
anh ách	*-ch*	*-nh*

Table 5: Transformation rules of final consonants

Root	Reduplicant	#
-p	*-m*	52
-t	*-n*	96
-c	*-ng*	56
-ch	*-nh*	28
	Sum	232

Table 6: Statistic of the third type reduplication

The transformation of final consonant occurs only with the roots having as final consonant *p*, *t*, or *c*. The principle of tone combination is the same as that of the second reduplication type.

A detailed statistic about these reduplicative words is given in the Table 6. There are 232 reduplicative words of the third type.

Briefly, the total number of reduplicative words of all the three types of reduplication is 813, making up about $813/28,416 \approx 2.86\%$ of the number of two-syllable words.

4 Implementation

We report in this section the construction of a computational model for recognition and production of the three types of reduplication presented in the previous section. We have implemented finite-state sequential transducers (FSTs) which are able to recognize and produce corresponding types of reduplicative words. These devices operate on the same input and output alphabets, say Σ, containing all Vietnamese characters.

FSTs are formal devices for encoding regular relations. A regular relation is a mapping between two regular languages. In our cases, these languages are sets of Vietnamese root and reduplicant syllables.

We adapted nice and efficient algorithms developed by (Daciuk et al., 2000) to incrementally construct minimal transducers from a source of data. These algorithms are originally designed to build optimal deterministic finite-state automata on-the-fly but they can also be used to construct optimal sequential transducers. We could consider simply that the alphabet of the automata would be $\Sigma \times \Sigma$; output strings of Σ^* are associated with the final states of the lexicon and they are only outputed once corresponding valid inputs from Σ are recognized. Interested readers are invited to refer to (Daciuk et al., 2000) for further detail of the algorithms for building optimal automata on-the-fly.

4.1 First Type Transducer

In the first type reduplication, the root and the reduplicant is completely identical in writing; they are only distinguished by a stress in pronunciation. We can simply construct a deterministic finite-state transducer (FST) f_1 that produces reduplicants from their roots in which the output string labeled on each arc is the same as its input character; that is $f_1(x) = x$ where x is a syllable in the first type duplication. As an illustration, the following minimal FST recognizes and generates three first type reduplicative words *luôn luôn* (always), *lừ lừ* (silently), *khàn khàn* (raucous).

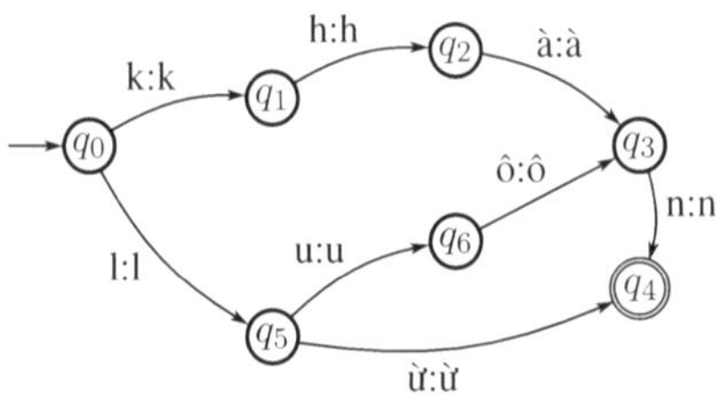

The minimal FST f_1 recognizing all 274 reduplicative words of the first type consists of 90 states in which 16 states are final ones. It has 330 transitions, the maximum number of outtransitions from a state is 28.

4.2 Second Type Transducer

In the second type reduplication, the root has an non-flat tone while its reduplicant has the corresponding flat tone. A root determines for it the unique reduplicant. Hence we can construct a sequential FST f_2 which is able to generate reduplicants from roots.

For instance, consider two reduplicative words of the second type *lem lém* (glib) and *lem lẻm* (voluble). They can be recognized by the minimal sequential FST f_2 such that f_2(*lém*) = *lem* and f_2(*lẻm*) = *lem* as depicted in the following figure:

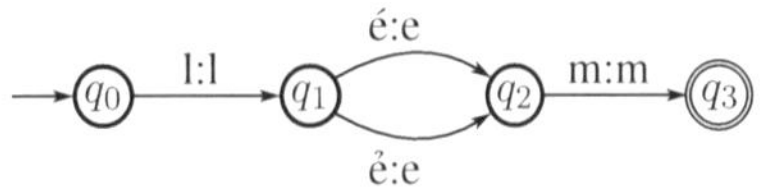

Similarly, the minimal FST f_2 which generates three reduplicative words *giông giống* (a little similar), *đằng đẵng* (interminable) and *đăm đắm* (fixedly) is as follows:

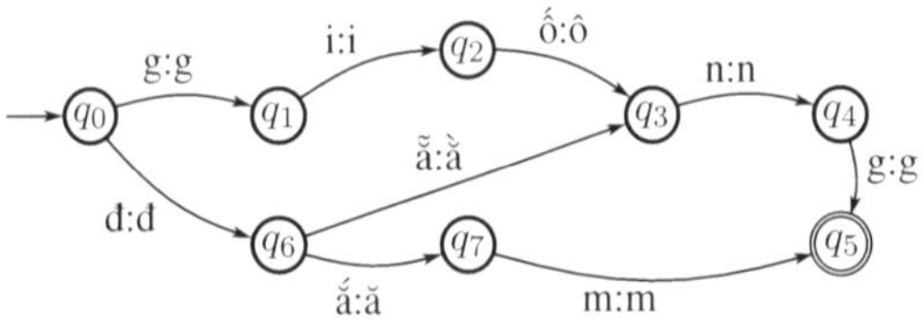

The minimal FST f_2 recognizing all 307 reduplicative words of the second type consists of 93 states in which 11 states are final ones. It has 371 transitions, the maximum number of outtransitions from a state is 22.

4.3 Third Type Transducer

The roots and reduplicants in the third type reduplication are not only combined by principles of flat and non-flat tones, they are also distinguised by last consonants. We know that in the case the root ends with *c*, its reduplicant is one character longer than it. The other three transformations of last consonants do not change the length of the reduplicants with respect to that of the roots.

Hence the FST f_3 which recognizes the third type reduplication is required to modify the tones of the reduplicants with respect to those of the roots on the one hand, and to transform last consonants of the roots on the other hand. For example, the minimal FST f_3 recognizing four reduplicative words *biêng biếc* (bluish green), *biền biệt* (leave behind no traces whatsoever), *bình bịch* (a series of thudding blows) and *bôm bốp* (pop pop) is given in the figure below:

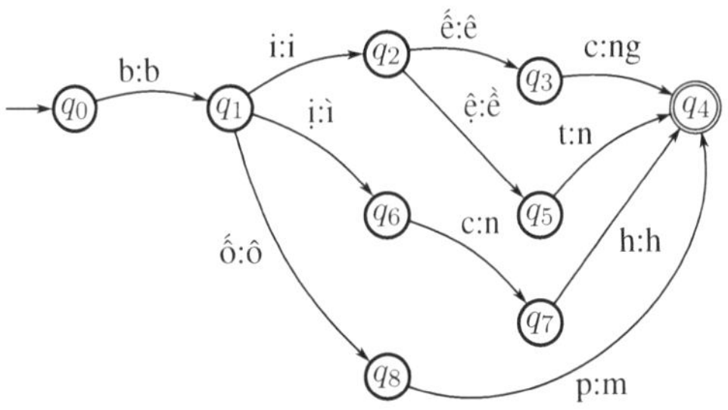

The minimal FST f_3 recognizing all 232 reduplicative words of the third type consists of 59

states in which 2 states are final ones. It has 262 transitions, the maximum number of outtransitions from a state is 19.

Once all the three transducers have been constructed, we can unify them by making use of the standard union operation on transducers to obtain a sequential FST which is able to recognize all the three class of reduplication presented above (Mohri, 1996; Mohri, 1997).

4.4 A Software Package

We have developed a Java software package named **vnReduplicator** which implements the above-mentioned computational model of Vietnamese reduplication. The core component of this package is a minimal FST which can recognize a substantial amount of reduplicative bi-syllabic words found in the Vietnamese language.

The first application of this core model which we have developed is a reduplication scanner for Vietnamese. We use the minimal FST of the core model to build a tool for fast detection of reduplication. The tool scans a given input text and produces a list of all the recognized reduplicative words. The detection process is very fast since the underlying transducer operates in optimal time in the sense that the time to recognize a syllable corresponds to the time required to follow a single path in the deterministic finite-state machine, and the length of the path is the length of the syllable measured in characters.

As an example, given the following input text

"Anh đi *biền biệt*. Cô vẫn chờ anh hơn 20 năm *đằng đẵng*."[2],

the scanner marks two reduplicative words as shown in the italic face.

We are currently investigating another useful application of the core model for a partial spell checking of Vietnamese text. It is observed that people may make typhographical errors in writing like *đằng đắng* instead of the correct word *đằng đẵng*. In such cases, the computational model can be exploited to detect the potential errors and suggest corrections.

The reduplication model could also help improve the accuracy of Vietnamese lexical recognizers in particular and the accuracy of Vietnamese word segmentation systems in general.

The reduplication scanner will be integrated to **vnTokenizer**[3] - an open source and highly accurate tokenizer for Vietnamese texts (Le et al., 2008).

The software and related resources will be distributed under the GNU General Public Lisence[4] and it will be soon available online[5].

5 Conclusion and Future Work

We have presented for the first time a computational model for the reduplication of the Vietnamese language. We show that a large class of reduplicative words can be modeled effectively by sequential finite-state string-to-string transducers.

The analysis of the various patterns of reduplication of the Vietnamese language has twofold contributions. On the one hand, it gives useful information on identification of spelling variants in Vietnamese texts. On the other hand, it gives an explicit formalization of precedence relationships in the phonology, and as a result helps ordering and modeling phonological processes before transfer of the presentation to the articulatory interface.

It is argued that the relation between morphology and phonology is an intimate one, both synchronically and diachronically. As mentioned earlier, Vietnamese reduplication is always accompanied by a modification of phone and tone for a symmetric and harmonic posture. We thus believe that the compact finite-state description of a large class of reduplication would help connect morphosyntactic attributes to individual phonological components of a set of Vietnamese word forms and contribute to the improvement of Vietnamese automatic speech recognition systems.

As mentioned earlier, the current work does not handle partial reduplication in which either the onset is repeated or the rhyme and the tone of syllables are repeated, for example *bồng bềnh* (bob), *chúm chím* (open slightly one's lips), *lẩm cẩm* (doting), *lúng túng* (perplexed, embarrassed). Partial reduplication is a topic which has been well studied for a long time by Vietnamese linguists community. It has been shown that partial reduplicative words also have certain principle formation rules (Diệp, 1999; UBKHXH, 1983). Hence, partial reduplicative words could also be generated and recognized by an appropriate finite-state

[2] He has left behind no traces whatsoever. She has been waiting for him for 20 years.

[3] *http://www.loria.fr/~lehong/tools/vnTokenizer.php*

[4] *http://www.gnu.org/copyleft/gpl.html*

[5] *http://www.loria.fr/~lehong/projects.php*

model which encodes precisely their formation rules. This is an interesting topic of our future work in constructing a rather complete computational model for Vietnamese bi-syllabic reduplication.

Furthermore, in addition to the bi-syllabic reduplication forms, there exists also three or four syllable reduplication forms, for example *cỏn còn con* (very little), *tẹo tèo teo* (very small), or *vội vội vàng vàng* (hurry), *đủng đà đủng đỉnh* (deliberate). These reduplication forms involve the copying operation of morphological structures which is a non-regular operation. Non-regular operations are problematic in that they cannot be cast in terms of composition – the regular operation of major importance in finite-state devices, while finite-state devices cannot handle unbounded copying. However, the question of the possibility for an elegant account to reduce these specific kinds of reduplication to purely regular mechanisms would be of interest for further research to extend and improve the core reduplication components for Vietnamese. Unknown reduplicative word guessing is another interesting and useful topic since the lexicon can never cover all reduplicative words.

Acknowledgement

We gratefully acknowledge helpful comments and valuable suggestions from three anonymous reviewers for improving the paper.

References

Yael Cohen-Sygal and Shuly Wintner. 2006. *Finite-State Registered Automata for Non-Concatenative Morphology*. Computational Linguistics, Vol. 32, No. 1, Pages 49–82.

Jan Daciuk, Stoyan Mihov, Bruce W. Watson and Richard E. Watson. 2000 *Incremental Construction of Minimal Acyclic Finite-State Automata*. Computational Linguistics, Vol. 26, No. 1, 2000.

Le H. Phuong, Nguyen T. M. Huyen, Roussanaly A., Ho T. Vinh. 2008 A hybrid approach to word segmentation of Vietnamese texts. *Proceedings of the 2nd International Conference on Language and Automata Theory and Applications, Tarragona, Spain*. Springer LNCS 5196, 2008.

Diệp Quang Ban and Hoàng Văn Thung. 1999 *Ngữ pháp Tiếng Việt (Vietnamese Grammar)*. NXB Giáo dục, Hà Nội, Việt Nam.

Đoàn Thiện Thuật. 2003 *Ngữ âm tiếng Việt (Vietnamese Phonetics)*. NXB Đại học Quốc gia Hà Nội, Hà Nội, Việt Nam.

Đoàn Thiện Thuật (Editor-in-chief) and Nguyễn Khánh Hà and Phạm Như Quỳnh. 2003 *A Concise Vietnamese Grammar (For Non-native Speakers))*. Thế Giới Publishers, Hà Nội, Việt Nam.

Hữu Đạt and Trần Trí Dõi and Đào Thanh Lan. 1998 *Cơ sở tiếng Việt (Basis of Vietnamese)*. NXB Giáo dục, Hà Nội, Việt Nam.

Ronald Kaplan and Martin Kay. 1994. *Regular Models of Phonological Rule Systems*. Computational Linguistics, Vol. 20, No. 3, Pages 331–378.

Koskenniemi Kimmo. 1983 *Two-Level Morphology: A General Computational Model for Word-Form Recognition and Production*. The Department of General Linguistics, University of Helsinki.

Mehryar Mohri. 1996 *On Some Applications of Finite-State Automata Theory to Natural Language Processing*. Natural Language Engineering, Vol. 2, No. 1, Pages 61–80.

Mehryar Mohri. 1997 *Finite-State Transducers in Language and Speech Processing*. Computational Linguistics, Vol. 23.

Nguyễn Thị Minh Huyền, Laurent Romary, Mathias Rossignol and Vũ Xuân Lương. 2006. *A Lexicon for Vietnamese Language Processing*. Language Resources and Evaluation, Vol. 40, No. 3–4.

Tokunaga T., Kaplan D., Huang C-R., Hsieh S-K, Calzolari N., Monachini M., Soria C., Shirai K., Sornlertlamvanich V., Charoenporn T., Xia Y., 2008. *Adapting international standard for Asian language technologies*. Proceedings of The 6th International Conference on Language Resources and Evaluation (LREC 2008)

Tokunaga T. et al. 2008. *Developing International Standards of Language Resources for Semantic Web Applications* Research Report of the International Joint Research Program (NEDO Grant) for FY 2007, *http://www.tech.nedo.go.jp/PDF/100013569.pdf*

Tran D. D. and Castelli E. and Serignat J. F. and Trinh V. L. and Le X. H. 2006. *Linear F_0 Contour Model for Vietnamese Tones and Vietnamese Syllable Synthesis with TD-PSOLA*. Proceedings of TAL2006, La Rochelle, France.

Thang Tat Vu, Dung Tien Nguyen, Mai Chi Luong and John-Paul Hosom. 2006. *Vietnamese Large Vocabulary Continuous Speech Recognition*. Proceedings of Eurospeech 2005, Lisboa.

Ủy ban Khoa học Xã hội Việt Nam. 1983. *Ngữ pháp tiếng Việt (Vietnamese Grammar)*. Nhà xuất bản Khoa học Xã hội – Hà Nội, Việt Nam.

Construction of Chinese Segmented and POS-tagged Conversational Corpora and Their Evaluations on Spontaneous Speech Recognitions

Xinhui Hu, Ryosuke Isotani, Satoshi Nakamura
National Institute of Information and Communications Technology, Japan
{xinhui.hu, ryosuke.isotani, satoshi.nakamura}@nict.go.jp

Abstract

The performance of a corpus-based language and speech processing system depends heavily on the quantity and quality of the training corpora. Although several famous Chinese corpora have been developed, most of them are mainly written text. Even for some existing corpora that contain spoken data, the quantity is insufficient and the domain is limited. In this paper, we describe the development of Chinese conversational annotated textual corpora currently being used in the NICT/ATR speech-to-speech translation system. A total of 510K manually checked utterances provide 3.5M words of Chinese corpora. As far as we know, this is the largest conversational textual corpora in the domain of travel. A set of three parallel corpora is obtained with the corresponding pairs of Japanese and English words from which the Chinese words are translated. Evaluation experiments on these corpora were conducted by comparing the parameters of the language models, perplexities of test sets, and speech recognition performance with Japanese and English. The characteristics of the Chinese corpora, their limitations, and solutions to these limitations are analyzed and discussed.

1. Introduction

In corpus-based machine translation and speech recognition, the performance of the language model depends heavily on the size and quality of the corpora. Therefore, the corpora are indispensable for these studies and applications. In recent decades, corpus development has seen rapid growth for many languages such as English, Japanese, and Chinese. For Chinese, since there are no plain delimiters among the words, the creation of a segmented and part-of-speech (POS)-tagged corpus is the initial step for most statistical language processes. Several such Chinese corpora have been developed since the 1990s. The two most typical are People's Daily corpus (referred to as PKU), jointly developed by the Institute of Computational Linguistics of Peking University and the Fujitsu Research & Development Center [1], and the Sinica Corpus (referred to as Sinica) developed by the Institute of Information Science and the CKIP Group in Academia Sinica of Taiwan [2]. The former is based on the *People's Daily* newspaper in 1998. It uses standard articles of news reports. The latter is a balanced corpus collected from different areas and classified according to five criteria: genre, style, mode, topic, and source. Although conversational text is also contained in this corpus, it has only 75K of utterances and the domains are limited to a few fields, such as academia and economics, and the style is mostly in address and seldom in conversation.

Since the features of conversation differ from written text, especially in news articles, the development of a segmented and POS-tagged corpus of conversational language is promising work for spontaneous speech recognition and speech-to-speech translation.

In the Spoken Communication Group of NICT, in order to study corpus-based speech translation technologies for the real world, a set of corpora on travel conversation has been built for Japanese, English, and Chinese [3]. These corpora are elaborately designed and constructed on the basis of the concept of variety in samples, situations, and expressions. Now these corpora have been used in the NICT speech-to-speech translation (S2ST) system [8] and other services.

In this paper, we introduce our work on this Chinese corpora development and applications in S2ST speech recognition using these corpora. In Section 2, we provide a brief description of the contents of the NICT corpora, then describe how the Chinese data were obtained. In Section 3, we illustrate the specifications for the segmentation and POS tagging designed for these corpora. Here, we explain the guidelines of segmentation and POS tagging, placing particular emphasis on the features of conversation and speech recognition application. In Section 4, we outline the development procedures and explain our methods of how to get the segmented and POS-tagged data. Some statistical characteristics of the corpora will be shown here. In Section 5, evaluation experiments of speech recognition utilizing these corpora are reported by comparing the results using the same data sets of

Proceedings of the 7th Workshop on Asian Language Resources, ACL-IJCNLP 2009, pages 70–75,
Suntec, Singapore, 6-7 August 2009. ©2009 ACL and AFNLP

Japanese and English. Finally, in Section 6, we discuss the performance of the corpora, the problems that remain in the corpora, and give our ideas concerning future work.

2. Current NICT Chinese Corpora on Travel Dialog Domain

At NICT, in order to deal with various conversational cases of S2ST research, several kinds of corpora were elaborately designed and constructed [3]. Table 1 gives a brief description of the data sets related to the development of the Chinese corpora. Each corpus shown in this table was collected using different methods, for different application purposes, and was categorized into different domains.

Table 1. NICT Corpora Used for Chinese Processing

Name	Collecting Method	Uttr.	Domain
SLDB	Bilingual conversation evolved by interpreters.	16K	Dialogues with the front desk clerk at a hotel
MAD	Bilingual conversation evolved by a machine translation system.	19K	General dialogues on travel
BTEC	Text in guidebooks for overseas travelers	475K	General dialogues on travel

The SLDB (Spoken Language Database) is a collection of transcriptions of spoken language between two people speaking different languages and mediated by a professional interpreter.

In comparison, the MAD (Machine Translation Aid Dialogue) is a similar collection, but it uses our S2ST system instead of an interpreter.

The BTEC (Basic Travel Expression Corpus) is a collection of Japanese sentences and their English translations written by bilingual travel experts. This corpus covers such topics related to travel as shopping, hotel or restaurant reservations, airports, lost and found, and so on.

The original data of the above corpora were developed in the form of English-to-Japanese translation pairs. The Chinese versions are mainly translated from the Japanese, but a small portion of BTEC (namely, BTEC4, about 70K of utterances) was translated from English. Every sentence in these corpora has an equivalent in the other two languages, and they share a common header (ID), except for the language mark. All the data in these three languages constitute a set of parallel corpora. The following shows examples of sentences in the three languages:

Chn.: BTEC1\jpn067\03870\zh\\\\我想喝浓咖啡。
Eng.: BTEC1\jpn067\03870\en\\\\I'd like to have some strong coffee.
Jap.:BTEC1\jpn067\03870\ja\\\\濃いコーヒーが飲みたい。

3. Specifications of Segmentation and Part-of-Speech Tagging

By mainly referring to the PKU and taking into account the characteristics of conversational data, we made our definitions for segmentation units and POS tags. Here, we explain the outlines of these definitions, then illustrate the segmentation and POS-tagging items relating to those considerations on conversations.

3.1. Guidelines of the Definitions

(1) Compatibility with the PKU and Taking into account the Demand of Speech Recognition of S2ST

Since the specification of segmentations and POS-tagging proposed by the PKU [4] has its palpability and maneuverability and is close to China's national standard [5] on segmentation and close to the specification on POS tags recommended by the National Program of China, namely, the 973-project [6], we mainly followed PKU's specification. We adopted the concept of "segmentation unit," i.e., words with disyllable, trisyllable, some compound words, and some phrases were regarded as segmentation units. The morpheme character (word) was also regarded as an independent unit.

However, we made some adjustments to these specifications. In the speech recognition phase of S2ST to deal with data sparseness, the word for "training" needed to be shortened. So a numeral was divided into syllabic units, while both the PKU and the Sinica took the whole number as a unit. For the same reason, the directional verbs (趋向动词), such as "上，下，来，去，进去，and 出来，" which generally follow another verb and express action directions, were divided from the preceding verb. The modal auxiliary verbs (能愿动词), such as "能，想，and 要，" which often precede another verb were separated and tagged with an individual tag set. Because the numeral can be easily reunited as an integrated unit, such a processing method for numerals does not harm the translation phase of S2ST. Moreover, if the directional verb and the modal auxiliary verb can be identified, they will help the syntactic analysis and improve the translation phrase. These two kinds of verbs, together with "是 (be)" and "有 (have)" are more frequently used in colloquial conversations than in written text, so we took them as an individual segmentation unit and assigned a POS tag to each. The special processes for these kinds of words aim at reflecting the features of spoken language and improve the performance of the S2ST system.

(2) Ability for Future Expansion

Although the corpora were developed for speech recognition in S2ST system, it is desirable that they can be used in other fields when necessary. This reflects in both segmentation and POS-tagging. In segmentation, the compound words with definitive suffix or prefix are divided, so they can be combined easily when necessary. In POS-tagging, the nouns and verbs are mainly further categorized into several sub-tags. We selected about 40 POS tags for our corpora, as shown in Table 1 in the Appendix. With such scale of tag sets, it is regarded to be suitable for language model of ASR. When necessary, it is also easy to choice an adequate tag set from it to meet the needs of other tasks.

(3) Relation with the Corpora of Other Languages in NICT

The original data of the corpora are in Japanese or English. It is meaningful to build connections at the morphological level among these trilingual parallel corpora at least for "named entities." For example, we adopted the same segmentation units as in Japanese, and we subcategorized these words into personal names, organization names, location names, and drink and food names and assigned them each an individual tag. Personal names were further divided into family names and first names for Chinese, Japanese, and Western names. These subclasses are useful in language modeling, especially in the travel domain.

3.2. Some Explanations on Segmentation and POS-tagging

(1) About Segmentation

In our definition of a segmentation unit, words longer than 4 Hanzis (Chinese characters) were generally divided into their syntactic units. Idioms and some greeting phrases were also regarded as segmentation units. For example: "你好/，欢迎光临/，再见/，好的/." Semantic information was also used to judge segmentation unit. For example:

- 我/ 想/ 去/ <u>**最/ 好/**</u> 的/ 餐馆/ 。/ *(Tell me the best restaurant around here.)*
- <u>**最好/**</u> 是/ 价钱/ 不太/ 贵/ 的/ 宾馆/ 。/ *(I'd like a hotel that is not too expensive.)*

For segmenting compound words with different structures, we constituted detailed items to deal with them. These structures include "coordinated (并列), modifying (偏正), verb-object (动宾), subject-predicate (主谓), and verb-complement (述补)." The main consideration for these was to divide them without changing the original meaning. For those words that have a strong ability to combine with others, we generally separated them from the others. This was due to the consideration that if it were done in another way, it would result in too many words. For example, in the verb-object (动宾) structure, "买 (buy)" can combine with many nouns to get meaningful words or phrases, such as "买书 (buy book), 买肉 (buy meat), 买票 (buy ticket), and 买衣服 (buy clothes)." We prescribed separating such active characters or words, no matter how frequently they are used in the real world, to ensure that the meaning did not change and ambiguity did not arise. So the above phrases should be separated in following forms: "买/ 书/ (buy book), 买/ 肉/ (buy meat), 买/ 票/ (buy ticket), and 买/ 衣服 /buy clothes)."

For the directional verbs, we generally separated them from their preceding verbs. For example:

我/ 可以/ 换/ <u>**到/**</u> 别的/ 座位/ 吗/ ？/ *(Is it all right to move to another seat?)*

请/ 把/ 这/ 个/ 行李箱/ 保管/ <u>**到/**</u> 一点钟/ 。/ *(Please keep this suitcase until one o'clock.)*

Prefix and appendix were commonly separated from the root words. For example:

学生/ <u>**们/**</u> 都/ 去/ 京都/ 吗/ ？/ *(Are all students going to Kyoto?)*

我/ 是/ 自由/ 职业/ <u>**者/**</u>. *(I do free-lance work.)*

(2) About POS-Tagging

The POS tag sets are shown in Table 1 in the Appendix. The POS tagging was conducted by the grammar function based on how the segmentation unit behaves in a sentence.

4. Procedure of Developing the Chinese Corpora

The segmented and POS-tagged data were obtained in two steps. The first step was to get the raw segmented and POS-tagged data automatically by computer. The second was to check the raw segmented and POS-tagged data manually.

(1) Getting Raw Segmented and POS-Tagged Data

The text data were segmented and POS tagged by using the language model shown in formula (1).

$$P(L) = \alpha P(w_i \mid w_{i-1} w_{i-2}) + (1-\alpha) P(w_i \mid c_i) P(c_i \mid c_{i-1} c_{i-2}) \quad (1)$$

Here w_i denotes the word at the *ith* position of a sentence, and c_i stands for the class to which the word w_i belongs. The class we used here is a POS-tag set, and α is set 0.9.

The initial data for training the model were from the Sinica due to their balanced characteristics. The annotated data were added to the training data when producing new data. When the annotated data reached a given quantity (here, the BTEC1 was finished, and the total words in the corpora exceeded 1M), the Sinica data were not used for training. We have conducted an experiment with this model for an open test text of 510 utterances from BTEC, and the segmentation and POS-tagging accuracy was more than 95%. Furthermore, proper noun information was extracted from Japanese corpora and marked in the corresponding lines of the Chinese segmented and POS-tagged data.

(2) Manual Annotation

The manual annotations were divided into two phases. The first was a line-by-line check of the raw segmented and POS-tagged data. The second was to check the consistency. The consistency check was conducted in the following manner:

- Find the candidates having differences between the manually checked data and the automatically segmented and POS-tagged data.
- Pick up the candidates having a high frequency of updating in the above step, and build an inconsistency table. The candidates in this table are the main objects of the later checks.
- Check the same sentences with different segmentations and POS tags.
- List all words having multiple POS tags and their frequencies. Determine the infrequent ones as distrustful candidates and add them into the inconsistency tables.

The released annotated data were appended with a header ID for each token (pair of word entry and POS tag) in an utterance including a start marker and end marker, shown as follows:

BTEC1\jpn067\03870\zh\\\00010\||||UTT-START||||
BTEC1\jpn067\03870\zh\\\00020\我|我||我|r||||
BTEC1\jpn067\03870\zh\\\00030\想|想||想|vw||||
BTEC1\jpn067\03870\zh\\\00040\喝|喝||喝|v||||
BTEC1\jpn067\03870\zh\\\00050\浓|浓||浓|a||||
BTEC1\jpn067\03870\zh\\\00060\咖啡|咖啡||咖啡|n||||
BTEC1\jpn067\03870\zh\\\00070\。||||UTT-END||||

Table 2 shows some of the statistics for the 510K utterances in Table 1 for different languages.

Table 2. Some Statistics of Each Corpora in NICT

	Utter.	Ave. words /Uttr.	Words	Vocab.
Chinese	510K	6.95	3.50M	47.3K
Japanese	510K	8.60	4.30M	45.5K
English	510K	7.74	3.80M	32.9K

Figure 1 shows the distributions of utterance length (words in an utterance) for 3 languages among the 510K annotated data. From Figure 1, we know that the Chinese has the fewest words in an utterance, followed by English, with the Japanese having the most.

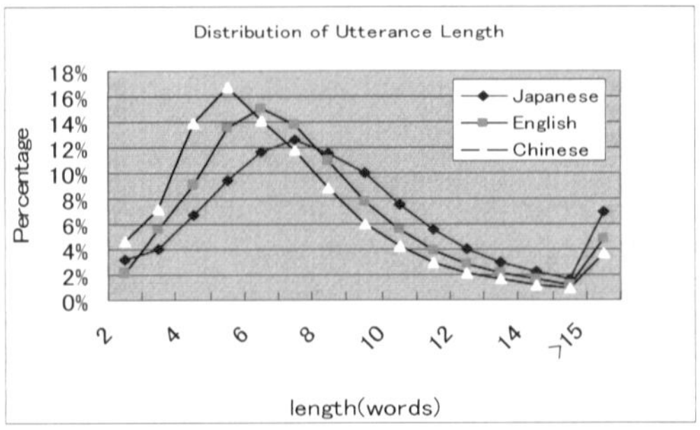

Figure 1. Distribution of utterance length

5. Evaluation Experiments

To verify the effectiveness of the developed Chinese textual corpora, we built a language model for speech recognition using these corpora. For comparisons with other languages, including Japanese and English, we also built language models for these two languages using the same training sets. Meanwhile, the same test set of each language was selected for speech recognition.

5.1. Data Sets for Language Models and Speech Recognitions

For simplicity, we adopted word 2-gram and word 3-gram for evaluating perplexities and speech recognition performance. The training data were selected from the 510K utterances in Table 1, while the test sets were also extracted from them, but they are guaranteed not to exist in the training sets. In evaluations of perplexity, 1524 utterances (a total of three sets) were chosen as the test set. In evaluation of recognition, 510 utterances were chosen as test set. For Japanese and English, the same data sets were also chosen for comparisons.

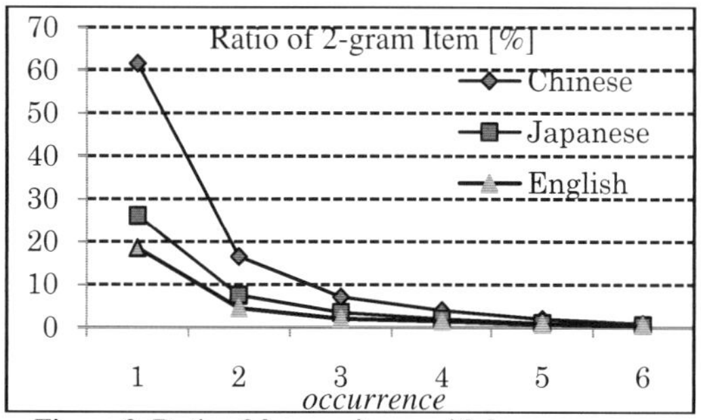

Figure 2. Ratio of 2-gram items with low occurrence

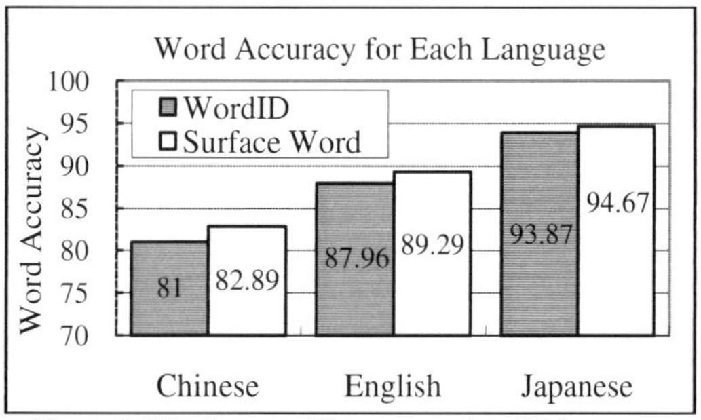

Figure 3. Word recognition accuracies of 3 languages

5.2. Comparisons of Language Models

Using the above utterances in the training sets, a word 2-gram and a 3-gram were built respectively for each language. The distributions of items inside these models were investigated. Figure 2 shows the ratios of 2-gram's items which have low occurrences (from 1 to 6) in the 2-gram model.

Compared with the other two languages, the Chinese has the biggest vocabulary. Moreover, it also has a large amount of low-frequency 1-gram, 2-gram, and 3-gram items. For example, more than 60% of its 2-gram entries appear only once. This can be regarded that the Chinese has more varieties when expressing a same meaning than the other two languages. It is also partly due to bias occurred in the translation process, compared to the original languages. So the probability computations in 2 or 3-gram related to these entries were estimated by using a smoothing approach, so the accuracy is not high.

Table 3 shows average sentence entropies (ASE) of the test sets to the 3-gram models. The ASE is obtained as follows: (1) first to get the product of average word entropy and the total word count in test set. (2) then divide the product by the total sentences in the test set. From the table, we know the Chinese has the maximal sentence entropy (or maximal perplexity) among the three languages. This means that when predicate a sentence in the recognition process, Chinese requires a much bigger search space than the other two languages.

Table 3. Average Sentence Entropy of the Test Sets to 3-gram Models

	Chinese	Japanese	English
Vocab. of Test Set	10,030	12,344	10,840
Ave. Sen. Entropy	294.58	165.80	202.92
Word Perplexity	45.0	20.1	28.5

5.3. Comparison of Speech Recognition Performances

The 2-gram language model was used for decoding recognition lattice, while the 3-gram model was used for rescoring process. The recognition results are shown in Figure 3. Here, WordID refers to the word's outer layer (entry) together with its POS tag, other information like conjugation of verbs, declension of nouns, etc., while the surface word contains only its outer layer, no POS tag is contained in this case .

The difference in word accuracy of speech recognition between these two forms is about 2% for Chinese, and 1% for English and Japanese.

6. Summary

This paper described the development of Chinese conversational segmented and POS-tagged corpora that are used for spontaneous speech recognition in S2ST system. While referring mainly to the PKU's specifications, we defined ours by taking into account the needs of S2ST. About 510K utterances, or about 3.5M words of conversational Chinese data, are contained in these corpora. As far as we know, they are presently the biggest ones in the domain of travel, with a style of conversations. Moreover, a parallel corpus was obtained using these 510K pairs of utterances of Chinese, Japanese, and English. These corpora now play a big role in spontaneous language and speech processing, and are used in the NICT/ATR Chinese-Japanese-English Speech-to-Speech Translation System [8] and other communication services. However, according to our evaluations in this paper, there are still some difference in performance among Chinese and other languages, especially Japanese. There is still some room to improve the quality of these corpora mainly because the Chinese text data were translated from other languages, mainly Japanese, with a few words from English. There is some bias in expression, especially for the transliterations of proper nouns. For examples, "Los Angles" is translated as "洛杉矶, 洛杉机, 洛杉基, and 洛山矶. " also, some utterances are not like those spoken by native speakers, like sentence of “非常感谢你的热情” which corresponds to the original sentence of “ご親切に感謝します(I appreciate your kindness).”

For future work, while continuing to improve the consistency of the corpora, we will expand the Chinese corpora from external data resource, such as Web sites and LDC databases, to extract original Chinese spontaneous text data.

7. References

[1] H.M. Duan, J. Song, G.W. Xu, G.X. Hu and S.W. Yu, “The Development of a Large-scale Tagged Chinese Corpus and Its Applications.” http://icl.pku.edu.cn/icl_tr

[2] C.R. Huang, and K.J. Chen, “Introduction to Sinica Corpus,” CKIP Technical Report 95-02/98-04, http://www.sinica.edu.tw/SinicaCorpus

[3] G. Kikui, E. Sumita, T. Takezawa, S. Yamamoto, “Creating Corpora for Speech-to-Speech Translation.” 8th European Conference on Speech Communication and Technology, Vol.1, pp.381-384, Sep., 2003

[4] S.W. Yu, X.F. Zhu, and H.M. Duan, “The Guideline for Segmentation and Part-Of-Speech Tagging on Very Large Scale Corpus of Contemporary Chinese.” http://icl.pku.edu.cn/icl_tr

[5] The National Standard of PRC, “Standardization of Segmentation for Contemporary Chinese.” GB13715, 1992.

[6] Institute of Applied Linguistics of the Ministry of Education, China, “Specification on Part-of-Speech Tagging of Contemporary Chinese for Information Processing (Draft).” 2002.

[7] H. Yamamoto, S. Isogai, and Y. Sagisaka, “Multi-class Composite N-gram Language Model,” Speech Communication, 2003, Vol.41, pp369-379.

[8] T. Shimizu, Y. Ashikari, E. Sumita, J.S. Zhang, S. Nakamura, “NICT/ATR Chinese-Japanese-English Speech-to-Speech Translation System.” Tsinghua Science and Technology, Vol.13, No.4, pp540-544, Aug. 2008.

Appendix Table 1. Chinese POS Tag Table

POS Tag		Description		POS Tag		Description	
		Chinese	English			Chinese	English
a		形容词	Adjective	n	nppx	人名中的姓	Chinese family name
b		区别词	Non-predicate adjective		nppm	人名中的名	Chinese first name
c		连词	Conjunction		nppxj	日本人的姓	Japanese family name
d		副词	Adverb		nppmj	日本人的名	Japanese first name
de		结构助词	Attributive		nppxw	欧美式人名的姓	Western family name
e		叹词	Interjection		nppmw	欧美式人名的名	Western first name
g		语素字	Morpheme Word		npl	地名	Place
h		前缀词	Prefix		npo	组织名	Organization
i		成语, 习用语	Idiom		npfd	饮食物名	Drink and food
j		简略语	Abbreviation	o		拟声词	Onomatopoeia
k		后缀词	Suffix	p		介词	Preposition
m	m	数词	Numeral	q		量词	Quantifier
	ma	数量定词	Numeral Classifier	r		代词	Pronoun
	mb	概数词	Approximate numeral	u		助词	Auxiliary
n	n	普通名词	Noun	v	v	普通动词	Verb
	nd	方位词	Directional locality		v1	系动词“是”等	Auxiliary verb
	ns	处所名	Space word		v2	动词“有“	Verb “Have”
	nt	时间词	Time word		vt	趋向动词	Directional verb
	nx	非汉字, 字符	Numeric, character string		vw	能愿动词	Modal verb
	np	专有名词	Proper noun	w		标点符号	Punctuation
	npp	人名	Personal name	y		语气助词	Modal particle

Bengali Verb Subcategorization Frame Acquisition - A Baseline Model

Somnath Banerjee **Dipankar Das** **Sivaji Bandyopadhyay**
Department of Computer Science & Engineering
Jadavpur University, Kolkata-700032, India
s.banerjee1980@gmail.com, dipankar.dipnil2005@gmail.com,
sivaji_cse_ju@yahoo.com

Abstract

Acquisition of verb subcategorization frames is important as verbs generally take different types of relevant arguments associated with each phrase in a sentence in comparison to other parts of speech categories. This paper presents the acquisition of different subcategorization frames for a Bengali verb *Kara* (*do*). It generates compound verbs in Bengali when combined with various noun phrases. The main hypothesis here is that the subcategorization frames for a Bengali verb are same with the subcategorization frames for its equivalent English verb with an identical sense tag. Syntax plays the main role in the acquisition of Bengali verb subcategorization frames. The output frames of the Bengali verbs have been compared with the frames of the equivalent English verbs identified using a Bengali-English bilingual lexicon. The flexible ordering of different phrases, additional attachment of optional phrases in Bengali sentences make this frames acquisition task challenging. This system has demonstrated precision and recall values of 77.11% and 88.23% respectively on a test set of 100 sentences.

1 Introduction

A subcategorization frame is a statement of what types of syntactic arguments a verb (or an adjective) takes, such as objects, infinitives, that-clauses, participial clauses, and subcategorized prepositional phrases (Manning,1993). The verb phrase in a sentence usually takes various types of subcategorization frames compared to phrases of other types and hence the acquisition of such frames for verbs are really challenging.

A subcategorization dictionary obtained automatically from corpora can be updated quickly and easily as different usages develop. Several large, manually developed subcategorization lexicons are available for English, e.g. the COMLEX Syntax (Macleod *et al.,* 1994), ACQUILEX (Copestake, 1992) and the ANLT (Briscoe *et al.*, 1987) dictionaries. VerbNet (VN) (Kipper-Schuler, 2005) is the largest online verb lexicon with explicitly stated syntactic and semantic information based on Levin's verb classification (Levin, 1993). It is a hierarchical domain-independent, broad-coverage verb lexicon with mappings to other lexical resources such as WordNet (Miller, 1990), XTAG (XTAG Research Group, 2001) and FrameNet (Baker *et al.*, 1998). But, there is no existing subcategorization lexicon available for Bengali language. The subcategorization of verbs is an essential issue in parsing for the free phrase order languages such as Bengali. As there is no such existing parser available in Bengali, the acquisition as well as evaluation of the acquired subcategorization frames are difficult but crucial tasks. The main difference between English and Bengali sentence is the variation in the ordering of various phrases. The pivotal hypothesis here is that the subcategorization frames obtained for a Bengali verb are same with the subcategorization frames that may be acquired for its equivalent verb with an identical sense tag in English.

The present work deals with the acquisition of verb subcategorization frames of a verb *kara* (do) from a Bengali newspaper corpus. This verb generates various types of compound verbs in combination with other preceding noun phrases in Bengali. The sentences containing these types of compound verb entries have been retrieved from the Bengali corpus. The Bengali verb subcategorization frame acquisition task has been carried out for the ten most frequent compound verbs that contain *kara* (do) as a component. The number of occurrences of other compound verbs

Proceedings of the 7th Workshop on Asian Language Resources, ACL-IJCNLP 2009, pages 76–83,
Suntec, Singapore, 6-7 August 2009. ©2009 ACL and AFNLP

is negligible in the corpus. So, for evaluation purpose, we have not considered those verbs. Each of the ten Bengali compound verbs has been searched in the Bengali-English bilingual lexicon[1] and the equivalent English verb meanings with its synonyms have been identified and retrieved. All possible subcategorization frames for each of the English synonyms of the Bengali verb have been acquired from the English VerbNet[2]. These frames have been mapped to the Bengali sentences that contain the compound verb. Evaluation results with a test set of 100 sentences show the effectiveness of the model with precision, recall and F-Measure values of 77.11%, 88.23% and 79.24% respectively. There are some frames that have not been identified due to their absence in the corpus. Linguists have suggested that these frames do appear in Bengali and hence can be acquired.

The rest of the paper is organized as follows. Section 2 gives the description of the related works carried out in this area. Section 3 describes the framework for the acquisition of subcategorization frames for ten compound Bengali verbs. Evaluation results of the system are discussed in section 4. Finally section 5 concludes the paper.

2 Related Work

One of the early works for identifying verbs that resulted in extremely low yields for subcategorization frame acquisition is described in (Brent, 1991). A rule based system for automatically acquiring six verb subcategorization frames and their frequencies from a large corpus is mentioned in (Ushioda *et al.*, 1993). An open class vocabulary of 35,000 words was analyzed manually in (Briscoe and Carroll, 1997) for subcategorization frames and predicate associations. The result was compared against associations in ANLT and COMLEX. Variations of subcategorization frequencies across corpus type (written vs. spoken) have been studied in (Carroll and Rooth, 1998). A mechanism for resolving verb class ambiguities using subcategorization frames is reported in (Lapata and Brew, 1999). All these works deal with English. Several works on the term classification of verb diathesis roles or the lexical semantics of predicates in natural language have been reported in ((McCarthy, 2001), (Korhonen, 2002), (Stevenson and Merlo, 1999) and (Walde, 1998)).

A cross lingual work on learning verb-argument structure for Czech language is described in (Sarkar and Zeman, 2000). (Samantaray, 2007) gives a method of acquiring different subcategorization frames for the purpose of machine aided translation system for Indian languages. The work on subcategorization frame acquisition of Japanese verbs using breadth-first algorithm is described in (Muraki *et al.*, 1997).

3 System Outline

We have developed several modules for the acquisition of verb subcategorization frames from the Bengali newspaper corpus. The modules consist of POS tagging and chunking, Identification and Selection of Verbs, English Verb Determination, Frames Acquisition from VerbNet and Bengali Verb Subcategorization Frame Acquisition.

3.1 POS Tagging and Chunking

We have used a Bengali news corpus (Ekbal and Bandyopadhyay, 2008) developed from the web-archives of a widely read Bengali newspaper. A portion of the Bengali news corpus containing 1500 sentences have been POS tagged using a Maximum Entropy based POS tagger (Ekbal *et al.*, 2008). The POS tagger was developed with a tagset of 26 POS tags[3], defined for the Indian languages. The POS tagger demonstrated an accuracy of 88.2%. We have also developed a rule-based chunker to chunk the POS tagged data with an overall accuracy of 89.4%.

3.2 Identification and Selection of Verbs

Our previous work (Das *et.al.*, 2009) on the acquisition of Bengali subcategorization frames from the same Bengali news corpus was carried out for the most frequent verb "দেখা" (*dekha*) (see) in that corpus. The next highest frequent verb in this corpus is "করা" (*kara*) (do) which is a special verb in Bengali. However to the best of our knowledge, no frame acquisition task has been carried out yet for this Bengali verb. The single occurrence of "করা" (*kara*) as a main verb in a sentence takes completely different subcategorization frames in comparison with the acquired frames for the compound verbs consisting of "করা" (*kara*) as a component. Hence, we have

[1] http://home.uchicago.edu/~cbs2/banglainstruction.html
[2] http://verbs.colorado.edu/~mpalmer/projects/verbnet.html
[3] http://shiva.iiit.ac.in/SPSAL2007/iiit_tagset_guidelines.pdf

concentrated our focus to acquire subcategorization frames for the Bengali verb "করা" (*kara*).

For this purpose, we have manually analyzed the tagged and chunked data to identify the word "করা" (*kara*) that are tagged as main verb (VM) and belong to the verb group chunk (VG) in the corpus. The preceding noun phrase of "করা" (*kara*) generally produces completely different verbs in Bengali (e.g. [তৈরি করা (*tairi*(NN) *kara*(VM))(*make*)], [ব্যবহার করা (*byabahar* (NN) *kara*(VM))(*use*)] etc.).

Bengali, like any other Indian languages, is morphologically very rich. Different suffixes may be attached to a verb depending on the various features such as Tense, Aspect, and Person. The Bengali stemmer uses a suffix list to identify the stem form of the verb "করা" (*kara*). Another table stores the stem form and the corresponding root form. Stemming process has correctly identified 234 occurrences of the verb "করা" (*kara*) from its 241 occurrences in the corpus with an accuracy of 97.09%. The sentences where the verb "করা" (*kara*) appears in any inflected form but has been tagged as main verb (VM) have been retrieved. These sentences have been considered for fine-grained analysis of verb subcategorization frames. It is expected that the corpus will have adequate number of occurrences for each subcategorization frame of the verb. The passive occurrences of "করা" (*kara*) such as "করানো" (*karano*), করিয়ে (*kariye*) have been filtered out and the sentences containing the passive entries of "করা" have not been considered in the present work.

The compound verb phrases with pattern such as {[XXX] (NN) [*kara*] (VM)} have been identified and retrieved from the Bengali POS tagged and chunked corpus. It has been observed that most of these compound verb phrases are individually different verbs in Bengali. Around 182 various kinds of verbs have been identified. Certain typical and distinct occurrences of "করা" (*kara*) have also been identified. But, linguistic verification shows that these typical verbs are formed by attaching the verb "করা" (*kara*) to an adjective or an adverb word, like ঝকঝক করা (*jhakjhak kara*) , তকতক করা (*taktak kara*), শীত করা (*sheet kara*) etc. Such types of around 48 verb entries have been identified and filtered out from the corpus. The rest 134 distinct types of Bengali compound verbs (CV) with "করা" (*kara*) as a component have been considered as target verbs for analysis.

We have identified the frequencies of these verbs in the corpus. It has to be mentioned that only a few verbs have an adequate number of sentences in the corpus. For this reason, only the top ten compound verbs that have the largest number of occurrences in the corpus have been selected. Table 1 represents the top 10 different Bengali compound verbs and their frequencies obtained from the corpus.

Bengali Verbs	**Freq.**
তৈরি করা (*tairi kara*) (make)	23
ব্যবহার করা (*byabahar kara*) (use)	18
বাস করা (*bas kara*) (live)	17
কাজ করা (*kaj kara*) (work)	15
সংগ্রহ করা (*sangraha kara*) (collect)	13
বন্ধ করা (*bandha kara*) (shut)	13
চিত্‌কার করা (*chitkar kara*) (shout)	3
ভুল করা (*bhul kara*) (mistake)	3
জিজ্ঞাসা করা (*jigyasa kara*) (ask)	3
পর্যবেক্ষণ করা (*parjabekkhan kara*) (observe)	3

Table 1. Top 10 Bengali Compound Verbs and their frequencies obtained from the corpus

3.3 English Verb Determination

The verb subcategorization frames for the equivalent English verbs (in the same sense) of a Bengali verb are the initial set of verb subcategorization frames that have been considered as valid for that Bengali verb. The root forms of the target verbs appearing in different inflected forms in the Bengali corpus have been identified by the process described in section 3.2. The determination of equivalent English verbs has been carried out using a Bengali-English bilingual lexicon. We have used the available Bengali-English bilingual dictionary that has been formatted for the text processing tasks. Various syntactical representations of a word entry in the lexicon have been analyzed to identify its synonyms and meanings. The example of an entry in the bilingual lexicon for our target verb "করা" (*kara*) is given as follows.

```
<করা [karā] v to do, to per-
form, to accomplish, to exe-
cute (কাজ করা); to build, to
make (তৈরি করা) ;.....>
```

But, the various distinct verbs, with "করা" (*kara*) as a component have individual separate entries in the bilingual dictionary. We have identified the equivalent English verbs from those Bengali verb entries in the dictionary. For example,

```
<তৈরি করা v. to build, to
make; ...>
<ব্যবহার করা v. to apply, to
use; to behave; to treat (a
person), to behave towards;
...>
<কাজ করা v. to work; to
serve; to be effective ;...>
```

Different synonyms for a verb having the same sense are separated using "," and different senses are separated using ";" in the lexicon. The synonyms including different senses of the target verb have been extracted from the lexicon. This yields a resulting set called Synonymous Verb Set (SVS). For example, the English synonyms (*apply, use*) and synonym with another sense (*behave*) have been selected for Bengali verb "ব্যবহার করা" (*byabahar kara*) and have been categorized as two different SVS for the Bengali verb "ব্যবহার করা". Two synonyms (*make, build*) for the Bengali verb "তৈরি করা" (*tairi kara*) are thus present in the same SVS. Now, the task is to acquire all the possible existing frames for each member of the SVS from the VerbNet. The "করা" (*kara*) verb may also appear in passive form in Bengali sentences. For example,

```
রামকে            কাজ
(Ramke)NNP    (kaj)NN
করানো           হয়েছিল
(karano)VM    (hayechilo)VAUX
```

The corresponding dictionary entry for the passive form of "করা" (*kara*) is as follows. But in this work, we have concentrated only on those sentences where "করা" (*kara*) appears in active form.

```
<করানো [karānō] v to cause to
do or perform or accomplish
or execute or build or
make...>
```

3.4 Frames Acquisition from VerbNet

VerbNet associates the semantics of a verb with its syntactic frames and combines traditional lexical semantic information such as thematic roles and semantic predicates, with syntactic frames and selectional restrictions. Verb entries in the same VerbNet class share common syntactic frames, and thus they are believed to have the same syntactic behavior. The VerbNet files containing the verbs with their possible subcategorization frames and membership information is stored in XML file format. The Bengali verb তৈরি করা (*tairi kora*) (make) has no direct class in VerbNet. The verb "make" and its synonymous verb "build" are members of one of the subclasses of the build-26.1 class and "make" is also a member of the dub-29.3 class. A snapshot of XML file for the build-26.1 class is given below.

```
.....
<VNCLASS ID="build-26.1"
.....<SUBCLASSES>
   <VNSUBCLASS ID="build-26.1-1">
<MEMBERS>
    <MEMBER name="build"
wn="build%2:36:00"/>
    <MEMBER name="make"
wn="make%2:36:01 make%2:36:05
.....
make%2:42:13 make%2:36:10"/>
.....
</MEMBERS>
.....
<FRAME>
    <DESCRIPTION descriptionNum-
ber="3.9" primary="NP-PP" secon-
dary="Asset-PP" xtag=""/>
<EXAMPLES>
    <EXAMPLE> The contractor
builds houses for $100,000.
    </EXAMPLE>
    .....
</EXAMPLES>
.....</FRAME>
.....
```

The verbs in VerbNet that take same type of subcategorization frames are stored in the <MEMBER> tag and the possible primary and secondary subcategorization frames are kept in <DESCRIPTION> tag with proper English examples for each frame. The example for each of the subcategorization frames for the English verb "make" has been given in the "build-26.1-1" subclass of the "build-26.1" class in the VerbNet. The sentence tagged within <EXAMPLE>.. </EXAMPLE> shows that after the occurrence of the verb "build/make", one noun phrase (NP) and one prepositional phrase (PP) have occurred as the arguments of the verb. The frame corresponding to this sentence has been described as the primary frame "NP-PP" in the frame description <DESCRIPTION> tag.

Sense wise separated SVS members occupy the membership of same class or subclass in VerbNet. It has been observed that the verbs "*build*" and "*make*" are members of the same SVS (extracted from the Bengali-English bilingual dictionary) and they are also members of the same subclass build-26.1-1. Therefore, both of the verbs take same subcategorization frames.

SVS (VerbNet classes)	Primary and *Secondary* Frames for a SVS
Make (build-26.1-1) Build (build-26.1-1)	NP-PP, NP, NP-NP, NP-NP-PP, *Asset-PP* *Asset-Subject*
Use (use-105, consume-66, fit-54.3) Apply (use-105)	NP-ADVP, NP-PP, NP-TO-INF-VC, Basic Transitive, NP-ING-SC, Location Subject Alternation, NP-PP *for-PP, Location-PP*
Behave (masquerade-29.6, 29.6-1)	PP, Basic Transitive *as-PP, like-PP, in-PP*

Table 2. The SVS members and their subcategorization frames for the corresponding Bengali verbs তৈরি করা (*tairi kara*) and ব্যবহার করা (*byabahar kara*)

The xml files of VerbNet have been preprocessed to build up a general list that contains all members (verbs) and their possible subcategorization frames (primary as well as secondary) information. This preprocessed list is searched to acquire the subcategorization frames for each member of the SVS of the ten Bengali verbs (identified in section 3.3). As the verbs are classified according to their semantics in the VerbNet, the frames for the particular Bengali verb are assumed to be similar to the frames obtained for the members of its SVS. It has also been observed that the same verb with a different sense can belong to a separate class in the VerbNet. For example, the acquired frames (primary and secondary) for each member of the SVS of the target verbs ("ব্যবহার করা" and "তৈরি করা") have been shown in Table 2. In this way, all possible subcategorization frames for each member of a SVS have been extracted from the generalized search list for our ten target verbs.

3.5 Bengali Verb Subcategorization Frames Acquisition

The acquired VerbNet frames have been mapped to the Bengali verb subcategorization frames by considering the position of the verb as well as its general co-existing nature with other phrases in Bengali sentences.

The syntax of "NP-PP" frame for a Bengali sentence has been acquired by identifying the target verb followed by a NP chunk and a PREP chunk. The sentences containing prepositional frame "PP" do not appear in the Bengali corpus, as there is no concept of preposition in Bengali. But, when we compare the sentences containing postpositional markers, i.e. PREP (postpositions) as a probable argument of the verb, the system gives the desired output.

যার থেকে হাতপাখা
(jar)PRP (theke)PREP (hat-pakha)NN
আর আচ্ছাদন তৈরি
(ar)CC (achhadon)QF (toiri)NN
করেছিলেন ম্যাক্স
(korechilen)VM (Max)NN

All the frames of a SVS corresponding to a Bengali verb have been considered. The Bengali verb "ব্যবহার করা" (*byabahar kara*) in the following sentence has taken the frame "ADVP-PRED" (the word with RB tag) from a different SVS.

কর্মচারীরা
(karmachari ra)NN
বন্ধুত্বপূর্ণ
(bondhuttwapurno)RB
ব্যবহার করেন
(byabahar)NN (karen)VM

Another form of "ADVP-PRED" frame has been obtained by considering the Bengali meaning of the corresponding English adverbial phrase. "There" is an adverbial phrase taken by the "live" verb in English. The corresponding representation in the equivalent Bengali verb is ওখানেই (*okhanei*) as shown in the following sentence. Hence, the frame has been identified.

ওখানেই বাস
(*okhanei*)RB (*bas*)NN
করতে হবে
(*karte*)VM (*habe*)VAUX

The NNPC (Compound proper noun), NNP (Proper noun), NNC (Compound common noun) and NN (Common noun) POS tags help to determine the subjects, objects as well as the locative information related to the verb. In simple sentences the occurrence of these POS tags preceded by the PRP (Pronoun) or NNPC tags and followed by the verb gives similar frame syntax for "Basic Transitive" frame of the VerbNet. Only the components like subject, object and a single verb in Bengali as well as in English sentence can be signified as simple "Basic Transitive" frame.

```
সে              রকম
(se)PRP    NP((rakam)NN
ডিজাইনের          কাজ        করে
(designer)NN) (kaj)NN (kare)VM
```

The following example shows that the frame identified from the sentence is also a "transitive frame" and the secondary frame component is a "material object" for that sentence.

```
 একটি          ব্যাগেজ
 (ekti)QC  (bagaze)NNP
      সংগ্রহ              করলাম
VGNF((sangroho)NN  (korlam)VM)
```

The PREP (postposition) followed by a NP phrase and the target verb gives similar syntax for a NP-PP frame but it has been noticed that the secondary frame here can be a component of "Location-PP".

```
 সেতু          থেকে
 (setu)NNP  (theke)PREP
       নানা         উদ্ভিদ
 NP((nana)JJ  (udvid)NN))
 প্রজাতি              পর্যবেক্ষণ
 (projati)JJ  (porjobekkhon)NN
 করলাম
 (korlam)VM
```

The sentences where the determiner (DEM) and a NP chunk follow the target verb the sequence (Target verb DEM NP) is considered as the frame of sentential complement "S" for that target verb.

```
 রাম           চিৎকার
 (Ram)NNP  (chitkar)(NN)
 করল                যে       সে
 (korlo)VM(je)(DEM)  (se)(PRP)
 আর               কখনও
 (ar)CC           (kokhono)NN
 আসবে          না
 (asbe)VM  (na)NEG
```

The presence of JJ (Adjective) generally does not play any role in the acquisition process of verb subcategorization frames. There are some frames that did not have any instance in our corpus. Such frames are "Asset-PP", "After-PP", "Location Subject Alternation" and "NP-TO-INF-VC" etc. A close linguistic analysis shows that these frames can also be acquired from the Bengali sentences. They have not occurred in the corpus that has been considered for the analysis in the present work.

4 Evaluation

The set of acquired subcategorization frames or the frame lexicon can be evaluated against a gold standard corpus obtained either through manual analysis of corpus data or from subcategorization frame entries in a large dictionary or from the output of the parser made for that language. As there is no parser available for the Bengali and also no existing dictionary for Bengali that contains subcategorization frames, manual analysis from corpus data is the only method for evaluation. The chunked sentences that contain the ten most frequent verbs have been evaluated manually to prepare the gold standard data.

We have identified 45 different kinds of verbs in the corpus. A detailed statistics of the verb "করা" (*kara*) is presented in Table 3. During the Bengali verb subcategorization frame acquisition process, it has been observed that the simple sentences contain most of the frames that the English verb form usually takes in VerbNet. Analysis of a simple Bengali sentence to identify the verb subcategorization frames is easier in the absence of a parser than analyzing complex and compound sentences. There are only three occurrences of "করা" (*kara*) as auxiliary in the corpus. These are chunking errors as the verb "করা" (*kara*) does not occur as auxiliary verb.

The verb subcategorization frames acquisition process is evaluated using type precision (the percentage of subcategorization frame types that the system proposes are correct according to the gold standard), type recall (the percentage of subcategorization frame types in the gold standard that the system proposes) and F-measure:

$$F = \frac{2 \cdot precision \cdot recall}{precision + recall}$$

The system has been evaluated with 100 gold standard test sentences containing ten most frequent verbs and the evaluation results are shown in Table 4. The recall of the system shows a satisfactory performance in producing Bengali verb subcategorization frames but the precision value requires more improvement.

Information	Freq.
Number of sentences in the corpus	1500
Number of different verbs in the corpus	45
Number of inflected forms of the verb "করা" in the corpus	49
Total number of occurrences of the verb "করা" (before stemming) in the corpus	241
Total number of occurrences of the verb "করা" (after stemming) in the corpus	234
Number of sentences where "করা" occurs as a Main Verb (VM)	206
Number of sentences where "করা" occurs as a Simple Main Verb (SVM)	2
Number of sentences where "করা" occurs as a Compound Main Verb (CVM)	204
Number of sentences where "করা" occurs as a Passive Verb (করানো)(done)	25
Number of sentences where "করা" occurs as a Auxiliary Verb (VAUX)	3
Number of simple sentences where "করা" occurs as a Simple Main Verb (SVM)	0
Number of simple sentences where "করা" occurs as a Compound Main Verb (CVM)	127

Table 3. The frequency information of the verb "করা" (*kara*) acquired from the corpus

Measures	Results
Recall	88.23%
Precision	71.11%
F-Measure	79.24

Table 4. The Precision, Recall and F-Measure values of the system

It has been noticed that the absence of other frames in the Bengali corpus is due to the free phrase ordering characteristics of Bengali Language. The proper alignment of the phrases is needed to cope up with this language specific problem. The number of different frames acquired for these ten verbs is shown in Table 5.

Bengali Verbs	Subcategory Frames	No. of Frames
তৈরি করা (*toiri kora*)	NP-PP NP-NP	15 3
ব্যবহার করা (*babohar kora*)	NP-ADVP NP-PP NP-ING-SC NP-PP Location-PP	1 2 1 1 1
বাস করা (*bas kora*)	Basic Transitive PP ADVP-PRED	 12 1 1
কাজ করা (*kaj kora*)	PP NP-PP	1 11
সংগ্রহ করা (*sangroho kora*)	Transitive (Material obj) PP	1 2
বন্ধ করা (*bondho kora*)	Basic Transitive NP-PP	 1 1
চিত্কার করা (*chitkar kora*)	S PP	1 1
ভুল করা (*bhul kora*)	Nil	0
জিজ্ঞাসা করা (*jigyasa kora*)	BT	1
পর্যবেক্ষণ করা (*porjobekkhon kora*)	Transitive (Location-PP) NP-PP	1 1

Table 5. The frequencies of different frames acquired from corpus

5 Conclusion

The acquisition of subcategorization frames for more number of verbs and clustering them will help us to build a verb lexicon for Bengali language. We need to find out Bengali verb subcategorization frames that may not be supported for the corresponding English verb with identical sense.

There is no restriction for domain dependency in this system. For the free-phrase-order languages like Bengali, the overall performance can be increased by proper assumptions, rules and implementation procedures. Verb morphological information, synonymous sets and their possible subcategorization frames are all important information to develop a full-fledged parser for Bengali. This system can be used for solving alignment problems in Machine Translation for Bengali as well as to identify possible argument selection for Question and Answering systems.

References

Anna Korhonen. 2002. Semantically motivated subcategorization acquisition. *ACL Workshop on Unsupervised Lexical Acquisition*. Philadelphia.

Anoop Sarkar and Daniel Zeman. 2000. Automatic extraction of subcategorization frames for czech. *COLING-2000*.

A. Ekbal and S. Bandyopadhyay. 2008. A Web-based Bengali News Corpus for Named Entity Recognition. *LRE Journal*. Springer.

A.Ekbal, R. Haque and S. Bandyopadhyay. 2008. Maximum Entropy Based Bengali Part of Speech Tagging. *RCS Journal*, (33): 67-78.

Akira Ushioda, David A. Evans, Ted Gibson, Alex Waibel. 1993. The Automatic Acquisition of Frequencies of Verb Subcategorization Frames from Tagged Corpora. *Workshop on Acquisition of Lexical Knowledge from Text*, 95-106. Columbus, Ohio.

B. K. Boguraev and E. J. Briscoe.1987. Large lexicons for natural language processing utilising the grammar coding system of the Longman Dictionary of Contemporary English. *Computational Linguistics*, 13(4): 219-240.

Christopher D. Manning. 1993. Automatic Acquisition of a Large Subcategorization Dictionary from Corpora. *31st Meeting of the ACL*, 235-242. Columbus, Ohio.

Collin F. Baker, Charles J. Fillmore, and John B. Lowe.1998. The Berkeley FrameNet project. *COLING/ACL-98*, 86-90. Montreal.

Copestake A.1992. The ACQUILEX LKB: Representation Issues in the Semi-automatic Acquisition of Large Lexicons. *ANLP*. Trento, Italy.

D.Das, A.Ekbal, and S.Bandyopadhyay. 2009. Acquiring Verb Subcategorization Frames in Bengali from Corpora. *ICCPOL-09*, LNAI-5459, 386-393.Hong Kong.

Dan Gusfield. 1997. *Algorithms on Strings, Trees and Sequences*. Cambridge University Press, Cambridge, UK.

Diana McCarthy. 2001. *Lexical Acquisition at the Syntax-Semantics Interface: Diathesis Alternations, Subcategorization Frames and Selectional Preferences*. University of Sussex.

Grishman, R., Macleod, C., and Meyers, A. 1994. Comlex syntax : building a computational lexicon. *COLING-94*, 268-272. Kyoto, Japan.

George A. Miller. 1990. WordNet: An on-line lexical database. *International Journal of Lexicography*, 3(4):235-312.

Glenn Carroll, Mats Rooth. 1998. Valence induction with a head-lexicalized PCFG. *EMNLP*. Granada.

Karin Kipper-Schuler.2005. VerbNet: *A broad-coverage, comprehensive verb lexicon*. Ph.D. thesis, Computer and Information Science Dept., University of Pennsylvania, Philadelphia, PA.

Kazunori Muraki, Shin'ichiro Kamei, Shinichi Doi.1997. *A Left-to-right Breadth-first Algorithm for. Subcategorization Frame Selection of Japanese Verbs*. TMI.

Levin, B. 1993. *English Verb Classes and Alternation: A Preliminary Investigation*. The University of Chicago Press.

Michael Brent.1991. Automatic acquisition of subcategorization frames from untagged text. *29th Meeting of the ACL*, 209-214. California.

Maria Lapata, Chris Brew.1999. Using subcategorization to resolve verb class ambiguity. *WVLC/EMNLP*, 266-274.

Suzanne Stevenson, Paola Merlo. 1999. Automatic Verb Classification using Distributions of Grammatical Features. *EACL-99*, 45-52. Norge.

Sabine Schulte im Walde. 1998. *Automatic Semantic Classification of Verbs According to Their Alternation Behavior*. Master's thesis, Stuttgart.

S.D. Samantaray.2007. A Data mining approach for resolving cases of Multiple Parsing in Machine Aided Translation of Indian Languages. *ITNG'07 © IEEE*.

Ted Briscoe, John Carroll.1997. Automatic Extraction of Subcategorization from Corpora. *ANLP-ACL*, 356-363. Washington, D.C.

XTAG Research Group. 2001. A lexicalized tree adjoining grammar for English. *IRCS*. University of Pennsylvania.

Phonological and Logographic Influences on Errors in Written Chinese Words

Chao-Lin Liu[1] Kan-Wen Tien[2] Min-Hua Lai[3] Yi-Hsuan Chuang[4] Shih-Hung Wu[5]
[1-4]National Chengchi University, [5]Chaoyang University of Technology, Taiwan
{[1]chaolin, [2]96753027, [3]95753023, [4]94703036}@nccu.edu.tw, [5]shwu@cyut.edu.tw

Abstract

We analyze a collection of 3208 reported errors of Chinese words. Among these errors, 7.2% involved rarely used character, and 98.4% were assigned common classifications of their causes by human subjects. In particular, 80% of the errors observed in the writings of middle school students were related to the pronunciations and 30% were related to the logographs of the words. We conducted experiments that shed light on using the Web-based statistics to correct the errors, and we designed a software environment for preparing test items whose authors intentionally replace correct characters with wrong ones. Experimental results show that using Web-based statistics can help us correct only about 75% of these errors. In contrast, Web-based statistics are useful for recommending incorrect characters for composing test items for "incorrect character identification" tests about 93% of the time.

1 Introduction

Incorrect writings in Chinese are related to our understanding of the cognitive process of reading Chinese (e.g., Leck et al., 1995), to our understanding of why people produce incorrect characters and our offering corresponding remedies (e.g., Law et al., 2005), and to building an environment for assisting the preparation of test items for assessing students' knowledge of Chinese characters (e.g., Liu and Lin, 2008).

Chinese characters are composed of smaller parts that can carry phonological and/or semantic information. A Chinese word is formed by Chinese characters. For example, 新加坡 (Singapore) is a word that contains three Chinese characters. The left (土) and the right (皮) part of 坡, respectively, carry semantic and phonological information. The semantic information, in turn, is often related to the logographs that form the Chinese characters. Evidences show that production of incorrect characters are related to phonological, logographic, or the semantic aspect of the characters. Although the logographs of Chinese characters can be related to the lexical semantics, not all errors that are related to semantics were caused by the similarity in logographs. Some were due to the context of the words and/or permissible interpretations of different words.

In this study, we investigate issues that are related to the phonological and logographical influences on the occurrences of incorrect characters in Chinese words. In Section 2, we present the details about the sources of the reported errors. We have collected errors from a published book and from a group of middle school students. In Section 3, we analyze the causes of the observed errors. Native speakers of Chinese were asked to label whether the observed errors were related to the phonological or the logographic reasons. In Section 4, we explore the effectiveness of relying on Web-based statistics to correct the errors. We submitted an incorrect word and a correct word separately to Google to find the number of web pages that contained these words. The correct and incorrect words differed in just the incorrect character. We examine whether the number of web pages that contained the words can help us find the correct way of writing. In Section 5, we employ Web-based statistics in the process of assisting teachers to prepare test items for assessing students' knowledge of Chinese characters. Experimental results showed that our method outperformed the one reported in (Liu and Lin, 2008), and captured the incorrect characters better than 93% of the time.

2 Data Sources

We obtained data from three major sources. A list that contains 5401 characters that have been believed to be sufficient for everyday lives was obtained from the Ministry of Education (MOE) of Taiwan, and we call the first list the **Clist**, henceforth. The 5401 characters form the core basis for the BIG-5 code, and an official introduction of these 5401 characters is available at http://www.cns11643.gov.tw/AIDB/encodings.do#encode4.

We have two lists of words, and each word is accompanied by an incorrect way to write the word. The first list is from a book published by MOE (1996). The MOE provided the correct words and specified the incorrect characters which were mistakenly used to replace the correct characters in the correct words. The second list was collected, in 2008, from the written essays of students of the seventh and the eighth grades in a middle school in Taipei. The incorrect characters were entered into computers based on students' writings, ignoring those characters that did not actually exist and could not be entered.

We will call the first list of word the **Elist**, and the second the **Jlist** from now on. Elist and Jlist contain, respectively, 1490 and 1718 entries. Each of these entries contains a correct word and the incorrect character. Hence, we can reconstruct the incorrect words

Proceedings of the 7th Workshop on Asian Language Resources, ACL-IJCNLP 2009, pages 84–91,
Suntec, Singapore, 6-7 August 2009. ©2009 ACL and AFNLP

easily. Two or more different ways to incorrectly write the same words were listed in different entries and considered as two entries for simplicity of presentation.

3 Error Analysis of Written Words

Two human subjects, who are native speakers of Chinese and are graduate students in Computer Science, examined Elist and Jlist and categorized the causes of errors. They compared the incorrect characters with the correct characters to determine whether the errors were **pronunciation-related** or logographs-related. Referring to an error as being "semantics-related" is ambiguous. Two characters might not contain the same semantic part, but are still semantically related, e.g., misusing "偷"(tou1) for "投"(tou2) in "投機取巧". In this study, we have not considered this factor. For this reason we refer to the errors that are related to the sharing of logographic parts in characters as **composition-related**.

Among the 1490 and 1718 words in Elist and Jlist, respectively, the two human subjects had consensus over causes of 1441 and 1583 errors. It is interesting to learn that native speakers had a high consensus about the causes for the observed errors, but they did not always agree. To have a common standard in comparison, we studied the errors that the two subjects had agreed categorizations.

The statistics changed when we disregarded errors that involved characters not included in Clist. An error would be ignored if either the correct or the incorrect character did not belong to the Clist. It is possible for students to write such rarely used characters in an incorrect word just by coincidence.

After ignoring the rare characters, there were 1333 and 1645 words in Elist and Jlist, respectively. The subjects had consensus over the causes of errors for 1285 and 1515 errors in Elist and Jlist, respectively.

Table 1 shows the percentages of five categories of errors: ***C*** for the composition-related errors, ***P*** for the pronunciation-related errors, ***C&P*** for the intersection of *C* and *P*, ***NE*** for those errors that belonged to neither *C* nor *P*, and ***D*** for those errors that the subjects disagreed on the error categories. There were, respectively, 505 composition-related and 1314 pronunciation-related errors in Jlist, so we see 505/1645=30.70% and 1314/1645=79.88% in the table. Notice that *C&P* represents the intersection of *C* and *P*, so we have to deduct *C&P* from the sum of *C*, *P*, *NE*, and *D* to find the total probability, namely 1.

It is worthwhile to discuss the implication of the statistics in Table 1. For the Jlist, similarity between pronunciations accounted for nearly 80% of the errors, and the ratio for the errors that are related to compositions and pronunciations is 1:2.6. In contrast, for the Elist, the corresponding ratio is almost 1:1. The Jlist and Elist differed significantly in the ratios of the error types. It was assumed that the dominance of pronunciation-related errors in electronic documents was a result of the popularity of entering Chinese with pronunciation-based methods. The ratio for the Jlist challenges this popular belief, and indicates that even though the errors occurred during a writing process, rather than typing on computers, students still produced more pronunciation-related errors than composition-related errors. Distribution over error types is not as related to input method as one may have believed. Nevertheless, the observation might still be a result of students being so used to entering Chinese text with pronunciation-based method that the organization of their mental lexicons is also pronunciation related. The ratio for the Elist suggests that editors of the MOE book may have chosen the examples with a special viewpoint in their minds – balancing pronunciation and composition related errors.

Table 1. Error analysis for Elist and Jlist

	C	*P*	*C&P*	*NE*	*D*
Elist	66.09%	67.21%	37.13%	0.23%	3.60%
Jlist	30.70%	**79.88%**	20.91%	2.43%	7.90%

4 Reliability of Web-based Statistics

In this section, we examine the effectiveness of using Web-based statistics to differentiate correct and incorrect characters. The abundant text material on the Internet gives people to treat the Web as a corpus (e.g., webascorpus.org). When we send a query to Google, we will be informed of the number of pages (**NOPs**) that possibly contain relevant information. If we put the query terms in quotation marks, we should find the web pages that literally contain the query terms. Hence, it is possible for us to compare the NOPs for two competing phrases for guessing the correct way of writing. At the time of this writing, Google found 107000 and 3220 pages, respectively, for "strong tea" and "powerful tea". (When conducting such advanced searches with Google, the quotation marks are needed to ensure the adjacency of individual words.) Hence, "strong" appears to be a better choice to go with "tea". This is an idea similar to the approach that compute collocations based on word frequencies (cf. Manning and Schütze, 1999). Although the idea may not work very well for small database, the size of the current Web should be considered large enough.

Using the quotation marks for the query terms enforced the influences of the surrounding characters in Chinese words, and provides a better clue for judging correct usage of Chinese characters. For instance, without the context, "每" and "美" might be used incorrectly to replace each other because they have the same pronunciation, i.e., Mei3. It is relatively unlikely for one to replace "每" with "美" when we write "每個" (*every one*), but these two characters can become admissible candidates when we write "美國" (*USA*) and "每國" (*every country*).

4.1 Field Tests

We test this strategy by sending the words in Elist and Jlist to Google to find the NOPs. We can retrieve the NOPs from the documents returned by Google, and compare the NOPs for the correct and the incorrect words to evaluate the strategy. Again, we focused on those in the 5401 words that the human subjects had consensus about their error types. Recall that we have 1285 and 1515 such words in Elist and Jlist, respectively. As the information available on the Web changes all the time, we also have to note that our experiments were conducted during the first half of March 2009. The queries were submitted at reasonable time intervals to avoid Google's treating our programs as malicious attackers.

Table 2 shows the results of our investigation. We considered that we had a correct result when we found that the NOP for the correct word was larger than the NOP for the incorrect word. If the NOPs were equal, we recorded an ambiguous result; and when the NOP for the incorrect word was larger, we recorded an incorrect event. We use '**C**', '**A**', and '**I**' to denote "correct", "ambiguous", and "incorrect" events in Table 2.

The column headings of Table 2 show the setting of the searches with Google and the set of words that were used in the experiments. We asked Google to look for information from web pages that were encoded in traditional Chinese (denoted **Trad**). We could add another restriction on the source of information by asking Google to inspect web pages from machines in Taiwan (denoted **Twn+Trad**). We were not sure how Google determined the languages and locations of the information sources, but chose to trust Google. The headings "**Comp**" and "**Pron**" indicate whether the words whose error types were composition and pronunciation-related, respectively.

Table 2 shows eight distributions, providing experimental results that we observed under different settings. The distribution printed in bold face showed that, when we gathered information from sources that were encoded in traditional Chinese, we found the correct words 73.12% of the time for words whose error types were related to composition in Elist. Under the same experimental setting, we could not judge the correct word 4.58% of the time, and would have chosen an incorrect word 22.30% of the time.

Statistics in Table 2 indicate that web statistics is not a very reliable factor to judge the correct words. The average of the eight numbers in the 'C' rows is only 71.54% and the best sample is 76.59%, suggesting that we did not find the correct words frequently. We would made incorrect judgments 24.75% of the time. The statistics also show that it is almost equally difficult to find correct words for errors that are composition and pronunciation related. In addition, the statistics reveal that choosing more features in the advanced search affected the final results. Using "Trad" offered better results in our experiments than using "Twn+Trad". This observation may arouse a perhaps controversial argument. Although Taiwan is the main area to use traditional Chinese, their web pages might not have used as accurate Chinese as web pages located in other regions.

Table 2. Reliability of Web-based statistics

		Trad		Twn+Trad	
		Comp	Pron	Comp	Pron
Elist	C	**73.12%**	73.80%	69.92%	68.72%
	A	**4.58%**	3.76%	3.83%	3.76%
	I	**22.30%**	22.44%	26.25%	27.52%
Jlist	C	76.59%	74.98%	69.34%	65.87%
	A	2.26%	3.97%	2.47%	5.01%
	I	21.15%	21.05%	28.19%	29.12%

4.2 An Error Analysis for the Field Tests

We have analyzed the reasons for why using Web-based statistics did not always find the correct words. Frequencies might not have been a good factor to determine the correctness of Chinese. However, the myriad amount of data on the Web should have provided a better performance.

The most common reason for errors is that some of the words are really confusing such that the majority of the Web pages actually used the incorrect words. Some of errors were so popular that even one of the Chinese input methods on Windows XP offered wrong words as possible choices, e.g., "雄赳赳" (the correct one) vs. "雄糾糾". It is interesting to note that people may intentionally use incorrect words in some occasions; for instance, people may choose to write homophones in advertisements.

Another popular reason is that whether a word is correct depends on a larger context. For instance, "小斯" is more popular than "小廝" because the former is a popular nickname. Unless we had provided more contextual information about the queried words, checking only the NOPs of "小斯" and "小廝" led us to choose "小斯", which happened to be an incorrect word when we meant to find the right way to write "小廝". Another difficult pair of words to distinguish is "紀錄" and "記錄".

Yet another reason for having a large NOP of the incorrect words was due to errors in segmenting Chinese character strings. Consider a correct character string "WXYZ", where "WX" and "YZ" are two correct words. It is possible that "XY" happens to be an incorrect way to write a correct word. This is the case for having the counts for "花海繽紛" to contribute to the count for "海繽" which is an incorrect form of "海濱".

5 Facilitating Test Item Authoring

Incorrect character correction is a very popular type of test in Taiwan. There are simple test items for young children, and there are very challenging test items for the competitions among adults. Finding an attractive incorrect character to replace a correct character to form a test item is a key step in authoring test items.

We have been trying to build a software environment for assisting the authoring of test items for incorrect character correction (Liu and Lin, 2008, Liu et al., 2009). It should be easy to find a lexicon that contains pronunciation information about Chinese characters. In contrast, it might not be easy to find visually similar Chinese characters with computational methods. We expanded the original Cangjie codes (OCC), and employed the expanded Cangjie codes (ECC) to find visually similar characters (Liu and Lin, 2008).

Cangjie encoding (Chu, 2009) is a special system for representing the formation of Chinese characters with a sequence of at most five basic symbols. For instance, "坡" and "波" are represented by "土木竹水" and "水木竹水", respectively. It is evident that the Cangjie codes are useful for finding visually similar characters.

With a lexicon, we can find characters that can be pronounced in a particular way. However, this is not enough for our goal. We observed that there were different symptoms when people used incorrect characters that are related to their pronunciations. They may use characters that could be pronounced exactly the same as the correct characters. They may also use characters that have the same pronunciation and different tones with the correct character. Although relatively infrequently, people may use characters whose pronunciations are similar to but different from the pronunciation of the correct character.

We reported that replacing OCCs with ECCs to find visually similar characters could increase the chances to find similar characters. Instead of saving "土木竹水" for "坡" directly, we divide a Chinese character into subareas systematically, and save the Cangjie codes for each of the subareas. A Chinese character is stored with the information about how it is divided into subareas and the Cangjie sequences for each of its subareas. The internal code for how we divide "坡" is 2, and the ECC for "坡" has two parts: "土" and "木竹水". Yet, it was not clear as to which components of a character should use ECCs (Liu and Lin, 2008; Liu et al., 2009).

5.1 Formalizing the Extended Cangjie Codes

We analyzed the OCCs for all the characters in Clist to determine the list of basic components, with computer programs. We treated a basic Cangjie symbol as if it was a word, and computed the number of occurrences of n-grams based on the OCCs of the characters in Clist. Since the OCC for a character contains at most five symbols, the longest n-grams are 5-grams. Because the reason to use ECCs was to find common components in characters, we saved n-grams that repeated no less than three times in a list. After obtaining this initial list of n-grams, we removed those n-grams that were substrings of longer n-grams in the list.

In addition, the n-grams that appeared no less than three times might not represent an actual part in any Chinese characters. This may happen by chance because we considered only frequencies of n-grams when we generated the initial list at the previous step. For instance, the OCC codes for "曬" (shai4), "晤" (wu4), and "晨" (chen2) are "日一一心", "日一一口", and "日一一女", respectively. Although the substring "日一一" appears three times, it does represent an actual part of Chinese characters. Hence, we manually examined all of the n-grams in the initial list, and removed such n-grams from the list.

In addition to considering the frequencies of n-grams formed by the basic Cangjie codes to determine the list of components, we also took advantage of radicals that are used to categorize Chinese characters in typical printed dictionaries. Radicals that are stand-alone Chinese words were included in the list of components.

After selecting the list of basic components with the above procedure, we encoded the words in Elist with these basic components. We inherited the 12 ways reported in a previous work (Liu and Lin, 2008) to decompose Chinese characters. There are other methods for decomposing Chinese characters into components. Juang et al. (2005) and their team at the Sinica Academia propose 13 different ways for decomposing characters.

At the same time when we annotated individual characters with their ECCs, we may revise the list of basic components. If a character that actually contained an intuitively "common" part and that part had not been included in the list of basic component, we would add this part into the list to make it a basic component and revised the ECC for all characters accordingly. The judgment of being "common" is subjective, but we still maintained the rule that such common parts must appear in more than three characters. When defining the basic components, not all judgments are completely objectively yet, and this is also the case of defining the original Cangjie codes. We tried to be as systematic as possible, but intuition sometimes stepped in.

We repeated the procedure described in the preceding paragraph five times to make sure that we were satisfied with the ECCs for all of the 5401 characters. The current list contains 794 components, and we can revise the list of basic components in our work whenever necessary.

5.2 Recommending Incorrect Alternatives

With the pronunciation of Chinese characters in a dictionary and with our ECC encodings for words in the Elist, we can create lists of candidate characters for replacing a specific correct character in a given word to create a test item for incorrect character correction.

There are multiple strategies to create the candidate lists. We may propose the candidate characters because their pronunciations have the same sound and the same tone with those of the correct character (denoted ***SSST***). Characters that have same sounds and different tones (***SSDT***), characters that have similar sounds and same tones (***MSST***), and characters that have similar sounds and different tones (***MSDT***) can be considered as candidates as well. It is easy to judge whether two Chinese characters have the same tone. In contrast, it is not trivial to define "similar" sound. We adopted the list of similar sounds that was provided by a psycholinguistic researcher (Dr. Chia-Ying Lee) at the Sinica Academia. "坡" (po) and "玻" (bo) and "犯"(fan4) and "患"(huan4) are pairs that have similar sounds. It was observed that these are four possible reasons that people used incorrect characters in writing.

Because a Chinese character might be pronounced in multiple ways, character lists generated based on these strategies may include the same characters. More specifically, the lists *SSST* and *SSDT* may overlap when a character that can be pronounced in multiple ways, and these pronunciations share the same sound and have different tones. The characters "待" and "好" are such examples. "待" can be pronounced as "dai1" or "dai4", and "好" can be pronounced as "hao3" or "hao4". Hence, characters that can be pronounced as "hao3" will be listed in both SSST and SSDT for "好".

In addition, we may propose characters that look similar to the correct character. Two characters may look similar for many reasons (Liu et al., 2009). The most common reason is that they contain the same components, and the other is that they belong to the same radical category and have the same total number of strokes (***RS***), e.g., the pairs "己" and "巳", "記" and "計", and "谿" and "豁". When two characters contain the same component, the shared component might or might not locate at the same position, e.g., "部" and "陪".

In an authoring tool, we could recommend a selected number of candidate characters for replacing the correct character. We tried two different strategies to compare and choose the visually similar characters. The similarity is computed based on the number and the locations of shared Cangjie symbols in the ECCs of the characters. The first strategy (denoted ***SC1***) gave a higher score to the shared component that located at the same location in the two characters being compared. The second strategy (***SC2***) gave the same score to any shared component even if the component did not reside at the same location in the characters. The characters "頸", "勁", and "徑" share the same component "巠". When computing the similarity between these characters with *SC1*, the contribution of "巠" will be the same for any pair. When computing with *SC2*, the contribution of "巠" will be larger for the pair "頸" and "勁" than for the pair "徑" and "勁". In the former case, "巠" appears at the same location in the characters.

When there were more than 20 characters that receive nonzero scores in the *SC1* and *SC2* categories, we chose to select at most 20 characters that had leading scores as the list of recommended characters.

We had to set a bound on the number of candidate characters, i.e., 20, for strategies *SC1* and *SC2*. The number of candidates generated from these two strategies can be large and artificial, depending on our scoring functions for determining similarities between characters. We did not limit the sizes of candidate lists that were generated by other strategies because those lists were created based on more objective methods. The rules for determining "similar" sounds were given by the domain experts, so we considered the rules objective in this research.

For the experiments that we reported in the following subsection, we submitted more than 300 thousand of queries to Google. As we mentioned in Section 4.1, a frequent continual submission of queries to Google will make Google treat our programs as malicious processes. (We are studying the Google API for a more civilized solution.) Without the bound, it is possible to offer a very long list of candidates. On the other hand, it is also possible that our program does not find any visually similar characters for some special characters, and this is considered a possible phenomenon.

5.3 Evaluating the Recommendations

We examined the usefulness of these seven categories of candidates with errors in Elist and Jlist. The first set of evaluation (the inclusion tests) checked whether the lists of recommended characters contained the incorrect character in our records. The second set of evaluation (the ranking tests) was designed for practical application in computer assisted item generation. Only for those words whose actual incorrect characters were included in the recommended list, we replaced the correct characters in the words with the candidate incorrect characters, submitted the incorrect words to Google, and ordered the candidate characters based on their NOPs. We then recorded the ranks of the incorrect characters among all recommended characters.

Since the same character may appear simultaneously in *SC1*, *SC2*, and *RS*, we computed the union of these three sets, and checked whether the incorrect characters were in the union. The inclusion rate is listed under ***Comp***, representing the inclusion rate when we consider only logographic influences. Similarly, we computed the union for *SSST*, *SSDT*, *MSST*, and *MSDT*, checked whether the incorrect characters were in the union, and recorded the inclusion rate under ***Pron***, representing the inclusion rate when we consider only phonological influences. Finally, we computed the union of the lists created by the seven strategies, and recorded the inclusion rate under ***Both***.

The second and the third rows of Table 3 show the results of the inclusion tests when we recommended candidate characters with the methods indicated in the column headings. The data show the percentage of the incorrect characters being included in the lists that

Table 3. Incorrect characters were contained and ranked high in the recommended lists

	SC1	*SC2*	*RS*	*SSST*	*SSDT*	*MSST*	*MSDT*	*Comp*	*Pron*	*Both*
Elist	73.92%	76.08%	4.08%	91.64%	18.39%	3.01%	1.67%	81.97%	99.00%	93.37%
Jlist	67.52%	74.65%	6.14%	92.16%	20.24%	4.19%	3.58%	77.62%	99.32%	97.29%
Elist	3.25	2.91	1.89	2.30	1.85	2.00	1.58			
Jlist	2.82	2.64	2.19	3.72	2.24	2.77	1.16			
Elist	19.27	17.39	11.34	19.13	8.29	19.02	9.15			
Jlist	17.58	16.24	12.52	22.85	9.75	22.11	7.68			

were recommended by the seven strategies. Notice that the percentages were calculated with different denominators. The number of composition-related errors was used for *SC1*, *SC2*, *RS*, and *Comp* (e.g., 505 that we mentioned in Section 3 for Jlist); the number of pronunciation-related errors for *SSST*, *SSDT*, *MSST*, *MSDT*, and *Pron* (e.g., 1314 mentioned in Section 3 for the Jlist); the number of either of these two types of errors for *Both* (e.g., 1475 for Jlist).

The results recorded in Table 3 show that we were able to find the incorrect character quite effectively, achieving better than 93% for both Elist and Jlist. The statistics also show that it is easier to find incorrect characters that were used for pronunciation-related problems. Most of the pronunciation-related problems were misuses of homophones. Unexpected confusions, e.g., those related to pronunciations in Chinese dialects, were the main reason for the failure to capture the pronunciation-related errors. (Namely, few pronunciation-related errors were not considered in the information that the psycholinguist provided.) *SSDT* is a crucial complement to *SSST*.

There is still room to improve our methods to find confusing characters based on their compositions. We inspected the list generated by *SC1* and *SC2*, and found that, although *SC2* outperformed *SC1* on the inclusion rate, *SC1* and *SC2* actually generated complementary lists in many cases, and should be used together. The inclusion rate achieved by the *RS* strategy was surprisingly high. We found that many of the errors that were captured by the *RS* strategy were also captured by the *SSST* strategy.

The fourth and the fifth rows of Table 3 show the effectiveness of relying on Google to rank the candidate characters for recommending an incorrect character. The rows show the average ranks of the included cases. The statistics show that, with the help of Google, we were able to put the incorrect character on top of the recommended list when the incorrect character was included. This allows us to build an environment for assisting human teachers to efficiently prepare test items for incorrect character identification.

Note that we did not provide data for all columns in the fourth and the firth rows. Unlike that we show the inclusion rates in the second and the third rows, the fourth and the fifth rows show how the actual incorrect characters were ranked in the recommended lists. Hence, we need to have a policy to order the characters of different lists to find the ranks of the incorrect characters in the integrated list.

However, integrating the lists is not necessary and can be considered confusing to the teachers. The selection of incorrect characters from different lists is related to the goals of the assessment, and it is better to leave the lists separated for the teachers to choose. The same phenomenon and explanation apply to the sixth and the seventh rows as well.

The sixth and the seventh rows show the average numbers of candidate characters proposed by different methods. Statistics shown between the second and the fifth rows are related to the recall rates (cf. Manning and Schütz, 1999) achieved by our system. For these four rows, we calculated how well the recommended lists contained the reported errors and how the actual incorrect characters ranked in the recommended lists. The sixth and the seventh rows showed the costs for these achievements, measured by the number of recommended characters. The sum of the sixth and the seventh rows, i.e., 103.59 and 108.75, are, respectively, the average numbers of candidate characters that our system recommended as possible errors recorded in Elist and Jlist. (Note that some of these characters were repeated.)

There are two ways to interpret the statistics shown in the sixth and the seventh rows. Comparing the corresponding numbers on the fourth and the sixth rows, e.g., 3.25 and 19.27, show the effectiveness of using the NOPs to rank the candidate characters. The ranks of the actual errors were placed at very high places, considering the number of the originally recommended lists. The other way to use the statistics in the sixth and the seventh rows is to compute the average precision. For instance, we recommended an average 19.13 characters in *SSST* to achieve the 91.64 inclusion rate. The recall rate is very high, but the averaged precision is very low. This, however, is not a very convincing interpretation of the results. Having assumed that there was only one best candidate as in our experiments, it was hard to achieve high precision rates. The recall rates are more important than the precision rates, particularly when we have proved that the actual errors were ranked among the top five alternatives.

When designing a system for assisting the authoring of test items, it is not really necessary to propose all of the characters in the categories. In the reported experiments, choosing the top 5 or top 10 candidates will contain the most of the actual incorrect characters based on the statistics shown in the fourth and the fifth rows. Hence the precision rates can be significantly increased practically. We do not have to merge the candidate characters among different categories because choosing the categories of incorrect characters depends on the purpose of the assessment. Reducing the length of the candidate list increases the chances of reducing the recall rates. Achieving the best trade off between precision and recall rates relies on a more complete set of experiments that involve human subjects.

Furthermore, in a more realistic situation, there can be more than one "good" incorrect character, not just one and only gold standard as in the reported experiments. It is therefore more reasonable the compute the precision rates based the percentage of "acceptable" incorrect characters. Hence, the precision rates are likely to increase and become less disconcerting.

We reported experimental results in which we asked 20 human subjects to choose an incorrect character for 20 test items (Liu et al., 2009). The best solutions were provided by a book. The recommendations provided by our previous system and chosen by the human subjects achieved comparable qualities.

Notice that the numbers do not directly show the actual number of queries that we had to submit to Google to receive the NOPs for ranking the characters. Because the lists might contain the same characters, the sum of the rows showed just the maximum number of queries that we submitted. Nevertheless, they still served as good estimations, and we actually submitted 103.59×1441(=149273) and 108.75×1583 (=172151) queries to Google for Elist and Jlist in experiments from which we obtained the data shown in the fourth and the fifth rows. These quantities explained why we had to be cautious about how we submitted queries to Google. When we run our program for just a limited number of characters, the problems caused by intensive queries should not be very serious.

5.4 Discussions

Dividing characters into subareas proved to be crucial in our experiments (Liu and Lin, 2008; Liu et al., 2009), but this strategy is not perfect, and could not solve all of the problems. The way we divided Chinese characters into subareas like (Juang et al., 2005; Liu and Lin, 2008) sometimes contributed to the failure of our current implementation to capture all of the errors that were related to the composition of the words. The most eminent reason is that how we divide characters into areas. Liu and Lin (2008) followed the division of Cangjie (Chu, 2009), and Juang et al. (2005) proposed an addition way to split the characters.

The best divisions of characters appear to depend on the purpose of the applications. Recall that each part of the character is represented by a string of Cangjie codes in ECCs. The separation of Cangjie codes in ECCs was instrumental to find the similarity of "苗" and "福" because "田" is a standalone subpart in both "苗" and "福". The Cangjie system has a set of special rules to divide Chinese characters (Chu, 2009; Lee, 2008). Take "副" and "福" for example. The component "畐" is recorded as an standalone part in "副", but is divided into two parts in "福". Hence, "畐" is stored as one string, "一口田", in "副" and as two strings, "一口" and "田", in "福". The different ways of saving "畐" in two different words made it harder to find the similarity between "副" and "福". An operation of concatenation is in need, but the problems are that it is not obvious to tell when the concatenation operations are useful and which of the parts should be rejoined. Hence, using the current methods to divide Chinese characters, it is easy to find the similar between "苗" and "福" but difficult to find the similar between "副" and "福". In contrast, if we enforce a rule to save "畐" as one string of Cangjie code, it will turn the situations around. Determining the similarity between "苗" and "福" will be more difficult than finding the similarity between "副" and "福".

Due to this observation, we have come to believe that it is better to save the Chinese characters with more detailed ECCs. By saving all detailed information about a character, our system can offer candidate characters based on users' preferences which can be provided via a good user interface. This flexibility can be very helpful when we are preparing text materials for experiments for psycholinguistics or cognitive sciences (e.g., Leck et al, 1995; Yeh and Li, 2002).

6 Summary

The analysis of the 1718 errors produced by real students show that similarity between pronunciations of competing characters contributed most to the observed errors. Evidences show that the Web statistics are not very reliable for differentiating correct and incorrect characters. In contrast, the Web statistics are good for comparing the attractiveness of incorrect characters for computer assisted item authoring.

Acknowledgments

This research was supported in part by the National Science Council of Taiwan under grant NSC-97-2221-E-004-007-MY2. We thank anonymous reviewers for their invaluable comments.

References

B.-F. Chu. 2009. *Handbook of the Fifth Generation of the Cangjie Input Method*, available at http://www.cbflabs.com/book/ocj5/ocj5/index.html. Last visited on 30 April 2009.

D. Juang, J.-H. Wang, C.-Y. Lai, C.-C. Hsieh, L.-F. Chien, J.-M. Ho. 2005. Resolving the unencoded character problem for Chinese digital libraries, *Proc. of the 5th ACM/IEEE Joint Conf. on Digital Libraries*, 311–319.

S.-P. Law, W. Wong, K. M. Y. Chiu. 2005. Whole-word phonological representations of disyllabic words in the Chinese lexicon: Data from acquired dyslexia, *Behavioural Neurology*, **16**, 169–177.

K. J. Leck, B. S. Weekes, M. J. Chen. 1995. Visual and phonological pathways to the lexicon: Evidence from Chinese readers, *Memory & Cognition*, **23**(4), 468–476.

H. Lee. 2008. *Cangjie Input Methods in 30 Days*, http://input.foruto.com/cjdict/Search_1.php, Foruto Company, Hong Kong. Last visited on 30 April 2009.

C.-L. Liu, K.-W. Tien, Y.-H. Chuang, C.-B. Huang, J.-Y. Weng. 2009. Two applications of lexical information to computer-assisted item authoring for elementary Chinese, *Proc. of the 22nd Int'l Conf. on Industrial Engineering & Other Applications of Applied Intelligent Systems*, 470–480.

C.-L. Liu, J.-H. Lin. 2008. Using structural information for identifying similar Chinese characters, *Proc. of the 46th ACL*, short papers, 93–96.

C. D. Manning, H. Schütze. *Foundations of Statistical Natural Language Processing*. The MIT Press. 1999.

MOE. 1996. *Common Errors in Chinese Writings* (常用國字辨似), Ministry of Education, Taiwan.

S.-L. Yeh, J.-L. Li. 2002. Role of structure and component in judgments of visual similarity of Chinese characters, *Journal of Experimental Psychology: Human Perception and Performance*, **28**(4), 933–947.

Resource Report: Building Parallel Text Corpora for Multi-Domain Translation System

Budiono, Hammam Riza, Chairil Hakim
Science and Technology Network Information Center (IPTEKnet)
Agency for the Assessment and Application of Technology (BPPT), Jakarta, INDONESIA
budi@iptek.net.id, hammam@iptek.net.id, chairil@iptek.net.id

Abstract

Parallel text is one of the most valuable resources for development of statistical machine translation systems and other NLP applications. However, manual translations are very costly, and the number of known parallel text is limited. Hence, our research started with creating and collecting a large amount of parallel text resources for Indonesian-English. We describe in this paper the creation of parallel corpora: ANTARA News, BPPT-PANL and BTEC-ATR. In order to be useful, these resources must be available in reasonable quantities and qualities to be useful for statistical approaches to language processing. We describe problem and solution as well robust tools and annotation schema to build and process these corpora.

1. Introduction

In recent years, our research focuses in developing Open Source Toolkit for English-Indonesian translation system. We need to build a good quality with reasonable size of parallel corpus in Indonesian-English. We started by collecting Indonesian corpus and perform raw corpus cleaning, translation, alignment and XML tagging. The alignment at sentence levels makes parallel corpora both more interesting and more useful. As long as parallel corpora exist, sentence aligned parallel corpora is an issue which is solved by sentence aligners. In our case, the alignment is performed manually by hand while doing the actual translation.

The task that was carried out by us in gathering corpus was conducted in several stages. Until now, we had several collections from various resources. Among them is the collection of ANTARA News corpus, collection of BPPT-PANL corpus and collection of BTEC-ATR corpus. Respectively this work had various Domain (National News, International News, Business/Economy, Politics, Science, Technology, and Sport) and different sources (News agency, Online Publisher, International institution) leading toward different handling and process.

2. Collection of ANTARA Corpus

ANTARA is the national news agency of Indonesia that has a collection of news articles available in two languages, Bahasa Indonesia and English. ANTARA develop a large news collection for the last 10 years, for various domains, i.e. political news, economics news, international news, national news, sport news, science news and entertainment news. All of these news articles were stored in a database system (Oracle) as comparable corpora and the structure of the database did not have the key pairs between one news article written in Indonesian and the one in English news article.

At the beginning, we had a long tedious process for reaching an agreement between the two sides, ANTARA and BPPT. We asked permission to use these data for our researches to develop automatic translation which in return will help ANTARA's journalist and reporters for translation. In addition, the resulting work will benefit both ANTARA and BPPT in the form of alignment of news articles and key pairs for database improvement.

The main problem is transforming this comparable corpus into parallel corpus. We should distinguish between Parallel Corpora with Comparable Corpora. The latter (comparable corpora) are texts in different

Proceedings of the 7th Workshop on Asian Language Resources, ACL-IJCNLP 2009, pages 92–95,
Suntec, Singapore, 6-7 August 2009.

languages with the same main topic. A set of news articles, from journals or news broadcast systems, as they refer the same event in different languages can be considered as Comparable Corpora. Consider a news item about the September 11 tragedy. Different newspapers, in different languages will refer the World Trade Center, airplanes, Bin Laden and a lot of other specific words. This is the case of Comparable Corpora which can be used by translators who know day-to-day language but need to learn how to translate a specific term.

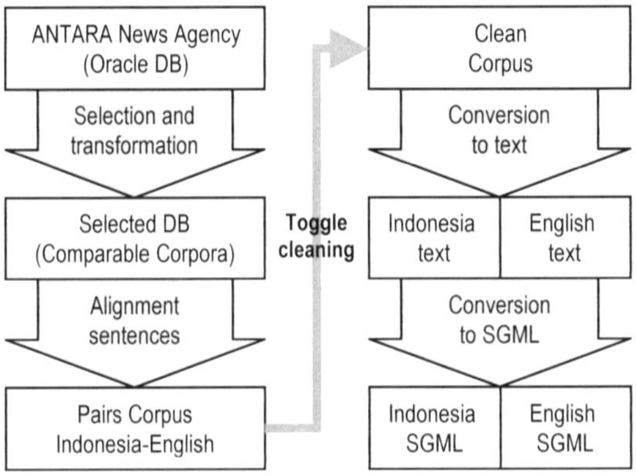

Figure 1. ANTARA Corpus Processing

The number of data's that was used is between the period of year 2000 to 2007 and the articles were taken in stages, in SQL format, amounting to 250.000 sentence pairs (2.5 Million words). These data, afterwards was processed by referring to the news title in respective article to become article pairs. After this article fitting was finished, the next step was to make the pairs of sentence and then the result was store in a new table of database. The work scheme of ANTARA corpus collection is given below in Figure 1.

During the alignment process, the sentences were reviewed manually, by means of election against the quality of the translations. The toggle cleaning stage is used for the process of cleaning of the punctuation mark like [? ! " " ' ' : ; {}]. Afterwards, these sentences pairs was separated into two documents, each for Indonesian and English and put into SGML format. Attention has to be made to keep the consistency of translation from the comparable corpora into parallel corpora.

The ANTARA corpus is used for building machine translation using an open source MOSES SMT. It can be reported here that the BLEU score of 0.76 can be reached by using 1 Million words training set.

3. Collection of BPPT-PANL Corpus

The creation of this corpus is divided into 3 steps [6]. First step is the translation of Indonesian corpus; the second step is the alignment process and resolving issues and followed by tagging of corpus using XML schema in step 3.

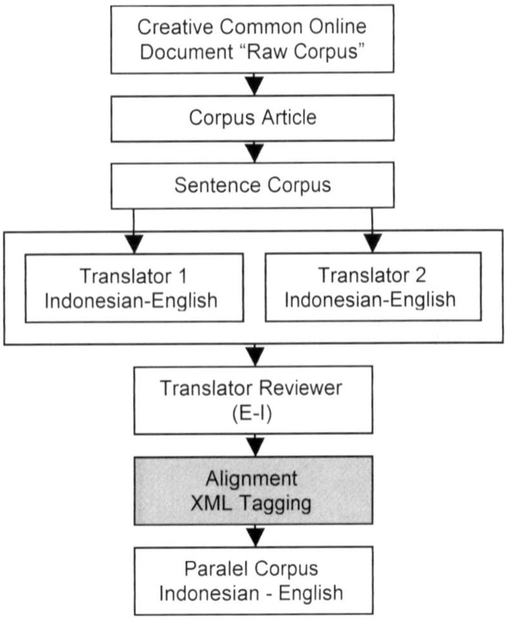

Figure 2. BPPT-PANL Corpus Development

3.1 Translation of Indonesian Corpus

We have collected corpora in Bahasa Indonesia covering various domains. This corpus is collected from various online sources which we can apply Creative Commons IPR to its content [2].

Translation, in our project definition, is the semantic and syntactic transfer from a sentence written in Bahasa Indonesia to a sentence in English language. This definition is rigidly constructed, in order to preserve sentence alignment between the original text and the target text in English.

If we are going to translate and align sentences, then obviously we must clarify what we understand by *sentence*. While most people have strong intuitions about what is a sentence and what is not, there is no universal definition of that notion. Before we set out on devising one, however, it should be noted that because PANL-BPPT Corpus is primarily intended to be used as a training text for statistical machine translation systems, both the exact translation and the actual segmentation of the text that results from translation are crucially important.

Our main concern in this regard was to come up with some guidelines for translation that would be both practical for the translators and aligners as well as it is useful for the end-users of the corpus. We started out with something relatively straightforward, which we then expanded as needed.

Of course, given the relative vagueness of the definitions of sentence and translation given above, it was clear that in many situations, arbitrary decisions would have to be made. Our human aligners were instructed to be as consistent as possible. But even then, because of the repetitive nature of the task, errors had to be expected.

3.2 Alignment of Parallel Texts

A parallel text alignment describes the relations that exist between a text and its translation. These relations can be viewed at various levels of granularity: between text divisions, paragraphs, sentences, propositions, words, even characters. While it would certainly have been interesting to produce finer-grain alignments, it was decided that BPPT-PANL Corpus would record correspondences at the level of sentences. This decision was based on a number of factors.

First, sentence-level alignments have so far proved very useful in a number of applications, which could be characterized as *high recall, low precision* applications, i.e. applications where it is more important to have all the answers to a specific question than to have only the good ones.

Secondly is the automatic acquisition of information about translation, as was proposed in [1] as part of a project to build a machine translation system entirely based on statistical knowledge. Such statistical models need to be *trained* with large quantities of parallel text. Intuitively, the ideal training material for this task would be parallel text aligned at the level of words. Yet, because these models picture the translation process in an extremely simplified manner, reliable statistical estimates can nevertheless be obtained from much less precise data, such as pairs of sentences.

For all these reasons, we decided that it would be more appropriate initially to concentrate on sentence-level alignments. Furthermore, we decided to restrict ourselves to "non-crossing" alignments, which is a parallel segmentation of the two texts, into an equal number of segments, such that the *nth* segment in one text and the *nth* segment in the other text are translations of one another [4].

It was suggested that all the texts would be aligned twice, each time by a different aligner. The resulting alignments would then be compared, so as to detect any discrepancies between the two. The aligners were then asked to conciliate these differences together. Because the entire BPPT-PANL corpus was aligned by the same two aligners, this way of proceeding not only minimized the number of errors; it also ensured that both aligners had the same understanding of the guidelines.

3.3 Corpus Tagging

SGML and XML played a major part in the BNC project [3] which serve as an interchange medium between the various data-providers, as a target application-independent format; and as the vehicle for expression of metadata and linguistic interpretations encoded within the corpus.

From the start of the project, it was recognized that we have to choose a standard format such as TEI P4 or XML in order to maintain the corpus for long term storage and also enable distribution of the data. The importance of XML as an application independent encoding format is also becoming apparent, as a wide range of applications for it begin to be realized.

The basic structural mark up of texts may be summarized as follows. Each of the documents or text source articles making up the corpus is represented by a single <corpus> element, containing a header <domain> and <language>, and followed by sentence ID <number>.

The header element contains detailed and richly structured metadata supplying a variety of contextual information about the document (its domain, source, encoding, etc., as defined by the Text Encoding Initiative).

Sample tagging for English as follows:

```
<?xml version="1.0" encoding="iso-8859-1" ?>
<corpus>
  <national>
    <language>english</language>
    <id>1</id>
    <sentence>The Indian government is
    providing scholarships to 20 Indonesian
    students annually including for university
    graduate and post-graduate
    studies.</sentence>
  </national>
</corpus>
```

4. Collection of BTEC-ATR Corpus

BTEC was the abbreviation from Basic Travel Expression Corpus. This corpus this was the everyday normal conversational speech mostly use in traveling and tourism. The source corpus was in monolingual English belonging to NICT-ATR Japan.

As part of A-STAR project cooperation [5], our task was to do the manual translation from English to Indonesian. Similar to the method that was used in developing BPPT-PANL corpus collection; we developed 153.000 utterances into parallel corpora. Additionally, we developed POS Tagging, syllabification and word-stress into this corpus. The main difference was BPPT-PANL originated in monolingual Indonesian that was taken from the domain international, national, economics, sport and science whereas BTEC-ATR originated in speech of English in the travel domain.

5. Summary

After many attempts for having a reasonable size of parallel text for statistical machine translation experiments, we are now having a good quality of parallel corpus collection in Bahasa Indonesia and English as follows:

Name	*Size*	*Domain*	*Origin*	*Annotation Scheme*
ANTARA	250K sentences	News (National Economy)	ANTARA News Agency	TEI P4
BPPT-PANL	500K words	News (Busines, Science)	Online Publisher	TEI, XML, TMX
BTEC-ATR	153K sentences	Travel	NICT-ATR	XML
INC-IX	100K sentences	Parliament Report	BPPT	GDA

References

[1] Brown, P. F., Pietra, S. A. D., Pietra, V. J. D., and Mercer, R. L. (1993). The Mathematics of Machine Translation: Parameter Estimation. Computational Linguistics, 19(2).

[2] Wikipedia Creative Commons Website, http://en.wikipedia.org/wiki/, retrieved August 08

[3] Aston, G. and Burnard, L. The BNC Handbook Edinburgh: Edinburgh University Press., 1998

[4] Simard, M. and Plamondon, P. (1996). Bilingual Sentence Alignment: Balancing Robustness and Accuracy. In Proceedings of AMTA-96, Montréal, Canada.

[5] Sakriani Sakti, Eka Kelana, Hammam Riza (BPPT), Satoshi Nakamura, Large Vocabulary ASR for Indonesian Language in the A-STAR Project, 2007.

[6] Riza, Hammam, et.al, PAN Localization Project Report. BPPT, 2008-2009.

A Syntactic Resource for Thai: CG Treebank

Taneth Ruangrajitpakorn **Kanokorn Trakultaweekoon** **Thepchai Supnithi**
Human Language Technology Laboratory
National Electronics and Computer Technology Center
112 Thailand Science Park, Phahonyothin Road, Klong 1,
Klong Luang Pathumthani, 12120, Thailand
+66-2-564-6900 Ext.2547, Fax.: +66-2-564-6772
{taneth.ruangrajitpakorn, kanokorn.trakultaweekoon, thepchai.supnithi}@nectec.or.th

Abstract

This paper presents Thai syntactic resource: Thai CG treebank, a categorial approach of language resources. Since there are very few Thai syntactic resources, we designed to create treebank based on CG formalism. Thai corpus was parsed with existing CG syntactic dictionary and LALR parser. The correct parsed trees were collected as preliminary CG treebank. It consists of 50,346 trees from 27,239 utterances. Trees can be split into three grammatical types. There are 12,876 sentential trees, 13,728 noun phrasal trees, and 18,342 verb phrasal trees. There are 17,847 utterances that obtain one tree, and an average tree per an utterance is 1.85.

1 Introduction

Syntactic lexical resources such as POS tagged corpus and treebank play one of the important roles in NLP tools for instance machine translation (MT), automatic POS tagger, and statistical parser. Because of a load burden and lacking linguistic expertise to manually assign syntactic annotation to sentence, we are currently limited to a few syntactical resources. There are few researches (Satayamas and Kawtrakul, 2004) focused on developing system to build treebank. Unfortunately, there is no further report on the existing treebank in Thai so far. Especially for Thai, Thai belongs to analytic language which means grammatical information relying in a word rather than inflection (Richard, 1964). Function words represent grammatical information such as tense, aspect, modal, etc. Therefore, to recognise word order is a key to syntactic analysis for Thai. Categorial Grammar (CG) is a formalism which focuses on principle of syntactic behaviour. It can be applied to solve word order issues in Thai. To apply CG for machine learning and statistical based approach, CG treebank, is initially required.

CG is a based concept that can be applied to advance grammar such as Combinatory Categorial Grammar (CCG) (Steedman, 2000). Moreover, CCG is proved to be superior than POS for CCG tag consisting of fine grained lexical categories and its accuracy rate (Curran et al., 2006; Clark and Curran, 2007).

Nowadays, CG and CCG become popular in NLP researches. There are several researches using them as a main theoretical approach in Asia. For example, there is a research in China using CG with *Type Lifting* (Dowty, 1988) to find features interpretations of undefined words as syntactic-semantic analysis (Jiangsheng, 2000). In Japan, researchers also works on Japanese categorial grammar (JCG) which gives a foundation of semantic parsing of Japanese (Komatsu, 1999). Moreover, there is a research in Japan to improve CG for solving Japanese particle shifting phenomenon and using CG to focus on Japanese particle (Nishiguchi, 2008).

This paper is organised as follows. Section 2 reviews categorial grammar and its function. Section 3 explains resources for building Thai CG treebank. Section 4 describes experiment result. Section 5 discusses issues of Thai CG treebank. Last, Section 6 summarises paper and lists up future work.

Proceedings of the 7th Workshop on Asian Language Resources, ACL-IJCNLP 2009, pages 96–102,
Suntec, Singapore, 6-7 August 2009. ©2009 ACL and AFNLP

2 Categorial Grammar

Categorial grammar (Aka. CG or classical categorial grammar) (Ajdukiewicz, 1935; Carpenter, 1992; Buszkowski, 1998; Steedman, 2000) is a formalism in natural language syntax motivated by the principle of constitutionality and organised according to the syntactic elements. The syntactic elements are categorised in terms of their ability to combine with one another to form larger constituents as functions or according to a function-argument relationship. All syntactic categories in CG are distinguished by a syntactic category identifying them as one of the following two types:

1. Argument: this type is a basic category, such as s (sentence) and np (noun phrase).
2. Functor (or functor category): this category type is a combination of argument and operator(s) '/' and '\'. Functor is marked to a complex lexicon to assist argument to complete sentence such as s\np (intransitive verb) requires noun phrase from the left side to complete a sentence.

CG captures the same information by associating a functional type or category with all grammatical entities. The notation α/β is a rightward-combining functor over a domain of α into a range of β. The notation $\alpha\backslash\beta$ is a leftward-combining functor over β into α. α and β are both argument syntactic categories (Hockenmaier and Steedman, 2002; Baldridge and Kruijff, 2003). The basic concept is to find the core of the combination and replace the grammatical modifier and complement with set of categories based on the same concept with fractions. For example, intransitive verb is needed to combine with a subject to complete a sentence therefore intransitive verb is written as s\np which means it needs a noun phrase from the left side to complete a sentence. If there is a noun phrase exists on the left side, the rule of fraction cancellation is applied as np*s\np = s. With CG, each lexicon can be annotated with its own syntactic category. However, a lexicon could have more than one syntactic category if it is able to be used in different appearances.

Furthermore, CG does not only construct a purely syntactic structure but also delivers a compositional interpretation. The identification of derivation with interpretation becomes an advantage over others.

Example of CG derivation of Thai sentence is illustrated in Figure 1.

Recently, there are many researches on combinatory categorial grammar (CCG) which is an improved version of CG. With the CG based concept and notation, it is possible to easily upgrade it to advance formalism. However, Thai syntax still remains unclear since there are several points on Thai grammar that are yet not completely researched and found absolute solvent (Ruangrajitpakorn et al., 2007). Therefore, CG is currently set for Thai to significantly reduce over generation rate of complex composition or ambiguate usage.

เขา ไป โรงเรียน
เขา /k^h ǎw/ 'He'
ไป /pai/ 'go'
โรงเรียน /roŋ riən/ 'school'
lit: He goes to school

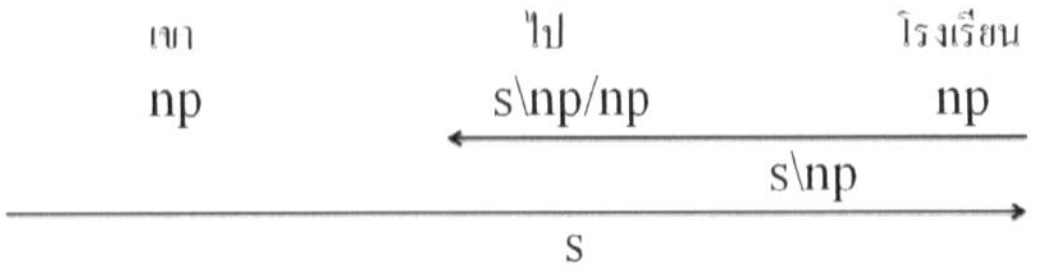

Figure 1. CG derivation tree of Thai sentence

3 Resources

To collect CG treebank, CG dictionary and parser are essentially required. Firstly, Thai corpus was parsed with the parser using CG dictionary as a syntactic resource. Then, the correct trees of each sentence were manually determined by linguists and collected together as treebank.

3.1 Thai CG Dictionary

Recently, we developed Thai CG dictionary to be a syntactic dictionary for several purposes since CG is new to Thai NLP. CG was adopted to our syntactic dictionary because of its focusing on lexicon's behaviour and its fine grained lexicalised grammar. CG is proper to nature of Thai language since Thai belongs to analytic language typology; that is, its syntax and meaning depend on the use of particles and word orders rather than inflection (Boonkwan, and Supnithi, 2008). Moreover, pronouns and other grammatical information, such as tenses, aspects, numbers, and voices, are expressed by function words such as determiners, auxiliary verbs, adverbs and adjectives, which are in fix word order. With CG, it is possible to well capture Thai grammatical information. Currently we only aim to improve an accuracy of Thai syntax parsing since it still remains unresearched ambiguities in Thai syntax. A list of grammatical Thai word orders which are handled with CG is shown in Table 1.

Thai utilisation	Word-order
Sentence	- Subject + Verb + (Object)[1] [rigid order]
Compound noun	- Core noun + Attachment
Adjective modification	- Noun + Adjective[2]
Predicate Adjective	- Noun + Adjective[3]
Determiner	- Noun + (Classifier) + Determiner
Numeral expression	- Noun + (Modifier) + Number + Classifier + (Modifier)
Adverb modification	- Sentence + Adverb - Adverb + Sentence
Several auxiliary verbs	- Subject + (Aux verbs) + VP + (Aux verbs)
Negation	- Subject + Negator + VP - Subject + (Aux verb) + Negator + (Aux verb) + VP - Subject + VP + (Aux verb) + Negator + (Aux verb)
Passive	- Actee + Passive marker + (Actor) + Verb
Ditransitive	- Subject + Ditransitive verb + Direct object + Indirect object
Relative clause	- Noun + Relative marker + Clause
Compound sentence	- Sentence + Conjunction + Sentence - Conjunction + Sentence + Sentence
Complex sentence	- Sentence + Conjunction + Sentence - Conjunction + Sentence + Sentence
Subordinate clause that begins with word "ว่า"	- Subject + Verb + "ว่า"+ Sentence

Table 1. Thai word orders that CG can solve

In addition, there are many multi-sense words in Thai. These words have the same surface form but they have different meanings and different usages. This issue can be solved with CG formalism. The different usages are separated because the annotation of syntactic information. For example, Thai word "เกาะ" /kɔʔ/ can be used to refer to noun as an *'island'* and it is marked as **np**, and this word can also be denoted an action which means *'to clink'* or 'to attach' and it is marked as **s\np/np**.

After observation Thai word usage, the list of CG was created according to CG theory explained in Section 2.

Thai argument syntactic categories were initially created. For Thai language, six argument syntactic categories were determined. Thai CG arguments are listed with definition and examples in Table 2. Additionally, **np**, **num**, and **spnum** are a Thai CG arguments that can directly tag to a word, but other can not and they can only be used as a combination for other argument.

With the arguments, other type of word are created as functor by combining the arguments together following its behaviour and environmental requirements. The first argument in a functor is a result of combination. There are only two main operators in CG which are slash '/' and backslash '\' before an argument. A slash '/' refers to argument requirement from the right, and a backslash '\' refers to argument requirement from the left. For instance, a transitive verb requires one **np** from the left and one **np** from the right to complete a sentence. Therefore, it can be written as **s\np/np** in CG form. However, several Thai words have many functions even it has the same word sense. For example, Thai word "เชื่อ"/cʰɯ̂ə/ (to believe) is capable to use as intransitive verb, transitive verb, and verb that can be followed with subordinate clause. This word therefore has three different syntactic categories. Currently, there are 72 functors for Thai.

With an argument and a functor, each word in the word list is annotated with CG. This information is sufficient for parser to analyse an input sentence into a grammatical tree. In conclusion, CG dictionary presently contains 42,564 lexical entries with 75 CG syntactic categories. All Thai CG categories are shown in Appendix A.

[1] Information in parentheses is able to be omitted.

[2] Adjective modification is a form of an adjective performs as a modifier to a noun, and they combine as a noun phrase.

[3] Predicate adjective is a form of an adjective acts as a predicate of a sentence.

Thai argument category	definition	example
np	a noun phrase	ช้าง (elephant), ผม (I, me)
num	A both digit and word cardinal number	หนึ่ง (one), 2 (two)
spnum	a number which is succeeding to classifier instead of proceeding classifier like ordinary number	นึง (one), เดียว (one)[4]
pp	a prepositional phrase	ในรถ (in car), บนโต๊ะ (on table)
s	a sentence	ช้างกินกล้วย (elephant eats banana)
ws	a specific category for Thai which is assigned to a sentence that begins with Thai word ว่า (that : sub-ordinate clause marker).	* ว่าเขาจะมาสาย [5] 'that he will come late'

Table 2. List of Thai CG arguments

3.2 Parser

Our implemented lookahead LR parser (LALR) (Aho and Johnson, 1974; Knuth, 1965) was used as a tool to syntactically parse input from corpus. For our LALR parser, a grammar rule is not manually determined, but it is automatically produced by a any given syntactic notations aligned with lexicons in a dictionary therefore this LALR parser has a coverage including a CG formalism parsing. Furthermore, our LALR parser has potential to parse a tree from sentence, noun phrase and verb phrase. However, the parser does not only return the best first tree, but also all parsable trees to gather all ambiguous trees since Thai language tends to be ambiguous because of lacking explicit sentence and word boundary.

3.3 Tree Visualiser

To reduce load burden of linguist to seek for the correct tree among all outputs, we developed a tree visualiser. This tool was developed by using an open source library provided by NLTK: The Natural Language Toolkit (http://www.nltk.org/Home; Bird and Loper, 2004).

A tree visualiser is a tool to transform a textual tree structure to graphic tree. This tool reads a tree marking with parentheses form and transmutes it into graphic. This tool can transform all output types of tree including sentence tree, noun phrase tree, and verb phrase tree. For example, Thai sentence "|การ|ล่า|เสือ|เป็น|การ|ผจญภัย|" /ka:n lâ: sɯ̌ə pɤn ka:n pʰaʔ con pʰai/ 'lit: Tiger hunting is an adventure' was parsed to a tree shown in Figure 2. With a tree visualiser, the tree in Figure 2 was transformed to a graphic tree illustrated in Figure 3.

4 Experiment Result

In the preliminary experiment, 27,239 Thai utterances with a mix of sentences and phrases from a general domain corpus are tested. The input was word-segmented by JwordSeg (http://www.suparsit.com/nlp-tools) and approved by linguists. In the test corpus, the longest utterance contains seventeen words, and the shortest utterance contains two words.

```
s
 (np
   (np/(s\np)[การ]
     s\np(
       (s\np)/np[ล่า]
       np[เสือ]
     )
   )
   s\np(
     (s\np)/np[เป็น]
     np(
       np/(s\np)[การ]
      s\np[ผจญภัย]
     )
   )
 )
```

Figure 2. An example of CG tree output

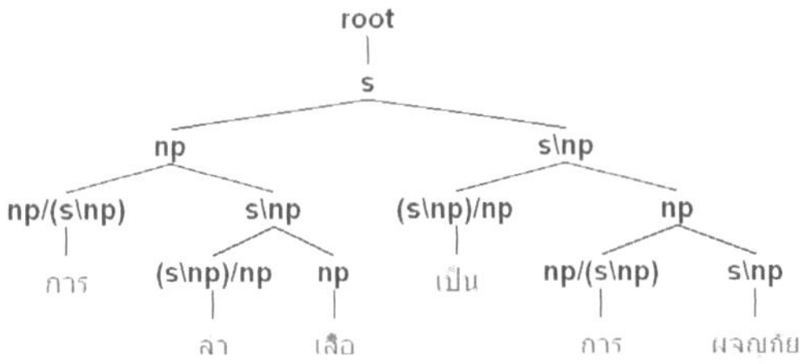

Figure 3. An example of graphic tree

[4] This spnum category has a different usage from other numerical use, e.g. ม้า[noun,'horse'] ตัว[classifier] เดียว[spnum,'one'] 'lit: one horse'. This case is different from normal numerical usage, e.g. ม้า[noun,'horse'] หนึ่ง [num,'one'] ตัว[classifier] 'lit: one horse'

[5] This example is a part of a sentence ฉันเชื่อว่าเขาจะมาสาย 'lit: I believe that he will come late'

All trees are manually observed by linguists to evaluate accuracy of the parser. The criteria of accuracy are:

- A tree is correct if sentence is successfully parsed and syntactically correct according to Thai grammar.
- In case of syntactic ambiguity such as a usage of preposition or phrase and sentence ambiguity, any tree following those ambiguity is acceptable and counted as correct.

The parser returns 50,346 trees from 27,239 utterances as 1.85 trees per input in average. There are 17,874 utterances that returns one tree. The outputs can be divided into three different output types: 12,876 sentential trees, 13,728 noun phrasal trees, and 18,342 verb phrasal trees.

From the parser output, tree amount collecting in the CG tree bank in details is shown in Table 3.

Tree type	Utterance amount	Tree amount	Average
Only S	8,184	12,798	1.56
Only NP	7,211	12,407	1.72
Only VP	8,006	11,339	1.42
Both NP and S	1,583	5,188	3.28
Both VP and S	1,725	6,816	3.95
Both NP and VP	397	1,140	2.87
S, NP, VP	133	658	4.95
Total	27,239	50,346	1.85

Table 3. Amount of tree categorised by a different kind of grammatical tree

5 Discussion

After observation of our result, we found two main issues.

First, some Thai inputs were parsed into several correct outputs due to ambiguity of an input. The use of an adjective can be parsed to both noun phrase and sentence since Thai adjective can be used either a noun modifier or predicate. For example, Thai input "|เด็กๆ|สดใส|บน|สนาม|" /dɛk dɛk sòd sǎi bon saʔ nǎ:m/ can be literally translated as follows:

1. Children is cheerful on a playground.
2. Cheerful children on a playground

For this problem, we decided to keep both trees in our treebank since they are both grammatically correct.

Second, the next issue is a variety of syntactic usages of Thai word. It is the fact that Thai has a narrow range of word's surface but a lot of polysymy words. The more the word in Thai is generally used, the more utilisation of word becomes varieties. With the several combination, there are more chances to generate trees in a wrong conceptual meaning even they form a correct syntactic word order. For example, Thai noun phrase "กำลัง|มหาศาล" /kam laŋ maʔ hǎ: sǎ:n/ 'lit: great power' can automatically be parsed to three trees for a sentence, a noun phrase, and a verb phrase because of polysymy of the first word. The first word "**กำลัง**" has two syntactic usages as a noun which conceptually refers to *power* and a pre-auxiliary verb to imply progressive aspect. The word "**มหาศาล**" is an adjective which can perform two options in Thai as noun modifier and predicate. These affect parser to result three trees as follows:

np: np(np[กำลัง] np\np[มหาศาล])
s: s(np[กำลัง] s\np[มหาศาล])
vp: s\np((s\np)/(s\np)[กำลัง] s\np[มหาศาล])

Even though all trees are syntactically correct, only noun phrasal tree is fully acceptable in terms of semantic sense as *great power*. The other trees are awkward and out of certain meaning in Thai. Therefore, the only noun phrase tree is collected into our CG treebank for such case.

6 Conclusion and Future Work

This paper presents Thai CG treebank which is a language resource for developing Thai NLP application. This treebank consists of 50,346 syntactic trees from 27,239 utterances with CG tag and composition. Trees can be split into three grammatical types. There are 12,876 sentential trees, 13,728 noun phrasal trees, and 18,342 verb phrasal trees. There are 17,847 utterances that obtain one tree, and an average tree per an utterance is 1.85.

In the future, we plan to improve Thai CG treebank to Thai CCG treebank. We also plan to reduce a variety of trees by extending semantic feature into CG. We will improve our LALR parser to be GLR and PGLR parser respectively to reduce a missing word and named entity problem. Moreover, we will develop parallel Thai-English treebank by adding a parallel English treebank aligned with Thai since parallel treebank is useful resource for learning to statistical machine translation. Furthermore, we will apply obtained CG treebank for automatic CG tagging development.

Reference

Alfred V. Aho, and Stephen C. Johnson. 1974 LR Parsing, In *Proceedings of Computing Surveys,* Vol. 6, No. 2.

Bob Carpenter. 1992. "Categorial Grammars, Lexical Rules,and the English Predicative", In R. Levine, ed., Formal Grammar: Theory and Implementation. OUP.

David Dowty, Type raising, functional composition, and non-constituent conjunction, In Richard Oehrle et al., ed., Categorial Grammars and Natural Language Structures. D. Reidel, 1988.

Donald E. Knuth. 1965. *On the translation of languages from left to right*, Information and Control 86.

Hisashi Komatsu. 1999. "Japanese Categorial Grammar Based on Term and Sentence". In *Proceeding of The 13th Pacific Asia Conference on Language, Information and Computation,* Taiwan.

James R. Curran, Stephen Clark, and David Vadas. 2006. Multi-Tagging for Lexicalized-Grammar Parsing. In *Proceedings of the Joint Conference of the International Committee on Computational Linguistics and the Association for Computational Linguistics (ACL)*, Paris, France.

Jason Baldridge, and Geert-Jan. M. Kruijff. 2003. "Multimodal combinatory categorial grammar". In *Proceeding of 10th Conference of the European Chapter of the ACL-2003,* Budapest, Hungary.

Julia Hockenmaier, and Mark Steedman. 2002. "Acquiring Compact Lexicalized Grammars from a Cleaner Treebank". In *Proceeding of 3rd International Conference on Language Resources and Evaluation (LREC-2002),* Las Palmas, Spain.

JWordSeg, word-segmentation toolkit. Available from: http://www.suparsit.com/nlp-tools), 2007.

Kazimierz Ajdukiewicz. 1935. *Die Syntaktische Konnexitat*, Polish Logic.

Mark Steedman. 2000. *The Syntactic Process*, The MIT Press, Cambridge Mass.

NLTK: The Natural Language Toolkit. Available from: http://www.nltk.org/Home

Noss B. Richard. 1964. *Thai Reference Grammar*, U. S. Government Printing Office, Washington DC.

Prachya Boonkwan, and Thepchai Supnithi. 2008. Memory-inductive categorial grammar: An approach to gap resolution in analytic-language translation. In *Proceeding of 3rd International Joint Conference on Natural Language Processing (IJCNLP-2008)*, Hyderabad, India.

Stephen Clark and James R. Curran. 2007. Formalism-Independent Parser Evaluation with CCG and DepBank. In *Proceedings of the 45th Annual Meeting of the Association for Computational Linguistics (ACL)*, Prague, Czech Republic.

Steven G. Bird, and Edward Loper. 2004. NLTK: The Natural Language Toolkit, In *Proceedings of 42nd Meeting of the Association for Computational Linguistics (Demonstration Track)*, Barcelona, Spain.

Sumiyo Nishiguchi. 2008. Continuation-based CCG of Japanese Quantifiers. In *Proceeding of 6th ICCS,* The Korean Society of Cognitive Science, Seoul, South Korea.

Taneth Ruangrajitpakorn, Wasan. na Chai, Prachya Boonkwan, Montika Boriboon, and Thepchai. Supnithi. 2007. The Design of Lexical Information for Thai to English MT, In *Proceeding of SNLP 2007*, Pattaya, Thailand.

Vee Satayamas, and Asanee Kawtrakul. 2004. Wide-Coverage Grammar Extraction from Thai Treebank. In *Proceedings of Papillon 2004 Workshops on Multilingual Lexical Databases,* Grenoble, France.

Wojciech Buszkowski, Witold Marciszewski, and Johan van Benthem, ed., *Categorial Grammar*, John Benjamin, Amsterdam, 1998.

Yu Jiangsheng. 2000. *Categorial Grammar based on Feature Structures*, dissersion in In-stitute of Computational Linguistics, Peking University.

Appendix A

Type	CG Category
Conjoiner	ws/s
Conjoiner	ws/(s/np)
Function word	spnum
Particle, Adverb	s\s
Verb	s\np/(s\np)/np
Verb	s\np
Function word, Particle	s/s
Function word	s/np
Auxiliary verb	s/(s/np)
Sentence	s
Conjoiner	pp/s
Conjoiner	pp/np
Conjoiner	pp/(s\np)
Function word	num
Classifier	np\num
Adjective	np\np
Noun, Pronoun	np/pp
Adjective, Determiner	np/np
Function word	np/(s\np)
Auxiliary verb	np/(np/np)
Function word	np/((s\np)/np)
Noun, Pronoun	np
Conjunction	(s\s)/s
Adverb, Auxiliary verb	(s\np)\(s\np)

Type	CG Category
Verb	(s\np)/ws
Verb, Adjective	(s\np)/pp
Determiner	(s\np)/num
Verb, Adjective	(s\np)/np
Function word, Verb, Adverb, Auxiliary verb	(s\np)/(s\np)
Function word	(s\np)/(np\np)
Auxiliary verb	(s\np)/((s\np)/np)
Conjunction	(s/s)/s
Function word	(s/s)/np
Function word	(s/s)/(s/np)
Classifier	(np\np)\num
Function word, Adverb, Auxiliary verb	(np\np)\(np\np)
Classifier	(np\np)/spnum
Function word	(np\np)/s
Determiner	(np\np)/num
Adjective, Conjoiner	(np\np)/np
Function word	(np\np)/(s\np)
Classifier, Function word, Adverb, Auxiliary verb	(np\np)/(np\np)
Auxiliary verb	(np\np)/((np\np)/np)
Adjective, Determiner	(np/pp)\(np/pp)
Determiner	(np/pp)/(np/pp)
Classifier	((s\np)\(s\np))\num
Classifier	((s\np)\(s\np))/spnum
Function word	((s\np)\(s\np))/np
Conjoiner	((s\np)\(s\np))/(s\np)

Type	CG Category
Function word	((s\np)\(s\np))/(np\np)
Function word	((s\np)\(s\np))/((s\np)\(s\np))
Verb	((s\np)/ws)/pp
Verb	((s\np)/ws)/np
Adverb, Auxiliary verb	((s\np)/pp)\((s\np)/pp)
Verb	((s\np)/pp)/np
Function word, Adverb	((s\np)/pp)/((s\np)/pp)
Auxiliary verb	((s\np)/np)\((s\np)/np)
Verb	((s\np)/np)/np
Verb	((s\np)/np)/(s\np)
Adverberb	((s\np)/(s\np))\((s\np)/(s\np))
Function word	((np\np)\(np\np))/np
Conjoiner	((np\np)\(np\np))/(np\np)
Adverb, Auxiliary verb	((np\np)/pp)\((np\np)/pp)
Adverb, Function word	((np\np)/pp)/((np\np)/pp)
Auxiliary verb	((np\np)/np)\((np\np)/np)
Conjoiner	((np/pp)\(np/pp))/(np/pp)
Verb	(((s\np)\np)
Verb	(((s\np)/ws)/pp)/np
Conjoiner	(((s\np)/pp)\((s\np)/pp))/((s\np)/pp)
Function word	(((s\np)/pp)\((s\np)/pp))/(((s\np)/pp)\((s\np)/pp))
Verb	(((s\np)/pp)/np)/np
Function word	(((s\np)/pp)/np)/(((s\np)/pp)/np)
Verb	(((s\np)/np)/(s\np))/pp
Conjoiner	(((np\np)/pp)\((np\np)/pp))/((np\np)/pp)

Part of Speech Tagging for Mongolian Corpus

Purev Jaimai and **Odbayar Chimeddorj**
Center for Research on Language Processing
National University of Mongolia
{purev, odbayar}@num.edu.mn

Abstract

This paper introduces the current result of a research work which aims to build a 5 million tagged word corpus for Mongolian. Currently, around 1 million words have been automatically tagged by developing a POS tagset and a bigram POS tagger.

1 Introduction

In the information era, language technologies and language processing have become a crucial issue to our social development which should benefit from the information technology. However, there are many communities whose languages have been less studied and developed for such need.

Mongolian is one of the Altaic family languages. It has a great, long history. Nonetheless, till now, there are no corpora for the Mongolian language processing (Purev, 2008). Two years ago, a research project to build a tagged corpus for Mongolian began at the Center for Research on Language Processing, National University of Mongolia. In the last year of this project, we developed a POS tagset and a POS tagger, and tagged around 1 million words by using them.

Currently, we have manually checked 260 thousand automatically tagged words. The rest of the tagged words have not checked yet because checking the tagged corpus needs more time and effort without any automatic or semi-automatic tool and method.

The statistical method is used in our POS tagger. The rule based method requires the Mongolian language description which is appropriate to NLP techniques such as POS tagger. But, the current description of Mongolian is quite difficult to model for the computer processing. The tagger is based on a bigram method using HMM. The tagger is trained on around 250 thousand manually tagged words, and its accuracy is around 81 percent on tagging around 1 million words.

2 POS Tagset Design

We designed a POS tagset for Mongolian corpus by studying the main materials in Mongolia (PANLocalization, 2007). According to the agglutinative characteristics of Mongolian, the number of tags is not fixed, and it is possible to be created a lot of combinations of tags.

The POS tagset consists of two parts that are a high-level tagset and a low-level tagset. The high-level tagset is similar to English tags such as noun, verb, adword etc. It consists of 29 tags (see Table 1), while the low-level tagset consists of 22 sub tags (see Table 2). The annotation of our tagset mainly follows the tagsets of PennTreebank (Beatrice, 1990) and BNC (Geoffrey, 2000).

No.	**Description**	**Tag**
	Noun	
1.	Noun	N
2.	Pronoun	PN
3.	Proper noun	RN
4.	Adjective	JJ
5.	Pro-adjective	PJ
6.	Ad-adjective	JJA
7.	Superlative	JJS
8.	Number	CD
9.	Preposition	PR
10.	Postposition	PT
11.	Abbreviation	ABR
12.	Determiner	DT
13.	Morph for possessive	POS
	Verb	
14.	Verb	V

Proceedings of the 7th Workshop on Asian Language Resources, ACL-IJCNLP 2009, pages 103–106,
Suntec, Singapore, 6-7 August 2009.

15.	Proverb	PV
16.	Adverb	RB
17.	Ya pro-word	PY
18.	Ad-adverb	RBA
19.	Modal	MD
20.	Auxiliary	AUX
21.	Clausal adverb	SRB
22.	Ge-rooted verb	GV
23.	Co-conjunction	CC
24.	Sub-conjunction	CS
	Others	
25.	Interjection	INTJ
26.	Question	QN
27.	Punctuation	PUN
28.	Foreign word	FW
29.	Negative	NEG

Table 1. High-Level Tagset for Mongolian

No.	Description	Tag
	Noun	
1.	Genitive	G
2.	Locative	L
3.	Accusative	C
4.	Ablative	B
5.	Instrumental	I
6.	Commutative	M
7.	Plural	P
8.	Possessive	S
9.	Approximate	A
10.	Abbreviated possessive	H
11.	Direction	D
	Verb	
12.	Past	D
13.	Present	P
14.	Serial verb	S
15.	Future	F
16.	Infinitive/Base	B
17.	Coordination	C
18.	Subordination	S
19.	1st person	1
20.	2nd person	2
21.	3rd person	3
22.	Negative	X

Table 2. Low-Level Tagset for Mongolian

The high-level tags are classified into noun, verb and others as shown in Table 1. In the noun column, parts of speech in the noun phrase such as adjective, number, abbreviation and so on are included. In the verb column, parts of speech in the verb phrase are included. In the other column, the parts of speech except those of the noun and verb phrases are included.

The low-level tagset is divided into two general types: noun phrase and verb phrase. It also consists of sub tags for inflectional suffixes such as cases, verb tenses etc. These tags are used mainly in combination with high-level tags.

Currently, around 198 combination tags have been created. Most of them are for noun and verb inflections. Tag marking length is 1 – 5 letters. Below we show some tagged sentences (see Figure 1).

Би	морь	унддаг
PN	**N**	**VP**
I	horse	ride
	I ride a horse	

Би	мориноос	айдаг
PN	**NB**	**VP**
I	from horse	fear
	I fear horses	

Би	мориноосоо	буулаа
PN	**NBS**	**VD**
I	from my horse	got off
	I got off my horse	

Figure 1. Mongolian Tagged Sentences

Three example sentences are shown in Figure 1. Mongolian sentence is placed in the first line, and the following lines, second, third and fourth are POS tags, English parts of speech translation and English translation, respectively. A word '*морь*' (horse) is used with different morphological forms such as nominative case in the first sentence, ablative case in the second sentence and ablative case followed by possessive in the last sentence. The noun inflected with nominative case is tagged N, the noun inflected with ablative case is tagged NB, and the noun inflected with ablative case and possessive is tagged NBS according to the two level tagset.

3 Bigram-POS Tagger

Although the statistical method needs a tagged corpus which takes a lot of time and effort, it is more reliable for languages whose linguistic descriptions have difficulties in NLP and CL purposes. Thus, we are developing a statistical POS tagger for the project.

The statistical method has been used on POS taggers since 1960s (Christopher, 2000). Some of these kinds of methods use HMM (Hidden Markov Model). The main principle of HMM is to assign the most possible tag to an input word in a sentence by using the probabilities of training data (Brian, 2007 and Daniel, 2000).

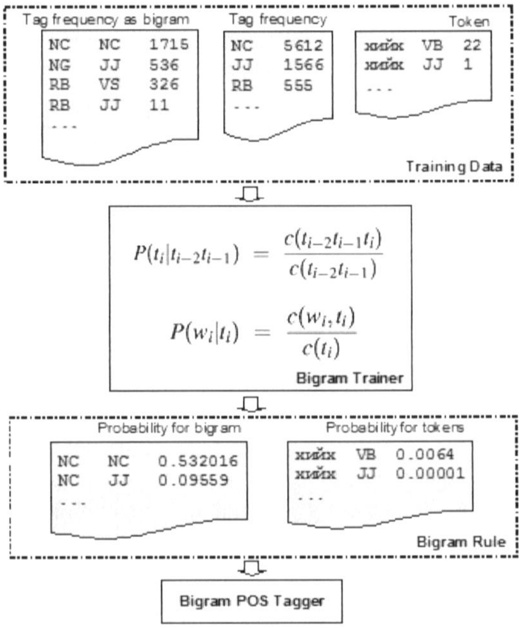

Figure 2. Overview of Mongolian Bigram tagger

The probabilities for the bigram tagger are calculated with the uni-tag frequency, the bi-tag frequency and the tokens from the training data (see Figure 2 for more detail).

4 Automatic POS Tagging

One million words of the Mongolian corpus have been tagged as the current result of the project. The tagging procedure is shown in Figure 3.

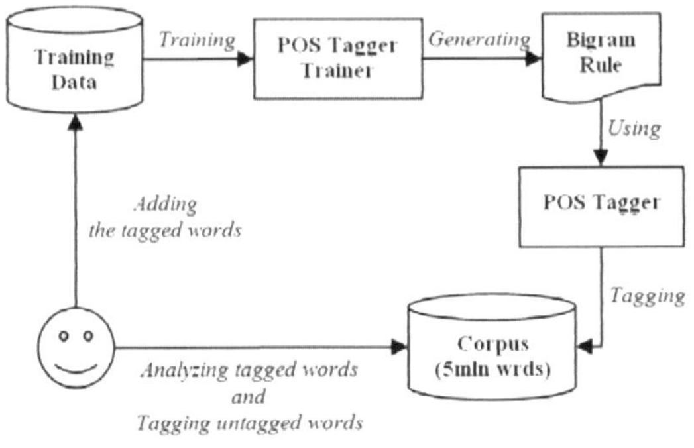

Figure 3. Automatic Tagging Procedure for Mongolian Corpus

When using the statistical POS tagger, the corpus tagging needs a training data. We have manually tagged around 110 thousand words. These 110 thousand words are used as the first training data. The statistical information on the first training data is shown in Table 3.

Words	Word type	Texts	Tags
112,754	21,867	200	185

Table 3. First Training Data

As shown in Table 3, the training data consists of 112,754 words. These words are divided into 21,867 types. This training data can be a good representative of the corpus because the texts in which distinct to total word ratio is higher are chosen (see Table 4).

No.	Texts (Files)	Distinct Words	Total Words	Percent
1.	MNCPR00320	113	125	0.9
2.	MNCPR00312	157	179	0.87
3.	MNCPR00118	118	136	0.86
4.	MNCPR00384	162	187	0.86
5.	MNCPR00122	238	279	0.85
6.	MNCPR00085	190	224	0.84
7.	MNCPR01190	320	379	0.84
8.	MNCPR00300	159	189	0.84
9.	MNCPR00497	241	288	0.83
10.	MNCPR00362	251	300	0.83

Table 4. Some Texts Chosen for Training Data

In Table 4, some of the texts that are chosen for the training data are shown. The most appropriate text that should be tagged at first is MNCPR00320 because its total words are 125 and distinct words are 113. Consequently, its equality of words types and total word is almost the same, 0.9. The first 200 texts from the corpus are manually tagged for the training data.

After training the bigram POS tagger, the corpus is tagged with it by 100 texts by 100 texts. After that, we manually checked the automatically tagged texts, and corrected the incorrectly tagged words and tagged the untagged words, in fact, new words to the training data. After manually checking and tagging, the automatically tagged texts are added to the training data for improving the tagger accuracy. Then, this whole process is done again and again. After each cycle, the training data is increased, and the accuracy of the tagger is also improved. The statistics of automatic tagging the first 100 texts is shown in Table 5.

Words	Word type	Texts	Tags	Untagged word
73,552	9,854	100	108	16,322

Untagged word type	Mistagged words	Accuracy
3,195	310	76.5

Table 5. First 100 Texts Automatically Tagged

As shown in Table 5, the untagged words are 22 percent of the total words, and 0.5 percent is tagged incorrectly. Incorrectly tagged words are manually checked. The mistagged words are caused from the insufficient training data. In the result of the first automatic tagging, the tagger that is trained on around 110 thousand words can tag 76.5 percent of around 73 thousand words correctly.

In tagging the second 100 texts, the accuracy is almost the same to the previous one because the training data is collected from texts containing more word types. The correctly tagged words are 78 percent. After checking and tagging the automatically tagged 400 texts, the training data is around 260 thousand words as shown in Table 6.

Words	Word types	Texts	Tags
260,312	27,212	400	198

Table 6. Current Training Data

We tagged another 900 texts based on the training data in Table 6. They consist of around 860 thousand words, and 81 percent is tagged. The statistics is shown in Table 7.

Words	Word type	Texts
868,258	41,939	900

Untagged words	Untagged word types	Accuracy
168,090	19,643	81

Table 7. Automatically tagged words

As shown in Table 7, the bigram POS tagger trained on 260 thousand words has tagged around 700 thousand of 868 thousand words. The accuracy is nearly the same to the previous tagging accuracy. That means the first training data is well selected, and includes main usage words. Therefore the accuracy of the first tagged 200 texts is very close to that of 900 texts tagged later.

5 Conclusion

A research project building a 5 million word corpus is in its last phase. We have automatically tagged 1 million words of the corpus by developing a POS tagset and a bigram-POS tagger for Mongolian. The tagging accuracy is around 81 percent depending on the training data. Currently, the training data is around 260 thousand words. As increasing the training data, the accuracy of the tagger can be up to 90 percent. However, the increasing training data takes a lot of time and effort. The tagset currently consists of 198 tags. It may increase in the further tagging. In this year, we are planning to tag and check the 5 million word corpus.

Acknowledgments

Here described work was carried out by support of PAN Localization Project (PANL10n).

References

Brian Roark and Richard Sproat. 2007. *Computational Approaches to Morphology and Syntax*. Oxford University Press.

Christopher D. Manning and Hinrich Schutze. 1999. *Foundations of Statistical NLP*. MIT Press.

Daniel Jurafsky, James H. Martin. 2000. *Speech and Language Processing*. Singapore.

PANLocalization Project. 2007. *Research Report on Tagset for Mongolian*. Center for Research on Language Processing, National University of Mongolia.

Purev Jaimai and Odbayar Chimeddorj. 2008. *Corpus Building for Mongolian*. The Third International Joint Conference on Natural Language Processing, Hyderabad, India.

Interaction Grammar for the Persian Language: Noun and Adjectival Phrases

Masood Ghayoomi
Nancy2 University
54506 Vandoeuvre, Nancy cedex, France
masood29@gmail.com

Bruno Guillaume
LORIA - INRIA, BP 239
54506 Vandoeuvre, Nancy cedex, France
Bruno.Guillaume@loria.fr

Abstract

In this paper we propose a modelization of the construction of Persian noun and adjectival phrases in a phrase structure grammar. This modelization uses the Interaction Grammar (IG) formalism by taking advantage of the polarities on features and tree descriptions for the various constructions that we studied. The proposed grammar was implemented with a Metagrammar compiler named XMG. A small test suite was built and tested with a parser based on IG, called LEOPAR. The experimental results show that we could parse the phrases successfully, even the most complex ones which have various constructions in them.

1 Introduction

Interaction Grammar (IG) is a grammatical formalism which is based on the notions of polarized features and tree descriptions.

Polarities express the resource sensitivity of natural language by modeling the distinction between saturated and unsaturated syntactic construction (Guillaume and Perrier, 2008).

IG focuses on the syntactic level of a natural language. This formalism is designed in such a way that it can be linked with a lexicon, independent of any formalism. The notion of polarity that is at the heart of IG will be discussed in section 2.2. In IG, the parsing output of a sentence is an ordered tree where nodes represent syntactic constituents described by feature structures.

What we are interested in is studying the construction of constituencies of the Persian language according to IG. Among various constituencies in the language, we have focused on the construction of Persian noun phrases and adjectival phrases as the first step to build a grammar for this language.

The current work covers only noun and adjectival phrases; it is only a first step toward a full coverage of Persian grammar. The grammar presented here could have been expressed in Tree Adjoining Grammar (TAG) or even in Context Free Grammar with features, but we strongly believe that the modelization of the verbal construction of Persian, which is much more complex, can benefit from advanced specificities of IG, like polarities, underspecifications and trees.

2 Previous Studies

2.1 IG for French and English

The first natural language considered within IG was French. A large coverage grammar which covers most of the frequent constructions of French, including coordination, has been built (Perrier, 2007; Le Roux and Perrier, 2007).

Recently, using the fact that the French and English languages have many syntactic similarities, Planul (2008) proposed an English IG built by modifying the French one. These two grammars were tested on the Test Suite for Natural Language Processing (TSNLP; Oepen et al, 1996). Both cover 85% of the sentences in the TSNLP.

2.2 Polarity

The notion of polarity is based on the old idea of Tesnière (1934), Jespersen (1935), and Adjukiewicz (1935) that a sentence is considered as a molecule with its words as the atoms; every word is equipped with a valence which expresses its capacity of interaction with other words, so that syntactic composition appears as a chemical reaction (Gaiffe and Perrier, 2004). Apparently, it seems Nasr (1995) was the first to propose a

Proceedings of the 7th Workshop on Asian Language Resources, ACL-IJCNLP 2009, pages 107–114,
Suntec, Singapore, 6-7 August 2009. ©2009 ACL and AFNLP

formalism that explicitly uses the polarized structure in computational linguistics. Then researches such as Muskens and Krahmer (1998), Duchier and Thater (1999), and Perrier (2000) proposed grammatical formalisms in which polarity is also explicitly used. However, Categorial Grammar was the first grammatical formalism that exploited implicitly the idea of polarity (Lambek, 1958). Recently, Kahane (2006) showed that well-known formalisms such as CFG, TAG, HPSG, and LFG could be viewed as polarized formalisms.

IG has highlighted the fundamental mechanism of neutralization between polarities underlying CG in such a way that polarities are attached to the features used for describing constituents and not to the constituents themselves. Polarization of a grammatical formalism consists of adding polarities to its syntactic structure to obtain a polarized formalism in which neutralization of polarities is used to control syntactic composition. In this way, the resource sensitivity of syntactic composition is made explicit (Kahane, 2004).

In trees expressing syntactic structures, nodes that represent constituents are labeled with polarities with the following meanings: A constituent labeled with a negative polarity (<-) represents an expected constituent, whereas a constituent labeled with the positive polarity (->) represents an available resource. Both of these polarities can unify to build a constituent which is labeled with a saturated neutral polarity (<=>) that cannot interact with any other constituents. The composition of structures is guided by the principle of neutralization that every positive label must unify with a negative label, and vice versa. Nodes that are labeled with the simple neutral polarity (=) do not behave as consumable resources and can be superposed with any other nodes any number of times; they represent constituents or features indifferently.

The notion of saturation in terms of polarity is defined as a saturated structure that has all its polarities neutral, whereas an unsaturated structure keeps positive or negative polarities which express its ability to interact with other structures. A complete syntactic tree must be saturated; that means it is without positive or negative nodes and it can not be composed with other structures: so all labels are associated with the polarity of = or <=>.

The set of polarities {-> , <- , = , <=>} is equipped with the operation of compositional unification as defined in the table below (Bonfante et al, 2004):

	<-	->	=	<=>
<-		<=>	<-	
->	<=>		->	
=	<-	->	=	<=>
<=>			<=>	

Table 1. Polarity compositions on the nodes

2.3 Tree Description Logic in IG

Another specification of IG is that syntactic structures can be underspecified: these structures are trees descriptions. It is possible, for instance, to impose that a node dominates another node without giving the length of the domination path. Guillaume and Perrier (2008) have defined four kinds of relations:

- Immediate dominance relations: $N > M$ means that M is an immediate sub-constituent of N.
- Underspecified dominance relations: $N >^{*} M$ means that the constituent N includes another constituent M at a more or less deep level. (With this kind of node relations, long distance dependencies and possibilities of applying modifiers could be expressed.)
- Immediate precedence relations: $N << M$ means that the constituent M precedes the constituent N immediately in the linear order of the sentence.
- Underspecified precedence relations: $N <<^{+} M$ means that the constituent M precedes the constituent N in the linear order of the sentence but the relation between them cannot be identified.

3 The Persian Language Properties

Persian is a member of the Indo-European language family and has many features in common with the other languages in this family in terms of morphology, syntax, phonology, and lexicon. Although Persian uses a modified version of the Arabic alphabet, the two languages differ from one another in many respects.

Persian is a null-subject language with SOV word order in unmarked structures. However, the word order is relatively free. The subject mood is widely used. Verbs are inflected in the language and they indicate tense and aspect, and agree with subject in person and number. The language does not make use of gender (Māhootiān, 1997).

In noun phrases, the sequence of words is around at least one noun, namely the head word. So, the noun phrase could be either a single unit noun, or a sequence of other elements with a noun. The syntax of Persian allows for having elements before a noun head _prenominal, and after the noun head _postnominal.

To make a phrase, there are some restrictions for the elements surrounding a head to make a constituent; otherwise the sequence of elements will be ill-formed, that is, ungrammatical.
Nouns belong to an open class of words. The noun could be a common noun, a proper noun, or a pronoun. If this noun is not a proper noun or a pronoun, some elements can come before it and some after it (Māhootiān, 1997). Some of the prenominal elements coming before a noun head are cardinal numbers, ordinal numbers, superlative adjectives, and indefinite determiners; post-nominal elements are nouns and noun phrases, adjectives and adjectival phrases, adjectival clauses with conjunctions, indefinite post-determiners, prepositional phrases, adverbs of place and time, ordinal numbers, possessive adjectives, and Ezafeh.
The syntactical structure of an adjectival phrase is simple. It is made up of a head adjective and elements that come before and after the head. An adjectival phrase is a modifier of a noun. The elements coming before a simple adjective are adverbs of quantity and prepositional phrases.

4 Required Tools

4.1 Test Suite

The test suite is a set of controlled data that is systematically organized and documented. In this case, the test suite is a kind of reference data different from data in large collections of text corpora. A test suite should have the following advantages: it should have a broad coverage on the structural level, so you can find many structures of a language with a minimal lexicon; it could be multilingual, so the structure of the languages could be compared; it should be a consistent and highly structured linguistic annotation. The differences between a test suite and a corpus are: that in test suite there is a control on the data, that the data has a systematic coverage, that the data has a non-redundant representation, that the data is annotated coherently, and that relevant ungrammatical constructions are included intentionally in a test suite (Oepen et al, 1996).
Since our end goal is to develop a fragment of Persian grammar, to the best of our knowledge no already developed test suite for our target constructions was available; so we built a very small test suite with only 50 examples based on a small lexicon _only 41 entries.

4.2 XMG

The XMG system is usually called a "metagrammar compiler" is a tool for designing large-scale grammars for natural language. This system has been designed and implemented in the framework of Benoit Crabbé (2005).
XMG has provided a compact representation of grammatical information which combines elementary fragments of information to produce a fully redundant, strongly lexicalized grammar. The role of such a language is to allow us to solve two problems that arise while developing grammars: to reach a good factorization in the shared structures, and to control the way the fragments are combined.
It is possible to use XMG as a tool for both tree descriptions in IG and TAG. Since there isnot any built-in graphical representation for IG in XMG, LEOPAR is used to display the grammar. LEOPAR is a parser for processing natural languages based on the IG formalism.

4.3 LEOPAR

LEOPAR is a tool chain constructed based on IG (Guillaume et al, 2008). It is a parser for IG that can be used as a standalone parser in which inputs are sentences and outputs are constituent trees. But it also provides a graphical user interface which is mostly useful for testing and debugging during the stages of developing the grammar. The interface can be used for interactive or automated parsing. LEOPAR also provides several visualization modes for the different steps in the parsing process. Furthermore, it offers some tools to deal with lexicons: they can be expressed in a factorized way and they can be compiled to improve parsing efficiency.
LEOPAR is based on UTF8 encoding, so it supports Persian characters. It is also modified to take into account the right-to-left languages. For our designed grammar we have taken the advantage of this parser for IG.

5 Designing the Grammar

In this section we explicitly describe the tree construction of the Persian noun and adjectival phrase structures which are polarized. We have provided the elementary syntactic structures derived from the existing rules in the language and then polarized the features in the trees which are named *initial polarized tree descriptions*.

To be more comprehensible and clear, nodes are indexed for addressing. More importantly, the trees should be read from right-to-left to match the writing system in the right-to-left language.
For clarity in the tree representations in this paper, no features are given to the nodes. But while developing the grammar with XMG, polarized features are given to the nodes to put a control on constructing the trees and avoid over-generating some constructions.
There are some constructions whose tree representations are the same but represent two different constructions, so they could be described from two different points of views. Such trees are described in the sections corresponding to the relevant constructions. Some morphophonemic phenomena were considered at the syntactic level, while developing our grammar. Such a phenomenon is defined at the feature level for the lexicon which will be described in their relevant sections.

5.1 Noun Construction

A noun phrase could consist of several elements or only one head noun element. If the element of a noun phrase (N1) is a noun, it is anchored to a lexicon item (N2) which could be a common noun, or a proper noun. The symbol ◊ has been used for the nodes that are anchored to a lexical item.

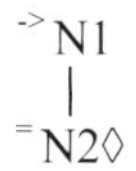

The tree of a common noun and a proper noun are the same, but features should be given to the tree to make a distinction between the anchored nouns. With the help of features, we can make some restrictions to avoid some constructions. Features and their values are not fully discussed here.

5.2 Pronoun Construction

A pronoun can appear both in subject and object positions to make a noun. In this construction, node N3 is anchored to a pronoun:

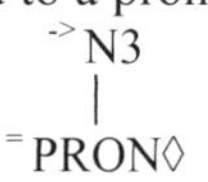

A pronoun cannot be used in all constructions. For example, N3 cannot be plugged into N5 in a determiner construction because a determiner could not come before a pronoun. To avoid this construction, some features have been used for the node N5 to stop the unification with some N nodes like N3.

5.3 Determiner Construction

In Persian a determiner comes before a common noun or a noun phrase, and not a proper noun or a pronoun.
Persian does not benefit from the definite determiner, but there are two kinds of indefinite determiners: one comes before a noun as a separate lexical item and the other one comes after a noun (post-determiner) which is joined to the end of the noun as described below:
If the determiner comes before a noun, there must be a tree in which a Det node is anchored to a lexicon item that is a determiner and which comes immediately before a noun. In other words, some lexical items which are determiners could attach to this node:

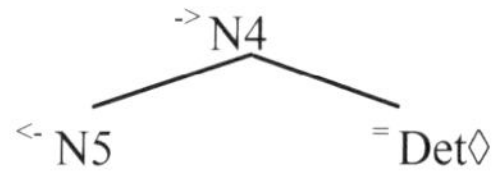

If the determiner comes after a noun (i.e. if it is a post-determiner), then it can be joined to the end of a noun. The post-determiner (P-Det) and the preceding noun (N7), make a noun (N6):

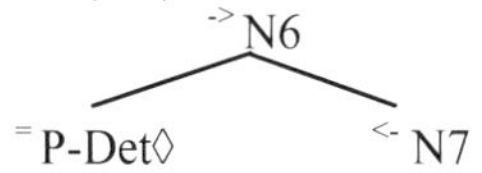

The post-determiner has three different written forms: 'ی' /i/, 'یی' /yi/, and 'ای' /?i/. The reason to have them is phonological. In our formalism we have considered this phonological phenomenon at a syntactic level.
If the post-determiner construction is used after an adjective in the linguistic data, it does not belong to the adjective (since the adjective is only the modifier of the noun), but it belongs to the noun. According to the phonological context and the final sound of the adjective, the post-determiner that belongs to the noun changes and takes one of the written forms.

5.4 Ezafeh Construction

One of the properties of Persian is that usually short vowels are not written. In this language, the Ezafeh construction is represented by the short vowel 'ِ-' /e/ after consonants or 'ی' /ye/ after vowels at the end of a noun or an adjective.
Here we try to give a formal representation of such construction that is described from a purely syntactical point of view. Ezafeh (Ez) appears on (Kahnemuyipour, 2002): a noun before another noun (attributive); a noun before an adjective; a noun before a possessor (noun or pronoun); an adjective before another adjective; a pronoun

before an adjective; first names before last names; a combination of the above.

Note that Ezafeh only appears on a noun when it is modified. In other words, it does not appear on a bare noun (e.g. 'کتاب' /ketāb/ 'book'). In Ezafeh construction, the node Ez is anchored to the Ezafeh lexeme. The below tree could make a noun phrase (N8) with Ezafeh construction, in which a common noun or a proper noun on N9 is followed by an Ezafeh (Ez) and another common noun, proper noun, pronoun or another noun phrase plugs to the node N10:

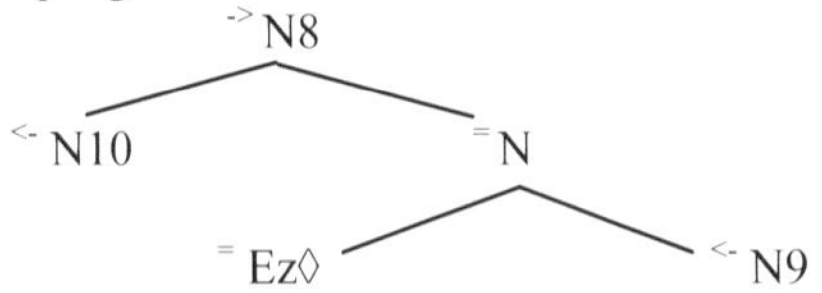

The below tree could make a noun phrase (N11) with Ezafeh construction in which a common noun or a proper noun on N12 is modified by an adjectival phrase on node ADJ1. Ezafeh has to be used after the noun to link it to the adjective:

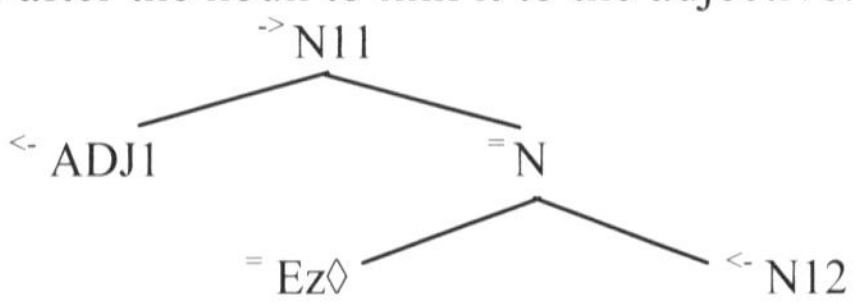

Based on the final sound of the word which is just before Ezafeh, there are two written forms for Ezafeh, depending on whether the noun ends with a consonant or a vowel.

As we have already said, Ezafeh contraction could be used for an adjective (ADJ1). After this construction, another adjectival phrase (ADJ3 and ADJ4) with Ezafeh could appear too. It should be mentioned that ADJ4 is plugged into an adjective without Ezafeh construction:

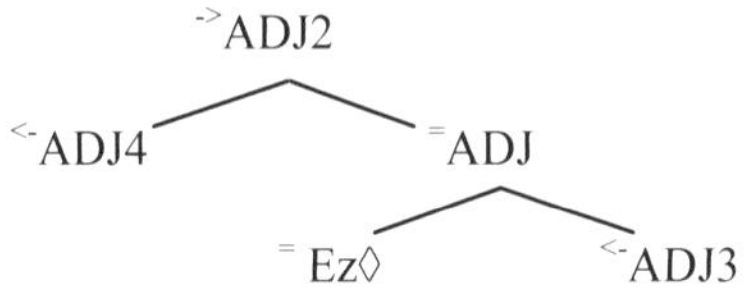

5.5 Possessive Construction

In Persian there are two different constructions for possessive. One is a separate lexical item as a common noun, a proper noun, or a pronoun. The second is a possessive pronoun that is a kind of suffix which attaches to the end of the noun. In the first construction, a noun with an Ezafeh construction is used and then a common noun, a proper noun, or a pronoun as a separate lexical item follows. In the latter construction, there is a common noun and the joined possessive pronoun. The two constructions are discussed here:

In section 5.4 we described Ezafeh construction (N8). This tree could be used for possessive construction, too. In this tree an Ezafeh is used after a common noun and Ezafeh is followed by either a common noun or a proper noun. A pronoun could not be used in N9 with Ezafeh. Such a kind of construction is avoided by defining features.

The possessive construction as a suffix could come after both a noun and an adjective. The general property of the joined possessive pronouns is that there is an agreement between the subject and the possessive pronoun in terms of number and person, no matter whether it is used after a noun or an adjective.

If the joined possessive pronoun (S-P) is used after a noun (N14), we would have the tree N13 in which the possessive pronoun is anchored to the suffix (S-P):

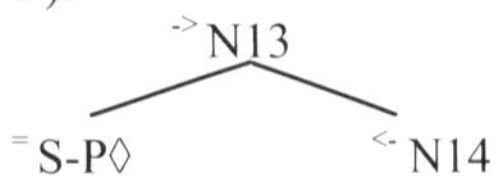

Based on the phonological reasons and considering Persian syllables, as was discussed previously in section 5.3, this suffix would have different written forms based on the phonological context it appears in: after a consonant, the vowel /ā/, or any other vowels except /ā/. For adjectives, there is no suffix possessive pronoun. In the linguistic data, this pronoun could appear after the adjective. But the point is that the adjective is only the modifier of the noun. This possessive pronoun, in fact, belongs to the noun and not the adjective, but based on the phonological rules (i.e. the final sound of the adjective) only one of the written forms would appear after that.

5.6 Count noun Construction

There are some nouns in Persian referred to as count nouns which have collocational relations with the head noun that is counted. So, in such a construction, the node C-N is anchored to a lexical item that is a count noun:

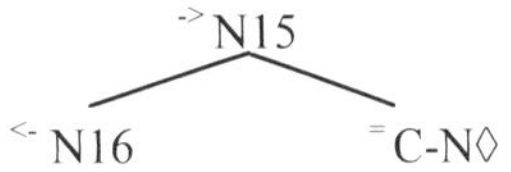

5.7 Object Construction

In Persian, a noun phrase can appear both in subject and object positions. If the noun phrase appears in a subject position, it does not require any indicator. But if the noun phrase appears in the direct object position (N18), the marker 'را' /rā/ is used to indicate that this noun phrase (N17) is a direct object. We call this marker 'Object Indicator' (O-I) so the node is anchored to the object maker. The representation of the tree for the object construction (N17) is the followings:

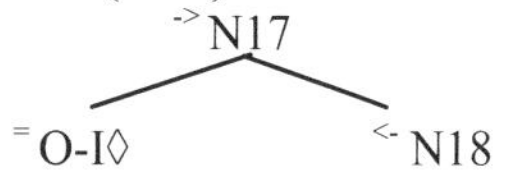

5.7 Conjunction Construction

In Persian, there is a construction to modify the preceding noun phrase with an adjective clause which we have named the Conjunction construction. In such a construction, there are a noun phrase (N20), a conjunctor (Conj), and a clause to modify the noun phrase (S1). In the tree, the conjunction node is anchored to a conjunctor:

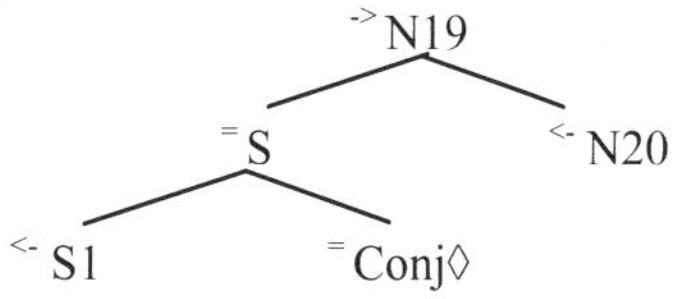

5.8 Adjective Constructions

There are two classes of adjectives: the first class comes before a noun head, the second one after.
There are three kinds of adjectives in the first class which can be differentiated from each other with the help of features. The first class of adjectives contains superlative adjectives, cardinal numbers, and ordinal numbers that modify a noun, a count noun, or a noun phrase. Usually, the adjectives coming before a noun phrase are in complementary distribution; i.e. the presence of one means the absence of the two others.
The following tree represents the adjective construction coming before a noun (N22). The adjective ADJ5 is anchored to a lexical item:

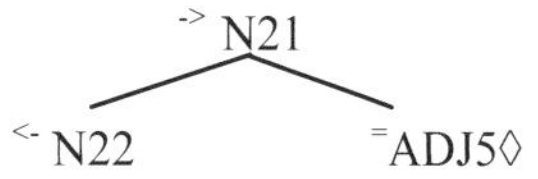

The second class of adjectives (which comes after a noun) contains mostly simple adjectives, ordinal numbers and comparative adjectives.
As we have already described tree N11 in section 5.4, to have an adjective after a noun the noun must have an Ezafeh construction. So, this tree represents a construction where an adjective (ADJ1) comes after a noun (N12).
To saturate ADJ1, the tree ADJ6 is required which is anchored to an adjective lexical item:

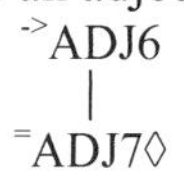

In some adjective constructions, a prepositional phrase could be used which comes before or after some adjective constituents. With the help of some features, we have made restrictions on the kind of adjective and the preposition lexical item that could plug into this node.
If a preposition is used before the adjective (ADJ9), it is a comparative adjective:

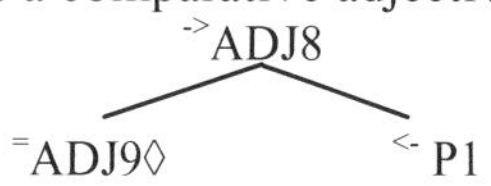

If the preposition is used after the adjective (ADJ11), it is either a comparative or a simple adjective:

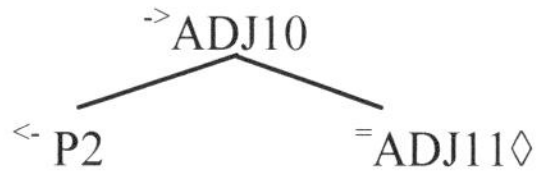

5.9 Preposition Construction

In Persian a common noun, a proper noun, a pronoun, or a noun phrase could come after a preposition (P4) to make a prepositional phrase (P3):

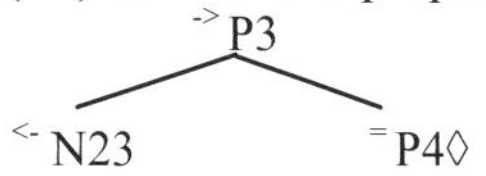

If the preposition construction is used in an adjective construction, only some specific prepositions can be used. Once again, the restrictions are encoded with features.

6 Implementation and Results

So far we have explicitly described the noun and adjectival phrase constructions in Persian according to the constituency rules that are extracted from the linguistic data. These rules are represented by polarized trees. Since we wanted to study the noun and adjectival phrase structures, they required data. We have gathered this data for our purpose as a test suite.
To design IG for the constructions that were described, we have used XMG as the basic tool to have the initial tree descriptions. While describing the trees in XMG, several operators will be used to polarizing features. The categories of the nodes are considered as features, so the nodes are polarized. Using XMG, we have done factorizations and defined classes for general trees. Three factorized general trees are defined in our XMG coding. We have also defined 17 classes for coding of trees to represent the constructions as described.
The output of XMG is given to LEOPAR to display the graphical representations of the tree structures and also parse the data. The test suite is given to LEOPAR for parsing.
Having the developed trees and the test suite, we successfully parsed all available phrases, from

the simplest to the most complex ones that had a variety of constructions in them. Example 1 has a simple construction, example 2 is of medium complexity, and example 3 is the most complex:

1. کتاب دانیال
/ketāb/ (/e/) /dāniyāl/
book (Ez) Daniel
'the book of Daniel / Daniel's book'

2. همزمان با انتشار اولین کتاب او
/hamzamān/ /bā/ /entešār/ (/e/) /avvalin/
in coincidence with publishing (Ez) the first
/ketāb/ (/e/) /?u/
book (Ez) his/her
'in coincidence with the publishing of his/her first book'

3. آن دو جلد کتاب جدید مهم دانیال را که
/ān/ /do/ /jeld/ /ketāb/ (/e/) /jadid/ (/e/)
that two volume book (Ez) new (Ez)
/mohem/ (/e/) /dāniyal/ /rā/ /ke/
important (Ez) Daniel POBJ that
'the two new important book volumes of Daniel that'

We know from section 5.4 that Ezafeh is pronounced but not written. Since the anchored nodes require a lexical item, we put the word 'اضافه' /ezāfe/ 'Ezafeh' in the lexicon to have a real representation of Ezafeh. Also, wherever Ezafeh is used in the test suite, this word is replaced.
As a sample, we give a brief description of parsing the phrases 1 and 2 with LEOPAR and display the outputs.
In our test suite, phrase 1 is found as 'کتاب اضافه دانیال'. In this phrase, the common noun /ketāb/ is followed by a proper noun /dāniyāl/ with Ezafeh. The possessive construction (N8) would be used to parse this phrase.
In parsing this phrase, firstly LEOPAR reads the words and matches them with the lexical items available in the lexicon to identify their categories. Then it plugs these words into the nodes in the trees that have the same syntactic category and have an anchored node. Finally, it gives the parsed graphical representation of the phrase.
For this phrase, the Ezafeh construction tree is used in such a way that N2 is anchored to the word /ketāb/ and N1 plugs into N9 to saturate it. Then, N2 is again anchored to the word /dāniyāl/ and N1 plugs in to saturate N10. The final parsed phrase is such that all internal nodes are saturated and have neutral polarity, as shown in Figure 1.
As another example, consider phrase 2, which is

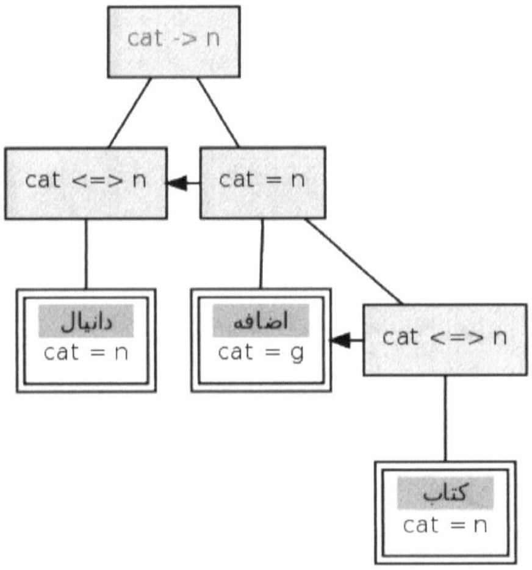

Figure 1: Parsing the phrase 'کتاب دانیال' with LEOPAR

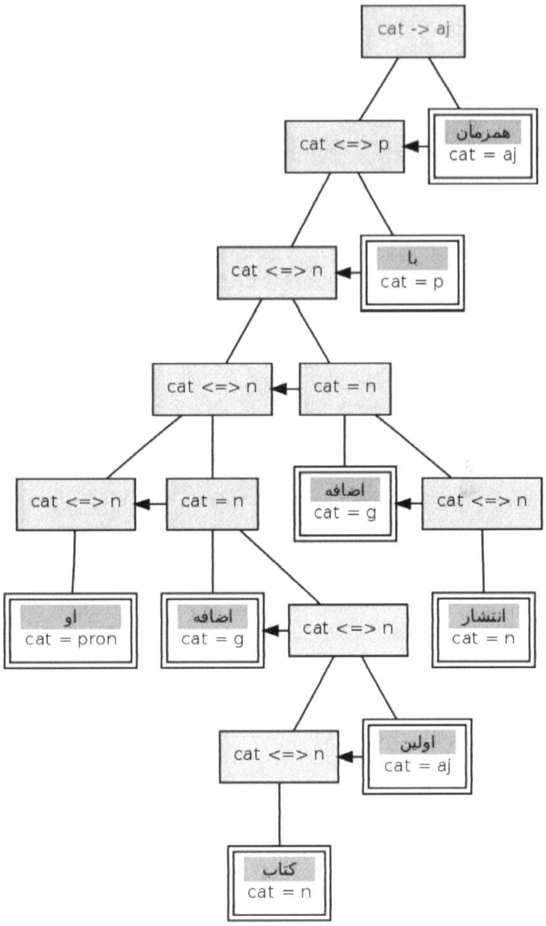

Figure 2: Parsing the phrase 'همزمان با انتشار اولین کتاب او' with LEOPAR

found as 'همزمان با انتشار اضافه اولین کتاب اضافه او' in our test-suite. Since some various constructions are used to build this phrase, we could say that it is a complex phrase. Firstly it takes the adjective phrase construction (ADJ10). P3, the prepositional phrase, plugs into P2. Since a noun or a noun phrase could be used after a preposition (N23), the Ezafeh construction (N8) that takes the noun plugs to this node. Another Ezafeh construction (N8) will be plugged into N10. The adjective construction (ADJ5) for ordinal numbers as the modifier of a noun (N22) could be used while a noun (N1) would plug into N22. Finally, the pronoun (N3) plugs into the unsaturated noun position in the second Ezafeh construction. Parsing the phrase with LEOPAR, the result has all internal nodes saturated and neutralized, and no polarities on the nodes are left unsaturated, as shown in Figure 2.

7 Conclusion and Future Work

In our research we have used IG to represent the construction of Persian noun and adjectival phrases in trees. XMG was used to represent the constructions using factorization and inherited hierarchy relations. Then, with the help of XMG, we defined IG by taking advantage of polarities on the features and tree descriptions for the various constructions that are introduced. Then, we used LEOPAR for the graphical representations of the trees and parsing the phrases. Finally, we applied our test suite to the parser to check whether we had the correct parsing and representation of the phrases. The experimental results showed that we could parse the phrases successfully, including the most complex ones, which have various constructions in them.

In the next step of our research, we would like to study the construction of prepositions and, more importantly, verbs in depth to make it possible to parse at the sentence level.

References

Adjukiewcz K., 1935. "Die syntaktiche konnexität" *Studia Philadelphica* 1, pp. 1-27.

Bonfante G. and B. Guillaume and G. Perrier, 2004. "Polarization and abstraction of grammatical formalism as methods for lexical disambiguation" In *Proc.s of 20th Int. Conf. on CL, Genève.*

Candito, M. H., 1996. 'A principle-based hierarchical representa-tion of LTAGs'. *COLING-96.*

Crabbé, B., 2005. "Grammatical development with XMG". *LACL 05.*

Duchier and Thater, 1999. "Parsing with tree descriptions: A constraint based approach" In *Proc.s of NLU and Logic Programming, New Mexico.*

Gaiffe, B. and G. Perrier, 2004. 'Tools for parsing natural language' *ESSLLI 2004.*

Guillaume B. and G. Perrier, 2008. "Interaction Grammars" INRIA Research Report 6621: http://hal.inria.fr/inria-00288376/

Guillaume B. and J. Le Roux and J. Marchand and G. Perrier and K. Fort and J. Planul, 2008, "A Toolchain for Grammarians" *CoLING 08, Manchester.*

Jesperson , O., 1935. *Analytic Syntax.* Allen and Uwin, London.

Kahane, S., 2004. "Grammaries d'unification polarisées" In *11iéme Conf. sur le TAL, Fés, Maroc.*

Kahane, S., 2006. "Polarized unification grammars". In *Proce.s of 21st Int. Conf. on CL and 44th Annual Meeting of the ACL. Sydney, Australia.*

Kahnemuyipour, A., 2000. "Persian Ezafe construction revisited: Evidence for modifier phrase," *Annual Conf. of the Canadian Linguistic Association.*

Lambek, J., 1958. "The mathematics of sentence structure", *The American Mathematical Monthly* 65: 154–170.

Leopar: a parser for Interaction Grammar http://leopar.loria.fr/

Le Roux, J. and G. Perrier, 2007. "Modélisation de la coordination dans les Grammaires d'Interaction", *Traitement Automatique des Langues* (TAL 47-3)

Māhootiān, Sh, 1997. *Persian.* Routledge.

Muskens and Krahmer, 1998. "Talking about trees and truth conditions". In *Logical Aspects of CL, Grenoble, France*, Dec 1998.

Nasr A., 1995. "A formalism and a parser for lexicalized dependency grammars" In *Proce.s of 4th Int. Workshop on Parsing Technologies, Prague.*

Oepen, S. and K. Netter and J. Klein, 1996. "TSNLP-Test suites for natural language processing". In *Linguistic Database*, CSLI Lecture Notes. Center for the Study of Language and information.

Perrier, G., 2000. "Interaction grammar" *Coling 2000.*

Perrier, G., 2007. "A French Interaction Grammar", *RANLP 2007, Borovets Bulgarie.*

Planul, J., 2008. *Construction d'une Grammaire d'Interaction pour l'anglais*, Master thesis, Université Nancy 2, France.

Tesnière L., 1934. "Comment construire une syntaxe" *Bulletin de la Faculté des Lettres de Strasbourg* 7-12iéme. pp. 219-229.

XMG Documentation http/wiki.loria.fr/wiki/XMG/Documentation

KTimeML: Specification of Temporal and Event Expressions in Korean Text

Seohyun Im
Dept. of Computer Science
Brandeis University
Waltham, MA, USA
ish97@cs.brandeis.edu

Hyunjo You, Hayun Jang, Seungho Nam, Hyopil Shin
Dept. of Linguistics
Seoul National University
Seoul, Korea
youhyunjo, hyan05, nam, hpshin@snu.ac.kr

Abstract

TimeML, TimeBank, and TTK (TARSQI Project) have been playing an important role in enhancement of IE, QA, and other NLP applications. TimeML is a specification language for events and temporal expressions in text. This paper presents the problems and solutions for porting TimeML to Korean as a part of the Korean TARSQI Project. We also introduce the KTTK which is an automatic markup tool of temporal and event-denoting expressions in Korean text.

1 Introduction

The TARSQI (Temporal Awareness and Reasoning systems for QA) Project[1] aims to develop technology for annotation, extraction, and reasoning of temporal information in natural language text. The main result of the TARSQI Project consists of TimeML (Pustejovsky et. al., 2003), TimeBank (Pustejovsky et. al., 2006), and TARSQI Toolkit (TTK, Verhagen and Pustejovsky, 2008). TimeML is a specification language for events and temporal expressions in text. TimeBank is an annotated corpus which was made as a proof of the TimeML specification. TTK is an automatic system to extract events and time expressions, creating temporal links between them[2].

TimeML is an ISO standard of a temporal markup language and has been being extended to other languages such as Italian, Spanish, Chinese, etc. (ISO/DIS 24617-1: 2008). TempEval-2, a task for the Semeval-2010 competition, has been proposed (Pustejovsky et. al. 2008). The task for the TempEval-2 is evaluating events, time expressions, and temporal relations. Data sets will be provided for English, Italian, Spanish, Chinese, and Korean.

The necessity of temporal and event expressions markup for any robust performance such as QA (for Korean QA system, refer to Han et. al., 2004), IE, or summarization is applied to Korean NLP applications as well. Recently, there have been TimeML-related studies for Korean: Jang et. al (2004) show an automatic annotation system of temporal expressions with Timex2 in Korean text. Lee (2008) argues about the semantics of Korean TimeML, specially the EVENT tag. Im and Saurí (2008) focus on the problems of TimeML application to Korean caused by typological difference between English and Korean. Motivated by them, the Korean TARSQI Project[3] started with the purpose of making TimeML, TimeBank and TTK for Korean text[4].

Porting TimeML to other languages can be challenging because of typological difference between languages. In this paper, we present the problems for TimeML application to Korean. Our solution is to change TimeML markup philosophy: a change from word-based in-line annotation to morpheme-based stand-off annotation. Based on the changed annotation philosophy, we decide how to annotate temporal and event-denoting expressions in Korean text. More specifically, it is challenging to decide whether we use LINK tags or attributes to annotate some

---

[1] Refer to www.timeml.org for details on the TARSQI.

[2] TTK contains GUTime (TIMEX3 tagging, Mani and Wilson, 2000), Evita (event extraction, Saurí et. al., 2005), Slinket (modal parsing, Saurí et. al., 2006b), S2T, Blinker, Classifier, Sputlink, Link Merger, etc.

[3] See http://word.snu.ac.kr/k-tarsqi/doku.php for more information about the KTARSQI Project.

[4] James Pustejovsky gave a talk about TARSQI for KTARSQI Project, visiting Korea for his invited talk at CIL 18 conference in 2008.

Proceedings of the 7th Workshop on Asian Language Resources, ACL-IJCNLP 2009, pages 115–122,
Suntec, Singapore, 6-7 August 2009.

temporal or event-denoting expressions (see examples in 3.2). In section 4, we describe the specification of Korean TimeML (KTimeML). Section 5 introduces Korean TTK (KTTK). Before discussing the issues of Korean TimeML, we briefly introduce TimeML.

2 The Basics of TimeML

TimeML features four major data structures: EVENT, TIMEX3, SIGNAL, and LINK. The **EVENT** tag encodes event-denoting expressions. The **TIMEX3** tag annotates temporal expressions of different sorts: fully specified dates, times, and durations, or just partially specified dates, times, and durations. The **SIGNAL** tag annotates elements that indicate how temporal objects are related among them (e.g., subordinating connectors such as *when* or *after*).

The LINK tag splits into three main types: (a) **TLINK**, which encodes temporal relations among EVENTs and TIMEX3s; (b) **ALINK**, representing aspectual information as expressed between an aspectual predicate and its embedded event; and (c) **SLINK**, encoding subordination relations conveying evidentiality (e.g. *Mary* ***said*** *[she bought some wine*]), factivity (*John* ***regretted*** *[Mary bought wine]*), or intensionality (*Kate* ***thought*** *[Mary bought beer]*).

Information relevant to each tag is characterized by means of attribute-value pairs (refer to Pustejovsky et. al. 2003 about specific attributes-value pairs). (1) illustrates an annotated sentence with the TimeML specification:

(1) *John* <u>*said*</u>$_{e1}$ *that Mary* <u>*began*</u>$_{e2}$ *to* <u>*work*</u>$_{e3}$

```
John
<EVENT id="e1" class="REPORTING"
tense="PAST" aspect="NONE" polar-
ity="POS">
said </EVENT>
that Mary
<EVENT id="e2" class="ASPECTUAL"
tense="PAST" aspect="NONE" polar-
ity="POS">
began </EVENT>
to
<EVENT id="e3" class="OCCURRENCE"
tense="NONE" aspect="NONE" polar-
ity="POS">
work </EVENT>

<TLINK eventID="e1" relatedToEvent="e2"
relType="AFTER"/>
<SLINK eventID="e1" subordinatedEvent="e2"
relType="EVIDENTIAL"/>
<ALINK eventID="e2" relatedToEvent="e3"
relType="INITIATES"/>
```

Sentence (1) presents three EVENT expressions (*said, began,* and *work*). SLINK conveys an evidential relation between *e1* (*said*) and *e2* (*began*). TLINK represents a temporal relation – `AFTER`– between the two same events. ALINK encodes an aspectual relation –`initiates`– between *e2* (*began*) and *e3* (*work*). Due to space limitations, some EVENT attributes are obviated.

3 Porting TimeML to Korean

3.1 The Characteristics of Korean

Korean is an agglutinative language whose words are formed by joining morphemes together, where an affix typically represents one unit of meaning and bound morphemes are expressed by affixes. For example, the sentence *John-i emeni-kkeyse o-si-ess-ta-te-ra* 'John-Nom mother-Nom come-Hon-Past-Quo-Ret-Dec [5] ' means that (I heard) (John said) that his mother came. Each morpheme has its own functional meaning or content.

As shown above, consideration of morphemes is important for TimeML markup of Korean text. Here, we summarize TimeML-related characteristics of Korean:

(i) In Korean, functional markers (tense, aspect, mood, modality, etc.) are represented morphologically. English as an isolating language uses periphrastic conjugation to represent functional categories.
(e.g. '*-keyss-*'is a conjectural modal morpheme in *pi-ka o-keyss-ta* 'it will rain'. While, '*will*' is an auxiliary verb in *it will rain.*)

(ii) Some subordination is realized morphologically via morpheme contraction.
(e.g. '*-ta-n-ta*' is a morphological contraction which denotes quotation in the sentence *John-i nayil o-n-ta-n-ta* 'John-Nom tomorrow come-Pres-Dec.Quo-Pres-Dec'. Its English counterpart is represented by subordination: *John* <u>*said*</u> *that he will* <u>*come*</u> *tomorrow*)

(iii) Some connectives in English correspond to morphemes in Korean.
(e.g. Korean counterpart of the English connective '*and*' in *I ate milk and went to sleep* is the morpheme '*-ko*' in the sentence *na-nun wuyu-rul masi-ko ca-re ka-ss-ta* 'I-Top milk-Acc drink-and sleep-ending go-Past-Dec')

(iv) The sentence type of English is represented by word order but that of Korean by ending morphemes
(e.g. Declarative: *pi-ka o-n-*<u>*ta*</u> 'it is raining' interrogative: *pi-ka o-*<u>*ni*</u>*?* 'Is it raining?')

---

[5] Nom: nominative case, Hon: honorific morpheme, Past: past tense morpheme, Quo: quotative mood morpheme, Ret: retrospective mood morpheme, Dec: declarative sentence ending

These properties of Korean make the porting of TimeML to Korean challenging. In the next section, we discuss the basic issues of KTimeML.

3.2 Basic Issues of Korean TimeML

3.2.1 Morpheme-based standoff annotation

TimeML employs word-based in-line annotation. It poses a challenge at the representation level, since it encodes information mainly based on the structure of the target language, and thus content equivalences among different languages are hard to establish. For example, indirect quotation in Korean offers an example of the mismatch of linguistic devices employed in different languages to express the same meaning. Quotation constructions in English use two predicates, the reporting and the reported, which TimeML marks up as independent EVENTs:

(2) *John <u>said</u>$_{e1}$ he <u>bought</u>$_{e2}$ a pen.*

```
<SLINK eventID="e1" subordinatedE-
vent="e2"relType="EVIDENTIAL"/>
```

TimeML uses a subordination link (SLINK) in order to convey the evidentiality feature that the reporting predicate projects to the event expressed by its subordinated argument.

On the other hand, a Korean quotative construction, as in (3), has only one verb stem, which corresponds to the subordinated predicate in English. Note that there is no reporting predicate such as *say* in English. Nevertheless, the sentence has a reporting interpretation.

(3) John-i ku-ka wine-ul sa-ss-ta-n-ta
J-Nom he-Nom wine-Acc buy-**Past**-Quo-**Pres**-Dec
'John **said** that he **bought** some wine'

The quotative expression *–ta-n-ta* above is a contracted form of *–ta-ko malha-n-ta* 'Dec-Quo say-Pres-Dec'. Although (3) is a simple sentence involving no subordination at the syntactic level, the two tense markers, '*-ss-*' and '*-n-*', are evidence of the existence of an implicit reporting event. Specifically, the past tense marker '*-ss-*' applies to the main event here (*sa-ss* 'buy-past'), while the present tense marker '*-n-*' is understood as applying to the implicit reporting event (*ta-n-ta* 'report-pres-Dec)[6].

Constructions presented above show a problem for the standard TimeML treatment of a Korean quotative sentence. The relationship between reporting and reported events is expressed morphologically, and thus the SLINK mechanism for word-based annotation is not adaptable here. Because Korean transfers meanings through morphological constructions, morpheme-based annotation is more effective than word-based for TimeML application to Korean[7].

For morpheme-based tagging, we propose stand-off annotation for Korean because it needs two-level annotation: the MORPH tag[8] and TimeML tags. Standoff annotation separates morphologically-annotated data from primary data and saves it in a different file, and then TimeML annotation applies to the data. The following is the proposed morpheme-based stand-off annotation for (3).

(4) Morpheme-based stand-off annotation for (3)

```
<MORPH id="m7" pos="PV"/>
<MORPH id="m8" pos="EFP"/>
<MORPH id="m9" pos="EFP"/>
<MORPH id="m10" pos="EFP"/>
<MORPH id="m11" pos="EF"/>
<EVENT id="e1" morph="m7 m8" yaleRo-
manization="sa-ss" pred="buy"
class="OCCURRENCE" tense="PAST" sen-
tenceMood="DEC"/>
<EVENT id="e2" morph="m9 m10 m11"
yaleRomanization="ta-n-ta" pred="say"
class="REPORTING" tense="PRESENT" sen-
tenceMood="DEC"/>
<SLINK eventID="e2" subordinatedE-
vent="e1" relType="EVIDENTIAL"/>
<TLINK eventID="e1" relatedToEvent="e2"
relType="BEFORE"/>
```

In (4), we show the example annotation of the MORPH tag for (3) to help readers to understand our proposal. Standoff annotation makes it possible to extract information about two events without using a non-text consuming EVENT tag. Moreover, each of the two tense morphemes is properly assigned to its related event. Our proposed TimeML annotation scheme is composed of two levels – morphological analysis and TimeML annotation.

[6] Tense markers of the construction can change: *sa-**ss**-tay-**ss**-ta* 'buy-**past**-quo-**past**-dec: *said_bought*'; *sa-**n**-ta-**n**-ta* 'buy-**pres**-quo-**pres**-dec: *say_buy*', etc.

[7] There can be several ways of annotating morphological constructions: morpheme-based, morpho-syntactic unit-based (refer to MAF: Clément and Clergerie, 2005), character-based, and bunsetsu-based. At present, we adopt morpheme-based annotation because it seems to be enough to introduce the required units for KTimeML markup and we want to avoid the possible redundancy of bunsetsu-based or morpho-syntactic unit-based annotation. Moreover, the criterion for separation of a morphological construction is related with tags such as EVENT, TIMEX3, or attributes like tense, aspect, mood, or modality in KTimeML, not with syntactic or phonological information. Standoff annotation makes it easy to mark up the interval of morphemes. Nevertheless, we consider the possible advantage of morpho-syntactic analysis positively for future work.

[8] The values of the POS attribute are based on a Korean Part_of_Speech Tag Set version 1.0 (Kim and Seo, 1994).

3.2.2 Surface-based annotation

KTimeML adopts the surface-based annotation philosophy of TimeML (Saurí et. al. 2006a), which does not encode the actual interpretation of the constructions it marks up, but their grammatical features. For example, the *leaving* event in the sentence *we are leaving tomorrow* is not annotated as expressing a future tense, but as expressed by means of a present tense form. Several considerations motivate this surface-based approach. As an annotation language, it must guarantee the marking up of corpora in an efficient and consistent way, ensuring high inter-annotator agreement. As a representation scheme, it needs to be used for training and evaluating algorithms for both temporal information extraction and temporal reasoning.

A surface-based approach is the suitable option for meeting such requirements. Nevertheless, it poses a challenge at the representation level. How to represent evidentiality in Korean and English shows the challenge.

(5) *I* *saw*$_{e1}$ *that John* *bought*$_{e2}$ *some wine.*
<SLINK lid="sl1" eventID="e1" subordinatedEvent="e2" relType="EVIDENTIAL"/>

English, as an isolating language, expresses evidentiality in a periphrastic manner. Hence, the TimeML treatment of these constructions consists in marking the two involved predicates as EVENTs, and introducing an SLINK between them. Korean has both periphrastic and morphological ways for expressing evidentiality. Annotating the periphrastic version with the standard TimeML treatment poses no problem because it has two predicates denoting events like its English counterpart. Morphological constructions however, are harder to handle, because the retrospective mood morpheme '*-te-*' brings about the implicit reference to a seeing event.

```
(6) Vietnam-un     tep-te-ra
    Vietnam-Top    hot-Ret-Dec
    '(as I saw) Vietnam was hot'
```

They are similar to quotative constructions in the sense that, although there is only one predicate expressed on the surface, the sentence refers to more than one event. Unlike quotative constructions, there is no morphological evidence of the implicit event; e.g. tense or sentence mood markers independent of those applied to the only verbal predicate in the sentence. The issue to consider is therefore whether to treat the evidential constructions by introducing an EVENT tag for the retrospective mood marker as in (7) or to handle them by specifying the evidential value of the main predicate at the MOOD attribute of its EVENT tag, as illustrated in (8).

(7) SLINK tagging for (6)

```
<EVENT id="e1" morph="m3" yaleRomanization="tep" class="STATE" pos="ADJECTIVE" tense="NONE"/>
<EVENT id="e2" morph="m4 m5" yaleRomanization="te-ra" class="PERCEPTION" pos="NONE" tense="NONE"/>
<SLINK lid="sl1" eventID="e2" subordinatedEvent="e1" relType="EVIDENTIAL"/>
```

(8) Mood-attribute tagging for (6)

```
<EVENT id="e1" morph="m3 m4 m5" yaleRomanization="tep-te-ra" pred="hot" class="STATE" pos="ADJECTIVE" tense="NONE" mood="RETROSPECTIVE"/>
```

As in (7), adding an EVENT tag for the retrospective morpheme corresponds semantically to English-based TimeML. However, it is not surface-based, because the perception event is an implicit event entailed by the retrospective morpheme. While, the annotation in (8) is a surface-based annotation of the evidential construction which uses the MOOD attribute for retrospective mood, thus respects the surface-based philosophy of TimeML. This is different from the English counterpart that presents two EVENTs related with a TLINK signaling their relative temporal order. KTimeML follows the surface-based annotation philosophy of TimeML ((8) here).

3.2.3 Cancellation of the head-only rule

TimeML employs the head-only markup policy in order to avoid problems derived from tagging discontinuous sequence (e.g. *we* **are** *not fully* **prepared**). If the event is expressed by a verbal phrase, the EVENT tag will be applied only to its head, which is marked in bold face in the examples (e.g. *has been* ***scrambling***, *to* ***buy***, *did not* ***disclose***). However, Korean does not have the discontinuity problem. See Korean examples:

```
(9) a.*na-nun cwunpitoy-e    wanpyekhakey  iss-ta
       I-Top  prepared-e     fully         exist-Dec
      'we are fully prepared'
    b. *John-un  ca-ko        anh-iss-ta
        J-Top    sleep-ko     Neg-exist-Dec
       'John is not sleeping'
```

In the above sentences, '*-e iss-*' and '*-ko iss-*' are respectively perfective and progressive aspect markers. No word can make discontinuous sequence by being embedded into the middle of the verb phrases. As we saw from the examples, Korean does not have discontinuity problem in verbal phrases. Thus, KTimeML does not need to follow the head-only annotation rule. By cancellation of the head-only rule, we annotate various verbal clusters (main verb + auxiliary verb construction: e.g. *mek-ko iss-ta* 'eat-progressive-dec'). It makes the KTimeML more readable by showing the progressive aspect-denoting expression *-ko iss-* in one unit of annotation.

4 Specification of the Korean TimeML

Based on the proposed annotation principles of KTimeML, we present the specification of the first version of KTimeML (KTimeML 1.1) with changed tags, attributes, and their values. We assume that the MORPH-tagged data are separately saved in a different file. KTimeML contains EVENT, TIMEX3, SIGNAL, and LINK tags. Some new attributes such as `mood` and `sType` are added to the attributes of the EVENT tag. The other tags have no changes from the TimeML tags[9].

KTimeML 1.1 adds the attributes of predicate_content (`pred`), `mood`, verb_form (`vForm`), and sentence type (`sType`) to the attributes of EVENT in TimeML (For Korean grammar, refer to Sohn, 1999, Nam and Ko, 2005). The BNF of EVENT is shown below:

```
attributes ::= id pred morph yaleRomanization
               class pos tense [aspect][mood]
               [sType][modality] vForm
id ::= ID
{id ::= EventID
 EventID ::= e<integer>}
morph ::= IDREF
{morph ::= MorphID}
yaleRomanization ::= CDATA
pred ::= CDATA
class ::= 'OCCURRENCE'|'ASPECTUAL'|'STATE'|
          'PERCEPTION'|'REPORTING'|'I_STATE'|
          'I_ACTION'
pos ::= 'ADJECTIVE'|'NOUN'|'VERB'|'OTHER'
tense ::= 'PAST' | 'NONE'
aspect ::= 'PROGRESSIVE'|'PERFECTIVE'|
           'DURATIVE' | 'NONE'
mood ::= 'RETROSPECTIVE' | 'NONE'
         {default, if absent, is 'NONE'}
sType ::= 'DECLARATIVE'|'INTERROGATIVE'|
          'IMPERATIVE'|'PROPOSITIVE'| 'NONE'
         {default, if absent, is 'DECLARATIVE'}
modality ::= 'CONJECTUAL'|'NONE'
         {default, if absent, is 'NONE'}
vForm ::= 'S_FINAL'|'CONNECTIVE'|'NOMINALIZED'|
          'ADNOMINAL'
         {default, if absent, is 'S_FINAL'}
polarity ::= 'NEG'|'POS'
         {default, if absent, is 'POS'}
```

KTimeML puts the semantic content of EVENT-tagged expressions for international communication. Because mood is not an important grammatical category for English, TimeML does not markup a mood attribute, but KTimeML adds the mood attribute since there are morphemes that express mood like many other languages. Unlike English, different sentence ending morphemes represent sentence types in Korean. Hence, KTimeML adds `sType` to attributes of the EVENT tag. We put `vForm` to distinguish between different subordinated clauses[10].

Event classes in KTimeML are the same as TimeML. Korean tense system does not have distinction between present and future unlike English, and thus the tense attribute has PAST and NONE values. We add DURATIVE to aspect attribute values in KTimeML for the durative expression such as combination of stative verb + progressive aspect marker (e.g. *al-ko iss-ta* 'know-durative-Dec').

For `mood`, KTimeML 1.1 puts the retrospective mood ('*-te-*'). The values of `vForm` attribute are S_FINAL, CONNECTIVE, and NOMINALIZED, and ADNOMINAL. The sentence types in Korean are DECLARATIVE, INTEROGGATIVE, IMPERATIVE, and PROPOSITIVE (e.g. *cip-ey ka-**ca*** 'Let's go home'). KTimeML puts CONJECTURAL (e.g. *nayil pi-ka o-**keyss**-ta* '(I guess) It will rain tomorrow') as a modality value and default is NONE. The sentence in (10) is an interesting example that includes all attributes of an EVENT tag for Korean TimeML except for aspect.

```
(10)ecey   Seoul-un  pi-ka  o-ass-keyss-te-ra
     yesterday Seoul-Top rain-Nom come-Past-Conj-Ret-Dec
     '(From that I saw), I guess that it rained in Seoul
      yesterday'

  <EVENT id="e1" morph="m6 m7 m8 m9 m10"
   yaleRomanization="wa-ss-keyss-te-ra"
   pred="come" pos="VERB"
   class="OCCURRENCE" tense="PAST"
   aspect="NONE" mood="RETROSPECTIVE"
   modality="CONJECTURAL" vForm="S_FINAL"
   sType="DECLARATIVE" polarity="POS"/>
```

Each of the morphemes above has its own functional meaning, which is represented as a value of an attribute in the EVENT tag.

The major types of TIMEX3 expressions are: (a) Specified Temporal Expressions, *2009-nyen 5-wol 1-il* '2009-year 5-month 1-day', (b) Underspecified Temporal Expressions, *wolyoil* 'Monday', *caknyen* 'last year', *ithul cen* 'two days ago'; (c) Durations, 2 *kaywol* '2 months', 10 *nyen* 'ten years'.

```
attributes ::= tid type [functionInDocument]
               [temporalFunction] morph
               yaleRomanization
               (value|valueFromFunction)
               [mod][anchorTimeID|anchorEventID]
```

[9] Nevertheless, how to annotate various morphological constructions in the specific texts is not trivial. The annotation guideline, which will be published on the web, will handle the issues in detail.

[10] ISO-TimeML also has `pred`, `mood`, and `vForm`.

```
tid ::= ID
{tid ::= TimeID
 TimeID ::= t<integer>}
morph ::= IDREF
{morph ::= MorphID}
yaleRomanization ::= CDATA
type ::= 'DATE'|'TIME'|'DURATION'
functionInDocument ::= 'CREATION_TIME'|
         'EXPIRATION_TIME'|'MODIFICATION_TIME'|
         'PUBLICATION_TIME'|'RELEASE_TIME'|
         'RECEPTION_TIME'|'NONE'
temporalFunction ::= 'true'|'false'
         {temporalFunction ::= boolean}
value ::= CDATA
         {value ::= duration|dateTime|
                    time|date|gYearMonth|
                    gYear|gMonthDay|
                    gDay|gMonth}
valueFromFunction ::= IDREF
{valueFromFunction ::= TemporalFunctionID
TemporalFunctionID ::= tf<integer>}
mod ::= 'BEFORE'|'AFTER'|'ON_OR_BEFORE'|
        'ON_OR_AFTER'|'LESS_THAN'|'MORE_THAN'|
        'EQUAL_OR_LESS'|'EQUAL_OR_MORE'|'START|
        'MID'|'END'|'APPROX'
anchorTimeID ::= IDREF
        {anchorTimeID ::= TimeID}
comment ::= CDATA
```

Although the BNF of TIMEX3 in Korean TimeML is same as that of TimeML, we point out that Korean time expressions also have the issue of how to treat morphological representations of temporal meaning. For example, *pwuthe* 'from' and *kkaci* 'to' in *3ilpwuthe* 5il*kkaci* 'From 3rd to 5th' both are the counterparts of prepositions in English (Jang et. al., 2004). We do not tag temporal morphemes as SIGNALs, in principle. Instead, we mark up *3ilpwuthe* 'from 3rd' with one TIMEX3 tag. However, temporal connectives such as *ttay* 'when' in *ku-ka o-ass-ul ttay younghee-nun ttena-ss-ta* 'When he came, Younghee left' are tagged as SIGNALs.

SIGNAL is used to annotate sections of text - typically function words - that indicate how temporal objects are to be related to each other. It includes temporal connectives (e.g. *ttay* 'when', *tongan* 'during'), and temporal noun (e.g. *hwu* 'after', *cen* 'before'). See the BNF of SIGNAL below:

```
attributes ::= sid morph yaleRomanization
sid ::= ID
{sid ::= SignalID
SignalID ::= s<integer>}
morph ::= IDREF
{morph ::= MorphID}
yaleRomanization ::= CDATA
```

We show an annotated example which describes the difference of Korean TimeML markup from the English-based TimeML. The sentence below is a compound sentence.

```
(11) ku-nun hankwuk panghan-ul maci-n hwu,
     Ku-Top  Korea    visit-Acc   finish  after
     onul  cwungkwuk-uro ttena-ss-ta
     today China-for      leave-Past-Dec
     'He finished his visit to Korea
     and left for China today'
```

```
<Document time: March, 20, 2009>
<EVENT id="e1" morph="m4 m5" yaleRomaniza-
   tion="pangmwun-ul"
 pred="visit" class="OCCURRENCE"/>
<EVENT id="e2" morph="m6 m7" yaleRomaniza-
   tion="machi-n" pred="finish"
   class="ASPECTUAL" pos="VERB"
   tense="NONE" vForm="ADNOMINAL"/>
<SIGNAL sid="s1" morph="m8" yaleRomaniza-
   tion="hwu"/>
<TIMEX3 tid="t1" morph="m9" yaleRomaniza-
   tion="onul" type="DATE" value="2009-03-
   20" temporalFunction="true"/>
<EVENT id="e3" morph="m14 m15 m16" yaleRo-
   manization="ttena-ss-ta"
 pred="leave" class="OCCURRENCE"
 tense="PAST" sType="DECLARATIVE"
 vForm="S_FINAL"/>
```

LINK types splits into TLINK, SLINK, and ALINK. The BNF of TLINK is as follows:

```
attributes ::= [lid] (eventID|timeID)
               [signalID] (relatedToEvent|
               relatedToTime) relType [comment]
lid ::= ID
{lid ::= LinkID
 LinkID ::= l<integer>}
eventID ::= IDREF
{eventID ::= EventID}
timeID ::= IDREF
{timeID ::= TimeID}
signalID ::= IDREF
{signalID ::= SignalID}
relatedToEvent ::= IDREF
{relatedToEvent ::= EventID}
relatedToTime ::= IDREF
{relatedToTime ::= TimeID}
relType ::= 'BEFORE'|'AFTER'|INCLUDES'|
            'IS_INCLUDED'|'DURING'|
            'SIMULTANEOUS'|'IAFTER'|'IBEFORE'|
            'IDENTITY'|'BEGINS'|'ENDS'|
            'BEGUN_BY'|'ENDED_BY'|'DURING_INV'
comment ::= CDATA
```

TLINK is a temporal link among EVENTs and TIMEX3s. For example, three TLINKs are tagged between the events in (11). We show those together with other LINKs in (12). Now, we show the BNF of SLINK.

```
attributes ::= [lid] eventID [signalID]
               subordinatedEvent relType
               [comment]
lid ::= ID
{lid ::= LinkID
 LinkID ::= l<integer>}
eventID ::= IDREF
{eventID ::= EventID}
subordinatedEvent ::= IDREF
{subordinatedEvent ::= EventID}
signalID ::= IDREF
{signalID ::= SignalID}
```

```
relType ::= 'INTENTIONAL'|'EVIDENTIAL'|
            'NEG_EVIDENTIAL'|'FACTIVE'|
            'COUNTER_FACTIVE'|'CONDITIONAL'
comment ::= CDATA
```

The subordination link is used for contexts involving modality, evidentials, and factives.

In Korean, various morphemes bring about subordination clauses. Nominal endings such as -*um/-ki* make nominal clauses (e.g. *na-nun John-i o-ass-**um**-ul al-ko iss-ta* 'I-Top John-Nom come-Past-Nominal ending-Acc know-Durative-Dec'; *na-nun kongpwuha-**ki**-ka shilh-ta* 'I-Top study-nominal ending-Nom hate-Dec'). Adnominal endings such as *-n/-un/-nun* make adnominal clauses (e.g. *na-nun John-i kaci-e-o-**n** kwaca-rul mek-ess-ta* 'I-Top John-Nom bring-adnominal ending cookies-Acc eat-Past-Dec'). Conditional clauses are also triggered by morphemes (e.g. *na-nun John-i o-**myen** ka-keyss-ta* 'I-Top John-Nom come-Conditional go-Conj-Dec'). All the above morphemes are not separately tagged as SIGNALs. The words with the morphemes – *o-ass-um-ul, kongpwuha-ki-ka, kaci-e-o-n,* and *o-myen* – are tagged as EVENTs.

ALINK is an aspectual link which indicates an aspectual connection between two events.

```
attributes ::= [lid] eventID [signalID]
               relatedToEvent relType
               [comment]
lid ::= ID
{lid ::= LinkID
 LinkID ::= l<integer>}
eventID ::= IDREF
{eventID ::= EventID}
relatedToEvent ::= IDREF
{relatedToEvent ::= EventID}
signalID ::= IDREF
{signalID ::= SignalID}
relType ::= 'INITIATES'|'CULMINATES'|
            'TERMINATES'|'CONTINUES'|
            'REINITIATES'
comment ::= CDATA
```

Now we show the ALINK and TLINKs of the sentence in (11).

```
(12) LINKs between the events in (11)
    <ALINK eventID="e2" relatedToEvent="e1"
    relType="CULMINATES"/>
    <TLINK eventID="e3" relatedToEvent="e2"
    relType="AFTER"/>
    <TLINK eventID="e2" relatedToEvent="e1"
    relType="ENDS"/>
    <TLINK eventID="e3" relatedToEvent="e1"
    relType="AFTER"/>
```

That is, the *visiting* event and the *finishing* are related aspectually and its relation type is culminating. The *finishing* event is related temporally with the *leaving* event by the signal '후'('after'). Naturally, the relation type of the TLINK is AFTER. From ALINK, additional TLINKs are derived between *visiting, finishing*, and *leaving* events.

5 Korean TARSQI ToolKit

Based on the specification of KTimeML, we started to develop KTTK[11].

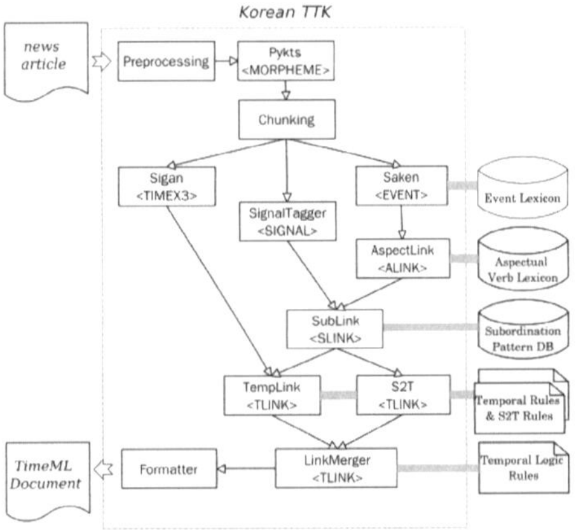

Figure 1. Korean TARSQI Architecture

At first, the normalization of the raw document is done in the preprocessor module. Here the raw text is separated into sentences, wide characters are substituted by regular characters, punctuation symbols are normalized (specially quotation marks), sino-korean characters (hanja) are transcribed in hangul, and, the encoding is also normalized to unicode.

The next module is called Pykts (Python Wrapper for KTS). Here, sentences are parsed in order to get their morphological components, which is achieved by means of a program called KTS. With the exception of this morphological parser, which was programmed in C, all the other components of our project are being written in Python in order to achieve good results in less time. The output of Pykts is a Document object composed by a hyerarchical data structure of document, sentences, words and morphemes, which is passed to the Event Tagger.

The Event Tagger consists of three modules: a preprocessor where the chunking of Time Expressions is done; a module called Saken, which does the tagging of events; and, a module called Sigan for TIMEX3 tagging. Then, LINK

[11] The architecture mainly relies on that of TTK. However, KTTK introduces a morphological analyzer for morpheme-based standoff annotation. KTTK uses the Aspectual Verb Lexicon for ALINK extraction.

taggers add TLINK, ALINK, SLINK tags. A module S2T changes the annotated SLINKs and ALINKs into TLINKs. In the final step, the LINK Merger merges all TLINKs with temporal closure.

6 Conclusion and Future Work

Temporal and event information extraction is an important step for QA and other inference or temporal reasoning systems. Korean TARSQI Project aims at (1) making KTimeML; (2) building Korean TimeBank as a gold standard, and (3) developing KTTK as an automatic markup tool of temporal and event expressions in Korean text.

In this paper, we presented problems in porting TimeML to Korean and proposed changes of TimeML philosophy. Since consideration of morphological issues is a basic step for KTimeML, we introduce a morpheme-based two-level stand-off annotation scheme. We adopt the surface-based annotation of TimeML, but do not follow the head-only annotation.

The tags of KTimeML are EVENT, TIMEX3, TLINK, ALINK, and SLINKs. The morphological annotation is saved as separate data. The EVENT tag has the attributes such as `vForm`, `sType`, `mood`, and `modality` in addition to the attributes of TimeML. We showed the architecture of KTTK.

This work will be a help for QA, IE, and other robust performance for Korean. In addition, KTimeML will be, hopefully, a model for porting TimeML to other agglutinative languages such as Japanese.

Aknowledgements

The authors wish to thank Kiyong Lee (ISO-TimeML) and James Pustejovsky, a director of the TARSQI Project, for their help for the specification of KTimeML.

References

Lionel Clément and Éric Villemonte de la Clergerie. 2005. MAF: a Morphosyntactic Annotation Framework. In *Proceedings of the Language and Technology Conference*, Poznan, Poland, pages 90-94.

Han, Kyoung-Soo, Hoojung Chung, Sang-Bum Kim, Young-In Song, Joo-Young Lee, and Hae-Chang Lim. 2004. TREC 2004 Question Answering System at Korea University. In *Proceedings of the 13rd Text REtrieval Conference*, Pages 446-455. Gettysburg, USA.

Im, Seohyun and Roser Saurí. 2008. TimeML Challenges for Morphological Lanuages: A Korean Case Study. In *Proceedings of CIL* 18, Seoul, Korea.

ISO DIS 24617-1:2008. *Language resources management – Semantic annotation framework (SemAF) – Part1: Time and events. ISO 2008*. Unpublished.

Jang, Seok-Bae, Jennifer Baldwin, and Inderjeet Mani, 2004. Automatic TIMEX2 Tagging of Korean News. In *Proceedings of ACM Transactions on Asian Language Information Processing*. Vol. 3, No. 1, Pages 51-65.

Kim, Jae-Hoon and Seo, Jung-yeon. 1994. ms. *A Korean Part-of-Speech Tag Set for Natural Language Processing* Version 1.0. KAIST. Seoul, Korea.

Kiyong, Lee, 2008. Formal Semantics for Temporal Annotation, An invited plenary lecture for CIL 18. In *Proceedings of the 18th International Congress of Linguists*, CIL 18, Seoul, Korea.

Inderjeet Mani and George Wilson. 2000. Processing of News. In *Proceedings of the 28th Annual Meeting of the Association for Computational Linguistics (ACL 2000)*, Pages 69-76.

Nam, Ki-Shim and Yong-Kun Ko, 2005. *Korean Grammar (phyojwun kwuke mwunpeplon).* Top Publisher. Seoul, Korea

Pustejovsky, J., M. Verhagen, X. Nianwen, R. Gaizauskas, M. Happle, F. Shilder, G. Katz, R. Saurí, E. Saquete, T. Caselli, N. Calzolari, K.-Y. Lee, and S.-H. Im. 2008. *TempEval2: Evaluating Events Time Expressions and Temporal Relations: SemEval Task Proposal.*

James Pustejovsky, Jessica Littman, Roser Saurí, Marc Verhagen. 2006. *TimeBank 1.2. Documentation.*

James Pustejovsky, José Castaño, Robert Ingria, Roser Saurí, Robert Gaizauskas, Andrea Setzer, and Graham Katz. 2003. TimeML: Robust Specification of Event and Temporal Expressions in Text. IWCS-5. *Fifth International Workshop on Computational Semantics.*

Roser Saurí, Jessica Littman, Bob Knippen, Robert Gaizauskas, Andrea Setzer, and James Pustejovsky. 2006a. *TimeML Annotation Guidelines* Version 1.2.1.

Roser Saurí, Marc Verhagen, and James Pustejovsky. 2006b. SlinkET: A Partial Modal Parser for Events. In *Proceedings of LREC* 2006. Genova, Italy.

Roser Saurí, Robert Knippen, Marc Verhagen and James Pustejovsky. 2005. Evita: A Robust Event Recognizer for QA Systems. In *Proceedings of HLT/EMNLP 2005*, Pages 700-707.

Sohn, Ho-Min. 1999. *The Korean Language*. Cambridge University Press.

Marc Verhagen and James Pustejovsky. 2008. Temporal Processing with the TARSQI Toolkit. In *proceedings Coling 2008: Companion volume - Posters and Demonstrations*, Pages 189-192.

CWN-LMF: Chinese WordNet in the Lexical Markup Framework

Lung-Hao Lee[1], Shu-Kai Hsieh[2], Chu-Ren Huang[1,3]

[1]Institute of Linguistics, Academia Sinica
[2]Department of English, National Taiwan Normal University
[3]Department of Chinese & Bilingual Studies, The Hong Kong Polytechnic University
[1]128 Academia Road, Section 2, Taipei 115, Taiwan
[2]162 He-ping East Road, Section 1, Taipei 106, Taiwan
[3]Hung Hom, Kowloon, Hong Kong
[1]{lunghao,churen}@gate.sinica.edu.tw
[2]shukai@ntnu.edu.tw
[3]churen.huang@inet.polyu.edu.hk

Abstract

Lexical Markup Framework (LMF, ISO-24613) is the ISO standard which provides a common standardized framework for the construction of natural language processing lexicons. LMF facilitates data exchange among computational linguistic resources, and also promises a convenient uniformity for future application. This study describes the design and implementation of the WordNet-LMF used to represent lexical semantics in Chinese WordNet. The compiled CWN-LMF will be released to the community for linguistic researches.

1 Introduction

Princeton WordNet[1] is an English lexical database that groups nouns, verbs, adjectives and adverbs into sets of cognitive synonyms, which are named as synsets (Fellbaum, 1998; Miller, 1995). The Global WordNet Association (GWA)[2] built on the results of Princeton WordNet and Euro WordNet (Vossen, 2004) is a free and public association that provides a platform to share and connect all languages in the world. For Mandarin Chinese in Taiwan, Huang et al. (2004) constructed the Academia Sinica Bilingual Ontological Wordnet (Sinica BOW) which integrates WordNet, English-Chinese Translation Equivalents Database (ECTED) and SUMO for cross-language linguistic studies. As a follow-up, Chinese WordNet (CWN) has been built as a robust lexical knowledge system which also embodies a precise expression of sense relations (Huang et al., 2008). In recent years, WordNet-like resources have become one of the most reliable and essential resources for linguistic studies for all languages (Magnini and Cavaglia, 2000; Soria et al. 2009; Strapparava and Valitutti, 2004).

Lexical Markup Framework (LMF, ISO-24613) is the ISO standard which provides a common standardized framework for the construction of natural language processing lexicons (Francopoulo et al., 2009). One important purpose of LMF is to define a standard for lexicons which covers multilingual lexical information (Francopoulo et al., 2006b). In this study, we describe the design and implementation of the Wordnet-LMF (Soria et al. 2009) to represent lexical semantics in Chinese WordNet.

The rest of this paper is organized as follows: Section 2 introduces Chinese WordNet and Lexical Markup Framework. Section 3 describes how we represent Chinese WordNet in the Lexical Markup Framework (CWN-LMF). Section 4 presents an example on Chinese word sense distinction using CWN-LMF format. Quantitative analysis of compiled CWN-LMF is presented in Section 5. We also describe the application scenario using CWN-LMF for information interoperability of lexical semantics in Section 6. Section 7 discusses the experience and difficulties of encoding CWN into Wordnet-LMF. Finally, Section 8 concludes this study with future research.

[1] Wordnet, available online at http://wordnetweb.princeton.edu/perl/webwn

[2] Global WordNet Association (GWA), available online at http://www.globalwordnet.org/

Proceedings of the 7th Workshop on Asian Language Resources, ACL-IJCNLP 2009, pages 123–130,
Suntec, Singapore, 6-7 August 2009. ©2009 ACL and AFNLP

2 Related Work

2.1 Chinese WordNet

Creating a semantic relation-based language resource is a time consuming and labor intensive task, especially for Chinese due to the unobvious definition and distinction among characters, morphemes and words. Chinese WordNet [3] (CWN) has been built by Academia Sinica and is successively extended its scope so far. Lemmas included in CWN mainly fall on the medium frequency words. Each lexical entry is analyzed according to the guidelines of Chinese word sense distinctions (CKIP, 2003; Huang et al. 2003) which contain information including Part-of-Speech, sense definition, example sentences, corresponding English synset(s) from Princeton WordNet, lexical semantic relations and so on. Unlike Princeton WordNet, CWN has not been constructed mainly on the synsets and semantic relations. Rather it focuses to provide precise expression for the Chinese sense division and the semantic relations needs to be based on the linguistic theories, especially lexical semantics (Huang et al., 2008). Moreover, Huang et al. (2005) designed and implemented the Sinica Sense Management System (SSMS) to store and manage word sense data generated in the analysis stage. SSMS is meaning-driven. Each sense of a lemma is identified specifically using a unique identifier and given a separate entry. There are 8,646 lemmas / 25,961 senses until December 2008 have been analyzed and stored in SSMS. Figure 1 shows the result of sense distinction for 足跡 zu-ji 'footprint' as an example in Chinese WordNet.

Huang et al. (2004) proposed Domain Lexico-Taxonomy (DLT) as a domain taxonomy populated with lexical entries. By using DLT with Chinese WordNet and Domain Taxonomy, there were 15,160 Chinese senses that linked and distributed in 463 domain nodes. In addition, Huang et al. (2005) further applied DLT approach to a Chinese thesaurus called as CiLin and showed with evaluation that DLT approach is robust since the size and number of domain lexica increased effectively.

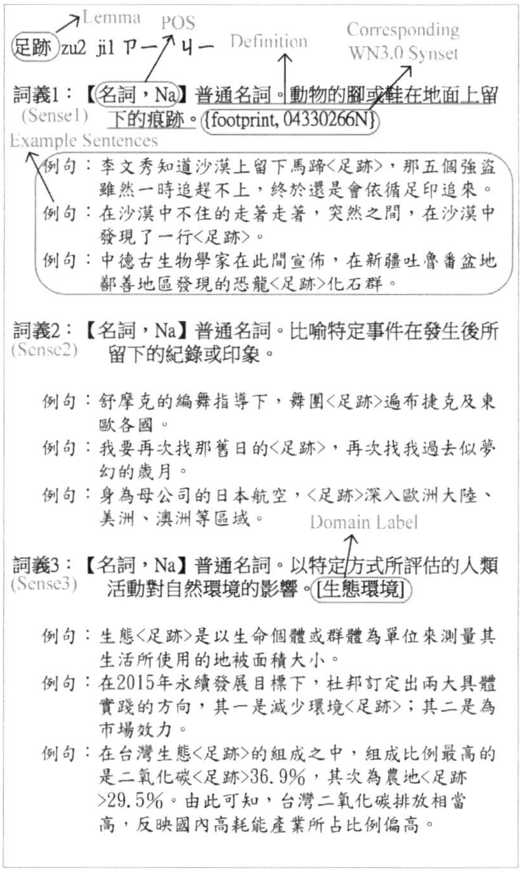

Figure1: The result of sense distinction for "zu2 ji1 (footprint)".

2.2 Lexical Markup Framework

Lexical Markup Framework (LMF, ISO-24613) is the ISO standard for natural language processing lexicons and machine readable dictionaries. The goals of LMF are to provide a common model for the creation and use of lexical resources, and to manage the exchange of data between them. Francopoulo et al. (2006a; 2009) offered a snapshot of how LMF represents multilingual lexicons. LMF facilitates data exchange among computational linguistic resources and also promises a convenient uniformity for future application. More updated information can be found online at http://www.lexicalmarkupframework.org .

Soria et al. (2009) proposed a Wordnet-LMF developed in the framework of the KYOTO [4] project as a standardized interoperability format for the interchange of lexico-semantic information. Wordnet-LMF is an LMF dialect tailored to encode lexical resources adhering to the Word-

[3] Chinese WordNet, available online at http://cwn.ling.sinica.edu.tw/

[4] KYOTO, available online at http://www.kyoto-project.eu/

Net model of lexical knowledge representation. Wordnet-LMF was designed by adhering to LMF principles yet taking into account on the one hand, the peculiarities of the Wordnet model, and on the other by trying to maximize the efficiency of the format.

If we take Princeton WordNet 3.0 synset {footprint_1} for example, a Wordnet-LMF representation can be found in Figure 2. The details will be explained in Section 3.

```
<Synset id="eng-30-06645039-n" baseConcept="1">
<Definition gloss="mark of a foot or shoe on a surface">
<Statement example="the police made casts of the
footprints in the soft earth outside the window"/>
</Definition>
<SynsetRelations>
<SynsetRelation target="eng-30-06798750-n"
relType="has_hyperonym">
</SynsetRelation>
<SynsetRelation target="eng-30-06645266-n"
relType="has_hyponym">
</SynsetRelation>
</SynsetRelations>
<MonolingualExternalRefs>
<MonolingualExternalRef externalSystem="Wordnet1.6"
externalReference="eng-16-01234567-n">
<MonolingualExternalRef externalSystem="SUMO"
externalReference="superficialPart" relType="at">
</MonolingualExternalRefs>
<Synset>
```

Figure 2: An example of Wordnet-LMF format.

3 CWN in the Lexical Markup Framework (CWN-LMF)

Wordnet-LMF is used to represent lexical semantics in Chinese WordNet. As *LexicalResource* is the root element in Wordnet-LMF, it has three children: one *GlobalInformation* element, one or more *Lexicon* elements, zero or *one SenseAxes* element. This means the object *LexicalResource* is the container for possibly more than one *lexicon;* inter-lingual correspondences are grouped in *SenseAxes* section. The details are presented as follows.

3.1 Global Information

The element named as *GlobalInformation* is used to describe general information about the lexical resource. The attribute "label" is a free text field. Example as follows:
<GlobalInformation label="Compile Chinese Wordnet entries using Wordnet-LMF">

3.2 Lexicon

In CWN-LMF, only one element *Lexicon* is used to contain a monolingual resource as a set of *LexicalEntry* instances followed by a set of *Synset* elements. The following attributes are specified:

- languageCoding: It has "ISO 639-3" as a fixed value.
- language: The standardized 3-letter language coding, e.g. zho, is used to specify the language represented by the lexical resource. It is a required attribute.
- owner: It is a required attribute to specify the copyright holder
- version: It is a required attribute to specify the resource version.
- label: It is used to record additional information that may be needed. This attribute is optional.

Example as follows:
<Lexicon languageCoding="ISO 639-3" label="Chinese WordNet 1.6" language="zho", owner="Academia Sinica", version="1.6">.

3.2.1 Lexical Entry

A *LexicalEntry* element can contain one lemma and one sense and has an optional attribute "id" which means a unique identifier.

The element, Lemma, represents a word form chosen by convention to designate the lexical entry. It contains the following attributes:

- partOfSpeech: It is a required attribute. This attribute takes as its value the part-of –speech value that according to WordNet conventions is usually specified for a synset. There are four part-of-speech notations that are used in CWN-LMF. The notation "n" is represented as a noun; the notation "v" is represented as a verb; the notation "a" is represented as an adjective; the notation "r" is represented as an adverb; and the other POS tags are represented as "s".
- writtenForm: It is added in case that "id" of *LexicalEntry* is numerical and it takes Unicode strings as values. This attribute is optional.

The *Sense* element represents one meaning of a lexical entry. For WordNet representation, it represents the variant of a synset. Required attributes are:

- id: It must be specified according to the convention used in Chinese WordNet, i.e. word_sense#nr.. For example, "環境_1" means that the first sense of lemma 環境 huan-jing 'environment'.
- synset: It takes as its value the ID of the synset to which the particular sense of the variant belongs. The ID of the synset will be described in the next subsection.

Take the first sense of lemma 環境 huan-jing 'environment' for example, it will be represented as follows:

```
<LexicalEntry>
   <Lemma writtenForm="環境" partOfS-
peech="n"></Lemma>
   <Sense id="環境_1" synset=" zho-16-
06640901-n"></Sense>
</LexicalEntry>
```

3.2.2 Synset

This element encodes information about a Chinese WordNet synset. *Synset* elements can contain one *Definition*, optional *SynsetRelations* and *MonolingualExternalRefs* elements. Required attributes for *Synset* element are the following:

- id: It is a unique identifier. The agreed syntax is "languageCode-version-id-POS". For example, "zho-16-06640901-n" is unique identifier of the first sense of lemma 環境 huan-jing 'environment'.
- baseConcept: Values for the *baseConcept* attribute will be numerical (1,2,3), which correspond to the BaseConcept sets. If the sense belongs to the first-class basic words of NEDO project (Tokunaga et al. 2006), we encode it as 1. Similarly, if the sense belongs to second-class basic words, we encode it as 2. The other senses will be encoded as 3 if they are not basic words.

The element *Definition* allows the representation of the gloss associated with each synset in attribute "gloss". The required attribute "example" of the element *Statement* contains the examples of use associated with the synset .

SynsetRelations is a bracketing element for grouping all *SynsetRelation* elements. Relations between synsets are codified by means of *SynsetRelation* elements, one per relation. Required attributes are:

- target: It contains the ID value of the synset that is the target of the relation.
- relType: It means the particular type. There are nine semantic relations in Chinese WordNet, including "has_synonym", "has_nearsynonym", "has_hypernym", "has_hyponym", "has_holonym", "has_meronym", "has_paranym", "has_antonym" and "has_variant". Among them, the semantic relation paranymy is used to refer to relation between any two lexical items belonging to the same semantic classification (Huang et al. 2008). For example, the set of "spring/summer/fall/winter" has paranymy relation of main concept of "seasons in a year".

MonolingualExternalRefs is a bracketing element to group all *MonolingualExternalRef* elements. *MonolingualExternalRef* elements must be used to represent links between a Sense or Synset and other resources, such as an ontology, a database or other lexical resources. Attributes are:

- externalSystem: It is a required attribute to describe the name of the external resource. For instance, possible values are "domain" (Magnini and Cavaglia, 2000), "SUMO" (Niles and Pease, 2001), and "Wordnet 3.0" for recording SenseKey values.
- externalReference: It means the particular identifier or node. This attribute is required.
- relType: It is optional attribute. If the "externalSystem" is "SUMO". "relType" is the type of relations with SUMO ontology nodes. Possible values are "at", "plus", and "equal".

We use the first sense of lemma 環境 huan-jing ‘environment’ to illustrate as follows:

```
<Synset id="zho-16-06640901-n" baseCon-
cept="2">
  <Definition gloss="普通名詞。人類及其他
  生物生存的空間。">
    <Statement example="人類與非人類都非
    常脆弱，常因自然環境改變而受到嚴重
    傷害。"/>
  </Definition>
  <SynsetRelations>
     <SynsetRelation target="zho-16-
     07029502-n" relType="has_synonym">
     </SynsetRelation>
  </SynsetRelations>
  <MonolingualExternalRefs>
     <MonolingualExternalRef externalSys
     tem="SUMO" externalRefe
     rence="GeographicArea" rel
     Type="plus"/>
   </MonolingualExternalRefs>
</Synset>
```

3.3 SenseAxes

SenseAxes is a bracketing element that groups together *SenseAxis* elements used for inter-lingual correspondences. The *SenseAxis* element is a means to group synsets belonging to different monolingual wordnets and sharing the same equivalent relation to Princeton WordNet 3.0. Required attributes are:

- id: It is a unique identifier.
- relType: It specifies the particular type of correspondence among synsets belonging to different resources. We use “eq_synonym” to represent equal synonym relation between Chinese Wordnet and Princeton WordNet.

For instance, Chinese synset zho-16-06640901-n maps onto English synset eng-30-08567235-n by means of an eq_synonym relation. This will be represented as follows:

```
<SenseAxes>
   <SenseAxis id="sa_zho16-eng30_5709" rel
   Type="eq_synonym">
      <Target ID="zho-16-06640901-n"/>
      <Target ID="eng-30-08567235-n"/>
   </SenseAxis>
</SenseAxes>
```

4 An Example of CWN-LMF Format

Take 自然 zi-ran ‘nature’ as an example shown in Figure 3. 自然 has six senses (some of them are abridged in the figure). Id attribute of the first sense is 自然_1 and its synset is called “zho-16-03059301-n”. This encoding of synset stands for 自然_1 with the unique ID 03059301 in Chinese WordNet version 1.6 and its part-of-speech is noun. Moreover, one can also learn that 自然_1 has a synonym, 大自然_1 (zho-16-06653601-n). Meanwhile, this sense is also corresponded to IEEE SUMO. Finally, this compiled CWN-LMF version is pointed to Princeton WordNet 3.0, i.e. Chinese synset “zho-16-03059301-n” maps onto English synset “eng-30-11408559-n” by means of an eq_synonym relation.

```
<?xml version="1.0" encoding="UTF-8"?>
<!DOCTYPE LexicalResource SYSTEM "kyoto_wn.dtd">
<LexicalResource>
   <GlobalInformation label="CWN-LMF" />
   <Lexicon languageCoding="ISO 693-3" label="Chinese
    Wordnet 1.6" language="zho" owner="Academia Sinica"
    version="1.6" >
     <LexicalEntry>
       <Lemma writtenForm="自然" partOfSpeech="n">
       </Lemma>
       <Sense id="自然_1" synset="zho-16-03059301-n">
       </Sense>
     </LexicalEntry>
     ...............
     <Synset id="zho-16-03059301-n" baseConcept="3">
       <Definition gloss="普通名詞。天然生成的環境與事物。">
         <Statement example="風景畫家走出工作室，開始描繪
         戶外的自然" />
       </Definition>
       <SynsetRelations>
         <SynsetRelation target="zho-16-06653061-n"
         relType="has_synonym">          (大自然_1)
       </SynsetRelation>
       <MonolingualExternalRefs>
          <MonolingualExternalRef externalSystem="SUMO"
          externalReference="(ComplementFn)InternationalProcess"
          relType="plus" />
       </MonolingualExternalRefs>
     </Synset>
     ...............
   </Lexion>
   <SenseAxes>
     <SenseAxis id="sa_zho16-eng30_17638" relType="eq_synonym">
       <Target ID="zho-16-03059301-n"> (自然_1)
       <Target ID="eng-30-11408559-n"> (nature)
     </SenseAxis>
     ...............
   </SenseAxes>
</LexicalResource>
```

Figure 3: The lemma 自然 in CWN-LMF format.

5 Quantitative Analysis of CWN-LMF

There are 8,646 lemmas / 25,961 senses until December 2008 have been analyzed in CWN 1.6. So far the work on Chinese word distinction is still ongoing. It is expected that there are more analyzed results in the next released version.

Among analyzed 25,961 senses, there are 268 senses and 1,217 senses that belong to the first-class and the second –class basic words, respectively. When part-of-speech is concerned, we can find most of these senses belong to nouns or verbs. There are 12,106 nouns, 10,454 nouns, 806 adjectives and 1,605 adverbs in CWN 1.6

We further distinguish semantic relations of CWN 1.6 and found that there are 3,328 synonyms, 213 near synonyms, 246 hypernyms, 38 hyponyms, 3 holonyms, 240 paranyms, 369 antonyms and 432 variants, respectively.

The IEEE SUMO is the only external system for monolingual references in CWN-LMF. There are 21,925 senses that were pointed to SUMO so far. In addition, there are 17,952 senses which shared the same equivalent relation to Princeton WordNet 3.0 in CWN-LMF.

6 Application Scenarios

The EU-7 project, KYOTO (Knowledge Yielding Ontologies for Transition-based Organization), wants to make knowledge sharable between communities of people, culture, language and computers, by assigning meaning to text and giving text to meaning (Vossen et al., 2008a; 2008b). The goal of KYOTO is a system that allows people in communities to define the meaning of their words and terms in a shared Wiki platform so that it becomes anchored across languages and cultures but also so that a computer can use this knowledge to detect knowledge and facts in text.

KYOTO is a generic system offering knowledge transition and information across different target groups, transgressing linguistic, cultural and geographic boundaries. Initially developed for the environmental domain, KYOTO will be usable in any knowledge domain for mining, organizing, and distributing information on a global scale in both European and non-European languages.

Whereas the current Wikipedia uses free text to share knowledge, KYOTO will represent this knowledge so that a computer can understand it. For example, the notion of environmental *footprint* will become defined in the same way in all these languages but also in such a way that the computer knows what information is necessary to calculate a *footprint*. With these definitions it will be possible to find information on footprints in documents, websites and reports so that users can directly ask the computer for actual information in their environment, for instance, what is the footprint of their town, their region or their company.

KYOTO's principal components are an ontology linked to WordNets in seven different languages (Basque, Chinese, Dutch, English, Italian, Japanese and Spanish). Due to different natures of languages, the different designed architectures were used to develop WordNets in theses languages. A unified framework is needed for information exchange. LMF is hence adopted as the framework at lexical semantic level in this project. The WordNet in these languages are compiled with designed WordNet-LMF format. CWN-LMF will also be involved and benefit for cross-language interpretabilities in semantic search field.

7 Discussion

Due to characters of Chinese language, there are some difficulties of encoding Chinese WordNet into Wordnet-LMF. A brief description is presented as follows.

Chinese WordNet was designed for Chinese word sense distinction and its lexical semantic relationships. The designed architecture belongs to word-driven, not synset-driven. So in CWN-LMF, we encoded a sense as an individual synset and marked up the "has_synonym" relation when senses belong to the same WordNet synset.

In addition, how to define the basic concept of Chinese language is difficult. So far the basic word lists of the NEDO project were used as preliminary basis. We need a further method to distinguish *baseConcept* attribute of word senses.

8 Conclusions

This study describes the design and implementation of how the Wordnet-LMF used to represent lexical semantics in Chinese WordNet. CWN-LMF is benefit for data exchange among computational linguistic resources, and also promises a convenient uniformity for domain-specific applications such as KYOTO in cross-language semantic search field.

Future work is investigated with several directions. We are planning to release Chinese WordNet 1.6 using CWN-LMF format in an xml file, including a XML DTD in the following days. In addition, the use of this lingual resource for further linguistic research is also under investigation.

Acknowledgements

The authors would like to thank Prof. Claudia Soria for her constructive comments. This work was funded by National Science Council, Taiwan under Grants NSC 97-2923-I-001-001-MY3., and also cooperated with EU-FP7 KYOTO project.

References

CKIP. 2003. Sense and Sensibility Vol. I. Technical Report 03-01. Taipei: Academia Sinica.

Fellbaum, C.. 1998. WordNet: an Electronic Lexical Database. The MIT Press.

Francopoulo, G., Bel, N., George, M., Calzolari, N., Monachini, M., Pet, M. and Soria, C.. 2006a. Lexical Markup Framework (LMF) for NLP Multilingual Resources. Proceedings of COLING-ACL Workshop on Multilingual Language Resources and Interoperability.

Francopoulo, G., Bel, N., George, M., Calzolari, N., Monachini, M., Pet, M. and Soria, C.. 2006b. LMF for Multilingual, Specialized Lexicons. Proceedings of the LREC Workshop on Acquiring and Representing Multilingual, Specialized Lexicons: the Case of Biomedicine.

Francopoulo, G., Bel, N., George, M., Calzolari, N., Monachini, M., Pet, M. and Soria, C.. 2009. Multilingual Resources for NLP in the Lexical Markup Framework (LMF). Language Resource and Evaluation. 43:57-70.

Huang, C.-R., Chang, R.-Y. and Lee, H.-P.. 2004. Sinica BOW (Bilingual Ontological Wordnet): Integration of Bilingual WordNet and SUMO. Proceedings of the 4th International Conference on Language Resources and Evaluation.

Huang, C.-R., Chen, C.-L., Weng, C.-X., Lee, H.-P., Chen, Y.-X. and Chen, K.-J.. 2005. The Sinica Sense Management System: Design and Implementation. Computational Linguistics and Chinese Language Processing. 10(4): 417-430.

Huang, C.-R., Hsieh, S.-K., Hong, J.-F., Chen, Y.-Z., Su, I.-L., Chen, Y.-X. and Huang, S.-W.. 2008. Chinese Wordnet: Design, Implementation, and Application of an Infrastructure for Cross-lingual Knowledge Processing. Proceedings of the 9th Chinese Lexical Semantics Workshop.

Huang, C.-R., Lee, H.-P. and Hong, J.-F.. 2004. Domain Lexico-Taxonomy: an Approach Towards Multi-domain Language Processing. Proceedings of the Asian Symposium on Natural Language Processing to Overcome Language Barriers.

Huang, C.-R., Lee, H.-P. and Hong, J.-F.. 2005. The Robustness of Domain Lexico-Taxonomy: Expanding Domain Lexicon with Cilin. Proceedings of the 4th ACL SIGHAN Workshop on Chinese Language Processing.

Huang, C.-R., Su, I.-L., Hsiao, P.-Y. and Ke, X.-L.. 2008. Paranymy: Enriching Ontological Knowledge in Wordnets. Proceedings of the 4th Global WordNet Conference.

Huang, C.-R., Tsai, D. B.-S., Weng, C.-X., Chu, N.-X., Ho, W.-R., Huang, L.-H. and Tsai, I.-N.. 2003. Sense and Meaning Facet: Criteria and Operational Guidelines for Chinese Sense Distinction. Proceedings of the 4th Chinese Lexical Semantics Workshop.

LMF. 2009. Lexical Markup Framework. ISO-24613. Geneva:ISO.

Magnini, B. and Cavaglia, G.. 2000. Integrating Subject Field Codes into WordNet. Proceedings of the 2nd International Conference on Language Resources and Evaluation.

Miller, G. A.. 1995. WordNet: a Lexical Database for English. Communications of the ACM. 38(11): 39-41.

Niles, I. and Pease, A.. 2001. Toward a Standard Upper Ontology. Proceedings of the 2nd International Conference on Formal Ontology in Information Systems.

Soria, C., Monachini, M. and Vossen, P.. 2009. Wordnet-LMF: Fleshing out a Standardized Format for Wordnet Interoperability. Proceedings of ACM Workshop on Intercultural Collaboration.

Soria, C., Monachini, M., Bertagna, F., Calzolari, N., Huang, C.-R., Hsieh, S.-K., Marchetti, A. and Tesconi, M.. 2009. Exploring Interoperability of Language Resources: the Case of Cross-lingual Semi-automatic Enrichment of Wordnets. Language Resource and Evaluation. 43:87-96.

Strapparava, C. and Valitutti, A.. 2004. WordNet-Affect: an Affective Extension of WordNet. Proceedings of the 4th International Conference on Language Resources and Evaluation.

Tokuaga, T., Sornlertlamvanich, V., Charoenporn, T., Calzolari, N., Monachini, M., Soria, C., Huang, C.-R., Yu, Y., Yu, H. and Prevot, L.. 2006. Infrastructure for Standardization of Asian Language Resources. Proceedings of the COLING/ACL Main Conference Poster Sessions.

Vossen, P.. 2004. EuroWordNet: a Multilingual Database of Autonomous and Language-specific Wordnets Connected via an Inter-Lingual-Index. International Journal of Linguistics. 17(2): 1-23.

Vossen, P., Agirre, E., Calzolari, N., Fellbaum, C., Hsieh, S.-K., Huang, C.-R., Isahara, H., Kanzaki, K., Marchetti, A., Monachini, M., Neri, F., Raffaelli, R., Rigau, G., Tescon, M. and VanGent, J.. 2008a. KYOTO: A System for Mining, Structuring, and Distributing Knowledge Across Languages and Cultures. Proceedings of 6th International Conference on Language Resource and Evaluation.

Vossen, P., Agirre, E., Calzolari, N., Fellbaum, C., Hsieh, S.-K., Huang, C.-R., Isahara, H., Kanzaki, K., Marchetti, A., Monachini, M., Neri, F., Raffaelli, R., Rigau, G., Tescon, M. and VanGent, J.. 2008b. KYOTO: A System for Mining, Structuring, and Distributing Knowledge Across Languages and Cultures. Proceedings of the 4th International Global WordNet Conference.

Philippine Language Resources: Trends and Directions

Rachel Edita Roxas **Charibeth Cheng** **Nathalie Rose Lim**
Center for Language Technologies
College of Computer Studies
De La Salle University
2401 Taft Ave, Manila, Philippines
rachel.roxas, chari.cheng, nats.lim@delasalle.ph

Abstract

We present the diverse research activities on Philippine languages from all over the country, with focus on the Center for Language Technologies of the College of Computer Studies, De La Salle University, Manila, where majority of the work are conducted. These projects include the formal representation of Philippine languages and the processes involving these languages. Language representation entails the manual and automatic development of language resources such as lexicons and corpora for various human languages including Philippine languages, across various forms such as text, speech and video files. Tools and applications on languages that we have worked on include morphological processes, part of speech tagging, language grammars, machine translation, sign language processing and speech systems. Future directions are also presented.

1 Introduction

The Philippines is an archipelagic nation in Southeast Asia with more than 7,100 islands with 168 natively spoken languages (Gordon, 2005). These islands are grouped into three main island groups: Luzon (northern Philippines), Visayas (central) and Mindanao (southern), and various Philippine languages distributed among its islands.

Little is known historically about these languages. The most concrete evidence that we have is the Doctrina Christiana, the first ever published work in the country in 1593 which contains the translation of religious material in the local Philippine script (the Alibata), Spanish and old Tagalog (a sample page is shown in Figure 1, courtesy of the University of Sto. Tomas Library, 2007). Alibata is an ancient Philippine script that is no longer widely used except for a few locations in the country. The old Tagalog has evolved to the new Filipino alphabet which now consists of 26 letters of the Latin script and “ng” and “ñ”.

The development of the national language can be traced back to the 1935 Constitution Article XIV, Section 3 which states that "...Congress shall make necessary steps towards the development of a national language which will be based on one of the existing native languages..." due to the advocacy of then Philippine President Manuel L. Quezon for the development of a national language that will unite the whole country. Two years later, Tagalog was recommended as the basis of the national language, which was later officially called *Pilipino*. In the 1987 Constitution, Article XIV, Section 6, states that “the National language of the Philippines is Filipino. As it evolves, it shall be further developed and enriched on the basis of existing Philippine and other languages.” To date, Filipino that is being taught in our schools is basically Tagalog, which is the predominant language being used in the archipelago.[1]

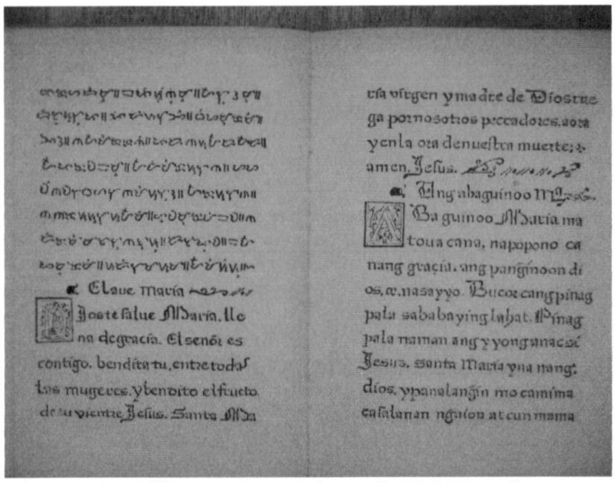

Figure 1: Alibata, Spanish and Old Tagalog sample page: Doctrina Christiana (courtesy of the University of Sto. Tomas Library, 2007)

Table 1 presents data gathered through the 2000 Census conducted by the National Statistics

[1] Thus, when we say Filipino, we generally refer to Tagalog.

Proceedings of the 7th Workshop on Asian Language Resources, ACL-IJCNLP 2009, pages 131–138,
Suntec, Singapore, 6-7 August 2009.

Office, Philippine government, on the Philippine languages that are spoken by at least one percent of the population.

Languages	Number of native speakers
Tagalog	22,000,000
Cebuano	20,000,000
Ilokano	7,700,000
Hiligaynon	7,000,000
Waray-Waray	3,100,000
Capampangan	2,900,000
"Northern Bicol"	2,500,000
Chavacano	2,500,000
Pangasinan	1,540,000
"Southern Bicol"	1,200,000
Maranao	1,150,000
Maguindanao	1,100,000
Kinaray-a	1,051,000
Tausug	1,022,000
Surigaonon	600,000
Masbateño	530,000
Aklanon	520,000
Ibanag	320,000

Table 1. Philippine languages spoken by least 1% of the population.

Linguistics information on Philippine languages are available, but as of yet, the focus has been on theoretical linguistics and little is done about the computational aspects of these languages. To add, much of the work in Philippine linguistics focused on the Tagalog language (Liao, 2006, De Guzman, 1978). In the same token, NLP researches have been focused on Tagalog, although pioneering work on other languages such as Cebuano, Hiligaynon, Ilocano, and Tausug have been made. As can be noticed from this information alone, NLP research on Philippine languages is still at its infancy stage.

One of the first published works on NLP research on Filipino was done by Roxas (1997) on IsaWika!, a machine translation system involving the Filipino language. From then on most of the NLP researches have been conducted at the Center for Language Technologies of the College of Computer Studies, De La Salle University, Manila, Philippines, in collaboration with our partners in academe from all over the country. The scope of experiments have expanded from north of the country to south, from text to speech to video forms, and from present to past data.

NLP researches address the manual construction of language resources literally built from almost non-existent digital forms, such as the grammar, lexicon, and corpora, augmented by some automatic extraction algorithms. Various language tools and applications such as machine translation, information extraction, information retrieval, and natural language database interface, were also pursued. We will discuss these here, the corresponding problems associated with the development of these projects, and the solutions provided. Future research plans will also be presented.

2 Language Resources

We report here our attempts in the manual construction of Philippine language resources such as the lexicon, morphological information, grammar, and the corpora which were literally built from almost non-existent digital forms. Due to the inherent difficulties of manual construction, we also discuss our experiments on various technologies for automatic extraction of these resources to handle the intricacies of the Filipino language, designed with the intention of using them for various language technology applications.

We are currently using the English-Filipino lexicon that contains 23,520 English and 20,540 Filipino word senses with information on the part of speech and co-occurring words through sample sentences. This lexicon is based on the dictionary of the Commission on the Filipino Language (Komisyon sa Wikang Filipino), and digitized by the IsaWika project (Roxas, 1997). Additional information such as synsetID from Princeton WordNet were integrated into the lexicon through the AeFLEX project (Lim, *et al.*, 2007b). As manually populating the database with the synsetIDs from WordNet is tedious, automating the process through the SUMO (Suggested Upper Merged Ontology) as an InterLingua is being explored to come up with the Filipino WordNet (Tan and Lim, 2007).

Initial work on the manual collection of documents on Philippine languages has been done through the funding from the National Commission for Culture and the Arts considering four major Philippine Languages namely, Tagalog, Cebuano, Ilocano and Hiligaynon with 250,000 words each and the Filipino sign language with 7,000 signs (Roxas, *et al.*, 2009). Computational features include word frequency counts and a concordancer that allows viewing co-occurring words in the corpus. Mark-up conventions followed some of those used for the ICE project.

Aside from possibilities of connecting the Philippine islands and regions through language, crossing the boundaries of time are one of the goals (Roxas, 2007a; Roxas, 2007b). An unexplored but equally challenging area is the collection of historical documents that will allow research on the development of the Philippine languages through the centuries, one of which is the already mentioned Doctrina Christiana which was published in 1593.

Attempts are being made to expand on these language resources and to complement manual efforts to build these resources. Automatic methods and social networking are the two main options currently being considered.

2.1 Language Resource Builder

Automatic methods for bilingual lexicon extraction, named-entity extraction, and language corpora are also being explored to exploit on the resources available on the internet. These automatic methods are discussed in detail in this section.

An automated approach of extracting bilingual lexicon from comparable, non-parallel corpora was developed for English as the source language and Tagalog as the target language (Tiu and Roxas, 2008). The study combined approaches from previous researches which only concentrated on context extraction, clustering techniques, or usage of part of speech tags for defining the different senses of a word, and ranking has shown improvement to overall F-measure from 7.32% to 10.65% within the range of values from previous studies. This is despite the use of limited amount of corpora of 400k and seed lexicon of 9,026 entries in contrast to previous studies of 39M and 16,380, respectively.

The NER-Fil is a Named Entity Recognizer for Filipino Text (Lim, *et al.*, 2007a). This system automatically identifies and stores named-entities from documents, which can also be used to annotate corpora with named-entity information. Using machine learning techniques, named entities are also automatically classified into appropriate categories such as person, place, and organization.

AutoCor is an automatic retrieval system for documents written in closely-related languages (Dimalen and Roxas, 2007). Experiments have been conducted on four closely-related Philippine languages, namely: Tagalog, Cebuano and Bicolano. Input documents are matched against the n-gram language models of relevant and irrelevant documents. Using common word pruning to differentiate between the closely-related Philippine languages, and the odds ratio query generation methods, results show improvements in the precision of the system.

Although automatic methods can facilitate the building of the language resources needed for processing natural languages, these automatic methods usually employ learning approaches that would require existing language resources as seed or learning data sets.

2.2 Online Community for Corpora Building

PALITO is an online repository of the Philippine corpus (Roxas, *et al.*, 2009). It is intended to allow linguists or language researchers to upload text documents written in any Philippine language, and would eventually function as corpora for Philippine language documentation and research. Automatic tools for data categorization and corpus annotation are provided by the system. The LASCOPHIL (La Salle Corpus of Philippine Languages) Working Group is assisting the project developers of PALITO in refining the mechanics for the levels of users and their corresponding privileges for a manageable monitoring of the corpora. Videos on the Filipino sign language can also be uploaded into the system. Uploading of speech recordings will be considered in the near future, to address the need to employ the best technology to document and systematically collect speech recordings especially of nearly extinct languages in the country. This online system capitalizes on the opportunity for the corpora to expand faster and wider with the involvement of more people from various parts of the world. This is also to exploit on the reality that many of the Filipinos here and abroad are native speakers of their own local languages or dialects and can largely contribute to the growth of the corpora on Philippine languages.

3 Language Tools

Language tools are applications that support linguistic research and processing of various language computational layers. These include lexical units, to syntax and semantics. Specifically, we have worked on the morphological processes, part of speech tagging and parsing. These processes usually employ either the rule-based approach or the example-based approach. In general, rule-based approaches capture language processes by formally capturing these processes which would require consultations and inputs from linguists. On the other hand, example-based approaches employ machine learning methodologies where automatic learning of rules is performed based on manually annotated data that are done also by linguists.

3.1 Morphological Processes

We have tested both rule-based and example-based approaches in developing our morphological analyzers and generators. Rule-based morphological analysis in the current methods, such as finite-state and unification-based, are predominantly effective for handling concatenative morphology (e.g. prefixation and suffixation), although some of these techniques can also handle limited non-concatenative phenomena (e.g. infixation and partial and full-stem reduplication) which are largely used in Philippine languages. TagMA (Fortes-Galvan and Roxas, 2007) uses a constraint-based method to perform morphological analysis that handles both concatenative and non-concatenative morphological phenomena, based on the optimality theory framework and the two-level morphology rule representation. Test results showed 96% accuracy. The 4% error is attributed to d-r alteration, an example of which is in the word *lakaran*, which is from the root word *lakad* and suffix *-an*, but *d* is changed to *r*. Unfortunately, since all candidates are generated, and erroneous ones are later eliminated through constraints and rules, time efficiency is affected by the exhaustive search performed.

To augment the rule-based approach, an example-based approach was explored by extending Wicentowski's Word Frame model through learning of morphology rules from examples (Cheng and See, 2006). In the WordFrame model, the seven-way split re-write rules composed of the canonical prefix/beginning, point-of-prefixation, common prefix substrings, internal vowel change, common suffix substring, point-of-suffixation, and canonical suffix/ending. Infixation, partial and full reduplication as in Tagalog and other Philippine languages are improperly modeled in the WordFrame model as point-of-prefixation as in the word *(hin)-intay* which should have been modeled as the word *hintay* with infix *–in-*. Words with an infix within a prefix are also modeled as point-of-prefixation as in the word *(hini-)hintay* which should be represented as infix *–in* in partial reduplicated syllable *hi-*. In the revised WordFrame model (Cheng and See, 2006), the non-concatenative Tagalog morphological behaviors such as infixation and reduplication are modeled separately and correctly. Unfortunately, it is still not capable of fully modeling Filipino morphology since some occurrences of reduplication are still represented as point-of-suffixation for various locations of the longest common substring. There are also some problems in handling the occurrence of several partial or whole-word reduplications within a word. Despite these problems, the training of the algorithm that learns these re-write rules from 40,276 Filipino word pairs derived 90% accuracy when applied to an MA. The complexity of creating a better model would be computationally costly but it would ensure an increase in performance and reduced number of rules.

Work is still to be done on exploring techniques and methodologies for morphological generation (MG). Although it could be inferred that the approaches for MA can be extended to handle MG, an additional disambiguation process is necessary to choose the appropriate output from the many various surface form of words that can be generated from one underlying form.

3.2 Part of Speech Tagging

One of the most useful information in the language corpora are the part of speech tags that are associated with each word in the corpora. These tags allow applications to perform other syntactic and semantic processes. Firstly, with the aid of linguists, a revised tagset for Tagalog has been formulated (Miguel and Roxas, 2007), since a close examination of the existing tagset for languages such as English showed the insufficiency of this tagset to handle certain phenomena in Philippine languages such as the lexical markers, ligatures and enclitics. The lexical marker *ay* is used in inverted sentences such as *She is good* (*Siya ay mabuti*). Ligatures can take the form of the word *na* or suffixes *–ng* (*-g*), the former is used if the previous noun, pronoun or adjective ends with a consonant (except for *n*), and the latter if the previous word ends with a vowel (or *n*).

Manual tagging of corpora has allowed the performance of automatic experiments on some approaches for tagging for Philippine languages namely MBPOST, PTPOST4.1, TPOST and TagAlog, each one exploring on a particular approach in tagging such as memory-based POS, template-based and rule-based approaches. A study on the performance of these taggers showed accuracies of 85, 73, 65 and 61%, respectively (Miguel and Roxas, 2007).

3.3 Language Grammars

Grammar checkers are some of the applications where syntactic specification of languages is necessary. SpellCheF is a spell checker for Filipino that uses a hybrid approach in detecting and correcting misspelled words in a document (Cheng, *et al.*, 2007). Its approach is composed of dictionary-lookup, n-gram analysis, Soundex and character distance measurements. It is implemented as a plug-in to OpenOffice Writer. Two spelling rules and guidelines, namely, the Komisyon sa Wikang Filipino 2001 Revision of the Alphabet and Guidelines in Spelling the Filipino Language, and the Gabay sa Editing sa Wikang Filipino rulebooks, were incorporated into the system. SpellCheF consists of the lexicon builder, the detector, and the corrector; all of which utilized both manually formulated and automatically learned rules to carry out their respective tasks.

FiSSAn, on the other hand, is a semantics-based grammar checker. Lastly, PanPam (Jasa, *et al.*, 2007) is an extension of FiSSAn that also incorporates a dictionary-based spell checker (Borra, *et al.*, 2007).

These systems make use of the rule-based approach. To complement these systems, an example-based approach is considered through a grammar rule induction method (Alcantara and Borra, 2008). Constituent structures are automatically induced using unsupervised probabilistic approaches. Two models are presented and results on the Filipino language show an F1 measure of greater than 69%. Experiments revealed that the Filipino language does not follow a strict binary structure as English, but is more right-biased.

A similar experiment has been conducted on grammar rule induction for the automatic parsing of the Philippine component of the International Corpus of English (ICE-PHI) (Flores and Roxas, 2008). The ICE-PHI corpora consist of English texts with indigenous words and phrases during speaker context switching. The markup language followed the standards specified by the ICE group, which is headed by ICE-GB. Constituent rule induction is performed from manually encoded syntactically bracketed files from the ICE-PHI, and will be used to parse the rest of the corpus. Manual post editing of the parse will be performed. The development of such tools will directly benefit the descriptive and applied linguistics of Philippine English, as well as other Englishes, in particular, those language components in the ICE.

Various applications on Philippine languages have been created at the Center for Language Technologies, College of Computer Studies, De La Salle University to cater to different needs.

4 Language Applications

4.1 Machine Translation

The Hybrid English-Filipino Machine Translation (MT) System is a three-year project (with funding from the PCASTRD, DOST), which involves a multi-engine approach for automatic language translation of English and Filipino Roxas, *et al.*, 2008). The MT engines explore on approaches in translation using a rule-based method and two example-based methods. The rule-based approach requires the formal specification of the human languages covered in the study and utilizes these rules to translate the input. The two other MT engines make use of examples to determine the translation. The example-based MT engines have different approaches in their use of the examples (which are existing English and Filipino documents), as well as the data that they are learning.

The system accepts as input a sentence or a document in the source language and translates this into the target language. If source language is English, the target language is Filipino, and vise versa. The input text will undergo preprocessing that will include POS tagging and morphological analysis. After translation, the output translation will undergo natural language generation including morphological generation. Since each of the MT engines would not necessarily have the same output translation, an additional component called the Output Modeler was created to determine the most appropriate among the translation outputs (Go and See, 2008). There are ongoing experiments on the hybridization of the rule-based and the template-based approaches where transfer rules and unification constraints are derived (Fontanilla and Roxas, 2008).

The rule-based MT builds a database of rules for language representation and translation rules from linguists and other experts on translation from English to Filipino and from Filipino to English. We have considered lexical functional grammar (LFG) as the formalism to capture these rules. Given a sentence in the source language, the sentence is processed and a computerized representation in LFG of this sentence is constructed. An evaluation of how comprehensive and exhaustive the identified grammar is will be considered. Is the system able to capture all possible Filipino sentences? How are all possible sentences to be represented since Filipino exhibits some form of free word order in sentences? The next step is the translation step, that is, the conversion of the computerized representation of the input sentence into the intended target language. After the translation process, the computerized representation of the sentence in the target language will now be outputted into a sentence form, or called the generation process. Although it has been shown in various studies elsewhere and on various languages that LFG can be used for analysis of sentences, there is still a question of whether it can be used for the generation process. The generation involves the outputting of a sentence from a computer-based representation of the sentence. This is part of the work that the group intends to address.

The major advantage of the rule-based MT over other approaches is that it can produce high quality translation for sentence patterns that were accurately captured by the rules of the MT engine; but unfortunately, it cannot provide good translations to any sentence that go beyond what the rules have considered.

In contrast to the rule-based MT which requires building the rules by hand, the corpus-based MT system automatically learns how translation is done through examples found in a corpus of translated documents. The system can incrementally learn when new translated documents are added into the knowledge-base, thus, any changes to the language can also be accommodated through the updates on the example translations. This means it can handle translation of documents from various domains (Alcantara, *et al.*, 2006).

The principle of garbage-in-garbage-out applies here; if the example translations are faulty, the learned rules will also be faulty. That is why, although human linguists do not have to specify and come up with the translation rules, the linguist will have to first verify the translated documents and consequently, the learned rules, for accuracy.

It is not only the quality of the collection of translations that affects the overall performance of the system, but also the quantity. The collection of translations has to be comprehensive so that the translation system produced will be able to translate as much types of sentences as possible. The challenge here is coming up with a quantity of examples that is sufficient for accurate translation of documents.

With more data, a new problem arises when the knowledge-base grows so large that access to it and search for applicable rules during translation requires tremendous amount of access time and to an extreme, becomes difficult. Exponential growth of the knowledge-base may also happen due to the free word order nature of Filipino sentence construction, such that one English sentence can be translated to several Filipino sentences. When all these combinations are part of the translation examples, a translation rule will be learned and extracted by the system for each combination, thus, causing growth of the knowledge-base. Thus, algorithms that perform generalization of rules are considered to remove specificity of translation rules extracted and thus, reduce the size of the rule knowledge-base.

One of the main problems in language processing most especially compounded in machine translation is finding the most appropriate translation of a word when there are several meanings of source words, and various target word equivalents depending on the context of the source word. One particular study that focuses on the use of syntactic relationships to perform word sense disambiguation has been explored (Domingo and Roxas, 2006). It uses an automated approach for resolving target-word selection, based on “word-to-sense” and “sense-to-word” relationship between source words and their translations, using syntactic relationships (subject-verb, verb-object, adjective-noun). Using information from a bilingual dictionary and word similarity measures from WordNet, a target word is selected using statistics from a target language corpus. Test results using English to Tagalog translations showed an overall 64% accuracy for selecting word translation.

Other attempts on MT are on Tagalog to Cebuano (Yara, 2007), and Ilocano to English (Miguel and Dy, 2008). Both researches focus on building the language resources for the languages Cebuano and Ilocano, respectively, since focus on the Philippine languages have so far been on Tagalog. It is also important to note that these contributions are local researches being done where the languages are actually spoken and actively in usage.

4.2 Sign Language Processing

Most of the work that we have done focused on textual information. Recently, we have explored on video and speech forms.

With the inclusion of the Filipino sign language in a corpora building project (Roxas, *et al.*, 2009), video formats are used to record, edit, gloss and transcribe signs and discourse. Video editing merely cuts the video for final rendering, glossing allows association of sign to particular words, and transcription allows viewing of textual equivalents of the signed videos.

Work on the automatic recognition of Filipino sign language involves digital signal processing concepts. Initial work has been done on sign language number recognition (Sandjaja, 2008) using color-coded gloves for feature extraction. The feature vectors were calculated based on the position of the dominant-hand's thumb. The system learned through a database of numbers from 1 to 1000, and tested by the automatic recognition of Filipino sign language numbers and conversion into text. Over-all accuracy of number recognition is 85%.

Another proposed work is the recognition of non-manual signals focusing on the various parts of the face; in particular, initially, the mouth is to be considered. The automatic interpretation of the signs can be disambiguated using the interpretation of the non-manual signals.

4.3 Speech Systems

PinoyTalk is an initial study on a Filipino-based text to speech system that automatically generates the speech from input text (Casas, *et al.,* 2004). The input text is processed and parsed from words to syllables, from syllables to letters, and assigned prosodic properties for each one. Six rules for Filipino syllabication were identified and used in the system. A rule-based model for Filipino was developed and used as basis for the implementation of the system. The following were determined in the study considering the Filipino speaker: duration of each phoneme and silences, intonation, pitches of consonants and vowel, and pitches of words with the corresponding stress. The system generates an audio output and able to save the generated file using the mp3 or wav file format.

A system has been developed at the Digital Signal Processing Laboratory at the University of the Philippines at Diliman to automatically recognize emotions such as anger, boredom, happiness and satisfaction (Ebarvia, *et al.*, 2008).

5 Future Directions

Through the Center for Language Technologies of the College of Computer Studies, De la Salle University, and our partners, varied NLP resources have been built, and applications and researches explored. Our faculty members and our students have provided the expertise in these challenging endeavors, with multi-disciplinary efforts and collaborations. Through our graduate programs, we have trained many of the faculty members of universities from various parts of the country; thus, providing a network of NLP researchers throughout the archipelago. We have organized the National NLP Research Symposium for the past five years, through the efforts of the CeLT of CCS-DLSU, and through the support of government agencies such as PCASTRD, DOST and CHED, and our industry partners. Last year, we hosted an international conference (the 22nd Pacific Asia Conference on Language, Information and Computation) which was held in Cebu City in partnership with UPVCC and Cebu Institute of Technology. We have made a commitment to nurture and strengthen NLP researches and collaboration in the country, and expand on our international linkages with key movers in both the Asian region and elsewhere. For the past five years, we have brought in and invited internationally-acclaimed NLP researchers into the country to support these endeavors. Recently, we have also received invitations as visiting scholars, and participants to events and meetings within the Asean region which provided scholarships, which in turn, we also share with our colleagues and researchers in other Philippine universities.

It is an understatement to say that much has to be explored in this area of research that interleaves diverse disciplines among technology-based areas (such as NLP, digital signal processing, multi-media applications, and machine learning) and other fields of study (such as language, history, psychology, and education), and cuts across different regions and countries, and even time frames (Cheng, *et al.*, 2008). It is multi-modal and considers various forms of data from textual, audio, video and other forms of information. Thus, much is yet to be accomplished, and experts with diverse backgrounds in these various related fields will bring this area of research to a new and better dimension.

References

D. Alcantara and A. Borra. 2008. Constituent Structure for Filipino: Induction through Probabilistic Approaches. *Proceedings of the 22nd Pacific Asia Conference on Language, Information and Computation (PACLIC).* 113-122.

D. Alcantara, B. Hong, A. Perez and L. Tan. 2006. *Rule Extraction Applied in Language Translation – R.E.A.L. Translation.* Undergraduate Thesis, De la Salle University, Manila.

A. Borra, M. Ang, P. J. Chan, S. Cagalingan and R. Tan. 2007. FiSSan: Filipino Sentence Syntax and Semantic Analyzer. *Proceedings of the 7th Philippine Computing Science Congress.* 74-78.

D. Casas, S. Rivera, G. Tan, and G. Villamil. 2004. *PinoyTalk: A Filipino Based Text-to-Speech Synthesizer.* Undergraduate Thesis. De La Salle University.

C. Cheng, R. Roxas, A. B. Borra, N. R. L. Lim, E. C. Ong and S. L. See. 2008. e-Wika: Digitalization of Philippine Language. *DLSU-Osaka Workshop.*

C. Cheng, C. P. Alberto, I. A. Chan and V. J. Querol. 2007. SpellChef: Spelling Checker and Corrector for Filipino. *Journal of Research in Science, Computing and Engineering.* 4(3), 75-82.

C. Cheng, and S. See. 2006. The Revised Wordframe Model for Filipino Language. *Journal of Research in Science, Computing and Engineering.* 3(2), 17-23.

D. Dimalen and R. Roxas. 2007. AutoCor: A Query-Based Automatic Acquisition of Corpora of Closely-Related Languages. *Proceedings of the 21st PACLIC.* 146-154.

E. Domingo and R. Roxas. 2006. Utilizing Clues in Syntactic Relationships for Automatic Target Word Sense Disambiguation. *Journal of Research for Science, Computing and Engineering.* 3(3), 18-24.

E. Ebarvia, M. Bayona, F. de Leon, M. Lopez, R. Guevara, B. Calingacion, and P. Naval, Jr. 2008. Determination of Prosodic Feature Set for Emotion Recognition in Call Center Speech. *Proceedings of the 5th National Natural Language Processing Research Symposium (NNLPRS).* 65-71.

D. Flores and R. Roxas. 2008. Automatic Tools for the Analysis of the Philippine component of the International Corpus of English. *Linguistic Society of the Philippines Annual Meeting and Convention.*

G. Fontanilla and R. Roxas. 2008. A Hybrid Filipino-English Machine Translation System. *DLSU Science and Technology Congress.*

F. Fortes-Galvan and R. Roxas. 2007. Morphological Analysis for Concatenative and Non-concatenative Phenomena. *Proceedings of the Asian Applied NLP Conference.*

K. Go and S. See. 2008. Incorporation of WordNet Features to N-Gram Features in a Language Modeller. *Proceedings of the 22nd PACLIC,* 179-188.

Gordon, R. G., Jr. (Ed.). 2005. *Ethnologue: Languages of the World*, 5th Ed. Dallas,Texas: SIL International. Online version: www.ethnologue.com.

M. Jasa, M. J. Palisoc and J. M. Villa. 2007. *Panuring Panitikan (PanPam): A Sentence Syntax and Semantics-based Grammar Checker for Filipino.* Undergraduate Thesis. De La Salle University, Manila.

H. Liao. 2006. *Philippine linguistics: The state of the art (1981-2005).* De La Salle University, Manila.

N. R. Lim, J. C. New, M. A. Ngo, M. Sy, and N. R. Lim. 2007a. A Named-Entity Recognizer for Filipino Texts. *Proceedings of the 4th NNLPRS.*

N. R. Lim, J. O. Lat, S. T. Ng, K. Sze, and G. D. Yu. 2007b. Lexicon for an English-Filipino Machine Translation System. *Proceedings of the 4th National Natural Language Processing Research Symposium.*

D. Miguel and M. Dy. 2008. Anglo-Cano: an Ilocano to English Machine Translation. *Proceedings of the 5th National Natural Language Processing Research Symposium.* 85-88.

D. Miguel and R. Roxas. 2007. Comparative Evaluation of Tagalog Part of Speech Taggers. Proceedings of the 4th *NNLPRS.*

R. Roxas, P. Inventado, G. Asenjo, M. Corpus, S. Dita, R. Sison-Buban and D. Taylan. 2009. Online Corpora of Philippine Languages. *2nd DLSU Arts Congress: Arts and Environment.*

R. Roxas, A. Borra, C. Ko, N. R. Lim, E. Ong, and M. W. Tan. 2008. Building Language Resources for a Multi-Engine Machine Translation System. Language Resources and Evaluation. Springer, Netherlands. 42:183-195.

R. Roxas. 2007a. e-Wika: Philippine Connectivity through Languages. *Proceedings of the 4th NNLPRS.*

R. Roxas. 2007b. Towards Building the Philippine Corpus. *Consultative Workshop on Building the Philippine Corpus.*

R. Roxas. 1997. Machine Translation from English to Filipino: A Prototype. *International Symposium of Multi-lingual Information Technology (MLIT '97)*, Singapore.

I. Sandjaja. 2008. *Sign Language Number Recognition.* Graduate Thesis. De La Salle University, Manila.

P. Tan and N. R. Lim. 2007. FILWORDNET: Towards a Filipino WordNet. *Proceedings of the 4th NNLPRS.*

E. P. Tiu and R. Roxas. 2008. Automatic Bilingual Lexicon Extraction for a Minority Target Language, *Proceedings of the 22nd PACLIC.* 368-376.

J. Yara. 2007. A Tagalog-to-Cebuano Affix-Transfer-Based Machine Translator. *Proceedings of the 4th NNLPRS.*

Thai WordNet Construction

Sareewan Thoongsup[1]
Kergrit Robkop[1]
Chumpol Mokarat[1]
Tan Sinthurahat[1]
[1] Thai Computational Linguistics Lab.
NICT Asia Research Center, Thailand
{sareewan, kergrit, Chumpol, tan, thatsanee, virach}@tcllab.org

Thatsanee Charoenporn [1,2]
Virach Sornlertlamvanich [1,2]
Hitoshi Isahara [3]
[2]National Electronics and Computer Technology Center Thailand, Thailand
[3]National Institute of Information and Communications Technology, Japan
isahara@nict.go.jp

Abstract

This paper describes semi-automatic construction of Thai WordNet and the applied method for Asian wordNet. Based on the Princeton WordNet, we develop a method in generating a WordNet by using an existing bi-lingual dictionary. We align the PWN synset to a bi-lingual dictionary through the English equivalent and its part-of-speech (POS), automatically. Manual translation is also employed after the alignment. We also develop a web-based collaborative workbench, called KUI (Knowledge Unifying Initiator), for revising the result of synset assignment and provide a framework to create Asian WordNet via the linkage through PWN synset.

1 Introduction

The Princeton WordNet (PWN) (Fellbuam, 1998) is one of the most semantically rich English lexical banks widely used as a resource in many research and development. WordNet is a great inspiration in the extensive development of this kind of lexical database in other languages. It is not only an important resource in implementing NLP applications in each language, but also in inter-linking WordNets of different languages to develop multi-lingual applications to overcome the language barrier. There are some efforts in developing WordNets of some languages (Atserias and et al., 1997; Vossen, 1997; Farrers and et al., 1998; Balkova and et al., 2004; Isahara and et al., 2008). But the number of languages that have been successfully developed their WordNets is still limited to some active research in this area. This paper, however, is the one of that attempt.

This paper describes semi-automatic construction of Thai WordNet and the applied method for Asian WordNet. Based on the Princeton WordNet, we develop a method in generating a WordNet by using an existing bi-lingual dictionary. We align the PWN synset to a bi-lingual dictionary through the English equivalent and its part-of-speech (POS), automatically. Manual translation is also employed after the alignment. We also develop a web-based collaborative workbench, called KUI (Knowledge Unifying Initiator), for revising the result of synset assignment and provide a framework to create Asian WordNet via the linkage through PWN synset.

The rest of this paper is organized as follows: Section 2 describes how we construct the Thai WordNet, including approaches, methods, and some significant language dependent issues experienced along the construction. Section 3 provides the information on Asian WordNet construction and progress. And Section 4 concludes our work.

2 Thai WordNet Construction Procedure

Different approaches and methods have been applied in constructing WordNet of many languages according to the existing lexical resources. This section describes how Thai WordNet is constructed either approach or method.

Proceedings of the 7th Workshop on Asian Language Resources, ACL-IJCNLP 2009, pages 139–144,
Suntec, Singapore, 6-7 August 2009.

2.1 Approaches

To build language WordNet from scratch, two approaches were brought up into the discussion: the merge approach and the expand approach.

The merge approach is to build the taxonomies of the language; synsets and relations, and then map to the PWN by using the English equivalent words from existing bilingual dictionaries.

The expand approach is to map or translate local words directly to the PWN's synsets by using the existing bilingual dictionaries.

Employing the merge approach, for Thai as an example, we will completely get synsets and relations for the Thai language. But it is time and budget consuming task and require a lot of skilled lexicographers as well, while less time and budget is used when employing the expand approach to get a translated version of WordNet. But some particular Thai concepts which do not occur in PWN will not exist in this lexicon. Comparing between these two approaches, the Thai WordNet construction intended to follow the expand approach by this following reasons;

- Many languages have developed their own WordNet using the PWN as a model, so we can link Thai lexical database to those languages.
- The interface for collaboration for other languages can be easily developed.

2.2 Methods

As presented above, we follow the expand approach to construct the Thai WordNet by translating the synsets in the PWN to the Thai language. Both automatic and manual methods are applied in the process.

2.2.1 Automatic Synset Alignment

Following the objective to translate the PWN to Thai, we attempted to use the existing lexical resources to facilitate the construction. We proposed an automatic method to assign an appropriate synset to a lexical entry by considering its English equivalent and lexical synonyms which are most commonly encoded in a bi-lingual dictionary. (Charoenporn 2008; Sornlertlamvanich, 2008).

	WordNet (synset)		TE Dict (entry)	
	total	Assigned	total	assigned
Noun	145,103	18,353 (13%)	43,072	11,867 (28%)
Verb	24,884	1,333 (5%)	17,669	2,298 (13%)
Adjective	31,302	4,034 (13%)	18,448	3,722 (20%)
Adverb	5,721	737 (13%)	3,008	1,519 (51%)
Total	207,010	24,457 (12%)	82,197	19,406 (24%)

Table 1. Synset assignment to entries in Thai-English dictionary

For the result, there is only 12% of the total number of the synsets that were able to be assigned to Thai lexical entries. And about 24% of Thai lexical entries were found with the English equivalents that meet one of our criteria. Table 1 shows the successful rate in assigning synsets to the lexical entry in the Thai-English Dictionary.

Considering the list of unmapped lexical entry, the errors can be classified into three groups, as the following.

1. The English equivalent is assigned in a compound, especially in case that there is no an appropriate translation to represent exactly the same sense. For example,
   L: ร้านค้าปลีก raan3-khaa3-pleek1
   E: retail shop
2. Some particular words culturally used I one language may not be simply translated into one single word sense in English. In this case, we found it explained in a phrase. For example,
   L: กรรเจียก kan0-jeak1
   E: bouquet worn over the ear
3. Inflected forms i.e. plural, past participle, are used to express an appropriate sense of a lexical entry. This can be found in non-inflection languages such as Thai and most of Asian languages, For example,
   L: ร้าวระทม raaw3-ra0-thom0
   E: greived

By using this method, a little part of PWN has been translated into Thai. About 88% of the total number of the synsets still cannot be assigned. Manual step is therefore applied.

2.2.2 Manual Construction

Human translation is our next step for synset translation. Two important issues were taken into discussion, when starting the translation process. Those are;

- How to assign or translate new concepts that still do not occur in the Thai lexicon. Compound word or phrase is acceptable or not.
- Which equivalent do we need to consider, synset-to-synset equivalent or word-to-word equivalent?

For the first issue, we actually intend to translate the PWN synsets into single Thai word only. But problems occurred when we faced with concept that has not its equivalent word. For example,

filly#1 -- (a young female horse under the age of four)
colt2#1 – (a young male horse under the age of four)
hog2#2, hogget#1, hogg#2 – (a sheep up to the age of one year: one yet to be sheared)

There is not any word that conveys the meaning of the above concepts. That is because of the difference of the culture. In this case, phrase or compound word will be introduced to use as the equivalent word of the concept. This phenomenon always occurs with cultural dependent concept, technical terms and new concepts.

As for the second issue, considering between (1) synset-to-synset equivalent assignment or (2) word-to-word equivalent assignment has to be discussed. Let consider the following concept of "dog" in the PWN.

<u>dog#1, domestic dog#1, Canis familiaris#1</u> -- (a member of the genus Canis (probably descended from the common wolf) that has been domesticated by man since prehistoric times; occurs in many breeds; "the dog barked all night")

The above synset consists of three words; dog, domestic dog, and Canis familiaris. The set of Thai synonyms that is equivalent to this English synset is the following.

Thai synset of 'dog'
{T1 หมา maa4 'dog' (normal word),
T2 สุนัข su1-nak3 'dog' (polite word),
T3 สุนัขบ้าน su1-nak3-baan0 'domestic dog',
T4 คานิส แฟมิเลียริส kha0-nis3-fae0-mi0-lia0-ris3 'Canis familiaris'}

These words have the same concepts but are different in usage. How do we choose the right Thai word for the right equivalent English word? It is a crucial problem. In the paragraph below, three English words which represent the concept "dog" are used in the different context and cannot be interchanged. Similarly, T1, T2 and T3 cannot be used substitutionally. Because it conveys different meaning. Therefore, word-to-word is our solution.

"**...Dog** usually means the **domestic dog**, Canis lupus familiaris (or "**Canis familiaris**" in binomial nomenclature)...."

Dog → T1 หมา maa4 'dog',
→ T2 สุนัข su1-nak3 'dog'
Domestic dog → T3 สุนัขบ้าน su1-nak4-baan0 'domestic dog'
Canis familiaris → T4 คานิส แฟมิเลียริส kha0-nis3-fae0-mi0-lia0-ris3 'Canis familiaris'

Consequently, word-to-word equivalent is very useful for choosing the right synonyms with the right context.

In conclusion, the main principle for the English to Thai translation includes

(1) "Single word" is lexicalized the existence of concepts in Thai.
(2) "Compound" or "Phrase" is represented some concepts that are not lexicalized in Thai.
(3) Synset-to-synset equivalent is used for finding Thai synset that is compatible with PWN synset.
(4) Word-to-word equivalent is used for finding the right Thai word that is compatible with PWN word in each synset.

2.3 Language Issues

This section describes some significant characteristics of Thai that we have to consider carefully during the translation process.

2.3.1 Out of concepts in PWN

There are some Thai words/concepts that do not exist in the PWN, especially cultural-related words. This is the major problem we have to solve during the translation.

One of our future plans is to add synsets that do not exist into the PWN.

2.3.2 Concept differentiation

Some concepts in the PWN are not equal to Thai concepts. For example, a synset {appear, come out} represents one concept "be issued or published" in English, but meanwhile, it represents two concepts in Thai, the concept of printed matter, and the concept of film or movie, respectively.

2.3.3 Concept Structure differentiation

In some cases, the level of the concept relation between English and Thai is not equal. For example, {hair} in the PWN represents a concept of "a covering for the body (or parts of it) consisting of a dense growth of threadlike structures (as on the human head); helps to prevent heat loss; ..." but in Thai, it is divided into two concepts;

T1 ขน khon4 'hair'
= "hair" that cover the body
T2 ผม phom4 'hair'
= "hair" that cover on the human head

This shows the nonequivalent of concept. Moreover, it also differs in the relation of concept. In PWN "hair" is a more general concept and "body hair" is more specific concepts. But in Thai T1 ขน khon4 'hair' (hair that covers the body) is more general concept and T2 ผม phom5 'hair' (hair that covers on the human head) is more specific one.

2.3.4 Grammar and usage differentiation

- Part of speech
    - "Classifier" is one of Thai POS which indicates the semantic class to which an item belongs. It's widely use in quantitative expression. For example, 'คน knon' used with 'person', 'หลัง lang' used with house.
    - Some adjectives in English, such as 'beautiful', 'red' and so on can function as the adjective and attribute verb in Thai.
- Social factors determining language usage
    - In Thai, some social factors, such as social status, age, or sex play an important role to determine the usage of language. For example, these following three words กิน kin0, ฉัน chan4 and เสวย sa0-waey4, having the same meaning 'eat', are used for different social status of the listener or referent. These words cannot be grouped in the same synset because of their usage.

3 From Thai to Asian WordNet

AWN, or Asian WordNet, is the result of the collaborative effort in creating an interconnected WordNet for Asian languages. Starting with the automatic synset assignment as shown in section 2, we provide KUI (Knowledge Unifying Initiator) (Sornlertlamvanich, 2006), (Sornlertlamvanich et al., 2007) to establish an online collaborative work in refining the WorNets. KUI is community software which allows registered members including language experts revise and vote for the synset assignment. The system manages the synset assignment according to the preferred score obtained from the revision process. As a result, the community WordNets will be accomplished and exported into the original form of WordNet database. Via the synset ID assigned in the WordNet, the system can generate a cross language WordNet result. Through this effort, an initial version of Asian WordNet can be fulfilled.

3.1 Collaboration on Asian WordNet

Followings are our pilot partners in putting things together to make KUI work for AWN.

- Thai Computational Linguistics Laboratory TCL), Thailand
- National Institute of Information and Communications Technology (NICT), Japan
- National Electronics and Computer Technology Center (NECTEC), Thailand
- Agency for the Assessment and Application of Technology (BPPT), Indonesia

- National University of Mongolia (NUM), Mongolia
- Myanmar Computer Federation (MCF), Myanmar

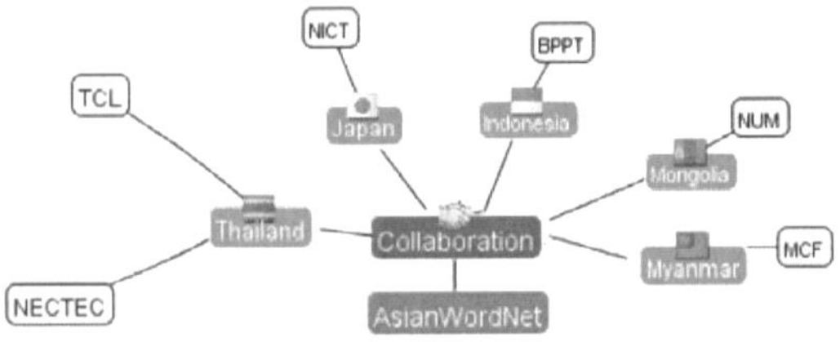

Figure 1. Collaboration on Asian WordNet

3.2 How words are linked

In our language WordNet construction, lexical entry of each language will be mapped with the PWN via its English equivalent. On the process of mapping, a unique ID will be generated for every lexical entry which contains unique sense_key and synset_offset from PWN. Examples of the generated ID show in Table 2. When a word with a unique ID is translated into any language, the same unique ID will be attached to that word automatically. By this way, the lexicon entry in the community can be linked to the each other using this unique ID.

id	sense_key	synset_offset
28259	car%1:06:00::	02929975
28260	car%1:06:01::	02931574
28261	car%1:06:02::	02931966
28262	car%1:06:03::	02932115
28263	car%1:06:04::	02906118

Table 2. Examples of the unique index with sense_key and synset_offset

3.3 Progress on Thai WordNet and Asian WordNet

This section presents the progress on Asian WordNet and Thai WordNet construction.

3.3.1 Current Asian WordNet

At present, there are ten Asian languages in the community. The amount of the translated synsets has been continuously increased. The current amount is shown in the table 3. As shown in the table, for example, 28,735 senses from 117,659 senses have been translated into Thai.

Language	Synset (s)	% of total 117,659 senses
Thai	28,735	24.422
Korean	23,411	19.897
Japanese	21,810	18.537
Myanmar	5,701	4.845
Vietnamese	3,710	3.153
Indonesian	3,522	2.993
Bengali	584	0.496
Mongolian	424	0.360
Nepali	13	0.011
Sudanese	11	0.009
Assamese	2	0.008
Khmer	2	0.002

Table 3. Amount of senses translated in each language

3.3.2 Sense Sharing

Table 4 shows the amount of senses that have been conjointly translated in the group of language. For example, there are 6 languages that found of the same 540 senses.

Language	Sense (s)	%
1-Language	27,413	55.598
2-Language	11,769	23.869
3-Language	5,903	11.972
4-Language	2,501	5.072
5-Language	1,120	2.272
6-Language	540	1.095
7-Language	53	0.107
8-Language	4	0.008
9-Language	2	0.004
10-Language	1	0.002
Total	49,306	100.000

Table 4. Amount of senses translated in each language

3.3.3 Amount of Words in Thai synsets

From the synset in Thai WordNet, there are the minimum of one word (W1) in a synset and the maximum of six words (W6) in a synset. The percentage shown in Table 5 presents that 89.78% of Thai synset contain only one word.

Amount of word in Thai Synset	Sense (s)	%
W1	19,164	89.78
W2	1,930	9.04
W3	211	0.99
W4	27	0.13
W5	4	0.02
W6	8	0.04
Total	21,344	100.00

Table 5. Amount of Word in Thai synsets

4 Conclusion

In this paper we have described the methods of Thai WordNet construction. The semi-auto alignment method constructed the database by using the electronic bilingual dictionary. The manual method has constructed by experts and the collaborative builders who works on the web interface at www.asianwordnet.org.

References

Christiane Fellbuam. (ed.). 1998. *WordNet: An Electronic Lexical Database.* MIT Press, Cambridge, Mass.

Xavier Farreres, German Rigau and Horacio Rodriguez. 1998. *Using WordNet for building WordNets.* In: *Proceedings of the COLING/ACL Workshop on Usage of WordNet in Natural Language Processing Systems*, Montreal.

Hitoshi Isahara, Francis Bond, Kiyotaka Uchimoto, Masao Utiyama and Kyoko Kanzaki. 2008. *Development of the Japanese WordNet.* In *LREC-2008*, Marrakech.

Jordi Atserias, Salvador Climent, Xavier Farreres, German Rigau and Horacio Rodriguez. 1997. Combinding multiple Methods for the automatic Construction of Multilingual WordNets. In proceedings of International Conference "Recent Advances in Natural Language Processing" (RANLP'97). Tzigov Chark, Bulgaria.

Piek Vossen, 1997. *EuroWordNet: a multilingual database for information retrieval.* In proceedings of DELOS workshop on Cross-language Information Retrieval, March 5-7, 1997, Zurich.

Thatsanee Charoenporn, Virach Sornlertlamvanich, Chumpol Mokarat, and Hitoshi Isahara. 2008. *Semi-automatic Compilation of Asian WordNet*, In proceedings of the 14th NLP2008, University of Tokyo, Komaba Campus, Japan, March 18-20, 2008.

Valenina Balkova, Andrey Suhonogov, Sergey Yablonsky. 2004. *Rusian WordNet: From UML-notation to Internet/Infranet Database Implementation.* In Porceedings of the Second International WordNet Conference (GWC 2004), pp.31-38.

Virach Sornlertlamvanich, Thatsanee Charoenporn, Chumpol Mokarat, Hitoshi Isahara, Hammam Riza, and Purev Jaimai. 2008. *Synset Assignment for Bi-lingual Dictionary with Limited Resource.* In proceedings of the Third International Joint Conference on Natural Language Processing (IJCNLP2008), Hyderabad, India, January 7-12, 2008.

Query Expansion using LMF-Compliant Lexical Resources

Tokunaga Takenobu — *Tokyo Inst. of Tech.*
Dain Kaplan — *Tokyo Inst. of Tech.*
Nicoletta Calzolari — *ILC/CNR*
Monica Monachini — *ILC/CNR*
Claudia Soria — *ILC/CNR*
Virach Sornlertlamvanich — *TCL, NICT*
Thatsanee Charoenporn — *TCL, NICT*
Xia Yingju — *Fujitsu R&D Center*
Chu-Ren Huang — *The Hong Kong Polytec. Univ.*
Shu-Kai Hsieh — *National Taiwan Normal Univ.*
Shirai Kiyoaki — *JAIST*

Abstract

This paper reports prototype multilingual query expansion system relying on LMF compliant lexical resources. The system is one of the deliverables of a three-year project aiming at establishing an international standard for language resources which is applicable to Asian languages. Our important contributions to ISO 24613, standard Lexical Markup Framework (LMF) include its robustness to deal with Asian languages, and its applicability to cross-lingual query tasks, as illustrated by the prototype introduced in this paper.

1 Introduction

During the last two decades corpus-based approaches have come to the forefront of NLP research. Since without corpora there can be no corpus-based research, the creation of such language resources has also necessarily advanced as well, in a mutually beneficial synergetic relationship. One of the advantages of corpus-based approaches is that the techniques used are less language specific than classical rule-based approaches where a human analyses the behaviour of target languages and constructs rules manually. This naturally led the way for international resource standardisation, and indeed there is a long standing precedent in the West for it. The Human Language Technology (HLT) society in Europe has been particularly zealous in this regard, propelling the creation of resource interoperability through a series of initiatives, namely EAGLES (Sanfilippo et al., 1999), PAROLE/SIMPLE (Lenci et al., 2000), ISLE/MILE (Ide et al., 2003), and LIRICS[1]. These continuous efforts have matured into activities in ISO-TC37/SC4[2], which aims at making an international standard for language resources.

However, due to the great diversity of languages themselves and the differing degree of technological development for each, Asian languages, have received less attention for creating resources than their Western counterparts. Thus, it has yet to be determined if corpus-based techniques developed for well-computerised languages are applicable on a broader scale to all languages. In order to efficiently develop Asian language resources, utilising an international standard in this creation has substantial merits.

We launched a three-year project to create an international standard for language resources that includes Asian languages. We took the following approach in seeking this goal.

- Based on existing description frameworks, each research member tries to describe several lexical entries and find problems with them.
- Through periodical meetings, we exchange information about problems found and generalise them to propose solutions.
- Through an implementation of an application system, we verify the effectiveness of the proposed framework.

Below we summarise our significant contribution to an International Standard (ISO24613; Lexical Markup Framework: LMF).

1st year After considering many characteristics of Asian languages, we elucidated the shortcomings of the LMF draft (ISO24613 Rev.9). The draft lacks the following devices for Asian languages.

[1] http://lirics.loria.fr/

[2] http://www.tc37sc4.org/

Proceedings of the 7th Workshop on Asian Language Resources, ACL-IJCNLP 2009, pages 145–152,
Suntec, Singapore, 6-7 August 2009.

(1) A mapping mechanism between syntactic and semantic arguments
(2) Derivation (including reduplication)
(3) Classifiers
(4) Orthography
(5) Honorifics

Among these, we proposed solutions for (1) and (2) to the ISO-TC37 SC4 working group.

2nd year We proposed solutions for above the (2), (3) and (4) in the comments of the Committee Draft (ISO24613 Rev. 13) to the ISO-TC37 SC4 working group. Our proposal was included in DIS (Draft International Standard).

(2') a package for derivational morphology
(3') the syntax-semantic interface resolving the problem of classifiers
(4') representational issues with the richness of writing systems in Asian languages

3rd year Since ISO 24613 was in the FDIS stage and fairly stable, we built sample lexicons in Chinese, English, Italian, Japanese, and Thai based on ISO24613. At the same time, we implemented a query expansion system utilising rich linguistic resources including lexicons described in the ISO 24613 framework. We confirmed that a system was feasible which worked on the tested languages (including both Western and Asian languages) when given lexicons compliant with the framework. ISO 24613 (LMF) was approved by the October 2008 ballot and published as ISO-24613:2008 on 17th November 2008.

Since we have already reported our first 2 year activities elsewhere (Tokunaga and others, 2006; Tokunaga and others, 2008), we focus on the above query expansion system in this paper.

2 Query expansion using LMF-compliant lexical resources

We evaluated the effectiveness of LMF on a multilingual information retrieval system, particularly the effectiveness for linguistically motivated query expansion.

The linguistically motivated query expansion system aims to refine a user's query by exploiting the richer information contained within a lexicon described using the adapted LMF framework. Our lexicons are completely complaint with this international standard. For example, a user inputs a keyword "ticket" as a query. Conventional query expansion techniques expand this keyword to a set of related words by using thesauri or ontologies (Baeza-Yates and Ribeiro-Neto, 1999). Using the framework proposed by this project, expanding the user's query becomes a matter of following links within the lexicon, from the source lexical entry or entries through predicate-argument structures to all relevant entries (Figure 1). We focus on expanding the user inputted list of nouns to relevant verbs, but the reverse would also be possible using the same technique and the same lexicon. This link between entries is established through the *semantic type* of a given sense within a lexical entry. These semantic types are defined by higher-level ontologies, such as MILO or SIMPLE (Lenci et al., 2000) and are used in semantic predicates that take such semantic types as a restriction argument. Since senses for verbs contain a link to a semantic predicate, using this semantic type, the system can then find any/all entries within the lexicon that have this semantic type as the value of the restriction feature of a semantic predicate for any of their senses. As a concrete example, let us continue using the "ticket" scenario from above. The lexical entry for "ticket" might contain a semantic type definition something like in Figure 2.

```
<LexicalEntry ...>
  <feat att="POS" val="N"/>
  <Lemma>
    <feat att="writtenForm"
          val="ticket"/>
  </Lemma>
  <Sense ...>
    <feat att="semanticType"
          val="ARTIFACT"/>
    ...
  </Sense>
  ...
</LexicalEntry>
```

Figure 2: Lexical entry for "ticket"

By referring to the lexicon, we can then derive any actions and events that take the semantic type "ARTIFACT" as an argument.

First all semantic predicates are searched for arguments that have an appropriate restriction, in this case "ARTIFACT" as shown in Figure 3, and then any lexical entries that refer to these predicates are returned. An equally similar definition would exist for "buy", "find" and so on. Thus, by referring to the predicate-argument structure of related verbs, we know that these verbs can take

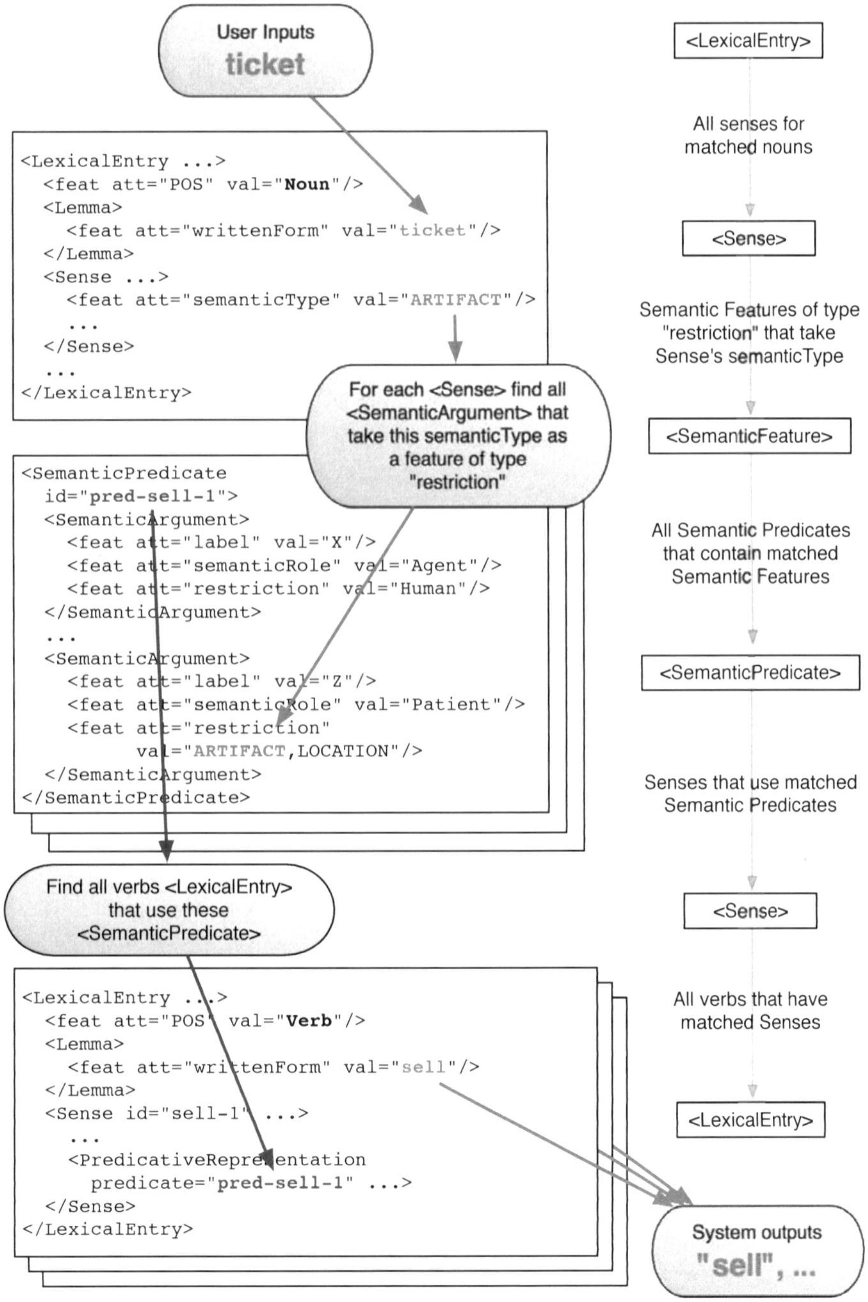

Figure 1: QE Process Flow

```
<LexicalEntry ...>
  <feat att="POS" val="V"/>
  <Lemma>
    <feat att="writtenForm"
          val="sell"/>
  </Lemma>
  <Sense id="sell-1" ...>
    <feat att="semanticType"
          val="Transaction"/>
    <PredicativeRepresentation
      predicate="pred-sell-1"
      correspondences="map-sell1">
  </Sense>
</LexicalEntry>

<SemanticPredicate id="pred-sell-1">
  <SemanticArgument ...>
    ...
    <feat att="restriction"
          val="ARTIFACT"/>
  </SemanticArgument>
</SemanticPredicate>
```

Figure 3: Lexical entry for "sell" with its semantic predicate

"ticket" in the role of object. The system then returns all relevant entries, here "buy", "sell" and "find", in response to the user's query. Figure 1 schematically shows this flow.

3 A prototype system in detail

3.1 Overview

To test the efficacy of the LMF-compliant lexical resources, we created a system implementing the query expansion mechanism explained above. The system was developed in Java for its "compile once, run anywhere" portability and its high-availability of reusable off-the-shelf components. On top of Java 5, the system was developed using JBoss Application Server 4.2.3, the latest standard, stable version of the product at the time of development. To provide fast access times, and easy traversal of relational data, a RDB was used. The most popular free open-source database was selected, MySQL, to store all lexicons imported into the system, and the system was accessed, as a web-application, via any web browser.

3.2 Database

The finalised database schema is shown in Figure 4. It describes the relationships between entities, and more or less mirrors the classes found within the adapted LMF framework, with mostly only minor exceptions where it was efficacious for querying the data. Due to space constraints, meta-data fields, such as creation time-stamps have been left out of this diagram. Since the system also allows for multiple lexicons to co-exist, a *lexicon_id* resides in every table. This foreign key has been highlighted in a different color, but not connected via arrows to make the diagram easier to read. In addition, though in actuality this foreign key is not required for all tables, it has been inserted as a convenience for querying data more efficiently, even within join tables (indicated in blue). Having multiple lexical resources co-existing within the same database allows for several advantageous features, and will be described later. Some tables also contain a *text_id*, which stores the original id attribute for that element found within the XML. This is not used in the system itself, and is stored only for reference.

3.3 System design

As mentioned above, the application is deployed to JBoss AS as an *ear*-file. The system itself is composed of java classes encapsulating the data contained within the database, a Parsing/Importing class for handling the LMF XML files after they have been validated, and JSPs, which contain HTML, for displaying the interface to the user. There are three main sections to the application: Search, Browse, and Configure. Explaining last to first, the Configure section, shown in Figure 5, allows users to create a new lexicon within the system or append to an existing lexicon by uploading a LMF XML file from their web browser, or delete existing lexicons that are no longer needed/used. After import, the data may be immediately queried upon with no other changes to system configuration, from within both the Browse and Search sections. Regardless of language, the rich syntactic/semantic information contained within the lexicon is sufficient for carrying out query expansion on its own.

The Browse section (Figure 6) allows the user to select any available lexicon to see the relationships contained within it, which contains tabs for viewing all noun to verb connections, a list of nouns, a list of verbs, and a list of semantic types. Each has appropriate links allowing the user to easily jump to a different tab of the system. Clicking on a noun takes them to the Search section (Figure 7). In this section, the user may select many lexicons to perform query extraction on, as is visible in Figure 7.

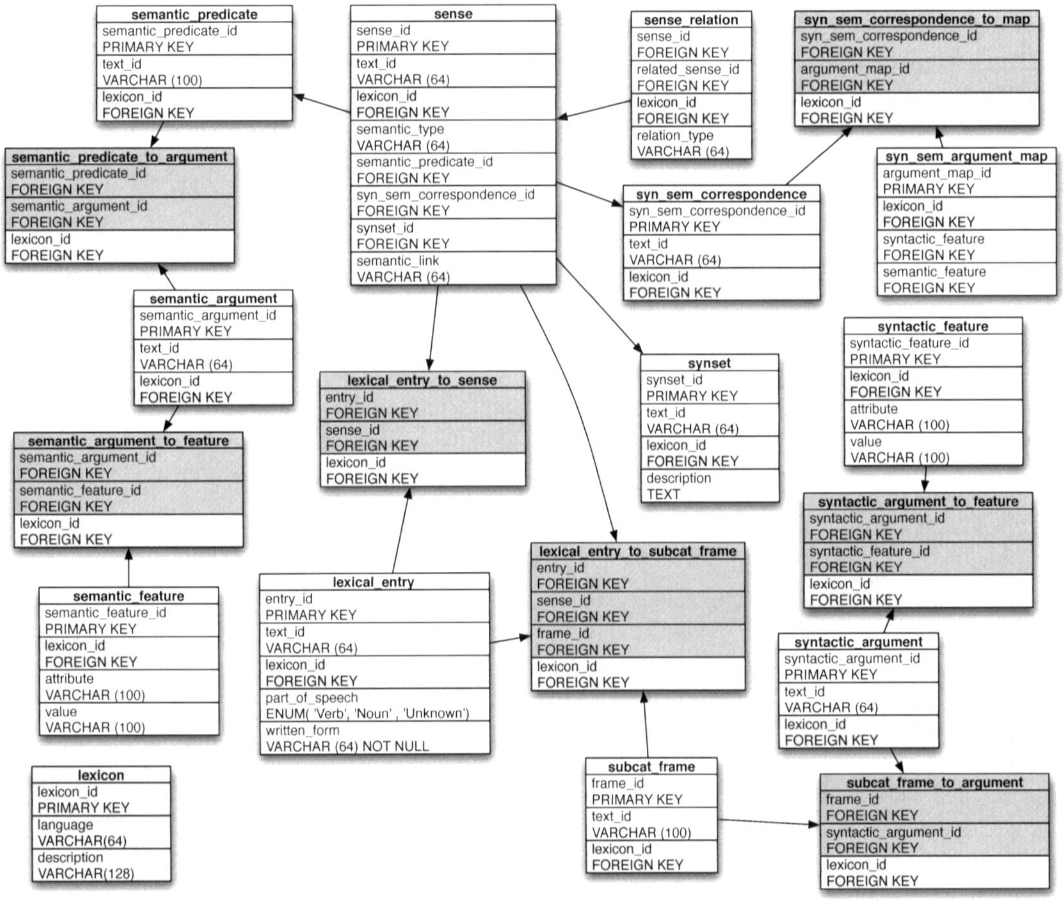

Figure 4: Database schema

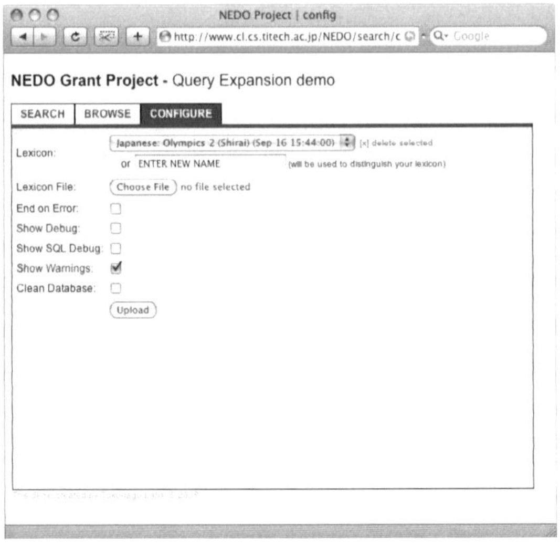

Figure 5: QE System - Configure

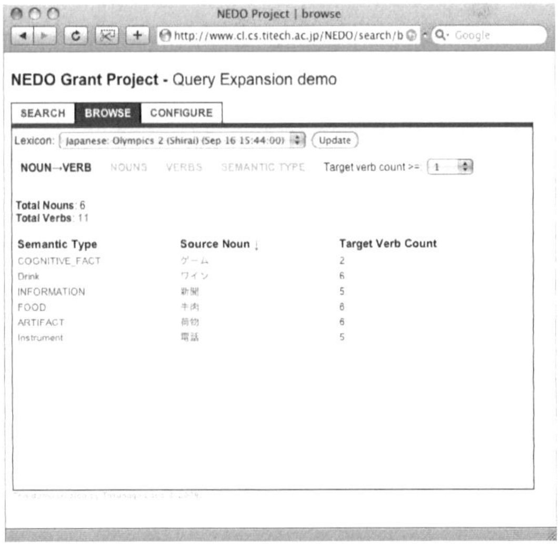

Figure 6: QE System - Browse

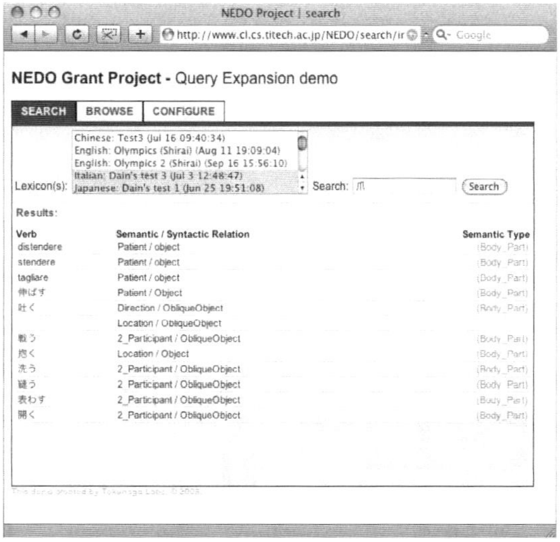

Figure 7: QE System - Search

3.4 Semantic information

This new type of query expansion requires rich lexical information. We augmented our data using the SIMPLE ontology for semantic types, using the same data for different languages. This had the added benefit of allowing *cross*-language expansion as a result. In steps two and three of Figure 1 when senses are retrieved that take specific semantic types as arguments, this process can be done across all (or as many as are selected) lexicons in the database. Thus, results such as are shown in Figure 7 are possible. In this figure the Japanese word for "nail" is entered, and results for both selected languages, Japanese *and* Italian, are returned. This feature requires the unification of the semantic type ontology strata.

3.5 Possible extension

Next steps for the QE platform are to explore the use of other information already defined within the adapted framework, specifically sense relations. Given to the small size of our sample lexicon, data sparsity is naturally an issue, but hopefully by exploring and exploiting these sense relations properly, the system may be able to further expand a user's query to include a broader range of selections using any additional semantic types belonging to these related senses. The framework also contains information about the order in which syntactic arguments should be placed. This information should be used to format the results from the user's query appropriately.

4 An Additional Evaluation

We conducted some additional query expansion experiments using a corpus that was acquired from Chinese LDC (No. "2004-863-009") as a base (see below). This corpus marked an initial achievement in building a multi-lingual parallel corpus for supporting development of cross-lingual NLP applications catering to the Beijing 2008 Olympics.

The corpus contains parallel texts in Chinese, English and Japanese and covers 5 domains that are closely related to the Olympics: traveling, dining, sports, traffic and business. The corpus consists of example sentences, typical dialogues and articles from the Internet, as well as other language teaching materials. To deal with the different languages in a uniform manner, we converted the corpus into our proposed LMF-compliant lexical resources framework, which allowed the system to expand the query between all the languages within the converted resources without additional modifications.

As an example of how this IR system functioned, suppose that Mr. Smith will be visiting Beijing to see the Olympic games and wants to know how to buy a newspaper. Using this system, he would first enter the query "newspaper". For this query, with the given corpus, the system returns 31 documents, fragments of the first 5 shown below.

(1) I'll bring an English *newspaper* immediately.

(2) Would you please hand me the *newspaper*.

(3) There's no use to go over the *newspaper* ads.

(4) Let's consult the *newspaper* for such a film.

(5) I have little confidence in what the *newspapers* say.

Yet it can be seen that the displayed results are not yet useful enough to know how to buy a newspaper, though useful information may in fact be included within some of the 31 documents. Using the lexical resources, the query expansion module suggests "buy", "send", "get", "read", and "sell" as candidates to add for a revised query.

Mr. Smith wants to buy a newspaper, so he selects "buy" as the expansion term. With this query the system returns 11 documents, fragments of the first 5 listed below.

(6) I'd like some *newspapers*, please.

(7) Oh, we have a barber shop, a laundry, a store, telegram services, a *newspaper* stand, table tennis, video games and so on.

(8) We can put an ad in the *newspaper*.

(9) Have you read about the Olympic Games of Table Tennis in today's *newspaper*, Miss?

(10) *newspaper* says we must be cautious about tidal waves.

This list shows improvement, as information about newspapers and shopping is present, but still appears to lack any documents directly related to *how* to buy a newspaper.

Using co-occurrence indexes, the IR system returns document (11) below, because the noun "newspaper" and the verb "buy" appear in the same sentence.

(11) You can make change at some stores, just buy a *newspaper* or something.

From this example it is apparent that this sort of query expansion is still too naive to apply to real IR systems. It should be noted, however, that our current aim of evaluation was in confirming the advantage of LMF in dealing with multiple languages, for which we conducted a similar run with Chinese and Japanese. Results of these tests showed that in following the LMF framework in describing lexical resources, it was possibile to deal with all three languages without changing the mechanics of the system at all.

5 Discussion

LMF is, admittedly, a "high-level" specification, that is, an abstract model that needs to be further developed, adapted and specified by the lexicon encoder. LMF does not provide any off-the-shelf representation for a lexical resource; instead, it gives the basic structural components of a lexicon, leaving full freedom for modeling the particular features of a lexical resource. One drawback is that LMF provides only a specification manual with a few examples. Specifications are by no means instructions, exactly as XML specifications are by no means instructions on how to represent a particular type of data.

Going from LMF specifications to a true instantiation of an LMF-compliant lexicon is a long way, and comprehensive, illustrative and detailed examples for doing this are needed. Our prototype system provides a good starting example for this direction. LMF is often taken as a prescriptive description, and its examples taken as pre-defined normative examples to be used as coding guidelines. Controlled and careful examples of conversion to LMF-compliant formats are also needed to avoid too subjective an interpretation of the standard.

We believe that LMF will be a major base for various SemanticWeb applications because it provides interoperability across languages and directly contributes to the applications themselves, such as multilingual translation, machine aided translation and terminology access in different languages.

From the viewpoint of LMF, our prototype demonstrates the adaptability of LMF to a representation of real-scale lexicons, thus promoting its adoption to a wider community. This project is one of the first test-beds for LMF (as one of its drawbacks being that it has not been tested on a wide variety of lexicons), particularly relevant since it is related to both Western and Asian language lexicons. This project is a concrete attempt to specify an LMF-compliant XML format, tested for representative and parsing efficiency, and to provide guidelines for the implementation of an LMF-compliant format, thus contributing to the reduction of subjectivity in interpretation of standards.

From our viewpoint, LMF has provided a format for exchange of information across differently conceived lexicons. Thus LMF provides a standardised format for relating them to other lexical models, in a linguistically controlled way. This seems an important and promising achievement in order to move the sector forward.

6 Conclusion

This paper described the results of a three-year project for creating an international standard for language resources in cooperation with other initiatives. In particular, we focused on query expansion using the standard.

Our main contribution can be summarised as follows.

- We have contributed to ISO TC37/SC4 activities, by testing and ensuring the portability and applicability of LMF to the development of a description framework for NLP lexicons for Asian languages. Our contribution includes (1) a package for derivational morphology, (2) the syntax-semantic interface with the problem of classifiers, and (3) representational issues with the richness of writing systems in Asian languages. As of October 2008, LMF including our contributions has been approved as the international standard ISO 26413.

- We discussed Data Categories necessary for Asian languages, and exemplified several Data Categories including reduplication, classifier, honorifics and orthography. We will continue to harmonise our activity with that of ISO TC37/SC4 TDG2 with respect to Data Categories.

- We designed and implemented an evaluation platform of our description framework. We focused on linguistically motivated query expansion module. The system works with lexicons compliant with LMF and ontologies. Its most significant feature is that the system can deal with any language as far as the those lexicons are described according to LMF. To our knowledge, this is the first working system adopting LMF.

In this project, we mainly worked on three Asian languages, Chinese, Japanese and Thai, on top of the existing framework which was designed mainly for European languages. We plan to distribute our results to HLT societies of other Asian languages, requesting for their feedback through various networks, such as the Asian language resource committee network under Asian Federation of Natural Language Processing (AFNLP)[3], and the Asian Language Resource Network project[4]. We believe our efforts contribute to international activities like ISO-TC37/SC4[5] (Francopoulo et al., 2006).

Acknowledgments

This research was carried out through financial support provided under the NEDO International Joint Research Grant Program (NEDO Grant).

References

R. Baeza-Yates and B. Ribeiro-Neto. 1999. *Modern Information Retrieval*. Addison-Wesley.

G. Francopoulo, G. Monte, N. Calzolari, M. Monachini, N. Bel, M. Pet, and C. Soria. 2006. Lexical markup framework (LMF). In *Proceedings of LREC2006*.

N. Ide, A. Lenci, and N. Calzolari. 2003. RDF instantiation of ISLE/MILE lexical entries. In *Proceedings of the ACL 2003 Workshop on Linguistic Annotation: Getting the Model Right*, pages 25–34.

A. Lenci, N. Bel, F. Busa, N. Calzolari, E. Gola, M. Monachini, A. Ogonowsky, I. Peters, W. Peters, N. Ruimy, M. Villegas, and A. Zampolli. 2000. SIMPLE: A general framework for the development of multilingual lexicons. *International Journal of Lexicography, Special Issue, Dictionaries, Thesauri and Lexical-Semantic Relations*, XIII(4):249–263.

A. Sanfilippo, N. Calzolari, S. Ananiadou, R. Gaizauskas, P. Saint-Dizier, and P. Vossen. 1999. EAGLES recommendations on semantic encoding. EAGLES LE3-4244 Final Report.

T. Tokunaga et al. 2006. Infrastructure for standardization of Asian language resources. In *Proceedings of the COLING/ACL 2006 Main Conference Poster Sessions*, pages 827–834.

T. Tokunaga et al. 2008. Adapting international standard for asian language technologies. In *Proceedings of the Sixth International Language Resources and Evaluation (LREC'08)*.

[3]http://www.afnlp.org/

[4]http://www.language-resource.net/

[5]http://www.tc37sc4.org/

Thai National Corpus: A Progress Report

Wirote Aroonmanakun
Department of Linguistics
Chulalongkorn University
awirote@chula.ac.th

Kachen Tansiri
Thai National Corpus Project
Chulalongkorn University
kc.tansiri@gmail.com

Pairit Nittayanuparp
Thai National Corpus Project
Chulalongkorn University
cherngx@gmail.com

Abstract

This paper presents problems and solutions in developing Thai National Corpus (TNC). TNC is designed to be a comparable corpus of British National Corpus. The project aims to collect eighty million words. Since 2006, the project can now collect only fourteen million words. The data is accessible from the TNC Web. Delay in creating the TNC is mainly caused from obtaining authorization of copyright texts. Methods used for collecting data and the results are discussed. Errors during the process of encoding data and how to handle these errors will be described.

1 Thai National Corpus

Thai National Corpus (TNC) is a general corpus of the standard Thai language (Aroonmanakun, 2007). It is designed to be comparable to the British National Corpus (Aston and Burnard, 1998) in terms of its domain and medium proportions. However, only written texts are collected in the TNC, and the corpus size is targeted at eighty million words. In addition to domain and medium criteria, texts are also selected and categorized on the basis of their genres. We adopted Lee's idea of categorizing texts into different genres based on external factors like the purpose of communication, participants, and the settings of communication (Lee 2001). Texts in the same genre share the same characteristics of language usages, e.g. discourse structure, sentence patterns, etc. Moreover, since TNC is a representative of the standard Thai language at present, 90% of the texts will be texts produced before 1998. The rest 10% can be texts produced before 1998 if they are published recently. Therefore, the structure of TNC is shaped on the dimensions of domain, medium, genres and time (see Table 1). Texts that fit into the designed portion of these criteria will be selected. After that, copyright holders of each text will be contacted and asked to sign a permission form. To make this process easier, the same form is used for all copyright holders. When authorization is granted, texts are randomly selected either from the beginning, the middle, the end, or selected from many sections. Sampling size can vary, but the maximum size will not exceed 40,000 words or about 80 pages of A4 paper.

In this TNC project, we use the TEI guideline, "TEI P4", as the markup language. Three types of information are marked in the document: documentation of encoded data, primary data, and linguistic annotation. Documentation of encoded data is the markup used for contextual information about the text. Primary data refers to the basic elements in the text, such as paragraphs, sections, sentences, etc. Linguistic annotation is the markup used for linguistic analysis, such as parts of speech, sentence structures, etc. The first two types are the minimum requirements for marking up texts. The structure of each document is represented in the following tags:

<tncDoc xml:id="DocName">
<tncHeader> ...markup for contextual information ...
</tncHeader>
<text> ...body text, markup for primary data e.g. <p> and linguistic analysis e.g. <w>, <name> ....
</text>
</tncDoc>

For linguistic annotation, we mark word boundaries and transcriptions for every word. Information of parts-of-speech will not be marked at present. The following is an example of markup in a document.

<w tran="kot1maaj4">กฎหมาย</w><w tran="thaN3">ทั้ง</w> <w>3</w> <w tran="cha1bap1">ฉบับ</w><w tran="mii0">มี

Proceedings of the 7th Workshop on Asian Language Resources, ACL-IJCNLP 2009, pages 153–160,
Suntec, Singapore, 6-7 August 2009.

</w><w tran="lak3sa1na1">ลักษณะ</w><w tran="mUUan4">เหมือน</w><w tran="kan0">กัน </w><w tran="juu1">อยู่</w><w tran="jaaN1"> อย่าง</w><w tran="nUN1">หนึ่ง</w>

We recognize that marking tags manually is a difficult and a time-consuming task, so for this project, two programs are used for tagging language data and contextual information. TNC Tagger is used for segmenting words and marking basic tags <w> and <p> in the text. Word segmentation and transcription program proposed in Aroonmanakun and Rivepiboon (2004) is used as a tagger. TNC Header is used for inputting contextual information and generating header tag for each text. Output from TNC Tagger will be combined with the header tag as an XML document.

2 Data collection

This section explains methods of data collection and the outcomes. First, we thought that texts could be collected easily from publishers. So, we first wrote a letter to three major publishers asking for collaboration. We thought that they would be able to provide us lot of texts in electronic formats. So, we asked them to give us a list of their publications and mark for us items that they have in electronic forms. It turned out that they did not even understand much about the corpus and the purpose of collecting texts. Thus, we did not receive positive responses as expected. Only one publisher was able to give us the list of their publications. The rest asked us to be more specific about the texts we want. The fault is ours because we did not make clear what texts that we want and how their rights on the texts will be protected. Thus, corresponding with the publishers did not go smoothly and quickly as it should be. We also learned that the publishers are not the owners of all the texts. It depends on the agreement signed between the authors and the publishers. Normally, the author is the copyright holder. Publishers may hold the copyright for a certain period agreed by both parties.

Later, before we wrote to a publisher asking for their helps, we searched and listed the title and the number of pages that we want from each text. Project details and samples of concordance output were enclosed to give them a better understanding of the project. And we only asked the publishers to collaborate by providing us the contact address of the copyright holder of each text. This time we received a positive response from many publishers. From twenty two publishers we contacted, only one publisher officially refused to collaborate for their own reasons. Fourteen publishers did not response. Seven of them sent us the information we requested. After we received the contact addresses from the publishers, we then wrote a letter directly to the author. A permission form in which selected publications are listed was attached in the letter. We asked them to sign a permission form and return it in the enclosed envelope. To make them feel easier to support us, we informed them that they may remove their works from the TNC anytime by writing a letter informing us to do so. We did not even ask for a copy of the book or the article. We will look for those texts and typing them in ourselves. By doing this, we did not put a burden on the copyright owners. In addition, we contacted the P.E.N International-Thailand Centre, which is the association of publishers, editors, and novelists in Thailand, asking for contact addresses of novelists. For academic writers, we searched for their contact addresses from university websites. Of those 780 authors we had contacted, 250 of them granted us the permission to use their texts. We suspected that the address list we received from the P.E.N International-Thailand Centre may be out-of-date because we received only 41 replies from 278 requests to novelists.

For texts that are not copyrighted in Thai, e.g. news reports, documents from governments, laws and orders etc., they are collected preferably from those that are available in the internet.

After texts were saved in electronic format and catalogued in the database, they were parsed by the TNC Tagger program. Texts will be word segmented and marked basic tags as described in the previous section. The process is not fully automatic. The program will ask a user to make a correction if any chunk of texts could not be parsed. This usually happened because there was a spelling error within that text chunk. After the text is parsed, contextual information of the text will be inserted by using the TNC Header program. With these two programs, texts are converted into an XML format that conforms to the TEI P4 standard. Some problems occurred during this process will be discuss in section 4.

3 TNC web

It is now clear that collecting eighty million words is a long time process. At present, only fourteen million words are processed in the TNC. Nevertheless, it is a good idea to make the corpus accessible to the public. So, we had been developing a web interface to search the TNC, or the TNC web[1].

TNC web is a web interface for concordance software that will show not only keyword-in-context but also collocations and distributions of the keyword. When users enter a keyword, the distribution of keyword in five major genres will be shown on the right window. Users can click on the frequency of occurrence in any genre on this window. A concordance window will then be displayed underneath. Users can filter the search by specifying a genre, a domain, published year, authors' age range, and authors' gender. By doing this, users can search for the occurrence of the keyword in any specific context. Figure 1 shows the screen of concordance search from TNC web.

Collocation is searched by clicking on the icon "COLLOCATE". Collocations within 1-3 words on the left and right contexts will be ranked by statistical measure. Frequency of occurrence in five major genres will also be shown. Users can click on these numbers to see the concordance context. Figures 2 and 3 shows the collocation of the keyword วิ่ง – 'run' using log-likelihood and mutual information .

To make the processing time acceptable, the XML data was converted into MySQL database and PHP scripting language was used for web development. Co-occurrences of words are also stored as precache data. By doing this, the size of the data storage gets larger. The XML data of 14 million words, which is about 365 megabytes, is expanded to 2,064 megabytes on the server.

Though at present, the TNC is not balance and does not have a proportion of texts as planned, making it searchable through the web is still a useful idea. Users can get authentic data in various genres. And it would be easier for us to explain to the public what the TNC is and how it can be used.

4 Problems

The difficulties of creating the TNC are grounded on management rather than technical problems. The most difficult part is to get copyright texts. Unexpected errors during the process of creating an annotation text are also another problem causing a delay in creating the TNC.

[1] http://www.arts.chula.ac.th/~ling/ tnc2/

4.1 Getting more texts

Though the use of corpora is quite well known to academics, it is little known to the public at large. Without understanding from the people especially writers and publishers, it is not easy to get the support and collaboration from them. This is the main obstruction causing a delay in creating the TNC. Implementing TNC web is one method of getting TNC known to the public. Another strategy that we plan to do is to publicize the project and praise those who contributed their texts to the project. At this moment, a number of famous novelists had granted us the permission to include parts of their novels in the TNC. We could use these names to make other people feel that it is a privilege to have their texts as a part of TNC.

Another strategy of promoting TNC is to show its worth. We plan to publish a series of linguistic papers that use TNC as data of analysis, and demonstrate how basic information like word frequency and collocations in different genres can be used for teaching the Thai language.

4.2 Validating data

The delay in creating the TNC is also caused during the process of encoding data. As stated earlier in section 2, texts have to be parsed and encoded as XML data. During this process, different types of errors are found. These have to be handled to make the data correct and consistent.

System errors (unintentional): This is an unintentional typo that produces an ill-formed string. These errors are easier to detect and most people would agree that they should be corrected. For example, รถเสีเมื่อเช้า is ill-formed because a consonant character is missing after เสี . This string cannot be parsed and read. It should be edited as รถเสียเมื่อเช้า 'car, broken, this morning'.

System errors (intentional): This is an intentional typo that produces an ill-formed string. Even if the string produced from this type is ill-formed with respect to orthography rules, they are written intentionally to intensify meaning. For example, ยากกกกก -'difficult' is a word in which the last consonant is repeated to intensify the degree of difficulty.

Hidden errors: This is also an unintentional typo error because the actual text should be something else. But the error does not produce an ill-formed string. The string can be parsed and readable. But its meaning could be strange because the actual word is mistaken as another word. For example, the phrase รถตากลางถนน is well-formed because it can be read as four words รถ ตา กลาง ถนน, 'car, grandfather, middle, street'. But its meaning is anomalous. Thus, it should be changed to รถ ตาย กลาง ถนน, 'car, broken, middle, street' - 'the car was broken in the middle of the street. This type of error is called "hidden error" because it could not be detected by simply applying orthography rules. To correct this type of error, manual editing might be required.

Variation of writing: This type is not exactly an error. It is a variation of written form produced by different authors. From a prescriptive view, it could be viewed as an error and should be corrected. Some variations are a result of the lack of knowledge in spelling. For example, some people write the word โลกาภิวัตน์ 'globalization' incorrectly as โลกาภิวัฒน์. Some write the word that does not conform to orthographic rules, e.g. แซ่ด, which should be written as แซด 'buzzing'. It is possible that they do not know how to spell these words, which makes it an unintentional error. Preserving these errors would provide us authentic information, which will be very useful for studying spelling problems. Nevertheless, since the TNC is expected to be a reference of Thai language usages, keeping these variations could confuse users who want to know the correct or standard form of writing. Therefore, these variations should be corrected and removed from the TNC. However, these variations will be saved in an error log file for further use of spelling problems.[2]

However, we do not think that all variations of writing are errors. Variations caused by different transliteration methods should be kept as they are. When transliterating foreign words, it is likely that they are written differently despite the fact that a guideline for transliteration to Thai has been proposed by the Royal Institute. For example, the word "internet" is found written as "อินเตอร์เน็ต" , "อินเตอร์เนต" , "อินเตอร์เนท" , "อินเตอร์เน็ท" , "อินเทอร์เน็ต" , "อินเทอร์เนต" , or "อินเทอร์เน็ท. All of these variations are not seen as errors and therefore are not modified.

Segmentation errors: These are errors caused by the segmentation program. It is likely that the program would segment proper names incorrectly. For example, the name นายวันชัย กู้ประเสริฐ is segmented as <w tran="naaj0">นาย</w><w tran="wan0">วัน</w><w tran="chaj0">ชัย</w> <w tran="kuu2">กู้</w><w tran="pra1s@@t1"> ประเสริฐ</w>, instead of <w tran="naaj0">นาย </w><w tran="wan0chaj0">วันชัย</w> <w tran="kuu2pra1s@@t1">กู้ประเสริฐ</w>. A Thai named entity recognition module is needed to handle this problem. But before the module is included in the TNC tagger, these errors have to be manually corrected.

To correct errors caused by typos, we could compare the same text typed by two typists. But this method would double the expense of typing. Therefore, we seek to detect typos indirectly by using the TNC Tagger program. Basically, the program will segment words in the text. If a typo causes an ill-formed character sequence, the program will fail to segment that character sequence. Then, a pop-up screen asking for a correction of that string sequence will appear. If it is an unintentional system error, the correct word will be typed in. If it is an intentional system error, the intentionally incorrect word will be tagged manually. After the program finishes segmenting words, the program will create a list of unknown words (words that are not found in the dictionary) and words that occur only once in the file. This word list will be used by the TNC Editor program for spotting errors that are not typos. TNC Editor will be used for manually editing the document, especially the hidden, variation, and segmentation errors.

4.3 Obtaining authorization

Acquiring permission from the copyright holders is a time consuming process. We once thought of a way to use copyright text under a condition of "fair use" stated in the copyright protection act in Thailand. According to the act, any writing is automatically protected by the law throughout the life of the creator plus fifty years after the author dies. However, some works are not copyrighted, such as news reports which are facts rather than opinions; constitution and laws; rules, regulation, reports or documents issued by government organizations, etc.

On section 32 of the copyright protection act, certain uses of copyright materials are not considered a violation of copyright law, such as making a copy of text for research purpose without making a profit, making a copy for private use, for criticism with an acknowledgement of the writer, for teaching or educational purpose without making a profit, etc. But all these activities must not affect the benefits that the copyright holders should have received from their works.

[2] Thanks to Dr. Virach Sornlertlamvanich for making this suggestion.

In addition, on section 33, it is stated that a reasonable and acceptable part of a copyright work can be copied or cited if the copyright owner is acknowledged. Therefore, we had consulted an eminent law firm whether our project can make use of these exceptions of the Thai copyright law. Is it possible to argue that the texts we collected are used for educational/research purpose and no profit is generated from the TNC? In addition, users can see the bibliographic reference of each concordance line. Thus, is it possible to conclude that our uses of copyright texts are under the condition of "fair use"? However, the lawyers thought that we cannot use those argumentations since the text size we collected could be up to 40,000 words. Although the reference to the source text is shown to the users, the text length is greater than acceptable level. The TNC project is the project for creating a new database. Texts collected in this project are not used for criticism or for the study of those texts per se. Our activity in collecting copyright texts could affect the benefits the copyright holder should have. Thus, the creation of a corpus is not under the conditions of sections 32 and 33. At the end, the law firm advised us to continue asking for authorization from the copyright holder as we have been doing.

5 Future plan

We plan to run three tasks concurrently: cleaning up data, expanding data, and utilizing the corpus. For cleaning up data, Thai named entity recognition module will be implemented to reduce errors of word segmentation. But at the end, TNC Editor is needed to clean up segmented data manually. The program is now under development by IBM Thailand Co.,Ltd. For expanding data, more publishers and writers are being contacted. Copyright texts are now constantly being added into the corpus. But to increase the growth rate of the corpus size, we would prefer to have people submitting their works themselves. We hope that by making the corpus searchable online and revealing famous writers who had contributed their works will make people feel that it is the prestige to have their works included in the corpus. It remains to be seen whether our plan to publicize the TNC project will be successful. And finally, to increase the worth of TNC, we will encourage linguists to use TNC as the basis of Thai language studies. Basic facts like word lists in different genres will be released. We also hope that new Thai language resources like dictionaries and grammar books could be produced based on the actual usages found in the TNC.

6 Conclusion

In this paper we described the current status of the TNC project and the problems causing the delay of collecting data. The future work will still be focused on collecting more texts, both copyright and non-copyright material. We hope to fill the TNC with texts according to the designed proportion in the dimensions of domain, medium, and genres. We hope that our publicizing plan, making the TNC known to the public and praising those who contributed their texts, would easy the process of text collection.

Given that there are a huge number of texts available on the internet, it would be easier to collect texts from the internet without going through the process of obtaining authorization from the copyright holders. In fact, many corpora have been collected directly from the web (Baroni and Ueyama, 2006; Fletcher, 2007), or the web itself has been used as a corpus (Killgarriff and Grefenstettey, 2003). It might be true that natural language processing research can use web as data source for their works effectively. Nevertheless, we think that by getting authorization from text owners, we could fully distribute the source data. And this is necessary for linguistic analysis. In addition, by manually selecting and categorizing data to be included in the corpus, users can look for similarity and difference between different text settings. Therefore, we believe that the creation of TNC will still be fruitful for research especially on Thai linguistic analysis.

Acknowledgments

The TNC project is under the patronage of H.R.H Princess Maha Chakri Sirindhorn. It is conducted by the linguistics department, with collaboration from many researchers and publishers. Special thanks to Mr.Domnern Garden for actively supporting the project till the end of his life.

References

Aroonmanakun, W. 2007. Creating the Thai National Corpus. *Manusaya*. Special Issue No.13, 4-17.

Aroonmanakun, W., and W. Rivepiboon. 2004. A Unified Model of Thai Word Segmentation and Romanization. In *Proceedings of The 18th Pacific Asia Conference on Language, Information and*

Computation, Dec 8-10, 2004, Tokyo, Japan. 205-214.

Aston, G. and L. Burnard. 1998. *The BNC handbook: exploring the British National Corpus with SARA*. Edinburgh: Edinburgh University Press.

Baroni, M. and M. Ueyama. 2006. Building general- and special-purpose corpora byWeb crawling. In *Proceedings 13th NIJL International Symposium, Language Corpora: Their Compilation and Application*, Tokyo, Japan, 31-40.

Fletcher, William H. 2007. Implementing a BNC-Compare-able Web Corpus. In *Proceedings of the 3rd web as corpus workshop, incorporating cleaneval*, Louvain-la-Neuve, Belgium, 15-16 September 2007, 43-56.

Killgarriff, A, and G. Grefenstettey. 2003. Web as Corpus. In *Computational Linguistics* 9(3): 333-347.

Lee, D. 2001. Genres, registers, text types, domains and styles: clarifying the concepts and navigating a path through the BNC jungle. *Language Learning & Technology*, 5(3): 37-72.

TEI guidelines. http://www.tei-c.org/Guidelines/ [Accessed 2009-04-24].

TNC web. http://www.arts.chula.ac.th/~ling/TNC/ [Accessed 2009-04-24].

Domain		**Medium**	
Imaginative	25%	*Book*	60%
Informative	75%	*Periodical*	20%
Applied science		*Published miscellanea*	5-10%
Arts		*Unpublished miscellanea*	5-10%
Belief and thought		*Internet*	5%
Commerce and finance			
Leisure		**Time**	
Natural and pure science		*1998-present (2541-2550)*	90-100%
Social science		*1988-1997 (2531-2540)*	0-10%
World affairs		** before 1988 (-2531)*	0-5%

Genres	**Sub-genres**
Academic	*Humanities, e.g. Philosophy, History, Literature, Art, Music*
	Medicine
	Natural Sciences, e.g. Physics, Chemistry, Biology
	Political Science - Law – Education
	Social Sciences, e.g. Psychology, Sociology, Linguistics
	Technology & Engineering, e.g. Computing, Engineering
Non-Academic	*Humanities*
	Medicine
	Natural Sciences
	Political Science - Law – Education
	Social Sciences
	Technology & Engineering
Advertisement	
Biography - Experiences	
Commerce - Finance – Economics	
Religion	
Institutional Documents	
Instructional – DIY	
Law & Regulation	
Essay	*School*
	University
Letter	*Personal*
	Professional
Blog	
Magazine	
News report	
Editorial - Opinion	
Interview – Question & Answer	
Prepared speech	
Fiction	*Drama*
	Poetry
	Prose
	Short Stories
Miscellanea	

Table 1: Design of Thai National Corpus

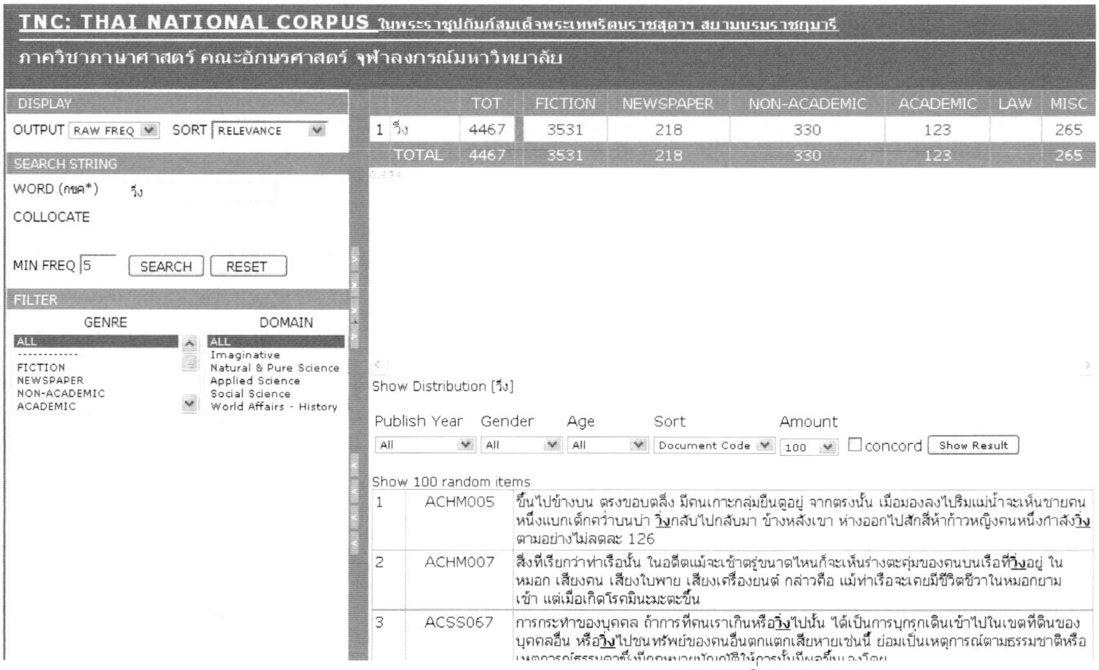

Figure 1: Concordance search result of the word วิ่ง 'run'

		TOT	FICTION	NEWSPAPER	NON-ACADEMIC	ACADEMIC	LAW	MISC	ALL	%	DL
1	ไป	1183	1009	25	72	17		60	159851	0.74	5473.54
2	หนี	326	222	43	27	9		25	3557	9.17	3087.76
3	มา	712	588	26	53	11		34	142992	0.50	2672.56
4	เข้า	470	410	19	24	2		15	39011	1.20	2541.20
5	รีบ	267	234	9	20			4	6075	4.40	2121.40
6	ออก	390	342	16	16	4		12	40169	0.97	1936.89
7	ตาม	370	303	9	24	4		30	53701	0.69	1590.33
8	ก็	419	363	3	29	4		20	128433	0.33	1217.25

Figure 2: Collocation of the word วิ่ง 'run' using Dunning's Log-likelihood

		TOT	FICTION	NEWSPAPER	NON-ACADEMIC	ACADEMIC	LAW	MISC	ALL	%	MI
1	จู๊ด	15	12		2			1	17	88.24	9.42
2	ตื๋อ	17	12		5				20	85.00	9.36
3	แจ้น	27	23	1	2			1	47	57.45	8.80
4	ปรู๊ด	14	14						27	51.85	8.65
5	กระหืดกระหอบ	22	22						46	47.83	8.53
6	เหยาะ	30	28					2	64	46.88	8.50
7	เร็ด	5	5						15	33.33	8.01
8	กวด	10	6			1		3	38	26.32	7.67

Figure 3: Collocation of the word วิ่ง 'run' using Mutual Information

The FLaReNet Thematic Network: A Global Forum for Cooperation

Nicoletta Calzolari
Consiglio Nazionale delle Ricerche
Istituto di Linguistica Computazionale
"A. Zampolli"
nicoletta.calzolari@ilc.cnr.it

Claudia Soria
Consiglio Nazionale delle Ricerche
Istituto di Linguistica Computazionale
"A. Zampolli"
claudia.soria@ilc.cnr.it

Abstract

The aim of this short paper is to present the FLaReNet Thematic Network for Language Resources and Language Technologies to the Asian Language Resources Community. Creation of a wide and committed community and of a shared policy in the field of Language Resources is essential in order to foster a substantial advancement of the field. This paper presents the background, overall objectives and methodology of work of the project, as well as a set of preliminary results.

1 Introduction

The field of Language Resources and Technologies has been developing for years to reach now a stable and consolidated status, attaining the right to be considered a discipline in itself, and as testified by the number of conferences and publications explicitly dedicated to the topic. Even if Language Resources (in the widest sense, i.e. spoken, written and multi-modal resources and basic related tools) have a rather short history, they are nowadays recognized as one of the pillars of NLP. The availability of adequate Language Resources for as many languages as possible is a pre-requisite for the development of a truly multilingual Information Society.

At the same time, however, the discipline has seen considerable fragmentation during those years of fast and enthusiast development, and the landscape is now composed by a kaleidoscope of different, often conflicting initiatives that vary as for research directions, theoretical approaches, implementation choices, distribution and access policies, languages, domain and modalities covered, etc.

The growth of the field in the last years should be now complemented by a common reflection and by an effort that identifies synergies and overcomes fragmentation. The consolidation of the area is a pre-condition to enhance competitiveness at EU level and worldwide. There is the need of working together to define common strategies and to identify priorities for the field to advance. Multiple concurring signs are now indicating that time is ripe for establishing an open language infrastructure, something that many of us have been pushing since some time and that is now increasingly recognized in the community at large as a necessary step for building on each other achievements.

Such an open infrastructure can only be realized if the Language Resources community is cohesive enough to be able to focus on a number or priority targets and collectively work towards them, and, at the same time, whether it is powerful enough to permeate the user community, the industry, and the policy-makers.

2 Why FLaReNet

Creation of the necessary conditions for the development of such an infrastructure cannot rely on research activities only and even more cannot rely on the initiative of individual groups. Instead, strategic actions are crucial, such as making contacts with and involving all interested parties, sensitize the policy makers and institutional bodies, involve associations and consortia, disseminating widely the results of common efforts. Only by mobilizing this wide and heterogeneous panorama of actors can such an ambitious goal be attained.

FLaReNet – Fostering Language Resources Network – is a Thematic Network funded by the

Proceedings of the 7th Workshop on Asian Language Resources, ACL-IJCNLP 2009, pages 161–164,
Suntec, Singapore, 6-7 August 2009. ©2009 ACL and AFNLP

European Commission under the eContentPlus framework (ECP-2007-LANG-617001) [1]. The FLaReNet Thematic Network was born with the specific aim – as required by the European Commission itself – to enhance European competitiveness in the field of Language Resources and Technologies, especially by consolidating a common vision and fostering a European strategy for the future. A major, long-term objective – as well as a powerful means for community creation – is creating the preparatory environment for making an open language infrastructure a reality.

3 Objectives

The objectives of FLaReNet are threefold:

- The creation and mobilization of a unified and committed community in the field of Language Resources and Technologies;
- The identification of a set of priority themes on which to stimulate action, under the form of a roadmap for Language Resources and Technologies;
- The elaboration of a blueprint of priority areas for actions in the field and a coherent set of recommendations for the policy-makers (funding agencies especially), the business community and the public at large.

3.1 Creation of a community

FLaReNet has the challenging task of creating a network of people around the notion of Language Resources and Technologies. To this end, FLaReNet is bringing together leading experts of research institutions, academies, companies, funding agencies, with the specific purpose of creating consensus around short, medium and long-term strategic objectives. It is of foremost importance that the FLaReNet Network be composed of the as widest as possible representation of experiences, practices, research lines, industrial and political strategies; this in order to derive an overall picture of the field of Language Resources and Technologies that is not limited to the European scenario, but can also be globally inspired. The Network is currently composed of around 200 individuals belonging to academia, research institutes, industries and government. Such a community also needs to be constantly increased in a concentric way that starts from the core disciplines but gradually projects itself towards "neighboring" ones, such as cognitive science, semantic web, etc.

3.2 Identification of priority themes

Language technologies and language resources are the necessary ingredients for the development of applications that will help bridging language barriers in a global single information space, in a variety of means (the Web as well as communication devices) and for a variety of channels (spoken and written language alike). It is of utmost importance, however, to identify priorities as well as short, medium, and long-term strategic objectives in order to avoid scattered or conflicting efforts.

The major players in the field of Language Resources and Technologies need to consensually work together and indicate a clear direction and priorities for the next years.

3.3 Elaboration of a blueprint of actions

However, whatever action cannot be implemented on a long term without the help of the necessary financial and political framework to sustain them. This is even most true for actions regarding Language Resources that typically imply a sustained effort at national level. To this end, the FLaReNet Network must propose the priority themes under the form of consensual recommendations and a plan of action for EC Member States, other European-wide decision makers, companies, as well as non-EU and International organizations.

FLaReNet goals are very ambitious and its objectives are to be seen in a more global framework. Although they are shaped by the European landscape of the field of LR&T, its mission is therefore inherently cross-boundary: in order to attain such goals getting a global view is fundamental.

To this end, it is important that FLaReNet is known by the Asian community, and it knows the Asian community. Some Asian community players are already members of the Network.

4 How FLaReNet works

Work in FLaReNet is inherently collaborative.
Its means are the following:

- Working groups
- Organization of workshops and meetings

[1] http://www.flarenet.eu

- External liaisons

4.1 Working Groups

Working Groups are intended as "think-tanks" of experts (researchers and users) who jointly reflect on selected topics and come up with conclusions and recommendations. The Working Groups are clustered in thematic areas and carry out their activities through workshops, meetings, and via a collaborative Wiki platform. The FLaReNet Thematic Areas are:

- The Chart for the area of Language Resources and Technologies in its different dimensions
- Methods and models for Language Resource building, reuse, interlinking, maintenance, sharing, and distribution
- Harmonization of formats and standards
- Definition of evaluation and validation protocols and procedures
- Methods for the automatic construction and processing of Language Resources.

4.2 Organization of workshops and meetings

Meetings and events lie at the core of FLaReNet action plan and dissemination strategies. They can either be specifically oriented to the dissemination of results and recommendations (*content-pushing* events) or, rather, to their elicitation (*content-pulling* events). Three types of meetings are envisaged:

- Annual Workshops, such as the "European Language Resources and Technologies Forum" held in Vienna, February 2009
- Thematic Workshops related to the work of Working Groups
- Liaison meetings (e.g. those with NSF-SILT, CLARIN, ISO and other projects as the need may arise).

Annual workshops are targeted to gather the broad FLaReNet community together. They are conceived as big events, and they aim at becoming major events in the Language Resources and Technology community of the kind able to attract a considerable audience. Given the success of the formula exploited for the FLaReNet "Vienna Event"[2], it is likely that Annual workshops will be organized along the same lines. However, this type of event cannot be repeated on a frequent schedule. At the same time, more focused events centered on specific topics and with extensive time allocated for discussion are essential.

To this end, Annual Workshops will be complemented by many Thematic workshops, i.e. more focused, dedicated meetings with a more restricted audience. These are directly linked to the work being carried out by the various Working Groups and are organized in a de-centralized manner, by direct initiative of the Working Group or Work package Leaders. In an attempt to increase FLaReNet sensitivity to hot issues, selection of topics and issues to be addressed will be also based on a bottom-up approach: FLaReNet members and subscribers are invited to submit topics of interest either freely or as a consequence of "Call for topics" related to particular events.

Finally, liaison meetings are those elicited by FLaReNet to make contact and create synergies with national and international projects that are partially overlapping with FLaReNet in either their objectives or the target audience. Examples of these are the FLaReNet-CLARIN and the FLaReNet-SILT liaison meetings.

4.3 External liaisons

For a Network like FLaReNet, whose aim is the development of strategies and recommendations for the field of Language Resources and Technologies, coordination of actions at a worldwide level is of utmost importance. To this end, FLaReNet is planning to establish contacts and liaisons with national and international associations and consortia, such as LDC, ISO, ALTA, AFNLP, W3C, TEI, COCOSDA, Oriental-COCOSDA. Specific actions of this kind have started already, such as the International Cooperation Round Table that took place in Vienna. The members of the International Cooperation Round Table will form the initial nucleus of the FLaReNet International Advisory Board.

5 First results and recommendations

More than a hundred players worldwide gathered at the latest FLaReNet Vienna Forum, with the

[2] http://www.flarenet.eu/?q=Vienna09, see the Event Program to get an idea of the event structure.

specific purpose of setting up a brainstorming force to make emerge the technological, market and policy challenges to be faced in a multilingual digital Europe.

Over a two-day programme, the participants to the Forum had the opportunity to start assessing the current conditions of the LR&T field and to propose emerging directions of intervention.

Some messages recurred repeatedly across the various sessions, as a sign both of a great convergence around these ideas and also of their relevance in the field. A clear *set of priorities* thus emerged *for fostering the field* of Language Resources and Language Technology.

Language Resource Creation. The effort required to build all needed language resources and common tools should impose on all players *a strong cooperation at the international level* and the community should define how to *enhance current coordination of language resource collection between all involved agencies* and ensure efficiency (e.g. through interoperability).

With data-driven methods dominating the current paradigms, *language resource building, annotation, cataloguing, accessibility, availability* is what the research community is calling for. Major institutional translation services, holding large volumes of useful data, seem to be ready to share their data and FLaReNet could possibly play a facilitating role.

More efforts should be devoted *to solve how to automate the production of the large quantity of resources demanded, and of enough quality to get acceptable results in industrial environments.*

Standards and Interoperability. In the long term, *interoperability will be the cornerstone of a global network of language processing capabilities*. The time and circumstances are ripe to take a broad and forward-looking view in order to establish and implement the standards and technologies necessary to ensure language resource interoperability in the future. This can only be achieved through a *coordinated, community-wide effort that will ensure both comprehensive coverage and widespread acceptance*.

Coordination of Language Technology Evaluation. Looking at the way forward, it clearly appears that *language technology evaluation needs coordination at international level*: in order to ensure the link between technologies and applications, between evaluation campaigns and projects, in order to conduct evaluation campaigns (for ensuring synchrony or for addressing the influence of a component on a system on the same data), in order to produce language resources from language technology evaluation, or to port an already evaluated language technology to other languages (best practices, tools, metrics, protocols…), in order to avoid "reinventing the wheel", while being very cautious that there are language and cultural specificities which have to be taken into account (tone languages, oral languages with no writing system, etc).

Availability of Resources, Tools and Information. *Infrastructure building* seems to be one of the main messages for FLaReNet. *For a new worldwide language infrastructure the issue of access to Language Resources and Technologies is a critical one* that should involve – and have impact on – all the community. There is the need to create the means to plug together different Language Resources & Language Technologies, in an *internet-based resource and technology grid*, with the possibility to easily create new workflows. Related to this is *openness and availability of information*. The related issues of *access rights and IPR* also call for cooperation.

6 Join FLaReNet

In order to constantly increase the community of people involved in FLaReNet, as well as to ensure their commitment to the objectives of the Network, a recruiting campaign is always open. People wishing to join the Network can do so by filling an appropriate web form available on the FLaReNet web site. The FLaReNet Network is open to participation by public and private, research and industrial organizations.

7 Conclusions

The field of Language Resources and Technologies needs a strong and coherent international cooperation policy to become more competitive and play a leading role globally. It is crucial to discuss future policies and priorities for the field of Language Resources and Technologies – as in the mission of FLaReNet – not only on the European scene, but also in a worldwide context. Cooperation is an issue that needs to be prepared. FLaReNet may become one of the privileged places where these – and future – initiatives get together to discuss and promote collaboration actions.

Towards Building Advanced Natural Language Applications - An Overview of the Existing Primary Resources and Applications in Nepali

Bal Krishna Bal
Madan Puraskar Pustakalaya
Lalitpur,Patan Dhoka,
Nepal
bal@mpp.org.np

Abstract

The paper gives an overview of some of the major primary resources and applications developed in the field of Natural Language Processing(NLP) for the Nepali language and their prospective for building advanced NLP applications. The paper also sheds light on the approaches followed by the current applications and their coverage as well as limitations.

1 Introduction

NLP is a relatively new area of involvement in the context of Nepal.The first ever NLP works in Nepal include the Nepali Spell Checker and Thesaurus that got released in the year 2005. The years after that saw an increasing amount of Research and Development of NLP resources and applications under different programs.This included **Dobhase**[1], an English to Nepali Machine Translation System, Stemmer and Morphological Analyzer, Parts-of-Speech(POS) Tagger, Chunker, Parser, a corpus-based on-line Nepali monolingual dictionary, Text-To-Speech etc. On the resources front, by 2008, we have had developed a Lexicon, Nepali Written Corpus,Parallel Corpus, POS Tagset,Speech Recordings etc. In the sections that follow, we will be discussing over the current achievements and the possible advanced applications that can be developed on the basis of the existing resources and applications.

2 Resources

2.1 Nepali Lexicon

The process of the development of the Nepali Lexicon(Bista *et al.*,2004-2007;2004-2007a) underwent several changes as the purpose of the lexicon was not very clear in the beginning.No doubt, we were aware that the usage of a lexicon would be basically a multi-purpose one, fitting to one or more NLP applications but we were a bit unsure about the actual format of the lexicon.As a result, the entries of the lexicon were maintained in different file formats ranging from plain spreadsheets to XML formatted data files. In the beginning, the attributes of the lexicon were decided to be as:

- Rootword
- Headword
- Pronunciation
- Syllablebreak
- Meaning
- PartsofSpeech
- Synonym
- Idiom

But later on, owing to time constraints and also taking into consideration the applicability of the lexicon to some of the immediate NLP applications being developed like the Spell Checker and the Stemmer/Morphological Analyzer, the entries were just made for the attributes - Rootword and PartsofSpeech. The file format was also fixed for the plain spreadsheet one, keeping into consideration the discomfort faced by the linguists and data entry persons with the XML data format.The latest size of the lexicon is 37,000 root words with their parts of speech category specified. Wherever more than one category is possible, multiple categories have been entered with the comma as the separator.

2.2 Nepali POS Tagset

The Nepali POS Tagset designed in the beginning consisted of 112 tags[2]. These tags were

[1]http://nlp.ku.edu.np/cgi-bin/dobhase

[2]http://www.bhashasanchar.org/pdfs/nelralec-wp-tagset.pdf

Proceedings of the 7th Workshop on Asian Language Resources, ACL-IJCNLP 2009, pages 165–170,
Suntec, Singapore, 6-7 August 2009. ©2009 ACL and AFNLP

used to manually and semi-automatically annotate the written corpus as well. Experiences, however, showed that error rates of annotation could be much higher when the size of the tagset was a big one, the reason primarily being the chances of assigning incorrect tags to the words out of confusion while manually annotating the the training data itself. It was with such motivations that a smaller sized POS Tagset[3] was later on developed that consists of just 43 tags. While developing the tagset, maximum care has been taken to ensure that this minimalist approach does not unnecessarily eliminate the unavoidable lexical categories of the language. The design of this Nepali POS Tagset was inspired by the PENN Treebank POS Tagset.Hence, whenever possible, the same naming convention has been used as in the case of the PENN Treebank Tagset. In Table 1, we provide the summary of the small sized POS Tagset. Owing to space constraints, we have just provided limited examples for each of the POS category.

2.3 Nepali Written Corpus

Different efforts have been put into developing the Nepali Written Corpus. We try to provide a brief overview on each of them below.

With an aim to facilitate linguistic and computational/corpus linguistic researches of the Nepali language,the compilation of different text corpora got initiated under the activity, **Nepali National Corpus**[4]. The Nepali National Corpus basically consists of three different types of corpora, namely, the Written Corpus(monolingual and parallel), the Spoken Corpus and the Speech Corpus. The monolingual Nepali Written Corpus was further sub-divided into two types - the Core Corpus and the General Corpus. The Core Corpus consists of 398 texts from about 15 different genres and amounting to 1 million words, has been collected from different books,journals,magazines and newspapers. The texts belong to the time period between 1990 and 1992. The Core Corpus has been converted into XML file format. In addition, the text has been annotated using the 112 Tagset. The General Corpus,on the other hand, is a collection of the written texts basically from the

Table 1: Summary of the Nepali POS Tagset

Tag	Description	Example
NN	Common Noun	Ghar
NNP	Proper Noun	Ram
PP	Personal Pronoun	Ma
PP$	Possessive Pronoun	Mero
PPR	Reflexive Pronoun	Afu
DM	Marked Demonstrative	Arko
DUM	Unmarked Demonstrative	Tyo
VBF	Finite Verb	Khayo
VBX	Auxiliary Verb	Thiyo
VBI	Verb Infinitive	Khana
VBNE	Prospective Participle	hidne manchhe
VBKO	Aspectual Participle	Thiyo
VBO	Other Participle Verb	Diyeko
JJ	Normal Unmarked Adjective	Asal
JJM	Marked Adjective	Ramro
JJD	Degree Adjective	Adhiktar
RBM	Manner Adverb	dhilo hidchha
RBO	Other Adverb	yaha basa
INTF	Intensifier	dherai chalaakh
PLE	Le-Postposition	Harile
PLAI	Lai-Postposition	Bhailai
KO	KO-Postposition	Ramko
POP	Other PostPositions	tabulmathi
CC	Co-ordinating Conjunction	ra
CS	Subordinating Conjunction	Kinabhane
UH	Interjection	Oho
CD	Cardinal Number	Ek
OD	Ordinal Number	Pahilo
HRU	Plural Marker	Haru
QW	Question Word	Ko
CL	Classifier	Dasjana
RP	Particle	Khai
DT	Determiner	Tyo keto
UNW	Unknown Word	Nekomprenas
FW	Foreign Word	good
YF	Sentence Final	? ! etc.
YM	Sentence Medieval	, ; : etc.
YQ	Quotation	' ' " "
YB	Brackets	() {} []
FB	Abbreviation	Ma.Pu.Pu
ALPH	Header List	Ka.
SYM	Symbol	%
NULL	<NULL>	

[3]http://nepalinux.org/downloads/nlp/nepali_pos_tagset.pdf

[4]The Nepali National Corpus was developed under the Nepali Language Resources and Localization for Education and Communication(NeLRaLEC)Project.For details, please visit http://bhashasanchar.org

internet. The collected texts amount to a size of 14 million words. Both the Core Corpus and the General Corpus above have been developed following the internationally accepted FLOB and FROWN framework for collecting text corpus.
Another set of collection under the Written Corpus is the Parallel Corpus. The Parallel Corpus consists of collections from two genres - computing and national development. The one on computing sizes to be 3 million words of English-Nepali parallel texts whereas the other one on national development amounts to about 966,203 words.
In another bid, a Nepali Corpora parallel to 100,000 words of common English source from PENN Treebank corpus, available through the Linguistic Data Consortium(LDC)has been developed[5].This Parallel Corpus has been also POS Tagged with the 43 POS Tagset as presented in Table 1.

2.4 Nepali Spoken Corpus

The Spoken Corpora has been designed on the basis of the Goteborg Spoken Language Corpus(GSLC). The Corpora have been collected from 17 social activities and contain about 2,60,000 words. These texts are audio-video recordings of the activities with their corresponding transcriptions and annotations about the participant's information. Each activity is stored in three separate files (.mpeg, .txt and .doc) respectively for recording,transcription and recording information.

2.5 Nepali Speech Corpus

The Speech Corpus is a specialized recordings of speech developed for the Nepali Text-To-Speech(TTS) application for enabling the software to speak Nepali from written texts.It consists of 1,880 sentences and 6053 words, extracted from the Core Corpus and later recorded in male and female voices. The recordings are approximately of 3-4 hours.

3 Applications

3.1 Nepali Thesaurus

For developing the Nepali Thesaurus, we have used the MyThes framework[6] developed by Kevin Hendricks. MyThes is incorporated with the OpenOffice.org suite.Originally, it did not support UTF-8 encoding but the support has been enabled after OpenOffice.org 2.0.2 onwards.The Nepali Thesaurus currently contains 5,500 entries with the attributes - POS Tag, Meaning and Synonym. This application has been released as an inbuilt package with OpenOffice.org Writer localized into Nepali for public usage since 2005.

3.2 Nepali Spell Checker

The Nepali Spell Checker follows the Hunspell framework[7]. In essence, Hunspell is a spell checker and morphological library.It is included in OpenOffice.org suite 2.0 onwards by default. Recently,it has also been adopted by the Google Search Engine as it's default Spell Checker. Depending upon the language specific terriotory, HunSpell may be customized by using the concerned locale file. HunSpell requires two files[8], respectively the dictionary file that contains the words for the language and the affix file that has rules associated to the words in the dictionary by using flags serving as pointers. The two files should be located in the folder openofficefolder/share/dic/ooo/. Spell checking is done using the affix file, locale and the dictionary file.While the affix file consists of affix rules, the dictionary file consists of root words. At the moment,the size of the dictionary file is about 37,000 entries whereas we have about 1,800 affix rules in the affix file. The word coverage in terms of spell checking is 6.2 million Nepali words. Random tests of the spell checker yielded accuracies of 90%(43 words unhandled out of 450 words),94%(25 words unhandled out of 400 words),89% accuracy(100 words unhandled out of 923 words) etc. By saying unhandled, we refer to the situation whereby the incorrect words are not provided appropriate suggestions.

3.3 Dobhase - English to Nepali Machine Translation System

With a view to aid to the majority of English unproficient Nepalis to some extent, this application was developed under a joint collaboration between Kathmandu University and Madan Puraskar Pustakalaya.The software currently is able to provide gist translations to simple declarative sentences.It

[5]This work has been developed with the support from the Language Resource Association (GSK) of Japan and International Development Research Center (IDRC) of Canada, through the PAN Localization Project(www.PANL10n.net)

[6]http://lingucomponent.openoffice.org/MyThes-1.zip

[7]http://hunspell.sourceforge.net

[8]The two files for Nepali is available at http://nepalinux.org/downloads/ne_NP_dict.zip

is a rule and transfer-based Machine Translation System. More information on the software is available at http://nlp.ku.edu.np/

3.4 The Online Nepali Dictionary

A Corpus based Online Nepali Dictionary has been developed for Nepali and is available in the following link http://nepalisabdakos.com
This dictionary differs from the existing ones(both hard and soft copy versions) in that this dictionary contains examples and meanings from the corpus itself. The XIARA software has been used to look for wordlists and concordances in due course of compiling the dictionary. The dictionary currently contains about 8,000 entries .

3.5 The Nepali Text-To-Speech

The Nepali Text-To-Speech Application has been developed following the Festival Speech Synthesis System.Currently, the Nepali Text-To-Speech works just in the Linux environment and has the basic capabilities of reading text from files.One may opt to hear the texts either from a male or a female voice.The application has been deemed useful not only to visually impaired but also to illiterates.Lately, there has been a growing demand of the application for extending it to a screen reader and making it work in cross-platforms.For more information, please visit http://bhashasanchar.org/textspeech_intro.php

3.6 Conversion Tools

Keeping into consideration that a lot of texts both in the government and the general public are still encoded in ASCII-based Nepali non-unicode fonts,we have developed the **Conversion Tools** both for converting non-unicode texts to unicode and vice versa.For details,please visit http://madanpuraskar.org/ Our efforts in the development of the tool have been supplemented by the Open Source Community as well.The latest information on the extended work is available at http://code.google.com/p/nepaliconverter/

3.7 The Nepali Stemmer and the Morphological Analyzer

The Nepali Stemmer and the Morphological Analyzer combines the results of the Stemmer and the Morphological Analyzer in the sense that besides producing the stem or root of any word, the associated bound morphemes and their grammatical category are also kept track of. The Nepali Stemmer and Morphological Analyzer is a rule-based one and makes use of the following resources:

- Free morpheme based lexicon
- Affix file or bound morpheme list
- Database of word breaking rules

The free morpheme based lexicon consists of free or unbound morphemes of the Nepali language together with their respective parts-of-speech information. Similarly, the affix file or bound morpheme list contains the prefix and the suffixes in Nepali.These affixes are further associated with numbers which point to the corresponding word breaking rules.Finally, the word breaking rules database basically represent the insertion and deletion rules applicable once a word breaks down into the root and the respective affixes. The application, which is still at a prototypical stage, is available at http://nepalinux.org/downloads/nlp/stemmer_ma.zip

3.8 The Nepali Computational Grammar Analyzer

The Nepali Computational Grammar Analyzer is an attempt to develop a basic computational framework for analyzing the correctness of a given input sentence in the Nepali language. While the primary objective remains in building such a framework, the secondary objective lies in developing intermediate standalone NLP modules like the POS Tagger,chunker and the parser.In Figure 1, we present the system architecture of the Nepali Computational Grammar Analyzer. Talking about the individual modules,for the POS Tagger,we have used TNT[9],a very efficient and state-of-the-art statistical POS tagger and trained it with around 82000 Nepali words.Currently the accuracy of the trained TnT POS Tagger for Nepali is 56% for unknown words and 97% for known words.
Similarly,for the chunker module, we have developed a hand-crafted linguistic chunk rules and a simple algorithm to process these rules.Currently, we have around 30 chunk rules, which have to be further optimized for better coverage and output.The chunkset consists of 11 chunk tags at the moment.
For the parser module, we have implemented

[9]http://coli.uni-saarland.de/ thorsten/tnt/

a constraint-based parser following the dependency grammar formalism[10] and in particular the Paninian Grammar framework(Bharati *et al.*,1993,1995;Pederson *et al.*,2004).A dependency parser gives us a framework to identify the relations between the verb(s) and the other constituents in a sentence. Such relations, which basically occur between verb(s) and nominal constituents are called **Karaka relations**.For Nepali, we have identified altogether six different Karaka relations, namely,Karta - K1, Karma - K2, Karan-K3, Sampradan - K4, Apadaan-K5, Others-KX.

The assumption is that if we can establish valid Karaka relations between the chunks of the sentence and the verb, then the given input sentence is valid.For example, in the Nepali sentence *Ram le bhaat khaayo (meaning Ram ate rice)*, there is a K1 relation between the verb *khaayo* and the noun chunk *Ram le*, and similarly K2 relation between the verb *khaayo* and the noun chunk *bhaat*. Next, the Karaka frame specifies what karakas are mandatory or optional for the verb and what vibhaktis(postpositions) they take respectively. Each verb belongs to a specific verb class (in our case, whether the verb is transitive or intransitive)and each class has a basic karaka frame. Each Tense,Aspect and Modality - TAM of a verb specifies a transformation rule. Based on the TAM of a verb, a transformation is made on the verb frame taking reference of the TAM frame. A detailed description of the Nepali Computation Grammar Analyzer is available at http://nepalinux.org/downloads/nlp/report_on _nepali_computational_grammar.pdf

The Grammar Analyzer for Nepali currently parses and analyzes simple declarative sentences with just one verb candidate.We have developed the karaka frame for around 700 Nepali verbs.An agreement module if added to the analyzer could further filter the parses returned by the parser module, this time taking the feature agreements like gender, number, person, tense, aspect and modality. Hence,with the possible addition of the agreement module, the robustness of the Grammar Analyzer is believed to significantly increase.

[10] http://w3.msi.vxu.se/nivre/papers/05133.pdf

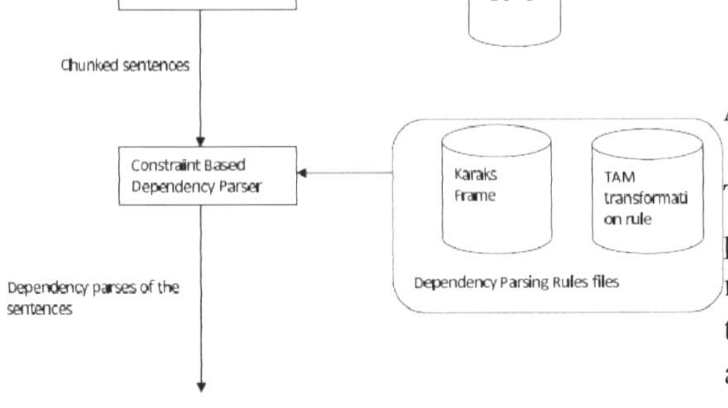

Figure 1: System Architecture of the Nepali Computational Grammar Analyzer

4 Conclusion

In this paper, we discussed on the different efforts put towards developing the basic NLP resources and applications.We also talked about the approaches followed by the applications and shed light on their current coverage and limitations. From the discussions above, it is quite clear that much work has been done in developing a basic NLP foundation for Nepali both from resource buiding and applications development perspectives. The way ahead is undoubtedly in refining the current achievements and building advanced NLP applications like Statistical Machine Translation System, Name Entity Recognition System, Question Answering System,Information Retrieval System, Information Extraction System etc. Another possibility is applying the expertise and experiences gathered while working for Nepali to other non-Nepali languages.

Acknowledgements

The works described in the paper have been partly supported by the International Development Research Center(IDRC), Canada through the PAN Localization Project(http://panl10n.net) and Asia IT & C Programme of the European Commission under the Bhasha Sanchar Project(http://bhashasanchar.org).

References

A.Bharati, V. Chaitanya, and R. Sangal, Natural Language Processing - A Paninian Perspective. New Delhi: Easter Economy Edition ed.Kantipur:Prentice Hall, 1995.

A.Bharati and R. Sangal, "Parsing free word order languages in the Paninian framework.," in Proceedings of the 31'st Annual Meeting on Association For Computational Linguistics (Columbus, Ohio, June 22, 1993).Annual Meeting of the ACL., Morristown, NJ, 1993, pp. 105-111.

A.Bharati, R. Sangal, and T. Reddy, "A Constraint Based Parser Using Integer Programming," in Proceedings of the ICON-2002, Mumbai, 2002, pp. 121-127.

B. K. Bal, B. Karki, and L. Khatiwada, "Nepali Spellchecker 1.1 and the Thesaurus, Research and Development," PAN Localization Working Papers 2004-2007.

B. K. Bal and P. Shrestha, "Nepali Spellchecker," PAN Localization Working Papers 2004-2007.

S. Bista, L. Kathiwada, and B. Keshari, "Nepali Lexicon," PAN Localization, Working Papers 2004-2007, pp.307-10.

S. Bista, L. Khatiwada, and B. Keshari, "Nepali Lexicon Development.," PAN Localization, Working Papers 2004-2007, pp.311-15.

M.Pederson, D. Eades, S. Amin, and L. Prakash, "Relative clauses in Hindi and Arabic:A paninian dependency grammar analysis. ," in Proceedings of the Twentiet International Conference on Computational Linguistics., Geneva, 2004, pp. 17-24.

Using Search Engine to Construct a Scalable Corpus for Vietnamese Lexical Development for Word Segmentation

Doan Nguyen
Hewlett-Packard Company
doan.nguyen@hp.com

Abstract

As the web content becomes more accessible to the Vietnamese community across the globe, there is a need to process Vietnamese query texts properly to find relevant information. The recent deployment of a Vietnamese translation tool on a well-known search engine justifies its importance in gaining popularity with the World Wide Web. There are still problems in the translation and retrieval of Vietnamese language as its word recognition is not fully addressed. In this paper we introduce a semi-supervised approach in building a general scalable web corpus for Vietnamese using search engine to facilitate the word segmentation process. Moreover, we also propose a segmentation algorithm which recognizes effectively Out-Of-Vocabulary (OOV) words. The result indicates that our solution is scalable and can be applied for real time translation program and other linguistic applications. This work is here is a continuation of the work of Nguyen D. (2008).

1 Introduction

The Vietnamese language as a minority language is gaining popularity including content and audience. It is important to emphasize a need for natural language such as search engines or translation tools to process the data correctly. With this emphasis, we need to have a way to improve and automate the training process as well as expanding its training data. Previous works in constructing segmentation systems for the Vietnamese language relied on single source of information such as newspapers or electronic dictionaries (Le H. Phuong et al. 2008, Dinh Dien and Vu Thuy, 2006, Le T. Ha et al., 2005). Mono-source corpora would work best within their domain, and might not work well externally per O'Neil (2007). Le A. Ha, (2003) described the dictionary based approach as problematic due to the lack of consistency and completeness. This speaks to the need of standardizations between dictionaries, concrete grammar theories, and being up-to-date with the arrival of new words. In the work of Nguyen C. T. et al. (2007), corpus training was done manually by linguists. This was very time-consuming and costly. Because the task is performed only once, a corpus will go stale and will get out-of-date. Dinh et al. (2008), in a comparison with major Vietnamese segmentation approaches, concluded that the handling of unknown compound words is a much greater source of segmenting errors and underscored that future effort should be geared at prioritizing towards the automatic detection of new compounds.

In this paper, we first present the main issues with the Vietnamese word segmentation problem. We describe the two approaches in obtaining raw text from the Web. Then, we present our approach in building a large web corpus for a word segmentation function and compare our result against a sophisticated algorithm built on a human trained corpus. Finally, we provide our conclusion and offer suggestions for future research directions.

2 Vietnamese Word Segmentation Problems

Vietnamese (Tiếng Việt) is the official language of Vietnam. The current writing system originates from the Latin alphabet, with diacritics for tones and certain letters. Vietnamese is often mistakenly judged as a "monosyllabic" language. However, the majority of the words are disyllabic (Le A. Ha, 2003) covering reduplication and adjectives. Its grammar depends on word ordering and sentence structure rather than morphology. Even though there is a space separating

Proceedings of the 7th Workshop on Asian Language Resources, ACL-IJCNLP 2009, pages 171–178,
Suntec, Singapore, 6-7 August 2009.

sound units, there is nothing used to identify word boundary.

Examples in Figure 1. are used to illustrate the difficulty of Vietnamese word segmentation when compared it to English. There are 256 possible sequences (2^{n-1}) of segmentation in this example.

English: A woman sells tea along the road .
A | woman | sells | tea | along |the | road . (1)

Vietnamese: Một người đàn bà bán nước trà ven đường .
Một | người đàn bà | bán | nước trà |ven | đường . (1)
Một | người đàn bà | bán nước | trà |ven | đường . (2)
Một | người |đàn bà | bán nước| trà | ven | đường . (3)
Một | người |đàn | bà | bán nước| trà | ven | đường . (4)
And many others combinations....

Figure 1. Ambiguity of word segmentation

The major segmentation problems with the Vietnamese word segmentation include: the handling of word ambiguities, detection of unknown words, and recognition of named entities.

2.1 Addressing Words Ambiguities

In a sequence of Vietnamese syllables, S, composing of two syllables A and B occurring next to one another, if S, A, and B are each words, then there is a conjunctive ambiguity in S. In contrast, in a sequence of Vietnamese syllables, S, composing of three syllables A, B, and C appearing contiguously, if A B and B C are each words, then there is a disjunctive ambiguity in S. In order to attain a higher precision rating, word ambiguity must be addressed.

2.2 Detection of Unknown Words

In a dictionary word segmentation based approach, only the words that are in the dictionary can be identified. The unknown words might belong to one of the following categories: (1) Morphologically Derived Word (MDW). There are some lexical elements that never stand alone, which express negation such as: "bất" in "bất quy tắc" (irregular) or transformation such as "hoá" in "công nghiệp hoá" (industrialize). (2) Interchanging usage of vowels i and y and changing in position of tone. For example: "dược sĩ" and "dược sỹ". Both mean "pharmacist". (3) Phonetically transcribed words. This can be seen in naturalized words like: "phô mai" (fromage), "híp hóp" (hip hop music), or "iPhône" (Apple iPhone).

2.3 Recognition of Named Entities

Unlike other Asian languages, Vietnamese personal, location, and organizational names all have the initial letter capitalized. For example: "Nguyễn Du" (a famous Vietnamese poet). Due to the language syntax standardization, a proper name could be written in many different forms. The following organizational name has three acceptable forms: Bộ Nông Nghiệp, Bộ Nông nghiệp, or Bộ nông nghiệp (Department of Agriculture). We use the following shape features (pattern) to assist with the recognition process:

Word Shape	Examples
Capitalized	Sài Gòn (Location)
All Caps	WTO (World Trade Organization)
Containing digit	H5N1 (Bird flu)
Containing hyphen	Vn-Index (Securities market of Việt Nam)
Mixed case	VnExpress (Vietnam News Daily)

Table 1. Word Shape features for identifying Vietnamese Name Entities

3 Using World Wide Web as a Resource to Build Corpora

There are two approaches to obtain linguistics data from the Web. The first approach is to crawl the web (Baroni et al., 2006 and O'Neil, 2007). This option gives flexibility in choosing or restricting sites to crawl upon. To have good coverage, it requires extensive hardware resource to support storage of content documented in the work of Baroni et al. (2006). Other complexities include a filtering capability to recognize content of a target language from crawling data, removing html code, and handling page duplication. The work of Le V. B (2003) indicated that it is very difficult to crawl on Web pages located in Vietnam due to a low network communication bandwidth.

A second approach is to use search engines via a web service API to find linguistic data. In the work of Ghani et al. (2001), a term selection method is used to select words from documents to use for a query. Documents from a search result list are downloaded locally to process and build corpus data. The technical challenges of this approach are: (1) Corpus being biased and being dictated by a ranking of a search engine. (2) Limited number of search queries is allowed by a search engine per day.

4 Our Approach to build corpus

We are structuring our system with two main components. The first component works as a word training and recognition system. The second component utilizes the training information provided from the first component to perform just a word segmentation task by leveraging the computed lexical statistics. This is a clear distinction between our work and Nguyen D. (2008). Because there is a limited number of search request imposed by commercial search engines each day, this approach is not practical for a condition where there is constant usage of search requests, for word segmentation purpose. Aside from this limitation, lexical statistics have to be recomputed for each new word segmentation request.

Figure 2. depicts the overall system consists of two components: The training Processing includes a new word discovery function and Normal Segmentation process. The training process would execute continuously and feed the lexical statistics to the second process for segmentation task purely.

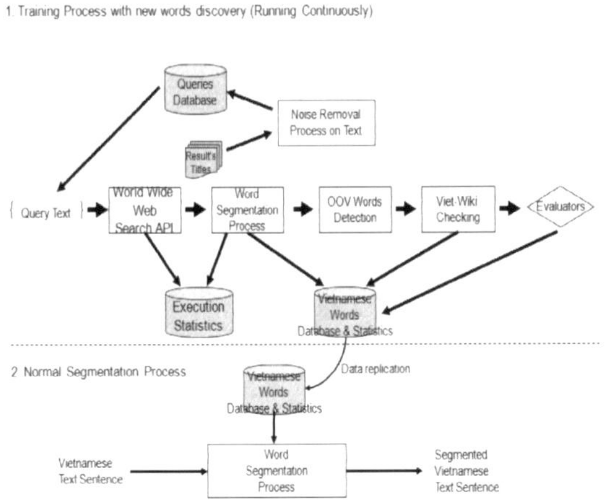

Figure 2. Vietnamese Words Corpus Construction Process

4.1 Word Training and Recognition System

This component trains identified words inside a Vietnamese Word Database with its frequency of occurrences. Newly encountered OOV words are recognized by the system then verified by a check against the Vietnamese Wikipedia programmatically. We do not wish to include all words from the Vietnamese Wikipedia as there are many foreign words. For examples: *St. Helens, Oregon*. The remained frequently found OOV words are evaluated by linguists for validity and will be included into the word database as confirmed. Unlike the work of Ghani (2001), in our work, a query to submit to an engine is a sentence derived from an unknown document title. The reason here is to enable the system to discover the unknown words and their frequencies naturally. This system performs:

- Seed the queries database with an initial set of queries, Q_n.
- Randomly select a query from Q_n and send to a search engine.
- From a search result list, process on document titles and snippet texts directly.
- Perform Vietnamese word segmentation on recognized sentences using question mark, exclamation mark, periods as separators. Update the word database with recognized segmented words and their computed frequencies and weights.
- Recognize and validate OOV words, using the Vietnamese Wikipedia or through morphological rules programmatically.
- Bootstrap Q_n with retrieved document titles.
- Return to step 2 above.

5 Word Segmentation System

In the Vietnamese language, as the white space cannot be used to denote word boundary, the function of a word segmentation system is to segment a sentence into a sequence of segmented words such that a context (or meaning) of a sentence is preserved.

5.1 Data Gathering and Words Extraction

In the first step, a search query is submitted to a search engine API and requests for **N** returned documents. The engine returns a search result list, which consists of document titles and their summary text. We parse the data and extract the required text. Syllables in the search query are then matched against the parsed text to extract potential words covering both monosyllabic and polysyllabic words. This function keeps track and counts their occurrences. At this stage, we also determine if a word is a proper name. We use the various word shape features in capitalization forms to assist with the recognition process. We compute the likelihood of extracted words to be proper names by taking the account of the number of identified capitalized words over the total of the same words in appearing the documents set, N documents. Once the extraction process is complete, we perform additional validation steps to discard incorrect generated words. To be accepted as a potential word, a word must satisfy one of the following rules: (1) It appears in the word database. (2) It is recognized as a proper name word. (3) It is a MDR word. (4) It is an OOV word with strong world collocation as defined below.

An OOV word is identified when there is a strong collocation (cohesion) attached between its syllables. That is the following condition(s) is/are met: (1) For two syllable words to collocate: $P(s_1\ s_2) > P(s_1)P(s_2)$, (2) For three syllable words to collocate: $P(s_1\ s_2\ s_3) > MAX\{ P(s_1)P(s_2)P(s_3), P(s_1)P(s_2s_3), P(s_1s_2)P(s_3) \}$ where $w = s_1\ s_2\ s_3$, $P(s_1 \ldots s_n) = Freq(s_1 \ldots s_n)/N$, and N is the number of documents returning from a search engine.

Collocation concept has been utilized in the merging syllables to determine the best possible segment in the work of Wirote (2002).

Suffix	Translation	Result Lexical Category	Morphological Rules	Examples
học	"'-logy, -ics"	Noun	**IF** Syllable_Suffix("học") **AND** Prefix_With_Word((Noun(W)) **THEN** WORD(W+ " "+ "học")	ngôn ngữ (language) + học → ngôn ngữ học (linguistics)
hóa	"-ize, -ify"	Verb	**IF** Syllable_Suffix("hóa") **AND** (Prefix_With_Word((NOUN(W)) **OR** Prefix_With_Word((ADJECTIVE(W))) **THEN** WORD(W+ " " +"hóa")	công nghiệp (industry) + hóa → công nghiệp hóa (industrialize)
Prefix	**Translation**	**Result Lexical Category**	**Morphological Rules**	**Examples**
sự	"Action-"	Noun	**IF** Syllable_Prexix("sự") **AND** (Suffix_With_Word((Verb(W)) **OR** Suffix_With_Word((Adjective(W))) **THEN** WORD(sự+ " "+ W)	sự + thảo luận (discuss, debate) → sự thảo luận (discussion)
bất	"Un-"	Noun	**IF** Syllable_Prexix("bất") **AND** (Suffix_With_Word((Verb(W)) **OR** Suffix_With_Word((Adjective(W))) **THEN** WORD(bất+ " "+ W)	bất + hợp pháp (legal, lawful) →bất hợp pháp (Not legal)

Table 2. Examples of derivational morphology and morphological rules to construct compound words

To recognize for morphological derived words (MDW), we have identified a range of prefixes and suffixes (Goddard, 2005). When a morpheme modifies another morpheme, it produces a subordinate compound word (Ngo, 2001). For example: nhà (as a prefix) + báo (newspaper) → nhà báo (journalist). The table 2. provides a few examples of Vietnamese suffixes, prefixes, and Morphological Rules to derive subordinate compound words.

5.2 Sentences Construction

Given a set of potential segmented words obtained from step 5.1, applied only for training process or for a normal segmentation process (Figure 2.), the task of sentences constructor is to assemble the identified words in such a way that they appear in the same order as the original query. We use Greedy algorithm to construct sentences using the following heuristic strategies: (1) Selection of polysyllabic words over monosyllabic words whenever possible. (2) Eliminating segments which have already examined. (3) Declaring a solution when a constructed sentence has all of segmented words appearing in the same order as in the original query text.

5.3 Sentences Refinement and Reduction through Ambiguity Resolution

Since there is only a single solution to present to a user, we need to have an algorithm to improve upon proposed sentences and reduce them to a manageable size. The algorithm **Sentences_Refine_Reduce** below describes the steps in refining the sentences to a finer solution(s).

Definition: Let the pipe symbol, |, be designated as a boundary of a segment. Two segments, in two sentences, are overlapped if their first and last syllables are: (1) located next to a segmented boundary. (2) Identical and positioned at the same location. For example, in the following two sentences:

Sentence #1: tốc độ | truyền | thông tin | sẽ | tăng | cao
Sentence #2: tốc độ | truyền thông | tin | sẽ | tăng | cao

The overlapped segments are: "tốc độ", "sẽ", "tăng", and "cao". We are now describing an algorithm to perform sentences refinement and reduction as follows:

Algorithm : Sentences_Refine_Reduce()
Input: SBuffer - for input sentences
Output: SBuffer - for output sentences

```
Until Converged(SBuffer) Do:
   Itr_Sentences_Buf = { }
   For si in SBuffer Do:
      Find sj such that Max {|Overlapped_Segment (si,sj)|} for sj ∈ SBuffer and si != sj
      Res_Segments=Overlapped_Segments(si,sj)
          U Conjunctive_Segments_Resolutions(si,sj)
          U Disjunctive_Segments_Resolutions(si,sj)
      Itr_Sentences_Buf = Itr_Sentences_Buf U
          Sentence(Res_Segments)
   SBuffer=(SBuffer!=Itr_Sentences_Buf)
      ? Itr_Sentences_Buf : SBuffer
```

For conjunctive ambiguity resolution, to determine if all syllables should be classified as a single word or appeared as individual words, we utilize word collocation strength. We define collocating strength as follows.

$$P(s_1...s_n) = \frac{Freq(s_1...s_n)}{N} \quad (2)$$

We compare it against a probability of finding the syllables occur independently in N documents as shown in equation (3). The outcome determines if the syllables should be collocated or separately appeared:

$$P(s_1)...P(s_n) = \frac{Freq(s_1)}{N} \times ... \times \frac{Freq(s_n)}{N} \quad (3)$$

For disjunctive ambiguity resolution, because a determination involves multiple words with overlapping text, we determine the best possible segments by computing their probability distribution of word segments to find out which one has the highest probability of success. This is discussed further in the section "Sentences Scoring and Ordering" below. Figure 3 illustrates a process where sentences are refined through disambiguating words.

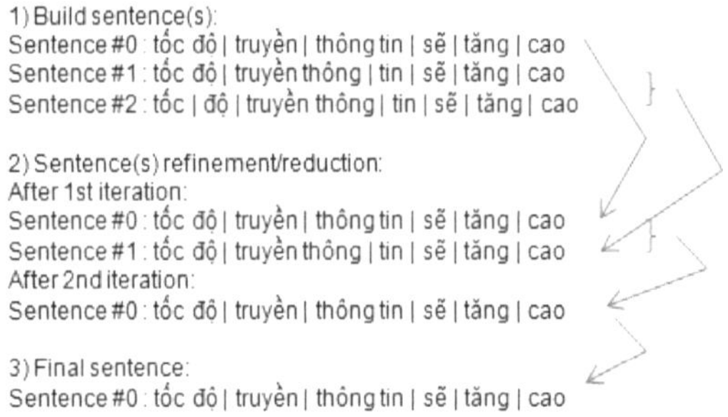

Figure 3. An Example of Sentences Refinement

After the 1st iteration, the sentences 1 and 2 are combined through a resolution of conjunctive ambiguity between "tốc độ" vs. "tốc | độ" . After the 2nd iteration, sentences 1 and 2 are combined through a resolution of disjunctive ambiguity between "truyền | thông tin" vs. "truyền thông | tin". The process exits when a converged condition is reached. The final segmented sentence is translated in English as "The speed of information transmission will increase".

5.4 Sentences Scoring and Ordering

The task in this phase is to score and order the candidates. A language model is usually formulated as a probability distribution p(s) over strings s that attempts to reflect how frequently a string s occurs as a sentence in a corpus, Chen et al. (1998). For a segmented sentence S $= w_1 w_2 ... w_n$, where w is an identified segmented word, using a bigram model, we compute the probability distribution of a sentence s as follows:

$$p(s) = \prod_{i=1}^{n} P(w_i \mid w_1 ... w_{i-1}) \approx \prod_{i=1}^{n} P(w_i \mid w_{i-1}) \quad (4)$$

However, there is an event such that $P(w_i \mid w_{i-1}) = 0$. To handle this condition, we applied Additive Smoothing to estimate its probability. The formula was experimented and slightly modified to fit our needs and defined as follows:

$$P_{Add\_Theta}(w_i \mid w_{i-1}) = \frac{\delta + Freq(w_{i-1} w_i)}{\delta |W| + \sum_{w_i} Freq(w_{i-1} w_i)} \quad (5)$$

We define δ parameter as Freq(w_i)/|W| where |W| is an estimate number of the total words appears in N returned documents and 0 < δ < 1.

6 Experimental Results

With no restriction, there were 167,735 searches performed using the Yahoo! Boss Web Service API. We bootstrapped the initial core lexicons from Ho's Word List (2004) and built up to gather lexical statistics and discovered new OOV words. The corpus syllables classifications and their occurrences are shown in Figure 4.

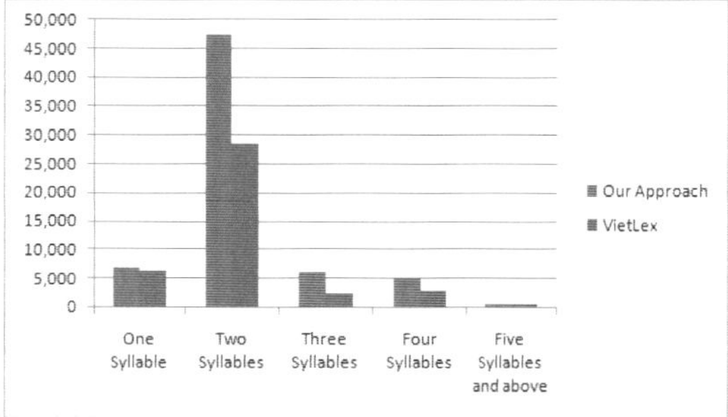

Figure 4. Syllables Types by Frequency

We compared our collected lexical data, using our approach, against VietLex (Dinh et al., 2008) and found a resembling to one, three, four, and five syllables. For the two syllables, there is a big difference: roughly about 19,000 words. This contributes to the fact that the original Ho's word list had already covered 49,583 two-syllable words to begin with. On top of it, we have included 3,000 additional new OOV words including MDW and proper names words. According to the Wiki's - Vietnamese_morphology, it estimates about 80% of the lexicon being disyllabic. In our corpus, we have 72% of disyllabic words.

1-Syllable	English Translation	Frequency
người *	person; people	571236
không *	not;negative	515704
những *	the;certain;some	446096
trong *	in;clear	439849
của *	of	356214
một *	one	330102
được *	able;possible	294234
cho *	give	220853
chúng	they, them, you	197476
cũng*	too;also	187149
tôi	I	183386
các *	every; all	176094
là *	to be; then	171868
có *	to be; to have	169001
nhưng	but	168465
và *	and	166743
với *	with	165368
thành *	to achieve; to make	158612
như	as;like	157848
phải *	must	155478

Table 3. The top 20th one-syllable words comparing with corpus of Le A. H[1] (2003)

[1] The star marker indicates the same word is co-occurred in Le's of top unigram listing.

Table 3 provides a top 20 one-syllable words obtained from our word database. The star marker indicates the same word is also co-occurred in Le's of top unigram listing.

The following disyllabic words, in Table 4, are a few of the new OOV words identified by our approach and absent from Ho's Word List (2004) .

Common Disyllabic Words	**Frequency**	**Uncommon Disyllabic Words**	**Frequency**
Việt Nam (Viet Nam)	206704	lan rộng (spread)	263
Người Việt (Vietnamese)	41260	ga lông (gallon)	14
Trung Quốc (China)	35345	Cồn Phụng (Island)	9
Tiếng Việt (Vietnamese)	28460	nghị sỹ (congress gressman)	22
Hoa Kỳ (America)	21262	công xôn (console)	2

Table 4. Some OOV disyllabic words

We evaluated our segmentation system against a popular Vietnamese word segmentation tool - the JVnSegmenter (Nguyen C. T, 2007): A Java-based Vietnamese Word Segmentation Tool (SVM). This tool was also a part of Dinh et al. (2008) evaluation aforementioned. With a source data provided by a neutral evaluator, and about 9600 sentences with an estimate of 100K words, we ran an experiment. The texts were input into both methods. To keep the fairness of the evaluation, the segmented output texts were sent out to a neutral assessor to analyze for results. The performance results are presented in Table 5. below.

Evaluation Areas	**JVnSegmenter**	**Our Approach**
Recall	0.814	0.821
Precision	0.883	0.897
F-Measure	0.847	0.857
OOV Rate	0.06	0.06
OOV Recall	0.921	0.951
IV Recall	0.807	0.813

Table 5. Performance Results Comparison

From the data above, the low OOV rate and high OOV recall in both systems could be explained by the nature of the testing corpus: Vietnamese novels/stories chosen by a neutral evaluator. With this type of content, the numbers of OOV words are much lesser when compared to other areas such as news, technology. Even though the results don't seem much higher than those obtained by JVnSegmenter, given the fact that JVnSegmenter used a manual trained corpus, our result is worth encouragements. Table 6 provides a few examples of the segmentation results.

Q1: tốc độ **truyền thông tin** sẽ tăng cao (Ambiguity) JVnSegmenter: [tốc độ] [**truyền thông tin**] [sẽ] [tăng] [cao] Our Approach: tốc độ | **truyền | thông tin** | sẽ | tăng | cao	Q2: **hàn mặc tử** là một nhà thơ nổi tiếng (Proper Name) JVnSegmenter: **[hàn mặc] [tử]** [là] [một] [nhà thơ] [nổi tiếng] Our Approach: **hàn mặc tử** | là | một | nhà thơ | nổi tiếng
Q3: một người đàn bà làm nghề **bán nước trà** ven đường (Ambiguity) JVnSegmenter: [một] [người đàn bà] [làm nghề] [**bán nước] [trà**] [ven đường] Our Approach: một | người đàn bà | làm nghề | **bán** | **nước trà** | ven đường	Q4: thủ tướng trung quốc **ôn gia bảo** (Proper name) JVnSegmenter: [thủ tướng] [trung] [quốc] **[ôn] [gia bảo]** Our Approach: thủ tướng | trung quốc | **ôn gia bảo**

Table 6. Sample outputs of the two approaches: Our approach vs. JVnSegmenter

7 Conclusion

We presented our approach to segment Vietnamese text and to build a web corpus for the function. We made use of the web document titles and their snippet text to build a scalable corpus for segmenting query text. The results so far have shown that this approach has the following benefits:

- From a practical and performance perspective, this approach does not require extended manual effort in building a corpus. The learning from the training engine, running continuously, discovers new OOV words and feeds them into a normal word segmentation process where it supplies solutions to requesters efficiently.
- The approach discovers new OOV words and disambiguates words. Additionally, we discovered new proper nouns which are not a part of any dictionaries continuously. We integrated the finding knowledge from the Vietnamese Wikipedia into our OOV words confirmation process automatically. This makes the validation of new words much easier as suppose to rely on word adjudicators manually as per O'Neil (2007). And last, the evaluation result is a better edge when comparing to a popular Vietnamese segmentation tool in all the metrics considered. This tool has a corpus trained manually.
- Frequently found OOV words identified by our process which are not available in the Vietnamese Wikipedia can be suggested to Wiki authors' communities to create content and make them available for the worldwide audiences for their benefit.

For future works, we would like to look into the possibility of applying grammatical rules in conjunction with our current statistical based system to obtain a higher identification rate. Spelling suggestion and cross-lingual search are other interesting aspects, as now words can be identified along with their lexical statistics.

Acknowledgement

Our work is credited from the works of Nguyen Bon et al. (2006), Ho Ngoc Duc (The Free Vietnamese Dictionary Project), Cam T Nguyen et al. (JVnSegmenter - 2007), O'Neil (2007), and Yahoo! Boss Web Service, which made the API available limitlessly during the course of the work, and many anonymous contributors and reviewers. A Special thank to Mr. Thuy Vu who contributed to an assessment of our approach and the JVnSegmenter.

Reference

C. T. Nguyen, T. K. Nguyen, X. H. Phan, L. M. Nguyen, and Q. T. Ha. 2006. Vietnamese word segmentation with CRFs and SVMs: An investigation. In Proceedings of the 20th Pacific Asia Conference on Language, Information and Computation (PACLIC 2006), Wuhan, CH.

Cliff Goddard. 2005. The Languages of East and Southeast Asia (pages 70-71)

Dinh Dien, Vu Thuy. 2006. A Maximum Entropy Approach for Vietnamese Word Segmentation. In Proceedings of the 4th IEEE International Conference on Computer Science- Research, Innovation and Vision of the Future 2006, HCM City, Vietnam, pp.247–252.

Dinh Quan Thang, et al, 2008. Word Segmentation of Vietnamese Texts: a comparison of approaches. LREC : 2008

Ghani, R., Jones, R., Mladenic, D. 2001. Using the Web to create minority language corpora'. Proceedings of the 10th International Conference on Information and Knowledge Management

Ho Ngoc Duc, 2004: Vietnamese word list: Ho Ngoc Duc's word list – http://www.informatik.uni-leipzig.de/~duc/software/misc/wordlist.html

John O'Neil. 2007. Large Corpus Construction for Chinese Lexical Development, Government Users Conference: http://www.basistech.com/knowledge-center/unicode/emerson-iuc29.pdf

Le Thanh Ha, Huynh Quyet Thang, Luong Chi Mai. 2005. A Primary Study on Summarization of Documents in Vietnamese. The First International Congress of the International Federation for Systems Research, Japan.

L. H. Phuong and H. T. Vinh, 2008, Maximum Entropy Approach to Sentence Boundary Detection of Vietnamese Texts, IEEE International Conference on Research, Innovation and Vision for the Future RIVF 2008, Vietnam.

L. A. Ha. 2003. A method for word segmentation in Vietnamese. In Proceedings of the International Conference on Corpus Linguistics, Lancaster, UK.

Marco Baroni, Motoko Ueyama. 2006. Building general and special-purpose corpora by Web Crawling. Proceedings of the 13th NIJL International Symposium, Language Corpora: Their Compilation and Application. 31-40.

Ngo. N. Binh, B. H. Tran. 2001. Vietnamese Language Learning Framework – Part One: s Linguistic.

Nguyen D. 2008. Query preprocessing: improving web search through a Vietnamese word tokenization approach. SIGIR 2008: 765-766.

Stanley F. Chen, J. Goodman. 1998. An empirical study of smoothing techniques for language modeling. Center Research in Computing Technology, Harvard University, TR-10-98

Thanh Bon Nguyen, Thi Minh Huyen Nguyen, Laurent Romary, Xuan Luong Vu. 2006. A lexicon for Vietnamese language processing. Language Resources and Evaluation. Springer Netherlands

V-B. Le, B. Bigi, L. Besacier, E. Castelli, 2003. Using the Web for fast language model construction in minority languages", Eurospeech'03, Geneva, Switzerland, September 2003

Wirote Aroonmanakun. 2002. Collocation and Thai Word Segmentation, Proceedings of SNLP-Oriental COCOSDA 2002

Vietnamese morphology: From Wikipedia: http://en.wikipedia.org/wiki/Vietnamese_morphology

Yahoo! Boss Web Service API http://developer.yahoo.com/search/boss

Word Segmentation Standard in Chinese, Japanese and Korean

Key-Sun Choi
KAIST
Daejeon Korea
kschoi@kaist.ac.kr

Hitoshi Isahara
NICT
Kyoto Japan
isahara@nict.go.jp

Kyoko Kanzaki
NICT
Kyoto Japan
kanzaki@nict.go.jp

Hansaem Kim
National Inst.
Korean Lang.
Seoul Korea
thesis00@korea.kr

Seok Mun Pak
Baekseok Univ.
Cheonan Korea
smpark@bu.ac.kr

Maosong Sun
Tsinghua Univ.
Beijing China
sms@tsinghua.edu.cn

Abstract

Word segmentation is a process to divide a sentence into meaningful units called "word unit" [ISO/DIS 24614-1]. What is a word unit is judged by principles for its internal integrity and external use constraints. A word unit's internal structure is bound by principles of lexical integrity, unpredictability and so on in order to represent one syntactically meaningful unit. Principles for external use include language economy and frequency such that word units could be registered in a lexicon or any other storage for practical reduction of processing complexity for the further syntactic processing after word segmentation. Such principles for word segmentation are applied for Chinese, Japanese and Korean, and impacts of the standard are discussed.

1 Introduction

Word segmentation is the process of dividing of sentence into meaningful units. For example, "the White House" consists of three words but designates one concept for the President's residence in USA. "Pork" in English is translated into two words "pig meat" in Chinese, Korean and Japanese. In Japanese and Korean, because an auxiliary verb must be followed by main verb, they will compose one word unit like "tabetai" and "meoggo sipda" (want to eat). So the word unit is defined by a meaningful unit that could be a candidate of lexicon or of any other type of storage (or expanded derived lexicon) that is useful for the further syntactic processing. A word unit is more or less fixed and there is no syntactic interference in the inside of the word unit. In the practical sense, it is useful for the further syntactic parsing because it is not decomposable by syntactic processing and also frequently occurred in corpora.

There are a series of linguistic annotation standards in ISO: MAF (morpho-syntactic annotation framework), SynAF (syntactic annotation framework), and others in ISO/TC37/SC4 [1]. These standards describe annotation methods but not for the meaningful units of word segmentation. In this aspect, MAF and SynAF are to annotate each linguistic layer horizontally in a standardized way for the further interoperability. Word segmentation standard would like to recommend what word units should be candidates to be registered in some storage or lexicon, and what type of word sequences called "word unit" should be recognized before syntactic processing.

In section 2, principles of word segmentation will be introduced based on ISO/CD 24614-1. Section 3 will describe the problems in word segmentation and what should be word units in each language of Chinese, Japanese and Korean. The conclusion will include what could be shared among three languages for word segmentation.

2 Word Segmentation: Framework and Principles

Word unit is a layered pre-syntactical unit. That means that a word unit consists of the smaller word units. But the maximal word unit is frequently occurred in corpora under the constraints that the syntactic processing will not refer the internal structure of the word unit

Basic atoms of word unit are word form, morpheme including bound morpheme, and non-lexical items like punctuation mark, numeric string, foreign character string and others as shown in Figure 1. Usually we say that "word" is lemma or word form. Word form is a form that a lexeme takes when used in a sentence. For example, strings "have", "has", and "having" are word forms of the lexeme HAVE, generally distinguished by the use of capital letters. [ISO/CD 24614-1] Lemma is a conventional form used to represent a lexeme, and lexeme is an abstract unit generally associated with a set of word forms sharing a common meaning.

[1] Refer to http://www.tc37sc4.org/ for documents MAF, SynAF and so on.

Proceedings of the 7th Workshop on Asian Language Resources, ACL-IJCNLP 2009, pages 179–186,
Suntec, Singapore, 6-7 August 2009.

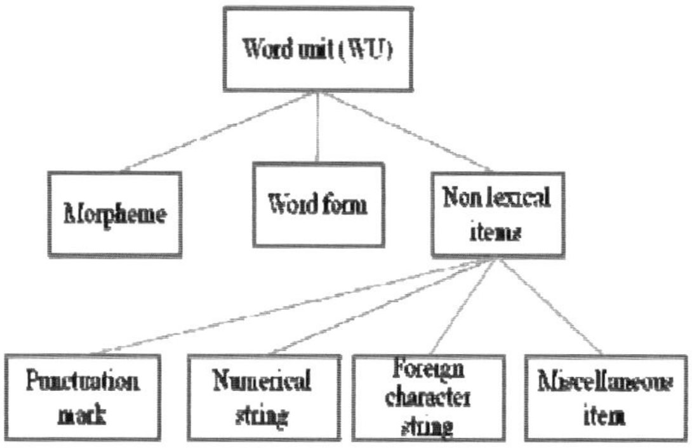

Figure 1. Configuration of Word Unit

BNF of word unit is as follows:

<*word unit*> ::= <*word form*> | <*morpheme*> | <*non lexical items*> | <*word unit*>,

where <*word unit*> is recursively defined because a longer word unit contains smaller word units.

Bunsetsu in Japanese is the longest word unit, which is an example of layered maximized pre-syntactical unit. *Eojeol* in Korean is a spacing unit that consists of one content word (noun, verb, adjective or adverb) plus a sequence of functional elements. Such language-specific word units will be described in section 3.

Principles for word segmentation will set the criteria to validate each word unit, to recognize its internal structure and non-lexical word unit, to be a candidate of lexicon, and other consistency to be necessitated by practical applications for any text in any language. The meta model of word segmentation will be explained in the processing point of view, and then their principles of word units in the following subsections.

2.1 Metamodel of Word Segmentation

A word unit has a practical unit that will be later used for syntactic processing. While the word segmentation is a process to identify the longest word unit and its internal structure such that the word unit is not the object to interfere any syntactic operation, "chunking" is to identify the constituents but does not specify their internal structure. Syntactic constituent has a syntactic role, but the word unit is a subset of syntactic constituent. For example, "blue sky" could be a syntactic constituent but not a word unit. Figure 2 shows the meta model of word segmentation. [ISO CD 24614-1]

2.2 Principles of Word Unit Validation

Principles for validating a word unit can be explained by two perspectives: one is linguistic one and the other is processing-oriented practical perspective.

In ISO 24614-1, principles from a linguistic perspective, there are five principles: principles of (1) bound morpheme, (2) lexical integrity, (3) unpredictability, (4) idiomatization, and (5) unproductivity.

First, bound morpheme is something like "in" of "inefficient". The principle of bound morpheme says that each bound morpheme plus word will make another word. Second, principle of lexical integrity means that any syntactic processing cannot refer the internal structure of word (or word unit). From the principle, we can say that the longest word unit is the maximal meaningful unit before syntactic processing. Third, another criterion to recognize a word is the principle of unpredictability. If we cannot infer the real fact from the word, we consider it as a word unit. For example, we cannot image what is the colour of blackboard because some is green, not black. [ISO 24614-1] The fourth principle is that the idiom should be one word, which could be a subsidiary principle that follows the principle of unpredictability. In the last principle, unproductivity is a stronger definition of word; there is no pattern to be copied to generate another word from this word formation. For example, in "白菜" (white vegetable) in Chinese, there is no other coloured vegetable like "blue vegetable."

Another set of principles is derived from the practical perspective. There are four principles: frequency, Gestalt, prototype and language economy. Two principles of frequency and language economy are to recognize the frequent occurrence in corpora. Gestalt and prototype principles are the terms in cognitive science about what are in our mental lexicon, and what are perceivable words.

Principle of language economy is to say about very practical processing efficiency: "if the inclusion of a word (unit) candidate into the lexicon can decrease the difficulty of linguistic analysis for it, then it is likely to be a word (unit)."

Gestalt principle is to perceive as a whole. "It supports some perceivable phrasal compounds into the lexicon even though they seem to be free combinations of their perceivable constituent parts," [ISO/CD 24614-1] where the phrasal compound is frequently used linguistic unit and its meaning is predictable from its constituent elements. Similarly, principle of prototype provides a rationale for including some phrasal compounds into lexicon, and phrasal compounds serve as prototypes in a productive word formation pattern, like "apple pie" with the pattern "fruit + pie" into the lexicon.

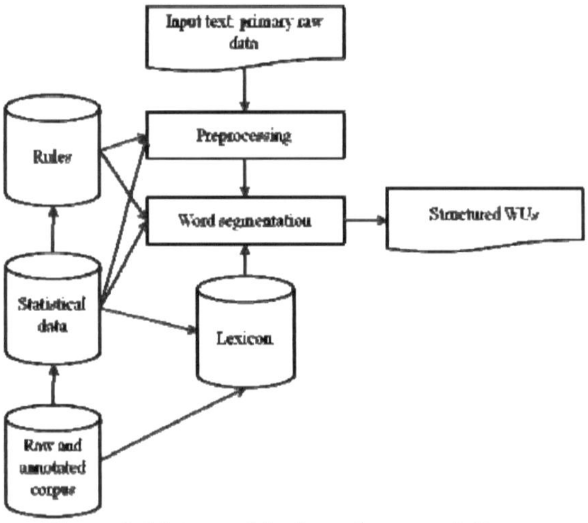

Figure 2. Meta model of word segmentation proess [ISO/CD 24614-1]

2.3 Principles for Word Unit Formation

As a result of word segmentation of sentence, we will get word units. These principles will describe the internal structure of word unit. They have four principles: granularity, scope maximization of affixations, scope maximization of compounding, and segmentation for other strings. In the principle of granularity, a word unit has its internal structure, if necessary for various application of word segmentation.

Principles of scope maximization of affixations and compounding are to recognize the longest word unit as one word unit even if it is composed of stem + affixes or compound of word units. For example, "unhappy" or "happy" is one word unit respectively. "Next generation Internet" is one word unit. The principle of segmentation for other strings is to recognize non-lexical strings as one word unit if it carries some syntactic function, for example, 2009 in "Now this year is 2009."

3 Word Segmentation for Chinese, Japanese and Korean

If the word is derived from Chinese characters, three languages have common characteristics. If their word in noun consists of two or three Chinese characters, they will be one word unit if they are "tightly combined and steadily used." Even if it is longer length, it will be a word unit if it is fixed expression or idiom. But if the first character is productive with the following numeral, unit word or measure word, it will be segmented. If the last character is productive in a limited manner, it forms a word unit with the preceding word, for example, "東京都" (Tokyo Metropolis), "8 月" (August) or "加速器" (accelerator). But if it is a productive suffix like plural suffix and noun for locality, it is segmented independently in Chinese word segmentation rule, for example, "朋友|们" (friends), "长江|以北" (north of the Yangtzi River) or "桌子|上" (on the table) in Chinese. They may have different phenomena in each language.

Negation character of verb and adjective is segmented independently in Chinese, but they form one word unit in Japanese. For example, "yasashikunai" (優しく無い, not kind) is one word unit in Japanese, but "不|写" (not to write), "不| 能" (cannot), "没|研究" (did not research) and "未| 完成" (not completed) will be segmented independently in Chinese. In Korean, "chinjeolhaji anhta" (친절하지 않다, not kind) has one space inserted between two eojeols but it could be one word unit. "ji anhta" makes negation of adjectival stem "chinjeolha".

We will carefully investigate what principles of word units will be applied and what kind of conflicts exists. Because the motivation of word segmentation standard is to recommend what word units should be registered in a type of lexicon (where it is not the lexicon in linguistics but any kind of practical indexed container for word units), it has two possibly conflicting principles. For example, principles of unproductivity, frequency, and granularity could cause conflicts because they have different perspectives to define a word unit.

3.1 Word Segmentation for Chinese

For convenience of description, the specification in this section follows the convention that classifies words into 13 types: noun, verb, adjective, pronoun, numeral, measure word, adverb, preposition, conjunction, auxiliary word, modal word, exclamation word, imitative word.

3.1.1 Noun

There is word unit specification for common nouns as follows:

- Two-character word or compact two-character noun phrase, e.g., 牛肉(beef) 钢铁(steel)

- Noun phrase with compact structure, if violate original meaning after segmentation, e.g., 有功功率 (Active power)
- Phrase consisting of adjective with noun, e.g., 绿叶 (green leave)
- The meaning changed phrase consisting of adjective, e.g., 小媳妇(young wife)
- Prefix with noun, e.g., 阿哥(elder brother) 老鹰(old eagle) 非金属(nonmetal) 超声波(ultrasonic)
- Noun segmentation unit with following postfix (e.g. 家 手 性 员 子 化 长 头 者), e.g., 科学家(scientist)
- Noun segmentation unit with prefix and postfix, e.g., 超导性(superconductance)
- Time noun or phrase, e.g., 五月(May), 11 时 42 分 8 秒(forty two minutes and eight seconds past eleven), 前天(the day before yesterday), 初一(First day of a month in the Chinese lunar calendar)

But the followings are independent word units for noun of locality (e.g., 桌子|上 (on the table), 长江|以北 (north of the Yangtzi River)), and the "们" suffix referring to from a plural of front noun (e.g., 朋友 们(friends)) except "人们", "哥儿们"(pals), "爷儿们"(guys), etc. Proper nouns have similar specification.

3.1.2 Verb

The following verb forms will be one word unit as:

- Various forms of reiterative verb, e.g., 看看(look at), 来来往往(come and go)
- Verb–object structural word, or compact and stably used verb phrase, e.g., 开会(meeting) 跳舞(dancing)
- Verb–complement structural word (two-character), or stably used Verb-complement phrase (two-character), e.g., 提高(improve)
- Adjective with noun word, and compact, and stably used adjective with noun phrase, e.g., 胡闹(make trouble) , 瞎说(talk nonsense)
- Compound directional verb, e.g., 出去(go out) 进来(come in).

But the followings are independent word units:

- "AAB, ABAB" or "A 一 A, A 了 A, A 了一 A", e.g., 研究|研究(have a discuss), 谈|一|谈 (have a good chat)
- Verb delimited by a negative meaning characters, e.g., 不|写(not to write) 不|能(cannot) 没|研究(did not research) 未|完成(not completed)
- "Verb + a negative meaning Chinese character + the same verb" structure, e.g., "说|没|说(say or not say)?"
- Incompact or verb–object structural phrase with many similar structures, e.g., 吃|鱼(Eat fish) 学|滑冰(learn skiing)
- "2with1" or "1with2" structural verb- complement phrase, e.g., 整理|好(clean up), 说|清楚(speak clearly), 解释|清楚(explain clearly)
- Verb-complement word for phrase, if inserted with "得 or 不", e.g., 打|得|倒 (able to knock down), and compound directional verb of direction, e.g., 出|得|去(able to go out)
- Phrase formed by verb with directional verb, e.g., 寄|来(send), 跑|出|去(run out)
- Combination of independent single verbs without conjunction, e.g., 苦|盖(cover with), 听|说, 读|写 (listen, speaking, read and write)
- Multi-word verb without conjunction, e.g., 调查|研究(investigate and research)

3.1.3 Adjective

One word unit shall be recognized in the following cases:

- Adjective in reiterative form of "AA, AABB, ABB, AAB, A+"里"+AB", e.g., 大大(big), 马里马虎(careless), except the adjectives in reiterative form of "ABAB", e.g., 雪白|雪白(snowy white)
- Adjective phrase in from of "一A一B，一A二B，半A半B，半A不B，有A有B", e.g., 一心一意(wholeheartedly)
- Two single-character adjectives with word features varied, 长短(long-short) 深浅(deep-shallow) 大小(big-small)
- Color adjective word or phrase, e.g., 浅黄(light yellow) 橄榄绿(olive green)

But the followings are segmented as independent word units:

- Adjectives in parataxis form and maintaining original adjective meaning, e.g., 大|小尺寸(size), 光荣 |伟大(glory)
- Adjective phrase in positive with negative form to indicate question, e.g., 容易| 不| 容易(easy or not easy), except the brachylogical one like 容不容易(easy or not).

3.1.4 Pronoun

The followings shall be one word unit:

- Single-character pronoun with "们", e.g.,我们 (we)
- "这、那、哪" with unit word "个" or "些、样、么、里、边", e.g., 这个(this)
- Interrogative adjective or phrase, e.g., 多少 (how many)

But, the following will be independent word units:

- "这、那、哪" with numeral , unit word or noun word segmentation unit, e.g., 这 |十 天 (these 10 days), 那| 人(that person)
- Pronoun of "各、每、某、本、该、此、全", etc. shall be segmented from followed measure word or noun, e.g., 各| 国 (each country), 每| 种(each type).

3.1.5 Numeral

The followings will be one word unit:

- Chinese digit word, e.g., 一亿八千零四万七百二十三(180,040,723)
- "分之" percent in fractional number, e.g., 五分之三(third fifth)
- Paratactic numerals indicating approximate number, e.g., 八九 公斤(eight or nine kg)

On the other hand, Independent word unit cases are as follows:

- Numeral shall be segmented from measure word, e.g., 三| 个(three)
- Ordinal number of "第" shall be segmented from followed numeral, e.g., 第 一 (first)
- "多、一些、点儿、一点儿", used after adjective or verb for indicating approximate number.

3.1.6 Measure word

Reiterative measure word and compound measure word or phrase is a word unit, e.g., 年年 (every year), 人年 man/year.

3.1.7 Adverb

Adverb is one word unit. But "越…越…、又…又…" , etc. acting as conjunction shall be segmented, e.g., 又 香 又 甜(sweet yet savory).

3.1.8 Preposition

It is one word unit. For example, 生于(be born in), and 按照规定(according to the regulations).

3.1.9 Conjunction

Conjunction shall be deemed as segmentation unit.

3.1.10 Auxiliary word

Structural auxiliary word "的、地、得、之" and tense auxiliary word "着、了、过" are one word unit, e.g., 他 | 的 | 书 (his book), 看 | 了 (watched). But the auxiliary word "所" shall be segmented from its followed verb, e.g., 所 想 (what one thinks).

3.1.11 Modal word

It is one word unit, e.g., 你好吗？(How are you?).

3.1.12 Exclamation word

Exclamation word shall be deemed as segmentation unit. For example, "啊，真美！" (How beautiful it is!)

3.1.13 Imitative word

It is one word unit like "当当" (tinkle).

3.2 Word Segmentation for Japanese

For convenience of description, the specification in this section follows the convention that classifies words into mainly 10 types: meishi (noun), doushi (verb), keiyoushi (adjective), rentaishi (adnominal noun: only used in adnominal usage), fukushi (adverb), kandoushi (exclamation), setsuzoushi (conjunction), setsuji (affix), joshi (particle), and jodoushi (auxiliary verb). These parts of speech are divided into more detailed classes in terms of grammatical function.

The longest "word segmentation" corresponds to "Bunsetsu" in Japanese.

3.2.1 Noun

When a noun is a member constituting a sentence, it is usually followed by a particle or auxiliary verb (e.g. "猫が" (neko_ga) which is composed from "Noun + a particle for subject marker"). Also, if a word like an adjective or adnominal noun modifies a noun, then a modifier (adjectives, adnominal noun, adnominal phrases) and a modificand (a noun) are not segmented.

3.2.2 Verb

A Japanese verb has an inflectional ending. The ending of a verb changes depending on whether it is a negation form, an adverbial form, a base form, an adnominal form, an assumption form, or an imperative form. Japanese verbs are often used with auxiliary verbs and/or particles, and a verb with auxiliary verbs and/or particles is considered as a word segmentation unit (e.g. "歩きました" (aruki_mashi_ta) is composed from "Verb + auxiliary verb for politeness + auxiliary verb for tense").

3.2.3 Adjective

A Japanese adjective has an inflectional ending. Based on the type of inflectional ending, there are two kinds of adjectives, "i_keiyoushi" and "na_keiyoushi". However, both are treated as adjectives.

In terms of traditional Japanese linguistics, “keiyoushi” refers to “i_keiyoushi”(e.g. 美しい, utsukushi_i) and “keiyoudoushi”(e.g. 静かな, shizuka_na) refers to “na_keiyoushi.” In terms of inflectional ending of “na_keiyoushi,” it is sometimes said to be considered as “Noun + auxiliary verb (da)”.

The ending of an adjective changes depending on whether it is a negation form, an adverbial form, a base form, an adnominal form, or an assumption form. Japanese adjectives in predicative position are sometimes used with auxiliary verbs and/or particles, and they are considered as a word segmentation unit.

3.2.4 Adnominal noun

An adnominal noun does not have an inflectional ending; it is always used as a modifier. An adnominal noun is considered as one segmentation unit.

3.2.5 Adverb

An adverb does not have an inflectional ending; it is always used as a modifier of a sentence or a verb. It is considered as one segmentation unit.

3.2.6 Conjunction

A conjunction is considered as one segmentation unit.

3.2.7 Exclamation

An exclamation is considered as one segmentation unit.

3.2.8 Affix

A prefix and a suffix used as a constituent of a word should not be segmented as a word unit.

3.2.9 Particle

Particles can be divided into two main types. One is a case particle which serves as a case marker. The other is an auxiliary particle which appears at the end of a phrase or a sentence.

Auxiliary particles represent a mood and a tense.

Particles should not be segmented from a word. A particle is always used with a word like a noun, a verb, or an adjective, and they are considered as one segmentation unit.

3.2.10 Auxiliary verb

Auxiliary verbs represent various semantic functions such as a capability, a voice, a tense, an aspect and so on. An auxiliary verb appears at the end of a phrase or a sentence. Some linguist consider “だ” (da), which is Japanese copura, as a specific category such as 判定詞(hanteishi).

An auxiliary verb should not be segmented from a word. An auxiliary verb is always used with a word like a noun, a verb, or an adjective, and is considered as one segmentation unit.

3.2.11 Idiom and proverb

Proverbs, mottos, etc. should be segmented if their original meanings are not violated after segmentation. For example:

Kouin	yano	gotoshi
noun	noun+particle	auxiliary verb
time	arrow	like (flying)

Time flies fast.

3.2.12 Abbreviation

An abbreviation should not be segmented.

3.3 Word Segmentation for Korean

For convenience of description, the specification in this section follows the convention that classifies words into 12 types: noun, verb, adjective, pronoun, numeral, adnominal, adverb, exclamation, particle, auxiliary verb, auxiliary adjective, and copula. The basic parts of speech can be divided into more detailed classes in terms of grammatical function. Classification in this paper is in accord with the top level of MAF.

In addition, we treat some multi-Eojeol units as the word unit for practical purpose. Korean *Eojeol* is a spacing unit that consists of one content word (like noun, verb) and series of functional elements (particles, word endings). Functional elements are not indispensable. Eojeol is similar with *Bunsetsu* from some points, but an Eojeol is recognized by white space in order to enhance the readability that enables to use only Hangul alphabet in the usual writing.

3.3.1 Noun

When a noun is a member constituting a sentence, it is usually followed by a particle. (e.g. “사자_가” (*saja_ga*, ‘a lion is’) which is composed from “Noun + a particle for subject marker”). Noun subsumes common noun, proper noun, and bound noun.

If there are two frequently concatenated Eojeols that consist of modifier (an adjective or an adnominal) and modificand (a noun), they can be one word unit according to the principle of language economy. Other cases of noun word unit are as follows:

1) Compound noun that consists of two more nouns can be a word unit. For example,

"손목" (*son_mok*, 'wrist') where *son+mok* = 'hand'+'neck'.

2) Noun phrase that denotes just one concept can be a word unit. For example, "예술의 전당" (*yesul_ui jeondang*, 'sanctuary of the arts' that is used for the name of concert hall).

3.3.2 Verb

A Korean verb has over one inflectional endings. The endings of a verb can be changed and attached depending on grammatical function of verb (e.g. "깨/뜨리/시/었/겠/군/요" (break [+emphasis] [+polite] [+past] [+conjectural] final ending [+polite]). Compound verb (verb+verb, noun+verb, adverb+verb) can be a segmentation unit by right. For example, "돌아가다" (*dola-ga-da*, 'pass away') is literally translated into 'go+back' (verb+verb). "빛나다" (*bin-na-da*, 'be shiny') is derived from 'light + come out' (noun+verb). "바로잡다" (*baro-jap-da*, 'correct') is one word unit but it consists of 'rightly+hold' (adverb+verb).

3.3.3 Adjective

A Korean adjective has inflectional endings like verb. For example, in "예쁘/시/었/겠/군/요" (pretty [+polite] [+past] [+conjectural] final ending [+polite]), one adjective has five endings. Compound adjective can be a segmentation unit by right. (e.g. "검붉다" (*geom-buk-da*, 'be blackish red'))

3.3.4 Adnominal

An adnominal is always used as a modifier for noun. Korean adnominal is not treated as noun unlike Japanese one. (e.g. "새 집" (*sae jip*, 'new house')" which consist of "adnominal + noun").

3.3.5 Adverb

An adverb does not have an inflectional ending; it is always used as a modifier of a sentence or a verb. In Korean, adverb includes conjunction. It is considered as one segmentation unit. Compound adverb can be a segmentation unit by right. Examples are "밤낮" (*bam-nat*, 'day and night'), and "곳곳" (*gotgot*, 'everywhere' whose literal translation is 'where where').

3.3.6 Pronoun

A pronoun is considered as one segmentation unit. Typical examples are "나" (*na*, 'I'), "너" (*neo*, 'you'), and "우리" (*uri*, 'we'). Suffix of plural "들" (*deul*, '-s') can be attached to some of pronouns in Korean. (e.g. "너희들" (*neohui-deul*, 'you+PLURAL'), "그들" (*geu-deul*, 'they' = 'he/she+PLURAL')).

3.3.7 Numeral

A numeral is considered as one segmentation unit: e.g. "하나" (hana, 'one'), "첫째" (*cheojjae*, 'first'). Also figures are treated as one unit like "2009 년" (the year 2009).

3.3.8 Exclamation

An exclamation is considered as one segmentation unit.

3.3.9 Particle

Korean particles can not be segmented from a word just like Japanese particles. A particle is always used with a word like a noun, a verb, or an adjective, but it is considered as one segmentation unit.

Particles can be divided into two main types. One is a case particle that serves as a case marker. The other is an auxiliary particle that appears at the end of a phrase or a sentence. Auxiliary particle represents a mood and a tense.

3.3.10 Auxiliary verb

A Korean auxiliary verb represents various semantic functions such as a capability, a voice, a tense, an aspect and so on.

Auxiliary verb is only used with a verb plus endings with special word ending depending on the auxiliary verb. For example, "보다" (*boda*, 'try to'), an auxiliary verb has the same inflectional endings but it should follow a main verb with a connective ending "어" (*eo*) or "고" ('*go*'). Consider "try to eat" in English where "eat" is a main verb, and "try" is an auxiliary verb with specialized connective "to". In this case, we need two Korean Eojeols that corresponds to "eat + to" and "try". Because "to" is a functional element that is attached after main verb "eat", it constitutes one Eojeol. It causes a conflict between Eojeol and word unit. That means every Eojeol cannot be a word unit. What are the word units and Eojeols in this case? There are two choices: (1) "eat+to" and "try", (2) "eat"+ "to try". According to the definition of Eojeol, (1) is correct for two concatenated Eojeols. But if the syntactic processing is preferable, (2) is more likely to be a candidate of word units.

3.3.11 Auxiliary adjective

Unlike Japanese, there is auxiliary adjective in Korean. Function and usage of it are very similar to auxiliary verb. Auxiliary adjective is considered as one segmentation unit.

Auxiliary verb can be used with a verb or adjective plus endings with special word ending depending on the auxiliary adjective. For example, in "먹고 싶다" (*meokgo sipda*, 'want to eat'), *sipda* is an auxiliary adjective whose meaning is 'want' while *meok* is a main verb 'want' and *go* corresponds to 'to'; so *meokgo* is 'to eat'.

3.3.12 Copula

A copula is always used for changing the function of noun. After attaching the copula, noun can be used like verb. It can be segmented for processing.

3.3.13 Idiom and proverb

Proverbs, mottos, etc. should be segmented if their original meanings are not violated after segmentation like Chinese and Japanese.

3.3.14 Ending

Ending is attached to the root of verb and adjective. It means honorific, tense, aspect, modal, etc.

There are two endings: prefinal ending and final ending. They are functional elements to represent honorific, past, or future functions in prefinal position, and declarative (*-da*) or concessive (*-na*)-functions in final ending. Ending is not a segmentation unit in Korean. It is just a unit for inflection.

3.3.15 Affix

A prefix and a suffix used as a constituent of a word should not be segmented as a word unit.

4 Conclusion

Word segmentation standard is to recommend what type of word sequences should be identified as one word unit in order to process the syntactic parsing. Principles of word segmentation want to provide the measure of such word units. But principles of frequency and language economy are based on a statistical measure, which will be decided by some practical purpose.

Word segmentation in each language is somewhat different according to already made word segmentation regulation, even violating one or more principles of word segmentation. In the future, we have to discuss the more synchronized word unit concept because we now live in a multi-lingual environment. For example, consider figure 3. Its English literal translation is "white vegetable and pig meat", where "white vegetable" (白菜) is an unproductive word pattern and forms one word unit without component word units, and "pig meat" in Chinese means one English word "pork". So "pig meat" (猪肉) is the longest word unit in this case. But in Japanese and Korean, "pig meat" in Chinese characters cannot be two word units, because each component character is not used independently.

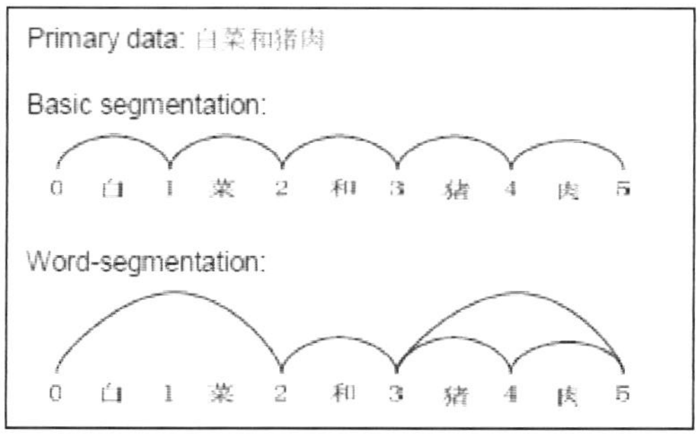

Figure 3. Basic segmentation and word segmentation [ISO/CD 24614-1]

What could be shared among three languages for word segmentation? The common things are not so much among CJK. The Chinese character derived nouns are sharable for its word unit structure, but not the whole. On the other hand, there are many common things between Korean and Japanese. Some Korean word endings and Japanese auxiliary verbs have the same functions. It will be an interesting study to compare for the processing purpose.

The future work will include the role of word unit in machine translation. If the corresponding word sequences have one word unit in one language, it is one symptom to recognize one word unit in other languages. It could be "principle of multi-lingual alignment."

The concept of "word unit" is to broaden the view about what could be registered in lexicon of natural language processing purpose, without much linguistic representation. In the result, we would like to promote such language resource sharing in public, not just dictionaries of words in usual manner but of word units.

Acknowledgement

This work has been supported by ISO/TC37, KATS and Ministry of Knowledge Economy (ROKorea), CNIS and SAC (China), JISC (Japan) and CSK (DPRK) with special contribution of Jeniffer DeCamp (ANSI) and Kiyong Lee.

References

ISO CD24614-1, Language Resource Management – Word segmentation of written texts for monolingual and multilingual information processing – Part 1: Basic concepts and general principles, 2009.

ISO WD24614-2, – Part 2: Word segmentation for Chinese, Japanese and Korean, 2009.

Author Index